W9-ADY-128

Dartnell's
Advertising Manager's
Handbook

DARTNELL is a publisher serving the world of business with books, manuals, newsletters and bulletins, and training materials for executives, managers, supervisors, salespeople, financial officials, personnel executives, and office employees. Dartnell also produces management and sales training videos and audiocassettes, publishes many useful business forms, and many of its materials and films are available in languages other than English. Dartnell, established in 1917, serves the world's business community. For details, catalogs, and product information, write to:

THE DARTNELL CORPORATION,
4660 N Ravenswood Ave,
Chicago, IL 60640-4595, U.S.A.
or phone (800) 621-5463, in U.S. and Canada.

Copyright 1997 in the United States, Canada, and Britain by
THE DARTNELL CORPORATION
Library of Congress Catalog Card Number: 96-71225
ISBN 0-85013-249-5

Printed in the United States of America

DARTNELL'S
ADVERTISING MANAGER'S
HANDBOOK

David Bushko
Editor

Fourth Edition

FIRST EDITION — 1969
SECOND EDITION — 1977
THIRD EDITION — 1982
Second Printing, 1985

Other Dartnell Handbooks:
Public Relations Handbook
Direct Mail and Mail Order Handbook
Marketing Manager's Handbook
Sales Manager's Handbook
Sales Promotion Handbook

CONTENTS

About the Editor

David Bushko is president of Aegis Communications in Greenwich, Connecticut. He combines in-depth theoretical expertise with 20 years of practical experience in corporate and marketing communications strategy, planning, creative development and implementation.

He has worked with management in major corporations, such as Digital Equipment Corporation, Dun & Bradstreet, GE, IBM, Pepsi-Cola and others.

Mr. Bushko is a member of the Institute of Management Consultants. He is also "Issues and Trends" editor for The Journal of Management Consulting.

He holds Ph.D., M.Phil., and M.A. degrees in English and Comparative Literature from Columbia, an M.Div. in theology from Yale, and a B.A. in psychology from Westminster College, Pennsylvania.

INTRODUCTION

In today's downsized, competitive, and frenetic business environment, advertising managers must wear many hats. In large companies, most ad managers have been downsized into a world that is outsized. It's a world of advertising that includes virtually every form of marketing communications, from print advertising to promotions, from business shows to kiosks and web sites. In smaller companies, the range of activities may be narrower, but it still extends well beyond the traditional boundaries of advertising.

From a budget point of view, the smaller company manager often has less to spend, but relative to what he or she needs to do with it, his or her position may well be the same as that of a manager at a large corporation. In both cases, much is usually expected from budgets that are severely constrained.

What to do? The clear assumption is that today's advertising manager will do more with less. This book can help, not by providing a lot of shortcuts, but by giving the reader proven solutions from recognized specialists. Consequently, the chapters in this handbook are not compilations of approaches. They are distillations of successful procedures, practical ideas, and useful techniques that experienced professionals have used to generate success for their companies and clients.

The book is organized to lead you through development of your advertising program, all the while recognizing that advertising may be a very broad term from your point of view.

The first chapter helps you begin where you should, i.e., with a plan. The chapter explains the key components of strategy in general, helps you understand their application to an advertising campaign, and gives you some visualization tools for helping you and your company make the right decisions.

The chapter on media planning leads you through the often tortuous road of media selection and measurement by explaining the terms and giving you practical advice for developing an approach to media that effectively supports your strategy.

The book offers a variety of ways to research and prepare for your campaign as well as for measuring its success. As senior management puts more pressure on advertising results, on knowing the return on its advertising investment, these topics are becoming increasingly important.

Another topic of considerable interest is the Internet. While widely publicized, for many, it is still a difficult concept. It is often even more puzzling to figure out how to develop and use Internet-based marketing communications. The chapter in this book offers a basic introduction, answers key questions and provides other essential information to get your advertising/marketing communications off on the right foot in this leading- edge medium.

In addition, there are chapters with practical suggestions and illuminating examples to help you generate creative ideas, evaluate copy and design, work with creative people, and sell the value of advertising to senior management.

In short, this book is intended as a practical guide for today's advertising manager — short of time, short of budget, but long on pressure- filled daily demands. In that spirit, those of us who have shared our expertise through the following pages offer you our best in the hope that it will help you give yours.

PREFACE

A book of this size, covering an extensive array of topics, requires the work of many hands and minds. I am, therefore, indebted to a number of people whose assistance and hard work have made this book possible.

First, I extend my appreciation to my friend, Joe Kreiner, formerly with Dartnell and now with Uarco, for asking me to take on the task of editing this book. In doing so, he gave me an occasion to share my experience and point of view with others. He also gave me a chance to meet a very interesting array of bright and successful individuals. I appreciate both opportunities.

When I first submitted an outline, there were several people who read it and responded with useful comments. Richard Costello, Manager, Corporate Marketing Communications, at GE; Michael Gury, Vice President of Product Marketing at BBC Worldwide/Americas; Jon Millenson, formerly Vice President at Young and Rubicam and now head of Delphi Strategic Development; and Joseph T. Plummer, formerly Vice Chairman, Worldwide Planning Director, D'Arcy, Massius, Benton and Bowles, now Vice Chairman, Audits and Surverys Worldwide, made valuable recommendations that helped clarify the organization and focus the content. They also helped me find writers for the various chapters. I appreciate the time and effort each spent on my behalf.

Two other executives were also instrumental in guiding me to informed and experienced resources. H. Paul Root, President of the Marketing Science Institute, and Phil Shyposh, Senior Vice President of Membership Services at the Association of National Advertisers, both directed me to expert professionals who have made substantial contributions to the content of this book. For these suggestions, I am grateful.

I also want to thank several people at Dartnell for their truly patient and long-suffering assistance at the publishing end of the operation. Keith Keller, Vice President and Group Director, Teamwork and Training Products, and Tracy Butzko, Group Director, Sales and Training Products, were both helpful and responsive in getting me over various hurdles along the way.

In addition to keeping the development process moving forward, Vera Derr, Product Development Manager, offered useful advice and encouragement during the writing and editing of manuscripts. And Kathleen Ineman and Bob Drake of Ineman Associates provided consistent and expert editorial assistance.

I would be remiss if I were not to thank those who have contributed chapters. All are very busy people with much to occupy them in both their business and personal lives. Yet, all took on the very difficult task of discussing subjects on which they are expert in language that is intelligible to more generalist practitioners. Virtually all told me the task was a challenge which, in the end, was both educational and rewarding. We all hope readers will share that experience.

Finally, I want to thank Ruth, my wife, and Margaret, my daughter, for listening as I played over various aspects of the contents and for providing insight and support. Their participation in the process was of greater assistance than they will ever know.

—D.B.

October, 1996

DARTNELL'S
ADVERTISING MANAGER'S
HANDBOOK

David Bushko is president of Aegis Communications in Greenwich, Connecticut. He combines in-depth theoretical expertise with 20 years of practical experience in corporate and marketing communications strategy, planning, creative development and implementation.

He has worked with management in major corporations, such as Digital Equipment Corporation, Dun & Bradstreet, GE, IBM, Pepsi-Cola and others.

Mr. Bushko is a member of the Institute of Management Consultants. He is also *"Issues and Trends" editor for* The Journal of Management Consulting.

He holds Ph.D., M.Phil., and M.A. degrees in English and Comparative Literature from Columbia, an M.Div. in theology from Yale, and a B.A. in psychology from Westminster College, Pennsylvania.

Chapter 1

STRATEGY: PLANNING TO WIN

The general who wins a battle makes many calculations in his temple before the battle is fought. The general who loses a battle makes but few calculations beforehand. Thus do many calculations lead to victory, and few calculations to defeat; how much more no calculation at all! It is by attention to this point that I can foresee who is likely to win or lose.

— Sun Tzu, *The Art of War*

What Is a Strategy and Why Is It Useful?

Simply put, a strategy describes how you plan to win. It is the hub around which all else revolves as you roll toward victory.

For this reason, your strategy must be clearly articulated (preferably in written form), comprehensible, and defensible. A defensible, information-based strategy built on a consensus helps ensure concentrated action, saves large amounts of time and money that would otherwise be wasted on "hit-or-miss" activities, and enables both immediate and long-term marketing efficiency.

Yet, in many companies, marketing and advertising strategies are either uncommon or very informal. It is virtually impossible to imagine a professional athletic team starting a game with only a vague idea of what the object of the game is, what its capabilities are, what its opponent's strengths and weaknesses are, and how they plan to match up against competitors to win.

Yet, corporations do this all the time, generally for either of two reasons. On the one hand, a company may be trapped in "paralysis by analysis." These companies can't get to the planning phase because they always find they "still need more information."

The way out of this trap is a negotiation process that allows you to define the information you need for a sound plan, get it, and get on with it. In this chapter, you should find considerable guidance about the information you need for a sound plan.

What you need in addition is explained in an article titled, "Between 'Paralysis by Analysis' and 'Extinction by Instinct'," by Ann Langley. As Langley notes, "In paralysis by analysis, checks and balances have become so dominant that it is virtually impossible to get anything done. In environments where speed to market is an important competitive advantage, this is a major problem. Efficient arbitration is needed to produce rapid, rational decisions."[1] This chapter also includes some tools you can use to increase the speed and efficiency of the arbitration process.

The second problem occurs when marketing executives believe they don't need to spend time developing a strategy, because after all "we know our market." Such is the view of intuitive marketers. They don't need a plan because they have already decided what the organization is going to do.

This is wrong. No one person, no matter how sound his or her intuitions, can take into account all of the factors that must be considered when planning strategy. That is why athletic teams often have a staff of coaches who help develop game plans. The cure for an excessively intuitive process is controls that keep the process informed without slowing it down.

As Langley explains, "The key element of any strategy for avoiding extinction by instinct is to install checks and balances into the system, so that people must think through their ideas."[2]

The discussion and tools provided in this chapter can be used as aids in this "thinking through" process. They can be of considerable help in avoiding both "paralysis" and "extinction," while developing a sound marketing and advertising strategy.

Consequently, we will do a number of things in this chapter. First, we will discuss the basic components of strategic thinking and what they mean from an advertising and communications point of view.

Then, we will concentrate on key elements of an advertising strategy. We will start by identifying the target audience and explaining the criteria needed to do that. We will then go on to explore potential marketing themes, showing you how to arrive at the one most likely to convey your message powerfully. We will also look at two ways to analyze your competition and assess how your marketing message will play in your competitive environment. And finally, we will discuss how to pull your strategic information together and evaluate your strategy.

Before we go further, a note about our approach is in order. There are those who will object that throughout this chapter two kinds of confusion exist. The first is between marketing and advertising strategies. For most people, these are two separate items. In theory, they are right.

In reality, however, the theory seldom holds. While the advertising (or the communications plan of which advertising is a part) should follow from the marketing plan, it seldom does. The reason? There is seldom a marketing plan. More accurately, there is seldom a marketing plan that people can use.

When there is a plan, it is usually a "numbers plan." In other words, it says, "Our strategy is to sell 400,000 widgets over the next 12 months." This is neither a strategy nor a basis for communications. It is a statement of objectives. No matter how detailed the level of breakdown that follows, for example, into regions, markets, etc., it is still a numbers plan.

When applied to communications, it becomes, "To do this, our strategy is to produce three ads, seven brochures, five direct mail campaigns, etc." Again, this is neither a strategy nor a basis for communications. It is a "wish list."

A marketing plan that is useful for communications must discuss audience segmentation, customer needs and the way in which the marketer plans to meet them, as well as the competition's strengths and weaknesses, potential moves and countermoves.

This kind of plan enables the implementation without which victory can't occur. Such a plan provides the information a marketer needs for "real life" action. It also allows the marketer to turn to communications with the kind of information copywriters and designers need for effective advertising, promotion and other communications activities. In short, such a plan, by building consensus and supplying the right information for action, provides both the way and the will to win.

Consequently, this chapter is aimed at both marketers and the communicator in need. Using the information you will gather here, you can build not only a communications strategy, but also much of the creative that will go into the materials upon which marketing must depend so heavily if it is to "make its numbers."

If the reader finds himself or herself in possession of a marketing plan that covers the points made in this chapter, it will simply be a matter of plugging the information into the framework provided within this chapter to arrive at an advertising strategy. Thus, the chapter will still be of value. If, however, you find very little of this information in your marketing plan, this chapter will be of use in helping you pull it together.

Another source of possible criticism is that this chapter confuses advertising strategy and communications strategy. Again, the criticism is true but not valid. Virtually everything written about advertising strategy and planning these days either discusses them in the context of overall communications or defines advertising as virtually all marketing communications.

This is not surprising. Advertising strategies are seldom standalone items these days. Nor should they be. If a marketer wants to communicate a message effectively to customers and prospects, he or she must certainly communicate through a variety of media. Thus, advertising must be integrated with a total communications approach. That approach is assumed here.

In this chapter, therefore, we will discuss general strategic principles and demonstrate how to apply them to develop a communications strategy. There are two additional reasons for doing this.

First, strategy is a unique discipline. While an advertising strategy may be presented as a simple one- or two-page document, advertisers need to develop that document through careful analysis underpinned by a well-grounded sense of what strategic thinking entails. Too often, "strategies" are actually tactical implementation plans.

Strategic thinking is something else. It is a discipline of its own with its own principles. These principles are the same regardless of whether you're applying them to military campaigns, political campaigns or advertising campaigns. Knowing these principles can make the critical difference between a strategy that wins and one that doesn't.

THE STRATEGIST'S FOUR BASIC TOOLS

Essentially, a strategy coordinates four factors implicit in any competitive situation — power, time, space and implementation capability. When you're thinking about these four factors and how to deploy them effectively, you're thinking strategically.

Power

All strategies tend to favor one component, usually power, over the others. However, you mustn't get too focused on any one factor, whatever it might be. It is important to do strategy spatially. That is you need to focus on your core strength and key objectives, while always seeing the whole playing field. This means you need to watch your competitors and know their moves. You must also watch for changes in your business's playing field, specifically the entry of new players, technologies, and product or service substitutes. Any of these might blindside you if care isn't taken.

To most people, for instance, power is what strategy is all about, getting it, using it, maintaining it. Yet, there are many examples of competitors who lost sight of some area of the playing field just long enough to let other competitors get a foothold that has proven difficult, if not impossible, to dislodge.

IBM, with its eye on the mainframe business, suddenly found the personal computer industry with Apple, Microsoft, Intel, Compaq, and others looming large. American automobile manufacturers failed to understand the Japanese threat to their high-end markets. By whittling away from the bottom up, foreign competitors gained strong positions that made ready bases for launches into the luxury class. There are many other examples of these kinds of competitive thrusts, all well-documented in business books.

In general, however, there are two ways marketers must wield their power. The market leader must maintain it. Those who rank second and lower must be alert for opportunities to weaken the leader by taking some of its power for themselves.

They must also keep careful track of how the leader wields its power so they aren't damaged or destroyed by it. This is the "9,000-pound gorilla" syndrome. "Where does a 9,000-pound gorilla sit? Anywhere it wants to." When it makes that decision, you must be sure you're not on *that* chair (unless you have attained 10,000-pound gorilla status by then).

When we consider advertising strategy, the primary source of advertising's power is its creative. This creative must grab your target audience's attention and deliver a memorable message in a way that motivates a prospect to buy. This is why advertising agencies talk so much about their "creative," call their employees "creatives," and focus so much time during their presentations on the "creative concept." It is the source of their — and their clients' — power. Thus, your advertising strategy, if it depends heavily upon a power thrust, will require a very strong creative concept.

Time

If power is the focus of most strategic thinking, "timing is everything."

Clearly, the most powerful time component in the marketing arsenal is speed. While power often seems to be the best — for some, the *only* — basis for strategic action, speed can spur greatness (and profits) as well. Ever since the great British navigator Sir Francis Drake pummeled the Spanish Armada with his lighter, faster vessels, strategists have known the value of speed. Applied relentlessly, speed can soon destroy an otherwise powerful competitor.

In the world of corporate marketing, for example, speed has proven to be a powerful ally of the niche marketer. Time and time again, small, alert companies that are quick on their feet, such as Dell Computers and Ben & Jerry's, have demonstrated an amazing ability to go toe-to-toe with larger, more powerful foes.

Speed, too, can shape your message. A small company that needs to offset the power of a much larger competitor will frequently find speed a friendly ally. And that usually shapes their advertising message.

Companies promote their speed from a variety of viewpoints. They may tout the speed of their service. They may emphasize their ability to "get there on time." They may extol their quick turnaround. All may be winning messages to those customers who "want it now."

In advertising, time has several ramifications. Most of these have to do with "frequency," a topic examined in greater detail in the media chapter of this book. Essentially, however, frequency is the number of times your audience sees your message.

You need to present your case to your target audience at the right time. In this, there is good news and bad news. The good news is that there is only one right time, and that is when your audience is receptive to your message. The bad news is that it is very difficult to know when that right time is.

Several things are critical when determining what time is the right time.

1. What is your objective? Is it to gain familiarity? Is it to drive sales? In general, the first is easier than the second, primarily because much of advertising's success in the second area depends upon its ability to catch people's attention close to the moment of sale.
2. How familiar is your audience with your company and its products? Generally, ads for very familiar brands have higher recall than those for less familiar brands.
3. How persuasive is your ad? This will depend upon the power of its creativity, its logic and its emotional appeal.

In short, when you introduce an ad campaign, determining how long it will run, whether your media placements will be sparse or intense, you are making strategic considerations. How you decide will depend upon your strategic objectives, your audience, your budget, and the nature of the media you're working with.

Space

Space can be a formidable competitive weapon. The way in which it is formidable, however, depends upon how "space" is defined. Al Ries and Jack Trout in their books, including both the renowned *Positioning* and *The 22 Immutable Laws of Marketing*, locate the appropriate "space" for marketing in the mind of the consumer. This is a legitimate starting point, especially for communications, where the audience should be your first consideration.

By locating marketing's space in the consumer's head, you focus on the key task of advertising, to win a mind for your product or service. If the mind is won, the purchase will follow.

Planning and other tactical marketing activities, however, require that we also consider aspects of external space. Depending upon your company and its marketing reach, you may locate your customers locally, regionally, nationally, or globally.

Your industry is also a space. It's a space that includes one or more products, buyers with their own usage and need profiles, and distribution traditions and innovations. All of these are spatial factors that need to be prioritized and considered in your strategic thinking because they will help determine which minds you need to win and where your advertising will be placed.

This is because, in advertising strategy, space is also something you buy. Especially true in print, this can also pertain to such items as billboards, point-of-sale (POS) materials, "yellow pages" advertising, and other items.

Advertisers refer to the spatial element of strategy as "reach." It requires locating your audience as specifically as possible, so that you can select the best possible media to "reach" them with your message. How well you do this will depend upon a combination of budget and media-buying creativity. In any case, where your ads will go, so that they will be seen by your target audience, is an essential strategic question.

Tactical Implementation Capability

Finally, in thinking of strategy, you need to consider your implementation capability. A strategy is only sound to the extent that it can be implemented.

This will have much to do with how you look at power, time, and space. Obviously, if your organization and people are bureaucratic, you probably can't choose speed as the keystone of your strategy. On the other hand, if you're the third-ranking competitor in your industry, it would be folly to choose power. It might give you an element of surprise, but odds are that you'll lose in the long run.

In developing your advertising strategy, you have to assess your tactical implementation capability right from the start. How good are your creative people? Are they highly creative or just so-so? How much money do you have? Plenty? Can you obtain the reach and frequency you need? How can you compensate? Will you have to innovate to meet your goals? If you rely on this, who will help? Your creative people? Your media planner? How much information will you have? Plenty of research? Just a little? None? What is the source of your power? Where can you find advertising leverage?

In advertising, assessing your implementation capability means realistically appraising your people and financial resources. If your agency or in-house talent is highly creative, for example, you may want to look at your company's strategic position and strengths, and find ways to match them with your creative power. If your strength is in financial rather than creative resources, you might want to push for the best creative you can get but plan on a strategy that relies more on shrewd use of space and time, that is, reach and frequency.

While strategies tend to emphasize one element over another, the fact is that the best strategies effectively deploy all four components, each one supporting the other. The ideal is a power-based strategy that relies on high-quality creative presented at maximum effective reach and frequency, all executed by knowledgeable, highly creative, and competent people for effective deployment.

Pulling this all together, however, requires a careful assessment of three primary elements — the target audience, the product and the needs it fulfills, and your competition.

IDENTIFYING AND ANALYZING YOUR TARGET AUDIENCE

In his book, *The Vest-Pocket Marketer*, Alexander Hiam discusses the "Chinese marketing" blunder. As he says, "the term comes from Carl Crow's classic *Four Hundred Million Customers* in which he argued that the Depression could be cured by exporting to a market as large as China."[3]

Hiam goes on to explain the fallacy. "The size of the market has little to do with its sales potential. But many marketers select target markets on the basis of size, and advertisers frequently rationalize media selections on the basis of number of exposures.... It usually works a lot better to focus more narrowly, to improve the quality of exposures or lists rather than the quantity, and to target the most receptive, least contested customer segments rather than the largest."[4] In light of this, how do you identify the "right" target audience? There are two approaches to this.

In their book, *The Portable MBA in Marketing*, Hiam and Charles D. Schewe discuss these approaches. The first they call "market aggregation." They note, "Marketers use this strategy when they believe enough consumers will buy the product as it is.... The market aggregation approach is used when consumers perceive little or no difference between the products of different firms, that is when competing products seem virtually the same physically and chemically."[5]

This approach enables lower production and marketing costs. "Only one product is made and production techniques do not have to be changed for different models, styles, and the like."[6]

Despite these benefits, there are some major disadvantages to the market aggregation strategy. "For this approach to be successful, therefore, a large number of people must have the same basic need or want. Also, the marketer must be able to design a single marketing mix that will satisfy various potential customers. If these two conditions are not met, mass marketing is doomed to failure."[7] In today's environment of rapidly customized products, in which choice in many product lines is extensive, the aggregate method seldom works.

The second approach, market segmentation, is generally more viable. This approach subdivides the market. While it can have significant expense implications in terms of research and production costs, it enables companies to "provide a product and marketing mix that 'fits' a relatively homogenous part of the total market. As a result, market segmentation results in a better match between what the marketer offers and what the market desires."[8] In many industries today, the sheer pressure of competition makes this approach a necessity.

But what criteria should you use for this subdividing process? There are four common criteria (Exhibit 1.1). First, the market must be definable (Exhibit 1.2). That is you must be able to specify which consumers comprise your market segment.

This definition can be done in a number of ways. You can define your audience demographically. "White males over 50," for example, is a demographic description. For further definition, you can add geographic categories, such as "white males over 50 living in or within a 50-mile radius of Chicago."

You might also define your audience in terms of usage, such as PC users, hand-cream users, etc. Or you can define your audience by

EXHIBIT 1.1

Market Segmentation

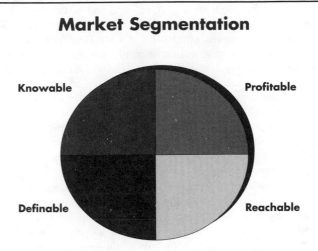

Knowable | Profitable

Definable | Reachable

EXHIBIT 1.2

Market Segmentation

DEFINABLE

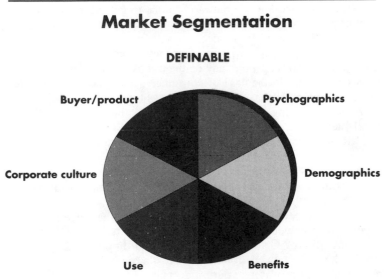

Buyer/product | Psychographics

Corporate culture | Demographics

Use | Benefits

the benefits they seek, such as car buyers in search of prestige or people who want foods that are both easy to prepare and healthy.

Second, your audience must be reachable (Exhibit 1.3). You must have ways of communicating with it specifically. It might be through trade or industry magazines. It might be through consumer publications targeted to your specific group. It might be through kiosks placed in locations your audience passes when going to and from work or during recreational activities. It might be television or radio commercials run when research shows your audience is tuned in.

Third, your audience must be knowable (Exhibit 1.4). This means knowing the target group's needs in relation to your product. How do they use it? Why do they use it? What are they trying to achieve? What are their primary buying criteria?

You may also want to know your audience's personality traits. What do these people think about themselves? Who are their heroes? Role models? What fantasies drive them? What dreams inspire them?

Beyond this, there are other levels of knowledge you might seek. What, for example, is the nature of the buying process? Is it an individual sell, or will several people be involved? The team sell is common in business-to-business, where companies subject buying decisions to review by multiple decision-makers. This has an impact upon marketing communications strategy, requiring that various tools be used to communicate with these diverse audiences in a sustainable way.

By comparison, consumer shopping is generally an individual sell. The decision process may go a lot faster, but a great deal more preparation and work might have to be done to get the individual to the point of purchase.

Another element in the decision process is decision influencers. These are not the people who buy, but they have a major influence on those who do. These people may be the trendsetters of fashion or trade press columnists. In the case of consumers, it might be friends, relatives, or others. In the world of business-to-business marketing, it might be purchasing agents, executives from other functions who will be affected by the sale, even employee groups.

Regardless, you need to identify decision influencers and include them in your strategic decision-making process. In both consumer and business-to-business marketing, it may be very important to reach and convince these people that influencing customers toward your products is a sound move on their part.

You also need to know the decision criteria that buyers use when buying your product. What needs do they expect to meet? Do they look for a certain size? Color? Speed? Shape? Do they want it to fit comfortably into a certain environment? Is cost a factor? By knowing these key criteria and measuring your products or services against them, you can ascertain potential sources of advertising messages.

EXHIBIT 1.3

Market Segmentation

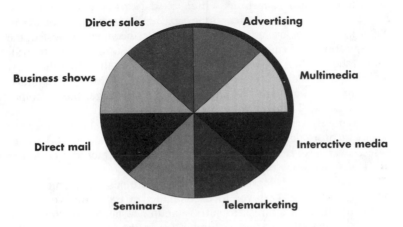

REACHABLE

Direct sales — Advertising

Business shows — Multimedia

Direct mail — Interactive media

Seminars — Telemarketing

EXHIBIT 1.4

Market Segmentation

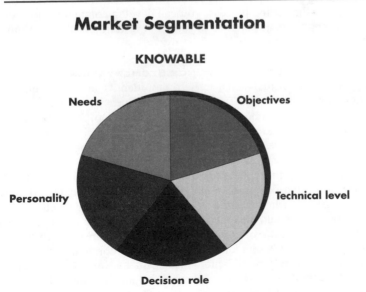

KNOWABLE

Needs — Objectives

Personality — Technical level

Decision role

You should also consider where your customer is in the buying cycle. Advertisers often refer to the AIDA model. The acronym stands for awareness, interest, desire, action. Sometimes this model is revised to awareness, interest, evaluation, trial, adoption.

According to the latter model, the prospect at each phase of the cycle asks specific questions which, as the theory goes, you must answer to move the customer to the next level. Awareness, for example, asks, "What's available?" As the customer becomes interested, the next question is, "What's in it for me?" As the customer moves to evaluation, the question becomes, "Which brand offers the best value?" At the trial stage, the customer asks, "How well does this specific brand meet my specific needs?" And at the adoption stage, the customer wants to know, "How much and how do I get one?"

While this model is convenient, the fact is that such linearity occurs inconsistently. Some buyers go from awareness to trial. In other cases, awareness is aroused by a specific brand, which the customer purchases, bypassing the other steps altogether.

This, however, doesn't diminish the usefulness of the model for planning. It still can keep you focused on the key issues that your communications must address to satisfy audience needs. If you know where the majority of your customers are in the buying cycle at the moment that advertising addresses them, you will have a clearer idea of what to say and how to structure the message effectively.

This model is also useful for structuring an overall communications approach. Again, by using research to assess where a given target market is in the buying process, you can develop communications that offer buyers different kinds of information at different times to move them along through the cycle efficiently.

TOOLS FOR AUDIENCE SEGMENTATION

Some useful tools exist to help you identify and focus on your most important audiences. Two simple ones are easy to build.

First, draw a circle (Exhibit 1.5). This is a tool that offers maximum ease-of-use and is as portable as a pen or pencil and a piece of paper. Circles are very useful tools for collecting things. In this one, you can collect audiences.

You can do this collection in several ways. The most effective is to meet with your marketing team. This team should include all those whose approval will be needed when you do advertising or other communications. It should also include people who talk to customers on a regular basis. If it doesn't, you should certainly plan research to corroborate the group's opinion. Your advertising/communications program will ultimately work better, in fact, if you include this kind of research, regardless of whether the group is familiar with its customers first-hand or further removed.

If bringing together a team of this sort isn't possible, you can talk

EXHIBIT 1.5

Market Segments

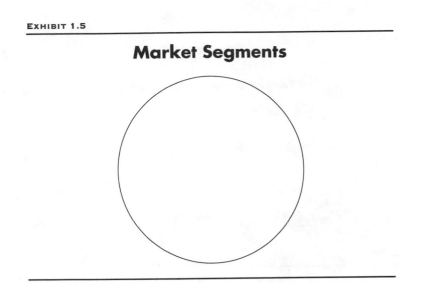

to people by phone or use electronic means, such as electronic mail, to find out to whom you should be addressing your messages. Whatever method you use to gather your audiences, write them inside your circle.

Once you've talked to everyone, you may want to circulate this circle for approval. Ask them to add any groups they think have been left out. This is also the time to start asking yourself and your marketing people whether these groups, though definable, are also knowable, reachable, and profitable.

These latter questions will generally lead to some further refinements. For a technology company, for example, the initial definition "Chief Information Officers" (CIOs), is probably way too broad, making the group difficult to reach profitably. The solution may be a more geographical and product-specific focus, such as "CIOs in *Fortune* top 250 companies with international responsibilities who are pursuing a client-server strategy."

Profitability may also be the problem with a perfume company's focus on "women 40–50." Targeting "women 40–50 with family incomes over $75,000 who prefer perfume to cologne and are looking for a sweet, flowerlike fragrance" may be much more effective.

Once the targets have all been identified, priorities should be the next order of business. For this, a simple triangle will do (Exhibit 1.6). Draw a triangle and ask your marketing group to select the most important audience in the circle. Put it at the top of the triangle. Use this process to prioritize at least your top three audiences.

This process will probably be more difficult than audience collection. To get the triangle filled out in a way that all can agree to will require the thinking through and negotiation process discussed at the

EXHIBIT 1.6

Markets

Ranked by marketing priority

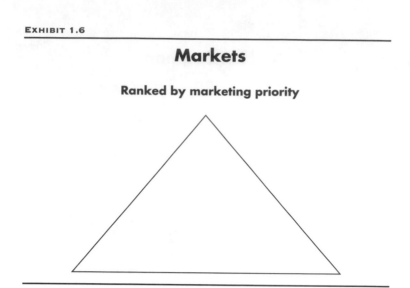

beginning of this chapter. The simple triangle forces a process of thinking through, while focusing the negotiation process. Thus, it enables a planning process that avoids "paralysis by analysis" on the one hand and "extinction by instinct" on the other.

There are two techniques you might use to move this process along. One is to fill out the triangle yourself, thus "driving a stake in the ground" against which others might react. Your choices might be made based upon the number of times each group was mentioned during the initial information-gathering. If "PC users," for example, were mentioned more than any other group, they would be a logical choice for the top of the pyramid.

Another prioritizing tool is "Worry Willy's Guide to Prioritizing," found in Michael Michalko's book, *Thinkertoys*.[9] Using this approach, you would list and number all of your potential audience groups.

For example:
1. end users
2. senior executives
3. chief information officers
4. department heads
5. columnists in technology magazines
etc.

Then, you can prepare a numbers grid by taking your first number and pairing it with all of the others. Begin a second column with your second number, pairing it with all of the numbers, except 1.

A grid for the above five numbers might look like this:

A	B	C	D
1 2			
1 3	2 3		
1 4	2 4	3 4	
1 5	2 5	3 5	4 5

Now you can make some simple decisions. Which of the first two is more important, end users or senior executives? Circle the one you and your group choose. Which is more important, end users or CIOs? Again, circle the one you and your group select. Continue to do this for each of the four columns.

When you are done, count how many times each number was selected. Then put the numbers in priority order from the one selected most often to the one selected the least. If there is a tie, leave them tied or make an intuitive decision to choose one over the other. Put the audience type beside each number, and your audiences are potentially prioritized.

Since this is just a tool, you need to check it against your intuition. If you've done this as a group, however, chances are it will hold. If it doesn't, change the priorities as necessary to achieve group consensus. You should use the tool; it should not use you.

Once you know where your markets are, you can focus on getting to know them better as individuals. Two types of charts can improve your acquaintance. The first is a "personality map." To use it, answer the questions along the left-hand column for each of your audiences (Exhibit 1.7).

The information you gather here can help you get a better sense of who your audiences are as people and how to speak to them effectively. This map can help with both strategy and tactical implementation. It can be used to generate ideas about what kinds of people to use as models in your ads, what sorts of settings you might show your product in to appeal to your audience and how to position your message.

Exhibit 1.8 is a decision map. It will help you understand how decisions are made and how to build your strategy so you can influence decisions effectively at the various stages of the decision-making process. Again, for each audience group, fill in the information requested along the left-hand column.

By this time, you and your marketing team should have a clear idea of whom you have to sell to, what kinds of people they are and how they buy. The next question is, "What do you have to offer them?"

IDENTIFYING THE RIGHT MESSAGE

Message strategy is at the heart of advertising. Advertising is a form of communication. Communication, when all is said and done, is a relatively straightforward process. A sender transmits a message that

EXHIBIT 1.7 PERSONALITY MAP

Audiences	Group A	Group B	Group C	Group D
Who will use your product?				
How will they use it?				
What benefits do they expect?				
How does the audience perceive itself in relation to your product?				
How would it like to perceive itself in relation to your product?				
What are the audience's goals and values?				

EXHIBIT 1.8 DECISION MAP

Audience Groups	Group A	Group B	Group C	Group D
Is yours a team or individual sell?				
Primary decision makers?				
Primary decision influencers?				
Primary buying criteria?				
Stage in the buying process (AIDA)?				
Length of average selling cycle?				

is evaluated by a recipient, who then responds. In doing advertising, your primary goal is to send the right message to the right people in the right way to generate the right response.

If it's that simple, you might ask, "Why is good advertising, memorable advertising, advertising that 'works,' so hard to find?" The answer is to be found in all of those little "rights."

In developing your message, you will confront several challenges. First, communicators often work in a context in which there is no clear marketing strategy. This happens for either of the two reasons stated at the beginning of this chapter: either there isn't enough research yet or everyone knows "intuitively" what the plan is. Therefore, it's impossible to know in any substantive way what the message should be. The result is "meandering" copy development.

This is a situation designed, as one writer put it, "to bring your old gray hairs in sorrow to the grave." You will discover this when you start the approval process. This is when lack of a plan will have a demoralizing impact. You'll know the curse is upon you when your reviewers respond to copy by saying things like, "I don't care for this word," or "This copy isn't 'punchy' enough for me."

What is happening here is that, having no clear strategic direction and criteria by which to judge what they see, executives take refuge in subjective reactions. Since there is no agreed-upon marketing theme, they can't judge the copy and graphics from a business perspective.

The result? Subjective judgments and an approval process that will very likely destroy your copy — and its message — in the end. It may see the light of day, but as far as its potential effectiveness is concerned, it will be sunset, not sunrise.

Another message development problem is "blinder vision." This occurs when virtually all marketing input comes from within the company — from engineers, development people, and marketing. All have their pet feature, function, and/or benefit. And all have their own views of how the product should be marketed.

It is surprising how many products are marketed on a basis that is truly divorced from market realities. Consider this tale. A major corporation was marketing a new technology. The marketing executive team agreed that it was a hot item for the busy executive. Ads were produced and placed. Collateral was created and distributed. Public relations sought to place stories in executive media.

Several months later, an entirely new marketing communications program was developed. The target audience? Mobile workers. Executives, it turned out, had no use for the product at all. The entire message was aimed at the wrong audience. When it came down to it, the reason was that one of the marketing executives thought it was the kind of "nifty gadget" he'd like to use, and, therefore, that an entire marketplace of executives would be eager to use it, too. As a result, all of the money, time and resources required to create the first campaign were wasted.

A third problem is the fear of being different, otherwise known as "me-too-ism." In a world in which only the unique gets attention, it is surprising how many millions of dollars corporations are willing to spend on saying the same thing as their competitors, rather than launching into something completely different. The way out of this and into stronger marketing communications is through positioning.

POSITIONING

"Positioning" is a marketing term originated by Al Ries and Jack Trout in their classic work, *Positioning*. In their book, they say, "Positioning starts with a product ... but positioning is not what you do with a product. Positioning is what you do in the mind of the prospect. That is, you position the product in the mind of the prospect."[10]

One of the main reasons this concept has stayed around for so long (the book's first printing was 1981) is that it addresses a problem that has gotten worse. "Positioning is the first body of thought that comes to grips with the difficult problem of getting heard in our over-communicated society."[11]

Positioning is based upon a concept of the way in which the mind works. Ries and Trout point out that the mind, unlike a computer, doesn't accept everything you try to put into it. It "accepts only that new information which matches its current state of mind. It filters out everything else."[12]

This has some ominous implications for advertising. In his book, *Strategy in Advertising*, Leo Bogart examines a range of advertising research and concludes, "The implication seems to be that most non-users have a penchant for tuning out the advertising for the brands they don't use."[13]

In fact, the mind only accepts what it wants to accept. As a general rule, when it accepts something, it relates it to something else that's already there. If it's something new, we relate it to a category; if it's something already in the category, we relate it to other items in that category.

For example, if your company introduces the first peanut-butter candy bar, those who like it will relate it to other candy bars. "This is better than candy bars that just have chocolate." If, on the other hand, yours is the second candy bar with peanut butter, they will relate it to others in the category. "This is better than the other peanut-butter candy bar."

How does this affect communications strategy? In many cases, as Ries and Trout note, marketers start with the premise that advertising simply tells people that you have what they want. Therefore, most advertising starts with research to find out what you should tell customers you have. Once discovered, it seems a simple matter to create an ad that tells people you have it.

What this fails to note is that someone else (often many people) has already told the customer that he or she has the same thing. This leaves the customer in a "whom should we believe" situation. So sales are made on the basis of other criteria, often price. The result is that advertising doesn't do its job, while the advertiser experiences price and margin pressure.

The ideal in positioning is to be first. In their book, *The 22 Immutable Laws of Marketing*, Ries and Trout discuss this desirable state. As they note, "Many people believe that the basic issue in marketing is convincing prospects that you have a better product or service. Not true.... The basic issue in marketing is creating a category you can be first in. It's the law of leadership: It's better to be first than to be better. It's much easier to get into the mind first than to try to convince someone you have a better product than the one that did get there first."[14]

Terry Richey in *The Marketer's Visual Tool Kit* points out, "In marketing, only one certainly, fatal decision exists: Become the second company to introduce a product or service not clearly better, faster, cheaper, or more reliable than the first company's. So days, months, and sometimes years are spent studying a product and why its features are better than the competition's. Ultimately (and in a surprisingly short time) the customers decide on their own, if you offer something better. Customers can be imaginative, smart, and quite cruel."[15]

The important issue here is not simply to be first, but to be first *in the mind*. IBM, for example, wasn't the first computer manufacturer. It was, however, and on a worldwide basis continues to be, first in the mind.

If you feel that you are doomed to languish in second place, however, consider Ries and Trout's second law. "If you didn't get into the prospect's mind first, don't give up hope. Find a new category you can be first in.... When you're first in a new category, promote the category. In essence, you have no competition."[16]

While this seems simple on the surface, it can be a lot more difficult than it might first appear to be. The mind is a terrible thing to try to comprehend. When Ries and Trout speak about "being first" and "categories," they are talking about someone else's mind, not yours or your CEO's. One person's self-evident category is not necessarily someone else's.

Here's an example: Suppose you're introducing a "light" mayonnaise. You survey your industry and discover that you are the first nonfat, dietetic mayonnaise on the market. You sally forth confident that you "have no competition," only to discover that customers see your product as another of many "light" salad dressings. Time to refine your ad message by more clearly defining your new category, not against all other mayonnaises, but against salad dressings.

"There's more to positioning than this, however. In the beginning is the word. A company can become incredibly successful if it can find a way to own a word in the mind of the prospect. Not a complicated word. Not an invented one. The simple words are best, words taken right out of the dictionary. This is the law of focus. You 'burn' your way into the mind by narrowing the focus to a single word or concept."[17] By way of examples, Ries and Trout note that, for most people, IBM owns computers, Hershey owns chocolate, and Coca-Cola owns colas.

Your word may be any of several types, including benefit-related (cavity prevention), service-related (overnight delivery), audience-related (younger people), or sales-related (preferred brand). And you can only own a word that has proponents for the opposing point of view. "High quality," for example, is a weak choice, because you are unlikely to have competitors proclaiming that they offer poor quality.

Perhaps the largest caveat for your intended word, however, is that it cannot already be owned. This is Ries and Trout's law of exclusivity. "When a competitor owns a word or position in the prospect's mind, it is futile to attempt to own the same word.... Despite the disaster stories, many companies continue to violate the law of exclusivity. You can't change people's minds once they are made up. In fact, what you often do is reinforce your competitor's position by making its concept more important."[18] A mail delivery company that promotes its overnight express capabilities, for example, might find itself promoting Federal Express's growth more than its own.

Richey broadens this to include all positioning. Like Ries and Trout, he sees positioning as a place in the customer's mind. This, he notes, "means *one* place. You can't own two positions with the same product and the same customer. This remains number one on the list of marketing law violations. You can't be perceived as both the premium option and the economical choice. You can't be the largest and at the same time offer the most custom service. Even if you could customers wouldn't believe you."[19]

Ries and Trout posit that people have a ranking, or "ladder," in their heads. "All products are not created equal. There's a hierarchy in the mind that prospects use in making decisions. For each category, there is a product ladder in the mind. On each rung is a brand name.... Your marketing strategy should depend on how soon you got into the mind and consequently which rung of the ladder you occupy."[20]

How many rungs are there on your product's ladder? "It depends on whether your product is a high-interest or low-interest product. Products you use every day (cigarettes, cola, beer, toothpaste, cereal) tend to be high-interest products with many rungs on their ladders. Products that are purchased infrequently (furniture, lawn mowers, luggage) usually have few rungs on their ladders.

"Products that involve a great deal of personal pride (automobiles, watches, cameras) are also high-interest products with many rungs on their ladders even though they are purchased infrequently.

"Products that are purchased infrequently and involve an unpleasant experience usually have very few rungs on their ladders. Automobile batteries, tires, and life insurance are three examples."[21]

TOOLS FOR POSITIONING AND MESSAGING

Several tools are available for helping you with positioning and messaging. Again, these are best used in conjunction with your marketing team. At the very least, fill them out from your point of view, circulate them, and get a consensus from all of those who will participate in approving your advertising. For positioning, you could use Richey's Positioning Cube (Exhibit 1.9). It assumes that customers give varying degrees of importance to two dimensions — cost and quality. If two other dimensions, reliability and innovation, for instance, are more important in your industry, you can substitute them.

To use the positioning cube, decide where to place each of the major products and competitors in your industry. Once you have done this, you need to find a place for yourself. This place should be along the edges; avoid the generic zone.

As Richey notes, "The center of the cube is dangerous territory where your product can become 'gray' and generic. Ironically, the forces at work pushing you in toward this danger zone are often aided by product managers themselves. It appears that the middle zone would hold the most business. It seems that that's where you could be more things to more people, where you are less vulnerable to competitive strategy shifts. Wrong. To differentiate your product, you must be known for something and fix a place in the customer's mind. You can't do that in the generic center zone."[22]

It's one thing, however, to know where the opportunities lie and another to exploit them effectively. Once you know what positions offer the greatest possibilities, you need to examine your product to see how its features, functions, and benefits message can be shaped to the opportunity the positioning cube has identified.

For this, you can use a simple grid on which you can list your product or service's features, functions and benefits (Exhibit 1.10). As you can see, the grid is comprised of three columns, one for each component. Filling in the features column should be easy. The product development group should be able to describe all of the primary and secondary features. Be sure you include all of them in the grid.

At the same time, be alert for additional features that the group may be overlooking. Consider this example from a campaign to sell computer printers. An agency was told that one of the printer's most impressive features was that it could print 16 items simultaneously. After hearing this feature described with a good deal of emphasis and watching a demonstration, the agency noted that on one demo run, the printer had printed 16 *different* items simultaneously. The engineer explained that this capability would be obvious to users, though it was

EXHIBIT 1.9 POSITIONING CUBE

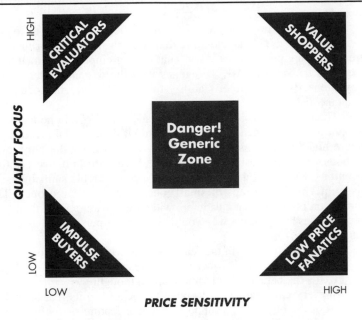

Excerpted by permission of the publisher, from The Marketer's Visual Tool Kit © 1994 Terry Richey. Published by AMACOM, a division of American Management Association. All rights reserved.

EXHIBIT 1.10 FEATURE GRID

Features	Functions	Benefits

not available on any competitive printer. The important thing was that it was 16 items across.

The agency suggested that it might not be all that obvious to customers and that the client should include it in the headline for this feature. Marketing people were wary. That kind of emphasis seemed to be overdoing it. Nevertheless, the agency won the day and noted — in a copy subhead — the printer's ability to print 16 *different* documents simultaneously.

The product was announced at a trade show. Within hours of the announcement, the agency got a call. Could it do a special piece of literature highlighting this feature only? It was virtually the only thing customers were interested in, especially those with mid-size printing operations who found that they could save considerable sums by using this printer to run groups of small jobs, as well as large ones. The moral: Don't assume that customers will view a feature from their perspective as users the same way you do from your perspective as manufacturer.

Once you've filled in the features, you need to go on to the next two columns. Functions — what the features do — are pretty straightforward. It's the benefits that require careful thought.

In every case, you need to push the benefit to its real appeal in the heart of the buyer. Let's suppose that your feature's benefit enables faster handling of customer calls, a fairly generic benefit. We can push this further to improved customer service, also fairly generic. Chances are most of your competitors are already saying something like this about what may be a similar feature.

Now, let's push improved customer service to its benefit, for example, more repeat business. Good, but could be better. More repeat business can be driven to more sales at lower costs. And if we push that benefit, the benefit will become more sales more profitably.

Even this can be improved upon, but it is far closer to a potential buyer's heart than simply faster handling of customer calls. In short, by continuing to push your benefits, you can close in on selling points that have a strong, immediate appeal to your audience.But a whole series of points doesn't necessarily lead to a strong ad. You need to select *one* as your key marketing theme. What is the "word" or "position" you want to own? This brings us to our second tool, the Feature Spectrum (Exhibit 1.11).

Another of Richey's tools, this is basically a simple nine-by-nine (nine spaces down and nine spaces across) grid. What makes this a valuable tool is the categories it forces you to think about: value and uniqueness. To fill in this grid, you need to locate each of the features from the feature grid on the value/uniqueness spectrum.

This is a useful exercise for two reasons. First, as Richey notes, "The Feature Spectrum brings the right marketing thought process quickly into play. And it's one of the surest ways to build consensus on

EXHIBIT 1.11 FEATURE SPECTRUM

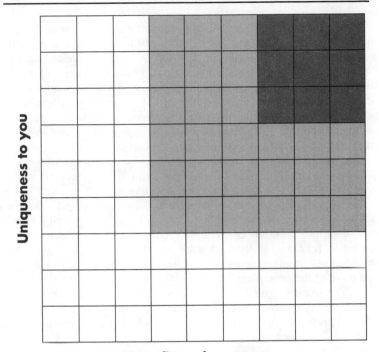

Benefit to the customer

direction."[23] The last point needs emphasis. Be sure that all of those who will approve your advertising have agreed to this chart. The next step is to prioritize those factors that appear in the upper three-by-three cube. One of these will be your strongest starting point for positioning. To help you prioritize, you can return again to "Worry Willie's Guide to Prioritizing." When applying this tool to identify your message, you should keep in mind the opportunities presented on the Positioning Cube (Exhibit 1.9). If your strongest selling point doesn't seem to fit the opportunity you identified on the cube, take another look to see if there's a more appropriate positioning. Or maybe, there's a creative opportunity you're missing.

You might also do well to consider your competition here.

COMPETITIVE ANALYSIS

You position yourself in relation to something. A pilot does not tell the tower that the plane is "here"; the pilot states a position in relation to various coordinates. When we position ourselves, we say who we are in relation to others. A vice president "position" says where someone fits in an organization in relation to other executives. "I live just north of the post office" positions your house.

The same is true of marketing positioning. It tells others where your company or product is in relation to something. That something is your competition. It is a frequently overlooked part of the marketing equation. Yet, a knowledge of your competition is essential for positioning.

Part of this knowledge can be obtained through research. This can tell you how your competitors are perceived by customers, what categories customers put you and your current and possible future products into, and what customers feel are your competitors' strengths and weaknesses within a given category or categories.

But what research provides is data. What you need is a framework within which you can place and analyze that data. Furthermore, such a framework should also give you most of the questions your research people should be asking.

The Porter Model for Competitive Analysis

There are two excellent models for this. One is Michael Porter's, and is found in his book, *Competitive Strategy* (Exhibit 1.12).[24] In this work, Porter first discusses the concept of competitor, noting that your analysis should include not only all significant existing competitors, but also potential ones.

Once these have been identified, you need to concentrate your efforts on four areas, two that pertain to what drives the competitor — future goals and assumptions — and two that pertain to what the competitor is doing and can do — current strategy and capabilities.

A knowledge of future goals can help you do several things. It

EXHIBIT 1.12 THE COMPONENTS OF A COMPETITOR ANALYSIS

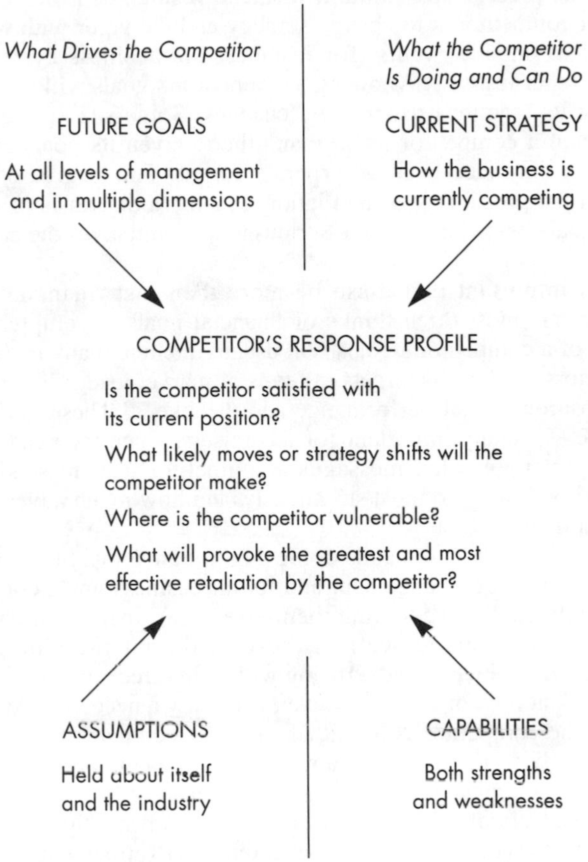

What Drives the Competitor

What the Competitor Is Doing and Can Do

FUTURE GOALS

CURRENT STRATEGY

At all levels of management and in multiple dimensions

How the business is currently competing

COMPETITOR'S RESPONSE PROFILE

Is the competitor satisfied with its current position?

What likely moves or strategy shifts will the competitor make?

Where is the competitor vulnerable?

What will provoke the greatest and most effective retaliation by the competitor?

ASSUMPTIONS

CAPABILITIES

Held about itself and the industry

Both strengths and weaknesses

Adapted and reprinted with the permission of The Free Press, a division of Simon & Schuster from *COMPETITIVE STRATEGY: Techniques for Analyzing Industries and Competitors* by Michael E. Porter. Copyright © 1980 by The Free Press.

will "allow predictions about whether or not each competitor is satisfied with its present position and financial results, and thereby, how likely that competitor is to change strategy and the vigor with which it will react to outside events (for instance, the business cycle) or to moves by other firms.... Knowing a competitor's goals will also aid in predicting its reactions to strategic changes. Some strategic changes will threaten a competitor more than others, given its goals and any pressures it may face from a corporate parent. This degree of threat will affect the probability of retaliation. Finally, a diagnosis of a competitor's goals helps interpret the seriousness of initiatives the competitor takes."[25]

It is important that these be more than just financial goals. "Although one most often thinks of financial goals, a comprehensive diagnosis of a competitor's goals will usually include many more qualitative factors, such as its targets in terms of market leadership, technological position, social performance and the like."[26] These qualitative factors are especially important for advertisers, since they can have a major impact upon what messages a competitor tries to send, what messages it will react to most strenuously, and how much advertising a competitor does.

While Porter recommends doing a thorough competitive analysis at multiple levels of management and for all business units, communicators will probably have to limit themselves to an analysis of competitors' corporate goals as well as those of the business unit(s), if applicable, with which the advertising will be in direct competition.

A look at both of those, however, is usually a necessity. As Porter notes, "If the competitor is a unit of a larger company, its corporate parent is likely to impose constraints or requirements on the business unit that will be crucial to predicting its behavior."[27]

An analysis of this sort can help you make intelligent assumptions about your competitor's likely marketing, advertising and marketing communications moves. Thus, it can lead to a better plan that is more clearly capable of identifying and exploiting both current and future opportunities.

But a firm grasp of a competitor's future goals isn't enough. You also need to look at the competitor's assumptions. These are of two kinds, assumptions about itself, and about its industry and the other companies in it.

In addition, your analysis might include two areas that prove to be key indicators of goals and assumptions. The first is history.

"What is the competitor's current financial performance and market share, compared to that of the relatively recent past?

What has been the competitor's history in the marketplace over time? Where has it failed or been beaten, and thus perhaps not likely to tread again?

In what areas has the company starred or succeeded as a company?

How has the competitor reacted to particular strategic moves or industry events in the past? Rationally? Emotionally? Slowly? Quickly? What approaches have been employed? To what sorts of events has the competitor reacted poorly, and why?"[28]

A second key area of indicators is managerial backgrounds and advisory relationships. Here, you need to look at several areas. These include:

"The functional background (finance, marketing, etc.) of top management;

The type of strategies that have worked or not worked for them personally in their careers;

The other businesses they have worked in, and what rules of the game and strategic approaches have been characteristic of those businesses;

Major events they have lived through, such as a sharp recession, traumatic energy shortage, major loss due to currency fluctuations, and so on;

Top managers' writing and speaking, their technical background or patent history where applicable, other firms they come into frequent contact with, their outside activities, and a range of other clues limited only by the imagination;

Advertising agencies and other marketing advisors used by the competitor."[29]

The third aspect of competitor analysis in Porter's framework is the competitor's current strategy, that is, how the business is currently competing. This consists of a statement of the competitor's "key operating policies in each functional area of the business and how it seeks to interrelate the functions. This strategy may be either explicit or implicit — one always exists in one form or the other."[30]

To help you focus on essentials in identifying this strategy, Porter provides a "wheel of competitive strategy" (Exhibit 1.13).[31] As Porter explains, "In the hub of the wheel are the firm's goals, which are its broad definition of how it wants to compete and its specific economic and noneconomic objectives. The spokes of the wheel are the key operating policies with which the firm is seeking to achieve these goals.

"Under each heading on the wheel a succinct statement of the key operating policies in that functional area should be derived from the company's activities. Depending on the nature of the business,

EXHIBIT 1.13 THE WHEEL OF COMPETITIVE STRATEGY

Adapted and reprinted with the permission of The Free Press, a division of Simon & Schuster from COMPETITIVE STRATEGY: Techniques for Analyzing Industries and Competitors by Michael E. Porter. Copyright © 1980 by The Free Press.

management can be more or less specific in articulating these key operating policies; once they are specified, the concept of strategy can be used to guide the overall behavior of the firm. Like a wheel, the spokes (policies) must radiate from and reflect the hub (goals), and the spokes must be connected with each other or the wheel will not roll."[32]

In other words, a company's strategy can be made explicit by looking at the goals it is seeking to achieve and then identifying the means it is using to do that. This kind of analysis can be especially valuable for those in marketing communications. It tells you what your competitor has decided to do and not do, which direction it has decided to take and which to abandon. This tells you what paths are likely to be most open, where the least resistance will be incurred. It may also give you hunches about vulnerabilities. Again, this can all be valuable information when you are identifying your key message, deciding what types of communications to integrate, and which media to buy.

The final component in Porter's framework is capabilities. "A realistic appraisal of each competitor's capabilities is the final diagnostic step in competitor analysis. Its goals, assumptions, and current strategy will influence the likelihood, timing, nature, and intensity of a competitor's reactions. Its strengths and weaknesses will determine its ability to initiate or react to strategic moves and to deal with environmental or industry events that occur."[33]

To perform this appraisal, you need to examine how the competitors' products are perceived from the user's perspective in each market segment. This means looking at the breadth and depth of your competitors' product lines, their channel coverage and quality, the strength of their channel relationships and their ability to service the channels. You should also look at your competitors' skills in each aspect of the marketing mix, market research and new product development, and the training and skills of their sales forces.

Once these components have been analyzed, it remains to synthesize them by asking questions about the competitor's potential offensive and defensive moves.

Offensively, you need to consider:

"Is the competitor dissatisfied in some way with its current position, so that it might initiate strategic change?

What are these changes likely to be?

How strenuous will these moves probably be and what would the competitor gain?"[34]

On the defensive side:

"Where are the competitor's vulnerabilities to strategic moves and to governmental, macroeconomic, or industry events?

What moves would be most likely to provoke retaliation because they threaten the competitor's goals or position?

Are there actions the competitor could not react to or would have difficulty reacting to because of its goals, strategy, existing capabilities and assumptions?"[35]

Answering these questions will help you synthesize your analytical information into a sound competitive profile.

On the surface, this process may appear more than a little daunting. However, you should remember several things.

1. This information should be readily available to you through your company's strategic marketing plan. (If it isn't, see the section on sources for competitive analysis.) It is worth using Porter's framework for competitive analysis as a guide to reading this plan. Go through the plan and see how it answers Porter's questions in each area. You might also use Porter's questions about offensive and defensive moves to assess your own company's approach. This might be a useful guide when deciding what type of advertising strategy will work best.

2. While the ideal is to use this framework for a process of rigorous analysis, practicality will limit the breadth and depth of your analysis. It is unlikely that you will have the time or resources to analyze all current and future competitors. Instead, consider the number of genuine competitors in your industry, based upon Ries and Trout's "ladder" concept discussed above. Then, limit your primary analysis to those on the rungs above you and perhaps those on the two or three rungs immediately below you.

It is a good idea, however, to keep Porter's broad definition of competitors in mind. Build a list of all of them and keep files of magazine clippings, downloaded articles, and other items. This can be a significant help during periodic communications strategy reviews.

The D'Aveni Model for Analyzing
Hypercompetitive Environments

Porter's is not the only worthwhile approach to competitive analysis. In his book, *Hypercompetition*, Richard D'Aveni proposes another model for fast-moving, hypercompetitive markets.

In his introduction to the book Ian C. MacMillen, from the Wharton School, defines hypercompetition as "an environment of intense change, in which flexible, aggressive, innovative competitors move into markets easily and rapidly, eroding the advantages of the large and established players."[36]

D'Aveni believes that the quest for a sustainable advantage, as Porter proposes, is an illusion. To him, all advantages erode. Therefore, the goal is not sustainable advantage but continuous disruption.

To know how to do this, D'Aveni presents an analytical model he calls Four Arena analysis. The four arenas are: cost and quality, timing and know-how, strongholds, and deep pockets. Each is a category of competitive moves.

Cost and quality refers to a company's ability to produce high-quality goods at a lower cost than its competitors.

Timing and know-how pertains to a company's ability to meet customers' needs faster than its competitors or provide unique expertise.

Strongholds alludes to a company's ability to create barriers to entry into a particular marketplace. This happens, for example, in some industrial markets where the sheer size of the initial investment in manufacturing facilities deters many from competing.

Deep pockets refers to a company's ability to use its vast capital resources to fend off competitive thrusts.

As D'Aveni says, Four Arena analysis "looks at the evolution of competition over time across the four arenas to identify trends and patterns of dynamic strategic interactions between competitors."[37] By performing this type of analysis, you can determine your "competitive situation, predict competitors' moves and identify the locus of competition; that is, which arena is the current or future battleground."[38]

To this, D'Aveni adds Four Lens analysis. "It looks at a single competitive move and analyzes its impact on each of the four arenas of competition."[39]

Using the hypercompetition model, you begin with a Four Arena analysis. This is essentially an analysis of trends or of the evolution of competition in your industry. It involves tracking the moves and countermoves made by competitors over a period of time.

This requires asking some key questions. What are the major competitive trends? Which arenas has your company dominated? Which have been dominated by your competitors? Which of these arenas will be the key arenas for future competition? What are the primary arenas in which you might have an opportunity to gain future advantages? How can you seize the advantage before your competitors?

This results in what D'Aveni calls "escalation ladders." "These ladders are actually cycles that can be restarted by actions of the firm. At each step of the ladder, companies move up a rung to gain advantage. Competitors are then forced to react to these moves, further escalating competition. If competitors do not react, if they fall behind on the ladder, they die…. These four escalation ladders — cost and quality, timing and know-how, stronghold creation/invasion, and deep pockets are, therefore, a conceptual way to understand market processes that occur naturally due to the competitive instincts of rivals."[40]

Once you've done this analysis, you need to determine your own competitive direction. As you consider specific steps, you can do a Four Lens analysis to help you determine what might result from those actions. To do this, you need to ask what impact the move will have on cost and quality. How it will affect timing and know-how? Strongholds? Deep pockets? What potential responses might you make to these results?

Finally, choose an arena on which to focus. To do this, look at each arena and determine if it is hyperactive (where there has been a lot of action over the past five years), erratic (big, but sporadic, moves), evolutionary (slow, continuous movement), temporarily dormant (inactive over a period of time) or arrested (nothing has happened and nothing is foreseen).

As D'Aveni notes, "In arenas that are dormant or arrested, the company should act to speed up competition, because these arenas offer the biggest opportunities for surprise. In very active arenas, the company should work to seize the initiative or shift attention elsewhere."[41] All of this can be useful in developing marketing communications messages.

Of further help is D'Aveni's assertion that not all disruptions are good. The ones that work are the ones that enable a company to serve its customers better. But by identifying customers as their primary stakeholders, companies relegate employees and shareholders to the back benches. Thus, the first task in achieving this critical strategic dimension is to find ways of putting customers first while satisfying employees and investors.

D'Aveni suggests that the key to achieving a real advantage for customers is to "identify customer needs that even the customer cannot articulate for him/herself, find new, previously unserved customers to serve, create customer needs that never existed before, and predict changes in customer needs before they happen."[42]

INFORMATION SOURCES FOR COMPETITIVE ANALYSIS

There is a variety of sources for competitive data. If you don't have a competitive intelligence or market research department to help you, consider these sources:

On-line databases today carry a wealth of information, including financial data, corporate profiles, speeches by executives, executive profiles, industry trend data and a great deal more. In fact, much of the information you need is available right at your computer. If you have an Internet connection or are connected to one of the major on-line services, chances are you can do virtually an entire competitive analysis at your desk.

Competitors themselves are good sources. Their annual and quarterly reports are public record and readily accessible. In addition, your salespeople can help you obtain competitors' marketing communications materials, such as brochures and fact sheets. You can also collect a great deal of this at major business shows. Simply go to the competitors' booths and pick it up.

Competitors' salespeople can also tell you a lot. Take a day or so and shop for competitors' products. This is especially useful when competitors sell through retail, distributors, dealers, or value-added resellers.

Competitors' former employees generally are very talkative about their former employers, including strengths and weaknesses. If you network around the business enough, you can probably find someone, maybe even someone in your own company, who used to work for a competitor. Glean what you can.

Federal, state and local government sources can be helpful. The Library of Congress, for example, has a referral service that can help you find the information you need about specific companies. There is also a Congressional Information Service Index available in many libraries. It can tell you about subjects and companies investigated by congressional committees. You may also want to check such places as the Commerce Department and publications from the United States Patent and Trademark Office. State labor departments, local chambers of commerce and better business bureaus are also good starting points.

Trade and industry associations publish directories with useful information about competitors. They also often have industry experts who can help you with industry practices and trends.

Investment analysts are constantly preparing reports for their customers on both industries and trends. Find out from your financial people or some other source who the top analysts are in your industry, give them a call or watch the financial papers for notice of available reports.

ADDITIONAL COMPETITIVE ANALYSIS TOOLS

The following charts can be useful to you in laying out your analyses in simple, easily accessible form.

The first is your Competitive Analysis Chart (Exhibit 1.14). It allows you to detail your findings from the Porter competitive analysis in a clear, readily usable format.

The second (Exhibit 1.15) is a chart for summarizing Porter's Competitor's Response Profile. Using the questions at the center of the Porter competitive framework, it lets you begin to focus on possible actions you can take and reactions competitors might make to your marketing activities.

Finally, as a guide and as a transition to the next section, we offer D'Aveni's own chart for strategy determination (Exhibit 1.16).

In addition to giving you a perspective on your industry and competitors, this type of competitive analysis can help with valuable forecasting that can lead to very effective advertising messages and strategies.

Competitive analysis of the sort and extent described in this sec-

EXHIBIT 1.14 COMPETITIVE ANALYSIS CHART

Topic	Competitor A	Competitor B	Competitor C	Competitor D
Current strategy?				
Capabilities?				
Future goals?				
Assumptions?				

EXHIBIT 1.15 COMPETITOR'S RESPONSE PROFILE

Question	Competitor A	Competitor B	Competitor C	Competitor D
Satisfied with current position?				
Likely moves or strategy shifts?				
Vulnerabilities?				
What will provoke the greatest and most effective retaliation?				

EXHIBIT 1.16 A HYPOTHETICAL FOUR-ARENA ANALYSIS

If the Firm Needs to Improve Its Competitive Position in Arena	Key Success Factors Are	The Most Critical New 7-S's Are
Cost/Quality	• Understanding customer needs • Cost reduction	• S-1 Shareholder Satisfaction • S-3 Speed
Know-how/Timing	• Becoming fast at market penetration • Building new know-how and innovation	• S-3 Speed • S-4 Surprise • S-2 Soothsaying
Stronghold Creation/Invasion	• Deterrence • Aggression	• S-6 Signals • S-7 Strategic Thrusts
Deep Pockets	• Use of brute force • Thwarting or out-maneuvering big opponents	• S-7 Strategic Thrusts • S-5 Shifting the Rules of Competition

Adapted and reprinted with the permission of The Free Press, a division of Simon & Schuster from HYPERCOMPETITION: Managing The Dynamics of Strategic Maneuvering by Richard A. D'Aveni with Robert Gunther. Copyright © 1994 by Richard A. D'Aveni.

tion can lead to better planning, more effective long-term positioning and more efficient expenditure of your advertising dollars.

PULLING IT ALL TOGETHER

If you've done the preceding phases well, you'll have both a comprehensive and a well-focused picture of your audience, your products and the needs they fulfill, and how they stand up to your competition. It is now time to pull it all together into an advertising strategy.

While we are focusing here on advertising, advertising needs to support—and be supported by—your other marketing communications. Therefore, our assumption is that we are talking not only about advertising, but about your total marketing communications package.

First, pulling it all together requires that you collect all of your audience segmentation, message development, and competitive analysis information. The development of these materials should have given you a sound grasp of your marketing playing field. Now, however, comes the final decision making. For this purpose, you might want to draw out the key visual material. This might include your audience segmentation charts, the circle of audiences and the pyramid of priorities, as well as your decision process and audience profile charts. You should also include your Feature Grid and Feature Spectrum. And you will also want your competitive analysis. These are your working tools.

Your next step is to decide how you will coordinate your strategic tools: power, space, time, and implementation capability. This means determining such factors as:

- The strength of your creative. Do you have a clear, strong, well-focused theme? Are you comfortable with your positioning?
- Your budget. Do you have enough money to achieve the reach and frequency you need? How does your budget compare with that of your competitors?
- Your people resources. Do you have confidence in your creative team? Is your media planner especially innovative? Will you get sound marketing communications advice from the people heading your effort on a day-to-day basis?

Your plan should begin with a clear statement of your objectives as specified at the beginning of the planning process. Winning means accomplishing these. Furthermore, you need to know that you are winning, so the objectives must be measurable.

Next, consider your marketing theme and its supporting argument. Include this in the plan. To win means communicating this message to your key audiences. This is the time to think in terms of integrated communications. Your message should be transmitted through various channels. You need to use several target advertising media. And you need to think of ways other than advertising to get your message into your audience's mind.

You need to ask, "What are the best channels of communication to use to reach each of my audiences?" In the case of advertising, this will certainly focus on types of media (newspapers, magazines, television, etc.) as well as specific publications, networks, and so on. However, your audience may also be reachable through your direct sales force, retail outlets, the mail, telemarketing, and a range of others. List them all.

Then in light of your budget and other resources, decide what kinds of communications you will create for each of these audiences in each of these channels. This process should include the type of communications (print ads, brochures, direct mail campaigns, etc.), the schedule for doing this and a general budget.

In considering your schedule, think in terms of the business year in your industry, its cycles and major events. If your fiscal year and calendar year are the same, you may find that things go with a rush in the second and fourth quarters. In the first quarter, people may just be doing their plans, while in the third quarter, summer vacation may slow things down.

This, of course, will be different for different industries. If you're in the patio and deck furniture business, the second and third quarters may be your busiest. If you're in the winter sportswear business, on the other hand, the first and fourth quarters may be your busiest times. In either case, the business cycle will determine the timing of your marketing communications effort.

In addition, you'll want to take into account trade and business shows, as well as other major industry events. You may, for example, want to announce a new product, ad campaign, or other activity before or during these events. In making these assessments, you should look at your competition. If a competitor with deep pockets is going to make a loud noise of its own during an industry or other event, you will want to time your announcement before or after this, so your message doesn't get lost in the blast.

To further refine your strategy, consider AIDA. This is the awareness-interest-desire-action model of the selling cycle mentioned earlier in this chapter. You may want to break it down further as awareness, interest, evaluation, test, action. This second model is especially useful in business-to-business.

You need to determine where each of your audiences is in this cycle. Then, identify the types of communications that will work best to answer the pertinent questions identified with each phase.

Finally, as you do this, consider the advice of some of the great strategists through the ages. One of these who is frequently quoted and widely read is Sun Tzu, a Chinese general who lived some 25 centuries ago. He identifies five essentials for victory. One essential has to do with power. "He will win who knows how to handle both superior and inferior forces."[43]

Two more have to do with timing. "He will win who knows when to fight and when not to fight."[44] And, "He will win who, prepared himself, waits to take the enemy unprepared."[45] The final two have to do with implementation capability. "He will win whose army is animated by the same spirit throughout all its ranks."[46] And, "He will win who has military capacity and is not interfered with by the sovereign.[47]

In more modern times, B.H. Liddell Hart in his book, *Strategy*, offers some additional matters of wisdom. Hart's book is a survey of military strategy from the fifth century B.C. through World War II. He concludes it with what he calls "the concentrated essence of strategy and tactics."[48]

Hart divides his eight maxims into two sections, "positive" and "negative." His first piece of advice is essential for you to remember as you begin your planning process. "Adjust your end to your means." As Hart explains, "In determining your objective, clear sight and cool calculation should prevail. It is folly to 'bite off more than you can chew,' and the beginning of military wisdom is a sense of what is possible. So learn to face facts while still preserving faith: there will be ample need for faith — the faith that can achieve the apparently impossible — when action begins."

Hart then moves on to the need for a clear goal. "Keep your object always in mind, while adapting your plan to circumstances." Note the word "adapting." It is a verb of process. It implies that strategy is not a single event, but an ongoing process, a fact that we shall note again when we discuss evaluating your strategy.

This process, however, must always be aimed at the goal. Otherwise, the dangers are significant, because "to wander down a sidetrack is bad, but to reach a dead end is worse." Being driven by an enemy into a canyon from which there is no escape is an old strategy, a fatal one to you. Keeping your goal in mind will help you avoid this fate.

Having gotten by general principles, Hart moves on to specifics. His third maxim is, "Choose the line (or course) of least expectation." He advises, "Try to put yourself in the enemy's shoes, and think what course it is least probable he will foresee or forestall." Both Porter's and D'Aveni's competitive models can help you with this exercise. Both are aimed at anticipating your competition and seeing where your competitors are least likely to expect an attack.

The next maxim follows from this. "Exploit the line of least resistance." Again, both Porter's and D'Aveni's models can help you identify this. The critical success factor, however, is not only to see where the least resistance lies, but also to be quick enough to exploit it. As we noted earlier, "timing is everything."

Hart now pushes strategy to a more sophisticated level. "Take a line of operation which offers alternative objectives." To Hart, an object and an objective are different. An object is a goal; an objective is a subgoal needed to achieve the object.

He cautions, "There is no more common mistake than to confuse a single line of operation [toward a goal], which is usually wise, with a single objective, which is usually futile." Instead, he counsels you to find "alternative objectives" that put your opponent on the horns of a dilemma, "which goes far to assure the chance of gaining one objective at least — whichever he guards least (the line of least resistance, noted above [ed.]) — and may enable you to gain one after the other."

During Porter's analysis, you looked at market areas critical to your competitor's strategy. You can now apply Hart's maxim. For example, you might select two market areas that are critical to you. Your marketing communications strategy could attack both. As your competitor defends the one it believes is the more critical of the two, you can secure the other. If your competitor fails to defend the other adequately, you may even be able to take both. But you will surely get one.

Throughout this process, you need to keep in mind Hart's final "positive" maxim, "Ensure that both plan and dispositions are flexible, adaptable to circumstances." This means, "Your plan should foresee and provide for a next step in case of success or failure, or partial success — which is the most common in war." And he counsels you to be ready to respond "in the shortest possible time."

Finally, Hart provides two "do nots." First, "Do not throw your weight into a stroke whilst your opponent is on guard." This is an application of his maxim to exploit the line of least resistance. This is particularly appropriate when you are fighting a bigger opponent. "The experience of history shows that, save against a much inferior opponent, no effective stroke is possible until his power of resistance or evasion is paralyzed." What are the signs that the time is right? Hart specifies two: disorganization and demoralization.

The second "do not" further reinforces the need for flexibility and monitoring. Furthermore, while the other maxims are important and valuable, this is one advertising people seem to ignore constantly. "Do not renew an attack along the same line (or in the same form) after it has once failed."

The reason for this, as Hart explains, is that "A mere reinforcement of weight is not sufficient change, for it is probable that the enemy also will have strengthened himself in the interval. It is even more probable that his success in repulsing you will have strengthened him morally."

This kind of thinking gets in the way in advertising. It occurs when, instead of admitting that a campaign is based upon a bad idea or a weak creative concept, advertisers opine that it will work well if it just gets "a bit of tweaking." As Hart, explains, not so.

EVALUATING YOUR STRATEGY

In evaluating your strategy, it is important to remember that strategy development is not a one-time event. Strategy has to do with how you are going to win. In business, this is an ongoing matter.

As many of the people we've discussed in this chapter, from Michael Porter to Richard D'Aveni, from Sun Tzu to Hart, rightly recognize, strategy must be constantly evaluated and revised to respond to a continuously changing playing field. Once you launch your strategy, your competitors will respond. Then, you will need to review your strategy and make appropriate changes.

However, the first evaluation should come now, as you've completed the initial strategy. A variety of criteria can be used to do this, a number of which have already been discussed in this chapter. The chapters on research and measurement presented later in this book offer more quantitative means.

In the end, a strategy must answer "yes" to several key questions:

1. Have you assessed the situation realistically?
2. Have you assessed the competition properly?
3. Have you assessed your resources properly?
4. Do you have the resources to execute your strategy effectively?
5. Will effective execution achieve your goals satisfactorily?
6. Will effective execution leave you in a strong position to continue competing?

Building Consensus to Create Success

In keeping with the consensus-building theme of this chapter, we will close with an evaluation approach that combines two techniques from *Thinkertoys*. It should help you obtain some objective answers to these questions.

The first is called Murder Board:

"Seek out people in your network of friends, relatives, and coworkers who have a creative mindset or are knowledgeable about your idea's environment.

The perfect feedback person has good imagination, perception, vision, and is as cold-eyed and objective as a pawnbroker pricing a broken watch.

Select as many as you wish and ask each for his or her help in providing you with feedback (it is probably best to approach them one at a time). How you involve people in your idea can make or break the Board's effectiveness. Give each person your written proposal and listen carefully to what they say, without judging.

Encourage each person to articulate his or her thoughts as they ponder your proposal and brainstorm with you for ways to improve your idea or its implementation. Play devil's advocate. If you get objections, make them tell you why they feel it won't work. Get specifics."[49]

In terms of your advertising plan, you might go to each member of your marketing team who will be involved in developing and approving your marketing communications. Review your strategy with them. Explain how you came to your conclusions, so they can understand your reasoning.

When you are done with the Murder Board, ask individuals to fill out, or fill out with them, a questionnaire that calls for numerical indexing. Ask them to quantify their responses to each of the following questions on a scale of 1–10, with 10 being a clear "Yes." (The point spreads are purely subjective. You can change them to suit your needs.) Your questionnaire might ask such questions as:

1. Have we selected the right target audience(s)?
2. Is our theme appropriate?
3. Is our supporting material strong?
4. Is our competitive analysis correct?
5. Is our timing appropriate?
6. Are we going into the right media?
7. Have we integrated our advertising with the right communications of other kinds?
8. Are you confident that we are ready to execute our strategy?

If there are numbers on which you score especially low, ask for clarification.

When you have all of your feedback, revise the plan accordingly. You can decide whether you need another round of feedback or whether you should start to execute. If you do not do another round of feedback, at least make revisions and check back with people who had strong concerns and whose support you must have to implement your campaign effectively. When their concerns have been satisfied, start to execute.

NOTES

1. Ann Langley, "Between 'Paralysis by Analysis' and 'Extinction by Instinct'," The Sloan Management Review, Spring 1995:74 by permission of publisher. Copyright 1995 by Sloan Management Review Association. All rights reserved.

2. Ibid.

3. Alexander Hiam, The Vest-Pocket Marketer (Prentice Hall, 1991), 49. Used by permission of Prentice Hall/Career & Personal Development.

4. Ibid., 50.

5. Alexander Hiam and Charles D. Schewe, The Portable MBA in Marketing (Copyright © 1992 John Wiley & Sons, Inc.), 205. Reprinted by permission of John Wiley & Sons, Inc.

6. Ibid.

7. Ibid.

8. Ibid., 207.

9. Michael Michalko, Thinkertoys (Copyright © 1991 by Michael Michalko with permission from Ten Speed Press, P.O. Box 7123, Berkeley, CA 94707), 319–323.

10. Al Ries and Jack Trout, Positioning: The Battle for Your Mind (New York: McGraw-Hill, 1986), 2. Reprinted with permission of The McGraw-Hill Companies.

11. Ibid., 3.

12. Ibid., 29.

13. Leo Bogart, Strategy in Advertising (NTC Business Books, 1996), 185.

14. Al Ries and Jack Trout, The 22 Immutable Laws of Marketing. Copyright © 1993 by Al Ries and Jack Trout. (New York: HarperCollins), 3. Reprinted with permission of HarperCollins Publishers, Inc.

15. Terry Richey, The Marketer's Visual Tool Kit (New York: AMACOM, a division of American Management Association, 1994), 45. All rights reserved.

16. Al Ries and Jack Trout, The 22 Immutable Laws of Marketing. Copyright © 1993 by Al Ries and Jack Trout. (New York: HarperCollins, 1993), 11 and 13. Reprinted with permission of HarperCollins Publishers, Inc.

17. Ibid., 27.

18. Ibid., 35.

19. Terry Richey, The Marketer's Visual Tool Kit (New York: AMACOM, a division of American Management Association, 1994), 79.

20. Al Ries and Jack Trout, The 22 Immutable Laws of Marketing. Copyright © 1993 by Al Ries and Jack Trout. (New York: HarperCollins, 1993), 39. Reprinted with permission of HarperCollins Publishers, Inc.

21. Ibid., 41.

22. Terry Richey, *The Marketer's Visual Tool Kit* (New York: AMACOM, 1994), 89.

23. Ibid., 51.

24. Michael E. Porter, *Competitive Strategy* (New York: The Free Press, a division of Simon & Schuster, Copyright © 1980 by The Free Press), 49. Adapted and reprinted with the permission of The Free Press.

25. Ibid., 50.

26. Ibid., 51.

27. Ibid., 53.

28. Ibid., 61.

29. Ibid., 61–63.

30. Ibid., 63.

31. Ibid., xvii.

32. Ibid., xvii.

33. Ibid., 63.

34. Ibid., 67.

35. Ibid., 68.

36. Richard D'Aveni with Robert Gunther, *Hypercompetition: Managing The Dynamics of Strategic Maneuvering* (New York: The Free Press, a division of Simon & Schuster, Copyright © 1994 by Richard A. D'Aveni), ix. Adapted and reprinted with the permission of The Free Press.

37. Ibid., 179.

38. Ibid.

39. Ibid.

40. Ibid., 181.

41. Ibid., 209.

42. Ibid., 245.

43. Sun Tzu, *The Art of War.* James Clavell, ed. (New York: Delta, 1983), 17.

44. Ibid.

45. Ibid.

46. Ibid.

47 Ibid.

48. From *STRATEGY*, 2nd Revised Edition by B. H. Liddell-Hart, © by Faber & Faber Ltd., England, 1954, 1967. Reprinted by permission of Henry Holt & Co., Inc.

49. Michael Michalko, *Thinkertoys* (Copyright © 1991 by Michael Michalko with permission from Ten Speed Press, P.O. Box 7123, Berkeley, CA 94707), 328.

Anthony Adams is professor of marketing at the University of Pennsylvania's Wharton School. Before joining the Wharton faculty, he was director, Strategic Marketing Research at the Coca-Cola Company, where he managed a $40 million global information network, and vice president of marketing research and planning at Campbell Soup Company.

One of today's most frequently quoted marketers, Adams was chairman of the Board of Directors of the Advertising Research Foundation (ARF) and former chairman of the Research Committee and member of the Advertising Management Committee of the Association of National Advertisers (ANA).

As a consultant, Adams works on advertising and marketing issues with a range of corporations, including Baltimore Gas & Electric, Clorox, Colgate-Palmolive, CPC, GTE, and Motorola.

CHAPTER 2

ADVERTISING RESEARCH

*Research can be of incalculable help in producing more effective
advertising.*
—David Ogilvy
Ogilvy on Advertising

*A renaissance is emerging ... the balanced integration of the sci-
ence and art of advertising will be the catalyst. That is, new learning
about how advertising works is being systematically applied toward
developing and managing advertising that sells.*
—Anthony J. Adams and Margaret H. Blair
"Persuasive Advertising and Sales Accountability:
Past Experience and Forward Validation"

John Wanamaker once declared: "Half my advertising is wasted,
and the trouble is I don't know which half."

In 1990, Dr. Magid Abraham and Dr. Leonard Lodish, of
Information Resources, Inc., confirmed Wanamaker's hypothesis. Using
their BehaviorScan® advertising tests, they reported that "increased
advertising led to more sales only about half the time."

Because advertising's contribution to sales has long been
believed to be too complex to measure, it has traditionally managed to
escape close scrutiny. With an increasing focus on the bottom-line, corporations are now requiring marketing to become more accountable for
its expenditures. In their 1995 article on the current "crisis" in marketing, marketing professors Jagdish Sheth and Rajendra Sisodia wrote:
"Many marketing phenomena are still not accurately measurable.
Without reliable measurement, meaningful improvements in efficiency
levels are extremely difficult to achieve. Marketing is beginning to
resemble manufacturing in the 'pre-quality' days. Whereas the TQM
[Total Quality Management] philosophy resolved many of manufacturing's problems, a similar change still awaits marketing."

What does this mean to the advertising industry? Primarily, managers must be prepared to support advertising decisions with hard facts
and demonstrable success. To accomplish this goal, marketers must
embrace the proper measurements, ones that are not only accurate but
valuable: "Traditionally, productivity has been measured in terms of
the *quantity* of output for a given amount of input. However, such measures are unsatisfactory in that they fail to adjust for changes in the
desirability of the output" (Sheth and Sisodia, 1995).

When using valid and reliable measurement, the impact of advertising is predictable. Advertising *can* be a profitable marketing tool.

This chapter will examine:
- the field of advertising pretesting
- a process for advertising improvement
- success cases based on this process.

PRETESTING: BEFORE ADVERTISING GOES TO AIR

The role of advertising measurement should be to help the agency create more effective advertising and to aid management in making better business decisions. In 1982, top research professionals of 21 major agencies developed the Positioning Advertising Copy Testing (PACT) Principles. (See the Appendix to this chapter.) The PACT Principles state that "copy testing should and can provide guidance for both the advertiser and the agency. Both share the common goal of running effective advertising and learning how effective advertising works." Unfortunately, rather than aiming for this "common goal," it is often evident that the agency, advertiser, and researchers are working at cross-purposes.

Agencies' efforts are often evaluated based on pretesting scores. This has resulted in some resentment by ad agencies toward research. According to copy-testing historian Darrell Lucas: "Testing, in itself, is a reflection on the judgments of creative people. However, they are likely to be the first to endorse a test which confirms their own judgment." John Keil (1985) colorfully described the creative person's position by likening it to "sitting in Sardi's waiting for the first edition of *The New York Times* to find out how the critic reacts to a Broadway show." Paul Feldwick, head of account planning at BMP DDB Needham in London, put the research-agency relationship in a somewhat darker light: "The words 'quantitative pretesting' in an advertising agency produce a predictable reaction — the verbal equivalent of the garlic and the crucifix at the approach of the vampire."

Agencies' negative reactions to quantitative testing are understandable; it is all too often used to evaluate agencies without giving them feedback to help them succeed. At the same time, it is hard to dispute the value of pretesting if it can, in fact, predict advertising's in-market effects. The key to a successful, mutually beneficial advertising program is to provide a means of consistently *improving* advertising success as well as accurately *predicting* when in-market success will occur.

THE HISTORY OF PRETESTING

Because television did not enter into mainstream society until the late 1940s and early 1950s, the earliest advertising pretesting was conducted on print advertising. In the 1920s and 1930s, methods for measuring the recognition of print advertisements were used by George Gallup and Daniel Starch. In 1948, the first print-testing research company was founded by Gallup and Claude Robinson.

Gallup and Robinson (G&R) developed the day-after-recall method. This method was later refined by the Procter and Gamble Company and Compton Advertising, Inc., one of its agencies, and would eventually become the Burke Day-After-Recall (DAR) technique. Variations on this method are still widely used to measure *reception* of the advertising stimulus, or whether the ad captured enough attention for respondents to remember having seen or heard the commercial. Usually this is expressed as a percentage of the total number of respondents (for example, if 23 of 100 respondents "recalled" the commercial, the recall score would be 23 percent). Exactly how recall is defined and gathered varies by the research provider. The measure may be "aided" or "unaided," with "aided" meaning that the respondent is prompted for an answer using the brand name or category. Recall can be gathered at any time following exposure, but one to three days is the usual period.

Pre-post preference-shift measurement originated with U. S. Army research on motivation conducted by Horace Schwerin during World War II. According to a 1964 article in *Printers' Ink*, "During the second World War, Schwerin directed large-scale Army studies to develop methods for making training messages more effective" (Dodd, 1964). In 1946, Schwerin Research Corporation (SRC) was founded, with Horace Schwerin serving as the company's president.

Subsequently, SRC developed Competitive Preference, a pre-post method of measuring advertising's effectiveness. The objective of this measurement was to predict the in-market response to the advertising stimulus by determining whether the ad was successful in convincing respondents to choose the advertised brand over its competition. In his overview of copy-test methods, Darrell Lucas described the technique: "Schwerin devised a procedure in which test subjects were invited to choose a free sample from a group of competing brands, including the brand to be tested. Each group was then exposed to advertising of the test brand, after which they were invited to choose a second free sample from the competing brands. Changes between the first and second choices were used to measure the advertising effect." In addition to this measurement, SRC also provided measures of communications and liking. Liking (also referred to as likeability) simply measures how well the respondents liked a particular ad. Liking is usually obtained using a five-point scale ranging from "liked very much" to "disliked very much." Although many advancements and refinements have been made since the 1960s, variations on the same basic techniques are still used today.

EVALUATING SUPPLIERS AND THEIR MEASUREMENTS
How does one pick the right measurement to pretest advertising? To answer this question, we will examine the methodologies of four

major television advertising pretesting suppliers, as well as their measurements' reliability, validity, and improvement records.

Because print advertising is typically measured in terms of readership or direct response rather than sales, pretest measurements for print will not be covered in this chapter. However, it should be noted that some of the measurements used in print research — such as recall or intrusiveness, idea communication, and attitude — are similar to the ones offered by television advertising pretest suppliers. Thus, many of the principles discussed in this chapter should be relevant to print advertising testing.

METHODOLOGY

rsc: The Quality Measurement Company

In 1968, Schwerin Research Corporation was acquired by investors in Evansville, Indiana, and **research systems corporation (rsc)** was formed. Margaret H. Blair, Schwerin's former head of Basic Research, has served as president of **rsc** since its inception. The company's primary measurement is the *ARS Persuasion*® measure, which evolved from SRC's Competitive Preference measurement. The *ARS Persuasion* measurement is based on a pre-post shift in brand choice obtained in a secure, off-air, simulated-purchase environment. It is calculated by subtracting the percent of respondents choosing the advertised product over competition *before* exposure to the television material from the percent choosing the advertised product *after* exposure — the net effect of retention and attraction as a result of the advertising stimulus. In the United States, the *ARS Persuasion* sample consists of 800–1,000 respondents (aged 16+) randomly recruited by mail from four geographically dispersed markets. **rsc** *Validated*ˢᴹ diagnostics — based on the advertising's strategic, communication, and executional elements — are provided with each ARSˢᴹ test. **rsc** is also the originator and sole provider of the **rsc** *T. Q. Process*ˢᴹ for continuous improvement in the sales effectiveness of television advertising.

ASI Market Research, Inc.

Audience Studies, Inc. (ASI), formerly a part of Columbia Pictures Corporation, became an independent research organization in 1963, with Gerry Lukeman, a former Schwerin large-group moderator, as president. Unlike the ARS system, APEXˢᴹ respondents view the commercials in their homes on cable television. Tests are conducted in at least two of ASI's 12 to 14 available markets. On the day of the test, approximately 200 respondents are recruited to "preview" a new television program, and appointments are made for re-interviewing. In the Tru-Share® brand-choice test procedure, pre-exposure brand usage and brand preference are obtained during the initial contact. Within two hours after exposure, respondents are re-contacted to obtain their post-exposure brand preference. In the Recall Plus® test procedure, respondents are exposed to the test material and re-contacted the following day for interviewing. The Recall Plus tests are used to obtain recall and recognition, from which the commercial's Measured Attention level and Brand Linkage Ratio are computed. The resulting Attention/Linkage Analysis® is used to determine the effect of executional factors on commercial recall. ASI has combined its recall and Tru-Share measurements to create the Copy Effect Index℠. ASI also offers diagnostics through custom-designed questionnaires or its Structured Diagnostics℠, a standardized questionnaire for which norms are available. Other ASI services include print testing, infomercial testing, marketing-mix modeling, and brand-equity research.

McCollum Spielman Worldwide

McCollum Spielman was founded by former Schwerin vice-presidents Donald H. McCollum and Harold M. Spielman in 1968. McCollum Spielman conducts off-air testing in four geographically dispersed locations that have been "linked" together with video tape. The sample for the test consists of approximately 400 respondents. One of MSW's differentiating features is its use of a double-exposure methodology. Before exposure, respondents are asked demographic questions, including a brand-usage question to be used in determining pre-exposure brand preference. After the first exposure, Clutter Awareness (a form of unaided recall) and Main Idea Communication measurements are gathered. After the second exposure, respondents are asked to select one of a list of products to establish post-exposure brand preference (Attitude Shift). Diagnostic data are also gathered at this time. MSW also does print and radio testing, focus groups, concept testing, packaging studies, promotion and premium testing, and product testing.

Millward Brown International

Millward Brown was founded in the U.K in 1973 and began operating in the United States in 1986. The company's Link copy test is conducted at central locations among a custom sample of 150 respondents. The system consists of three parts: the Core Module, the Communication Module, and the Video Module. The Core Module includes two open-ended questions and four rating scales. The rating scales measure enjoyment, attention-getting, perceived branding, and perceived ease of following. The Communication Module consists of verbal diagnostics, including both open-ended and aided communication questions, detailed comprehension, likes and dislikes, and brand influence. Finally, the Video Module measures the respondent's continuous involvement in the ad by using a joy stick to produce an interest track.

RELIABILITY

In 1979, Michael Ray, editor of the *Journal of Marketing Research*, stated that "managerial objectives can be met only when measures are reliable (contain little irrelevant measurement error)." The PACT Agencies (1982) agreed: "A copy testing system...should yield the same results each time that the advertising is tested. If, for example, a test of multiple executions does not yield the same rank order of performance on test/retest, the test is not reliable and should not be used to judge the performance of commercials. Tests in which external variables are not held constant will probably yield unreliable results."

In the field of advertising pretesting, reliability is usually measured by testing the same advertisement twice among different samples. If the measurement is reliable, the two independently obtained scores should be comparable to each other (that is, they should not be statistically different more often than would be expected if only random sampling error is present in the test result).

Most of the major research suppliers conduct some sort of reliability program to ensure consistent results. rsc was the pioneer in this area with its ARSAR[SM] (ARS Automatic Retest) program. In this program, every "nth" commercial is retested. Three statistical methods are used to evaluate the test-retest results: an F-test (ratio of observed to expected variance), a chi-square analysis, and correlations. This reliability program has been conducted on an ongoing basis since 1971, and has been implemented in each country in which rsc operates (rsc, 1995).

ASI's reliability data are produced through ASISTR (ASI Systematic Test-Retest), which appears to be modeled after rsc's ARSAR program. In the ASI program, client tests (generally two or three Tru-Share tests and about five recall tests each month) are randomly selected and retested. Chi-square analyses are used to analyze the resulting data (ASI Market Research, Inc., 1991a and 1991b).

McCollum Spielman applies an Analysis of Variance to its test-retest data to measure the replicability of its Clutter Awareness and Motivation measurements. In addition, MSW measures the discrimination of the AC-T measurements by determining the percentage of executions tested within a campaign that obtain a significantly different score from the campaign norm. The basic purpose is to determine "whether the AC-T methodology yields a substantial enough range of scores so that discrimination occurs among a brand's alternative executions." (McCollum Spielman Worldwide, *AC-T Reliability and Discrimination of Primary Measures*) All three companies have published analyses examining the reliability levels of their primary measurements. No data are available for Millward Brown International.

VALIDITY

As stated by the PACT Agencies (1982): "A copy testing system ... should provide results which are relevant to marketplace performance. PACT Agencies recognize that demonstration of validity is a major and costly undertaking requiring industrywide participation. While some evidence of predictive validity is available, many systems are in use for which no evidence of validity is provided. We encourage the cooperation of advertisers and agencies in pursuit of this critical need."

In 1964, *Printers' Ink* published the first major study comparing advertising *quality* (defined as Schwerin Research Corporation's Relative Competitive Preference measurement) and advertising *weight* (as measured by media expenditures) to changes in market share for established products. The study found that 39 percent of the changes in market share could be attributed to changes in advertising, with ad quality accounting for more of the variance than weight (31 versus 8 percent) (Kelly, 1964). Regarding this study, Harvard's Bob Buzzell (1964) stated in the *Journal of Marketing Research*: "The content and presentation of advertising messages, as measured by the SRC commercial tests, is related to short-term changes in market share. If anything, advertising message quality is more important than the level of advertising expenditure." SRC replicated the study in West Germany in 1968 with similar results (Murphy, 1968).

rsc continued in the tradition of SRC with new-product ATU (Awareness, Trial, and Usage) studies in the 1970s, which also indicated that the measured quality of the ad (*ARS Persuasion* level) was more important than weight alone (**rsc**, 1983). In the 1980s, established-brand studies produced similar learning. "In split-cable copy tests, the panels exposed to commercials with higher *ARS Persuasion* scores had significantly higher sales. *ARS Persuasion* differences accurately predicted seven out of seven cases" (Adams and Blair, 1992, Exhibit 2.1). Related Recall was predictive in only two of the seven cases.

Split-cable advertising *weight* tests conducted in the 1980s again indicated the importance of advertising quality. As reported in the *Journal of Advertising Research*, "The 'no difference' tests employed advertising with low *ARS Persuasion* scores. In the cases where *[ARS] Persuasion* was higher, the weight increases did produce a positive sales response" (Blair, 1987, Exhibit 2.2). Based on these findings, **rsc** constructed elasticity ranges to help advertisers gauge the probability of an in-market effect given an ad's *ARS Persuasion* score:

- If an ad is in the elastic range (an *ARS Persuasion* score above 7.0), a sales or share change is expected.
- A sales or share change is possible for moderately elastic ads scoring between 4.0 and 6.9.

EXHIBIT 2.1

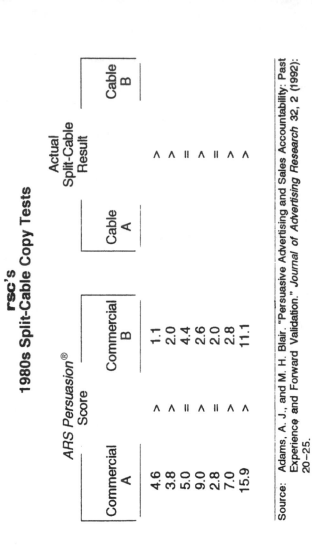

**rsc's
1980s Split-Cable Copy Tests**

ARS Persuasion® Score			Actual Split-Cable Result	
Commercial A		Commercial B	Cable A	Cable B
4.6	>	1.1		>
3.8	>	2.0		>
5.0	=	4.4		=
9.0	>	2.6		>
2.8	=	2.0		=
7.0	>	2.8		>
15.9	>	11.1		>

Source: Adams, A. J., and M. H. Blair. "Persuasive Advertising and Sales Accountability: Past Experience and Forward Validation." *Journal of Advertising Research 32,* 2 (1992): 20–25.

EXHIBIT 2.2

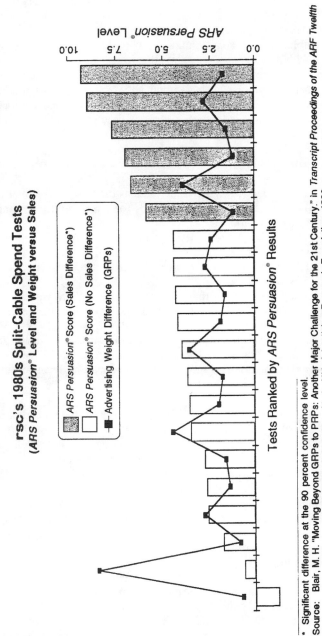

rsc's 1980s Split-Cable Spend Tests
(*ARS Persuasion*® Level and Weight versus Sales)

ARS Persuasion® Score (Sales Difference*)

ARS Persuasion® Score (No Sales Difference*)

Advertising Weight Difference (GRPs)

ARS Persuasion® Level

10.0   7.5   5.0   2.5   0.0

Tests Ranked by *ARS Persuasion*® Results

* Significant difference at the 90 percent confidence level.
Source: Blair, M. H. "Moving Beyond GRPs to PRPs: Another Major Challenge for the 21st Century." in *Transcript Proceedings of the ARF Twelfth Annual Electronic Media Workshop.* New York, NY: Advertising Research Foundation, 1993.

- Low elastic ads (with *ARS Persuasion* scores between 2.0 and 3.9) are not expected to produce a measurable sales or share change.
- Ads scoring below a 2.0 are in the inelastic range. No measurable sales or share changes have been observed among ads with *ARS Persuasion* scores this low.

rsc's most recent validation work involves a free-market analysis using 225 new- and established-brand ads. Note that other marketing variables, including media weight, price, promotions, and competitive activity *were not* factored into this analysis. Each case was examined to ensure that it met these criteria:

- The ad was tested before it began to air.
- The ad ran in at least two consecutive four-week periods when first aired.
- The case used scanner share data as the post-market metric.
- The brand did not drop coupons for a free product during the analysis period.
- The ad was the only one aired for the advertised product during the analysis period.
- Distribution levels were available over the analysis period (for new-brand cases).

"Among the 53 cases that met these criteria, there was a positive correlation of 0.67 between short-term market-share change and the *ARS Persuasion* level" (Kuse and Crang, 1995, Exhibit 2.3).

These cases were also evaluated relative to the elasticity levels derived from the 1980s split-cable studies. Each of the 53 free-market cases was classified on two dimensions: the elasticity level of the ad's *ARS Persuasion* score and the actual in-market share change. As reported by Kuse and Crang (1995): "All of the elastic ads produced at least a half-point share increase, with 91 percent of these ads producing an increase of a full share point. And while 70 percent of the elastic ads produced a two-share-point increase, none of the low elastic or inelastic ads produced a share change this large" (Exhibit 2.4).

In total, the *ARS Persuasion* measure has been shown to relate to in-market sales results in nearly 800 observations covering market share, new-product trial, sales volume, and category volume (Exhibit 2.5).

ASI's validation consists of 10 split-cable copy-test cases. In seven, sales results were correctly identified by recall scores. In six, sales results were correctly identified by Tru-Share scores. ASI has developed the Copy Effect Index, a model that combines recall and preference-shift scores. This combined measure was fitted to the ten cases, but no validation of this modeled measure on an independent data set has yet been published (Exhibit 2.6).

According to Peter Klein and Melvin Tainiter, "McCollum Spielman & Company (M/S/C) has had limited success in securing

EXHIBIT 2.3

rsc 1995 Free-Market Study:
Share Change versus *ARS Persuasion*® Level

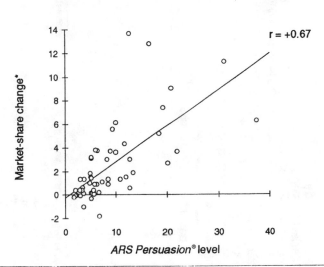

ARS Persuasion® level

* Source: InfoScan® or SCANTRACK®. (Four-week period after onset of advertising, versus four-week period before advertising.)

Source: Kuse, A. R., and D. E. Crang. "Some Universal Truths about Advertising: Conclusions from Three Major Independent Sources." Presented at the ARF Advertising and Copy Research Workshop. New York, NY: Advertising Research Foundation, 1995.

EXHIBIT 2.4

rsc 1995 Free-Market Study:
Elasticity and In-Market Results

Elasticity Range[1]	ARS Persuasion® Level	In-Market Implications	Odds of achieving a share-point difference[2] of:		
			+0.5	+1.0	+2.0 +
Elastic	≥ 7.0	Sales/share change expected	100%	91%	70%
Moderately elastic	4.0 – 6.9	Sales/share change possible	59	47	24
Low elastic	2.0 – 3.9	No measurable sales/share change expected	25	17	0
Inelastic	< 2.0	No measurable sales/share change observed	0	0	0

[1] rsc constructed these elasticity ranges from the 1980s split-cable findings to help advertisers gauge the probability of an in-market effect given an ad's *ARS Persuasion®* score.

[2] Four-week period after onset of advertising, versus four-week period before advertising.

Source: Kuse, A. R., and D. E. Crang. "Some Universal Truths about Advertising: Conclusions from Three Major Independent Sources." Presented at the ARF Advertising and Copy Research Workshop. New York, NY: Advertising Research Foundation, 1995.

EXHIBIT 2.5

ARS Persuasion® Measurement Relates to Sales
(Overview)

Study	Study Date(s)	Number of Cases	Sales Data Source
I	1964	67	Nielsen Store Audit (Market Share — USA)
II	1968	71	Nielsen Store Audit (Market Share — Germany)
III	1970s	28	New-Brand Test Markets (Reported ATU Trial)
IV	1980s	44	Split-Cable Studies (Sales Volume)
V	1990s	18	SCANTRACK® and InfoScan® (Market Share)
VI	1990s	157	SCANTRACK® (Category Volume)
VII	1995	53	National Scanner (Market Share)
VIII–XVI+	Multiple	350+	Unpublished/Proprietary Cases (Sales Volume)

788+	Market Share • Trial • Sales • Category Volume

CONTINUED ON NEXT PAGE

EXHIBIT 2.5 CONTINUED

Sources:
Study I: Dodd, A. R., Jr. "New Study Tells TV Advertisers How Advertising Builds Sales and Share of Market." *Printers' Ink* (May 8, 1964).
             Kelly, P. J. "The Schwerin Model: How You Can Use It to Build Your Share of Market." *Printers' Ink* (May 8, 1964).
             Buzzell, R. D. "Predicting Short-Term Changes in Market Share as a Function of Advertising Strategy." *Journal of Marketing Research* 1, 3 (1964): 27–31.

Study II: Murphy, M. P. "Empirical Evidence of the Effect of Advertising on Sales." Speech presented to the Professional Marketing Research Society. Toronto: 1968.

Study III: rsc. *Advertising Caused Awareness & Trial: ARS*[SM] *Predictive Validity for New Brand Advertising.* Evansville, IN: rsc, 1983.

Study IV: Blair, M. H. "An Empirical Investigation of Advertising Wearin and Wearout." *Journal of Advertising Research* 27, 6 (1987): 45–50.
             Blair, M. H., and K. E. Rosenberg. "Convergent Findings Increase Our Understanding of How Advertising Works." *Journal of Advertising Research* 34, 3 (1994): 35–45.

Study V: Unpublished study.

Study VI: Ashley, S. R. "How to Effectively Compete Against Private-Label Brands." In *Transcript Proceedings of the 181st ESOMAR Seminar on "Building Successful Brands."* Amsterdam: European Society for Opinion and Marketing Research, 1994.

Study VII: Kuse, A. R., and D. E. Crang. "Some Universal Truths about Advertising: Conclusions from Three Major Independent Sources." Presented at the ARF Advertising and Copy Research Workshop. New York, NY: Advertising Research Foundation, 1995.

EXHIBIT 2.6

ASI's Validation Cases

	Recall (A vs. B)	Tru-Share® (A vs. B)	Copy Effect Index® (A vs. B)	Sales (A vs. B)
1	36% > 25%	15% > 8%	238 > 101	A > B
2	27% < 36%	9% = 12%	121 < 204	A < B
3	14% < 27%	4% = 6%	60 < 138	A < B
4	37% > 27%	5% < 11%	135 < 208	A < B
5	27% > 15%	4% < 7%	100 = 92	A = B
6	22% = 20%	5% = 5%	100 = 88	A = B
7	31% = 27%	15% > 7%	193 > 99	A > B
8	28% < 35%	7% < 22%	85 < 254	A < B
9	39% > 28%	11% > 7%	164 > 65	A > B
10	41% > 28%	7% = 5%	198 > 110	A > B

Source: Walker, D. "Beyond Validation: Advertising Research for the 1990s." In *Transcript Proceedings of the Seventh Annual ARF Copy Research Workshop.* New York, NY: Advertising Research Foundation, 1990.

from clients confidential sales data firm enough to support a definitive study of the validity of [McCollum Spielman's] measurements." Thus, they developed a Quadrant Model to link their AC-T copy research measurements to their clients' reported marketplace objectives (Exhibit 2.7). These marketplace objectives were defined as "advertisers' assessments, by their own criteria, of their brands' market success during the period specific advertising was aired" and "advertisers' perceptions of the effect of TV advertising in a specific product category upon the consumers' decision-making process" (Klein and Tainiter, 1983). Klein and Tainiter concluded that "what this study conclusively demonstrates is that the key to a brand's market success is Attitude Shift, and to a significantly lesser degree, Clutter Awareness" (Exhibit 2.8). McCollum Spielman has more recently reported that BehaviorScan® micromarkets are being used to validate nine AD*VANTAGE/AC-T tests conducted by GfK, MSW's international affiliate (Klein and Tarr, 1992).

Validation of Millward Brown's LINK test is conducted indirectly through the company's Awareness Index, which is derived from brand-linked advertising awareness collected in-market as part of their Advanced Tracking Program. According to Millward Brown's Nigel Hollis (1994), "the LINK test was expressly designed to predict [the Millward Brown Awareness Index] and has proved remarkably successful." Hollis (1995) found that "where the Link forecast can be validated against tracking results [Millward Brown has] achieved an admirable record" (Exhibit 2.9). The Awareness Index, in turn, has been shown to relate to sales response (Exhibit 2.10).

APPLYING TOTAL QUALITY TO ADVERTISING

As stated in the introduction to this chapter, more and more companies are requiring a financial return from their advertising investment. If advertising does not produce increased sales and profits, it will lose its budget to other areas of the business which have proven their worth. For many of these corporate functions, increased productivity and return-on-investment are achieved through Total Quality Management (TQM). In the marketing function, a major stumbling block to TQM has been a resistance to statistical measurement, one of six basic ingredients of a successful Total Quality program (Exhibit 2.11).

Why this unwillingness to apply statistical measurement to advertising? Ogilvy and Raphaelson (1982) claim this phenomenon is due to creatives' rejection of research as an "inhibition to creativity." According to Blair (1994b), the reasons range from a disbelief in short-term sales effects (or the ability to measure them) to the claim that "advertising is an art, not a science." Blair also suggests that many popular advertising measurements (such as recall and liking) may be partly responsible for these beliefs, since they are predictive of adver-

EXHIBIT 2.7

McCollum Spielman Worldwide's Quadrant Model

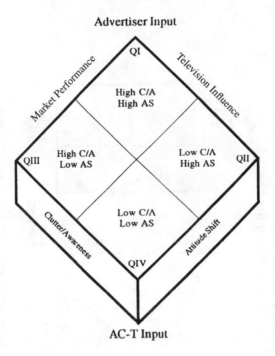

Source: Klein, P. R., and M. Tainiter. "Copy Research Validation: The Advertiser's Perspective." *Journal of Advertising Research* 23, 5 (1983): 9–17.

EXHIBIT 2.8

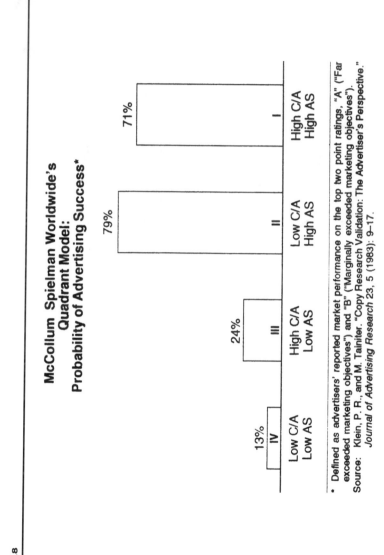

McCollum Spielman Worldwide's
Quadrant Model:
Probability of Advertising Success*

13%	24%	79%	71%
IV	III	II	I
Low C/A	High C/A	Low C/A	High C/A
Low AS	Low AS	High AS	High AS

* Defined as advertisers' reported market performance on the top two point ratings, "A" ("Far exceeded marketing objectives") and "B" ("Marginally exceeded marketing objectives").

Source: Klein, P. R., and M. Tainiter. "Copy Research Validation: The Advertiser's Perspective." *Journal of Advertising Research* 23, 5 (1983): 9–17.

EXHIBIT 2.9

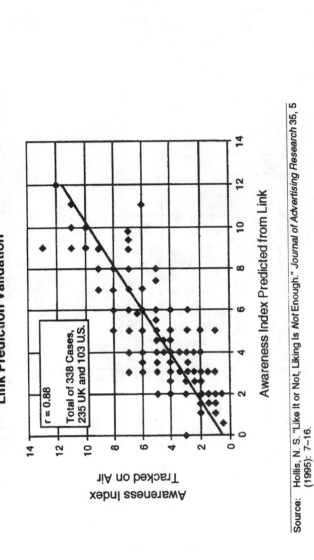

**Millward Brown International's
Link Prediction Validation**

r = 0.88

Total of 338 Cases,
235 UK and 103 U.S.

Awareness Index
Tracked on Air

Awareness Index Predicted from Link

Source: Hollis, N. S. "Like It or Not, Liking Is *Not Enough.*" *Journal of Advertising Research* 35, 5 (1995): 7–16.

EXHIBIT 2.10

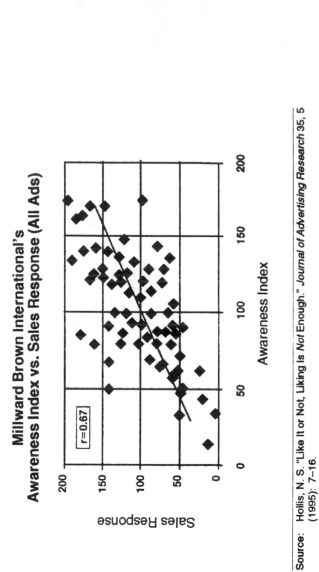

Millward Brown International's
Awareness Index vs. Sales Response (All Ads)

r=0.67

Sales Response

Awareness Index

Source: Hollis, N. S. "Like It or Not, Liking Is Not Enough." *Journal of Advertising Research* 35, 5 (1995): 7–16.

EXHIBIT 2.11

Six Impressive Concepts of Japanese TQM

➤ Focus on the Customer

➤ Long-Term Strategic Planning

? Measurement

➤ Empowerment

➤ Communication

➤ Education & Training

Source: McKee, M. "A North American Perspective of Japanese TQM." In *Conference Board Report 1048*. New York, NY: The Conference Board, 1993.

EXHIBIT 2.12

1980s Split-Cable Environments
(Overview)

Measurement	Study Source						Track Record
	Spend Test		Copy Test				
	rsc[1]	IRI[2]	rsc[1]	ARF[3]	IRI[2]	ASI[4]	
Liking	9/19	NA	0/5	3/5	NA	NA	12/29 = 41%
Brand-name recall	10/20	NA	2/7	2/5	NA	NA	14/32 = 44%
Recall	12/20	27/41	2/7	1/5	6/16	7/10	55/99 = 56%
Advertising weight	12/20	NA	NA	NA	NA	NA	12/20 = 60%
ARS Persuasion® measure	20/20	13/17	7/7	NA	NA	NA	40/44 = 91%

Sources:
[1] Kuse, A. R. "Measurement Tools for Ads That Sell." In *Transcript Proceedings of the Eighth Annual ARF Copy Research Workshop*. New York, NY: Advertising Research Foundation, 1991.
[2] McQueen, J. "Important Learning About How Advertising Works in Stimulating Long-Term Brand Growth." In *Transcript Proceedings of the ARF Marketplace Advertising Research Workshop*. New York, NY: Advertising Research Foundation, 1991.
[3] Haley, R. I., and A. L. Baldinger. "The ARF Copy Resea:ch Validity Project." *Journal of Advertising Research* 31, 2 (1991): 11–32.
[4] Walker, D. "Beyond Validation: Advertising Research for the 1990s." In *Transcript Proceedings of the Seventh Annual ARF Copy Research Workshop*. New York, NY: Advertising Research Foundation, 1990.

tising's in-market effects only about half the time, which is the same level of predictive ability as a coin toss (Exhibit 2.12).

The key to a profitable advertising investment is a means of *improving* advertising success, as well as accurately *predicting* when in-market success will occur. Until recently, measurement had not been used in an attempt to improve advertising. However, proper use of measurement is capable of dramatically increasing advertising's viability as an effective marketing tool.

Successful use of advertising measurement requires not only a valid and reliable primary measurement that accurately predicts an execution's in-market effect, but also application of this measurement at appropriate stages during the advertising development and airing processes. rsc has found that customers applying the *ARS Persuasion* measurement at key stages in the T. Q. Process have achieved over 160 percent improvement in their advertising (Blair, 1995). Percent improvement, in this case, was determined by examining the incidence of superior-selling ads (tested in the current year versus the previous year) for customers using *Firstep®* testing and rsc *Validated* diagnostics. Because the rsc *T. Q. Process*SM is the only one for which advertising improvement has been documented, we will examine it in greater detail.

Selling Proposition

The first stage in the T. Q. Process is identification of an effective selling proposition (or reason to buy). rsc's empirical evidence indicates that, among the factors in an advertiser's control, the basic selling proposition is the most powerful tool that can be used to increase selling power (Exhibit 2.13).

Although there are no "rules" for developing selling propositions, following some guidelines may increase the odds that they will be effective. Start with the product. What unique features does it have? What makes it different? What is its "reason for being"? Why should the consumer choose it? If no point-of-difference can be identified, it may be wise to meet with R&D for additional insight about the product (or ideas about how the product could be modified to give it a point-of-difference).

As stated in *Business Horizons* (Blair, Kuse, Furse, and Stewart, 1987), "Advertising's brand-differentiating role is the key to its performance. Competitors will chip away at the market shares of advertisers who forget to communicate the features that make their products superior." So focus on defining a concrete, brand-differentiating message, and try to avoid generic claims that are used by competitors. Don't send an ambiguous message — use clear language, be specific, and cite evidence to support the brand's claims. Use comparisons to demonstrate brand-differentiating claims. Tell the consumer if the product or some feature of the product is new. If a brand has more than one bene-

EXHIBIT 2.13

Summary of rsc Diagnostic Validation
(*ARS Persuasion*® Variance)

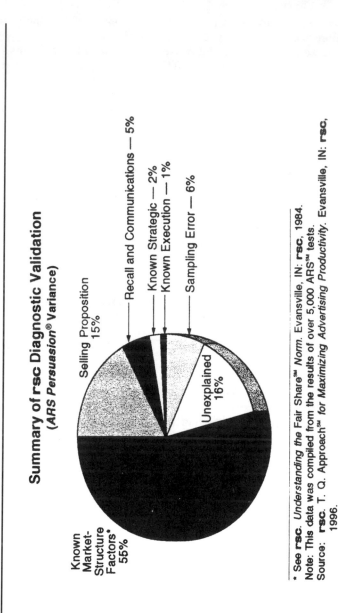

Selling Proposition
15%

Recall and Communications — 5%

Known Strategic — 2%
Known Execution — 1%

Sampling Error — 6%

Unexplained
16%

Known
Market-
Structure
Factors*
55%

* See **rsc**. *Understanding the* Fair Share℠ *Norm*. Evansville, IN: **rsc**, 1984.
Note: This data was compiled from the results of over 5,000 ARS℠ tests.
Source: **rsc**. T. Q. Approach℠ *for Maximizing Advertising Productivity*. Evansville, IN: **rsc**,
1996.

fit, selling propositions can be developed for each benefit separately — as well as for combinations of benefits — to determine which approach is most effective for the brand. Finally, don't confuse the consumer by sending "mixed messages"; make sure that the message is clearly communicated and that the visuals match the audio.

Although following these guidelines should provide a good start to finding a strong message, measurement is required to identify which messages are the most effective. **rsc**'s *T. Q. Process*^{SM} uses *Firstep* testing for this purpose. *Firstep* selling-proposition tests use the *ARS Persuasion* measurement (described in this chapter's "Pretesting" section), with the exception that the stimulus is a "bare bones" video without executional enhancements such as on-camera presenters, background sets, visual memory devices, music, and sound effects. The idea is to remove as much "execution" as possible while clearly focusing on the selling proposition. This allows the advertiser to isolate the strength of the basic selling idea.

Before undertaking *Firstep* testing, it is best to decide on action standards. The PACT Agencies (1982) support the use of action standards in that "the practice of specifying how the results will be used before the results are in insures that there is mutual understanding on the goals of the test — and it minimizes conflicting interpretations of the test once the results are in." **rsc** recommends that the *Firstep* level be superior. "Superior" is defined as statistically higher than the *Fair Share*^{SM} norm at the 90 percent confidence level. This "degree of difficulty" norm takes into consideration three market-structure factors: category brand loyalty, the number of brands in the category, and the advertised-brand's market share.

To avoid walking away from an effective proposition once found, the advertiser should re-evaluate the current selling proposition (along with alternative propositions) when having difficulty achieving superior executions.

Knowing the selling proposition's strength is essential as advertising development progresses from this stage to finished execution. If you begin with a strong selling proposition, 70 percent of the resulting executions will be strong. On the other hand, if you begin executing from a selling proposition that is not strong (or is inferior), the same high odds are associated with the resulting executions being weak (Exhibit 2.14). Thus, the sales-related measurement should be applied at the selling-proposition stage to increase the odds of attaining successful advertising executions.

Execution

First and foremost, executions should be based on a proven, sales-effective selling proposition. When executing, stay true to the original selling proposition. Use as much of the original wording as possible. If

EXHIBIT 2.14

Superior Selling Propositions
Lead to Superior-Selling Ads

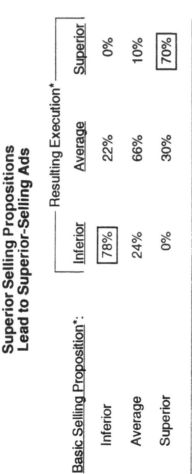

Basic Selling Proposition*:	Resulting Execution*		
	Inferior	Average	Superior
Inferior	78%	22%	0%
Average	24%	66%	10%
Superior	0%	30%	70%

* Selling propositions and executions are determined to be superior, average, or inferior based on their relationship to the market-structure "degree of difficulty" norm (*Fair Share*[SM]).

Note: Based on 163 execution tests.

Source: **rsc**. T. Q. Approach[SM] for *Maximizing Advertising Productivity*. Evansville, IN: **rsc**, 1996.

comparisons were used in the initial test, use those same comparisons in the ads. Maintain the same level of focus on the product and the brand-differentiating message. **rsc** *Validated* diagnostics indicate that when executing an ad, it is best to focus on the product, at the same time avoiding "superfluous" executional details that will serve to detract from the message. (See Exhibit 2.15 for a list of strategic, communication, and executional elements that help or hinder advertising effectiveness.) To measure this, **rsc** employs a quantitative approach that regularly evaluates more than 150 strategic, communication, and executional elements. To date, about 20 diagnostic elements have demonstrated a significant relationship with the *ARS Persuasion* measure and have helped explain 84 percent of the variation in *ARS Persuasion* levels.

Advertisers shouldn't feel they have to go overboard on production costs. Lower budget ads can (and do) achieve strong *ARS Persuasion* results. In his book *Ogilvy on Advertising*, David Ogilvy stated: "I have no research to prove it, but I suspect that there is a negative correlation between the money spent on producing commercials and their power to sell products. My partner Al Eicoff was asked by a client to remake a $15,000 commercial for $100,000. Sales went *down*."

rsc's research supports Ogilvy's hypothesis. A 1992 study of 56 commercials found a correlation between the cost of producing an ad and its *ARS Persuasion* level that is both *negative* and *significant*. Remember—the focus of the commercial is more important than exotic locations or state-of-the-art special effects. From the study results, **rsc** concluded: "Clearing away commercial clutter and focusing on brand differentiation appear to allow commercials to be produced at lower costs, providing more sales effective advertising for the money spent" (1992a). A final note: the emphasis placed on brand differentiation may seem to indicate that there is no place for emotion in advertising. This is not the case! According to Karl Rosenberg, Ron Arnold, and Pat Capetta (1991), "ads that use emotion to communicate brand differentiation have higher odds of superior *ARS Persuasion* than their purely rational counterparts."

Following production, each execution should be tested for its selling power prior to airing to ensure "fact-based" airing decisions. Although the track record is 70 percent superior executions from superior selling propositions, not all executions are strong; some enhance the proposition and some detract from it (Exhibit 2.16). Knowing which executions are stronger ensures that the media dollars will be spent behind the more sales-effective ones.

Airing

In 1984, **rsc** conducted a systematic tracking experiment in which *ARS Persuasion* levels were obtained for the same ads over time. Consistently, *ARS Persuasion* scores decreased when GRPs were spent

EXHIBIT 2.15

rsc Validated[SM] Diagnostics for the ARS Persuasion® Measure

Superior[1] Selling Proposition	Percent of Ads with Superior[1] ARS Persuasion® Results	
	When Element Is Present	When Element Is Absent
	70%	8%
Strategic elements:		
Brand-differentiating key message	28	12
New product or new/improved product features	30	12
Convenience in use	27	20
Competitive comparison	23	19
Superiority claim	22	19
Brand name reinforces product message[2]		
Total database	25	16
New brands	44	29
Established brands	13	12
Product is double-branded[3]		
Total database	27	19
New brands	41	36
Established brands	14	12
Communication factors:		
Related recall ≥ 23%[4]	25	10
Key message communication ≥ 16%[5]	32	14

Positive executional elements:

Demonstration of product in use or by analogy	23	13
Time actual product is on screen[6]	26	16
Product performance or benefits are main message	21	18
Results of using the product are demonstrated	22	19
Results of using (either tangible or intangible)	21	15
Setting directly related to use	22	19

Negative executional elements:

Slice-of-life format	13	22
Number of on-screen characters (four or more)	18	22
Vignettes (two or more)	16	21
Background cast	19	22

[1] Superiority is judged as a significant difference at the 90 percent confidence level relative to the *Fair Share*™ degree-of-difficulty norm.

[2] In order to be classified as containing this element, the brand name must reinforce, at least somewhat, what the product is or will do.

[3] In order to be classified as containing this element, the product must have two brand names (e.g., Goodyear Aquatred®).

[4] The 23% threshold was empirically determined to be the Related Recall level which yielded the best discrimination of superior and inferior *ARS Persuasion*® outcomes. Ads with a Related Recall level of less than 23 percent have 45 percent inferior persuaders and ten percent superior persuaders; ads with a Related Recall level of 23 percent or greater have 22 percent inferior persuaders and 25 percent superior persuaders.

- The key message is the sales point that is repeated most often or emphasized most strongly in the execution. The 16 percent threshold was empirically determined to be the playback level which yielded the best discrimination of superior and inferior *ARS Persuasion*® outcomes. Ads with key message playback of less than 16 percent have 35 percent inferior persuaders and 14 percent superior persuaders; ads with key message playback of 16 percent or greater have 18 percent inferior persuaders and 32 percent superior persuaders.

- Product is on screen for more than one-third of the commercial.

Source: **rsc** (personal communication, 1996).

EXHIBIT 2.16

Execution Can Enhance or Detract from Selling Proposition
(Examples)

Brand	ARS Persuasion® Level		Number of Executions
	Firstep®	Executions	
M	9.3	7.9 to 16.3	4
P	10.0	5.9 to 10.9	5
K	14.8	7.7 to 27.7	2

Source: Blair, M. H. "An Emerging Renaissance in Advertising through a T. Q. Approach for Maximizing Productivity." In *Transcript Proceedings of* rsc *T. Q. Advertising Success Forum I.* Evansville, IN: rsc. 1995.

behind the ad between the first test and the second test. With little spending, there was relatively little change in the *ARS Persuasion* level. Following heavy spending, *ARS Persuasion* scores dropped substantially. Ads with low *ARS Persuasion* scores in the initial test remained low in subsequent tests, regardless of spending levels.

Further, as GRPs were spent behind each commercial, the *ARS Persuasion* power declined consistently (for all types of commercials and products), and the relationship between spending and this decline in productivity was very strong, indicating the speed at which advertising's selling power was delivered to market (Exhibit 2.17). Since the discovery of the wearout function, over 100 tests have been conducted by **rsc** to verify the relationship, and the link between spending and the decline in *ARS Persuasion* power remains strong and consistent across countries (Exhibit 2.18).

These findings indicate that an ad's selling power is finite. As each execution goes on air, its *ARS Persuasion* power will decrease as media dollars are spent. This wearout phenomenon might be likened to drinking a glass of water. A full glass would represent a highly elastic ad, while an empty glass represents an inelastic ad. As media dollars are being spent, the water is being drunk — and selling power is being delivered to market. When the water is gone, so is the selling power.

As published in the *Journal of Advertising Research* (Blair, 1987): "Ads which are *not* Persuasive do not increase sales and do not improve over time — related to spending. Ads which *are* Persuasive *do* increase sales over time — related to spending; and they *wearout* in the process."

rsc research (1992b) also indicates that wearout affects each ad in a campaign individually, regardless of whether ads are aired sequentially or concurrently. Wearout is not a function of the cumulative GRPs spent behind a campaign, but rather the number of GRPs spent behind each ad. In addition, an airing hiatus does not affect the wearout of an ad, nor is there "recovery" of selling power while the ads are not on air.

rsc's wearout learning has been used to develop the *outlook®* wearout model, which combines media weight (GRPs) with the *ARS Persuasion* score to project *PRP®* (Persuasive Rating Point) delivery. A Persuasive Rating Point (or PRP) is simply a combination of media weight (GRPs) and the *ARS Persuasion* power of the executions on air during a particular period. For a given level of spending, the higher the *ARS Persuasion* score, the higher the *PRP* delivery.

In an example presented by Blair (1994a), a media plan called for heavy spending during periods five through seven. A single, moderately productive execution aired throughout the entire eight periods will deliver most of its *ARS Persuasion* power during the first four periods, leaving little selling power for the periods with the heaviest

EXHIBIT 2.17

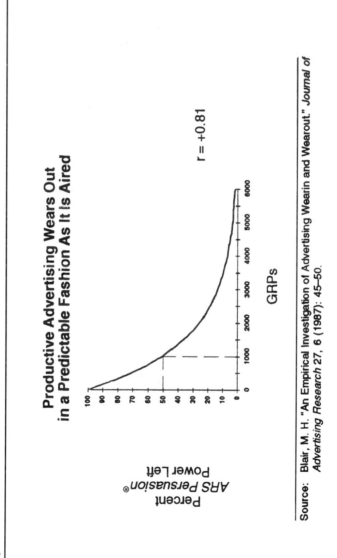

Productive Advertising Wears Out in a Predictable Fashion As It Is Aired

Percent
ARS Persuasion®
Power Left

GRPs

r = +0.81

Source: Blair, M. H. "An Empirical Investigation of Advertising Wearin and Wearout." *Journal of Advertising Research 27*, 6 (1987): 45–50.

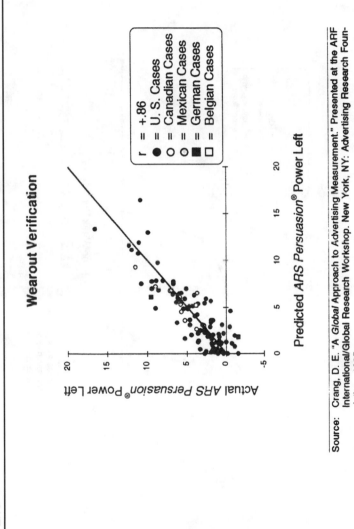

Wearout Verification

r	=	+.86
●	=	U. S. Cases
○	=	Canadian Cases
◎	=	Mexican Cases
■	=	German Cases
□	=	Belgian Cases

Actual ARS Persuasion® Power Left

Predicted ARS Persuasion® Power Left

Source: Crang, D. E. "A Global Approach to Advertising Measurement." Presented at the ARF International/Global Research Workshop. New York, NY: Advertising Research Foundation, 1995.

EXHIBIT 2.18

EXHIBIT 2.19

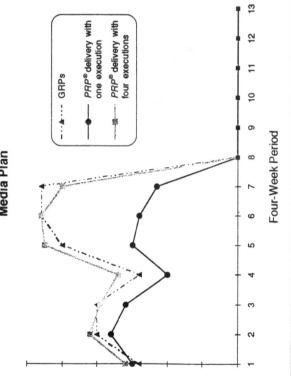

Media Plan

Four-Week Period

Legend:
- ····▲···· GRPs
- ──●── *PRP®* delivery with one execution
- ·····※····· *PRP®* delivery with four executions

Source: Blair, M. H. "Maximizing the Effectiveness of Television Advertising." In *Transcript Proceedings of the ESOMAR/ARF Worldwide Electronic and Broadcast Audience Research Symposium*. Amsterdam: European Society for Opinion and Marketing Research, 1994a.

spending. However, when three more executions (with similar *ARS Persuasion* levels) are used to refresh the media, the delivery of advertising's selling power is consistent with the timing of the media expenditures (Exhibit 2.19).

If superior advertising is desired, the recommended action standard would be to air only executions with *ARS Persuasion* levels at or above the absolute level of the *Firstep* score. Also keep in mind that as media dollars are spent, selling power is constantly declining. After 1,000 GRPs, about half of an ad's selling power has been spent. This generally means that ads should be taken off the air (and replaced with fresh, effective executions) before they wear down below the level of the degree-of-difficulty benchmark.

Therefore, this step in the T. Q. Process involves planning and implementing a refreshment schedule that takes into account the effectiveness of the final copy, expected media spending, and commercial wearout.

Tracking In-Market Results

As ads go to air, it is critical to link the pre-market measurements of ad effectiveness to the post-market measurements of sales and share. The case studies in the next section will highlight the importance of this step, as well as the other steps in this T. Q. Process.

APPLYING THE T. Q. PROCESS TO ADVERTISING: SUCCESS CASES

Campbell Soup's Prego®

The Campbell story is one of a brand group and agency which are advertising more confidently. They know how to develop and identify ads that sell; know how to leverage media dollars behind them; know when to refresh creative; know how to plan both sides of the advertising dimension simultaneously; and know how to achieve sales results with television advertising both short-term and over time. The implications from this story speak to the request for advertising accountability. Campbell and rsc are laying in the systems for improving advertising productivity and establishing advertising accountability.

— Adams and Blair (1992)

In late 1987, sales for Prego were soft. An ad called "Tastes Great :30" had been tested and, with an *ARS Persuasion* score of +5.8, met Campbell's airing standard of +4.0. This ad positioned Prego as tasting more like homemade because it is rich with herbs and spices. When "Tastes Great :30" went on air, Prego's market share increased almost two points; however, the *outlook* wearout projection indicated that the ad's selling power would wear down quickly.

In an effort to develop stronger advertising, the company changed Prego's strategy. They decided to retain the idea that Prego tastes more like homemade, but now emphasized Prego's thickness. "Beauty Shot :15," the first execution based on this new selling proposition, achieved an *ARS Persuasion* score of +4.5. This score was disappointing given expectations for the new strategy, so the ad was revised. The altered version, "Beauty Shot Rev. :15," achieved an *ARS Persuasion* score of +10.0. When the revised ad went to air, Prego share jumped four-and-a-half points (Exhibit 2.20).

Subsequently, two more executions, "Beauty Shot Poolout #1 :15" and "Beauty Shot Poolout #2 :15," were produced using the same effective selling proposition, and achieved scores of +6.0 and +10.9. "Beauty Shot Poolout #2," the stronger of the two ads, went to air, and once again share increased (Exhibit 2.20). Note: A poolout is one of a series of ads that are based on the same strategy but differ in execution, for example, the situation or characters. Poolouts are often produced from a single commercial shoot.

Between 1988 and 1992, Prego continued to air strong ads based on the same effective selling proposition. At the same time, there was significant new-product activity in the spaghetti-sauce category with Classico®, Hunt's®, Contadina®, Healthy Choice™, and Campbell's® brands entering the market. By 1992, the new brands gained about 25 percent share of market, in some cases with productive advertising (Exhibit 2.21). The brands were operating under a "traditional process." During the five-year case study, rsc's CATS® service was used to monitor the spaghetti-sauce category. Data gathered included market share/sales, the *ARS Persuasion* level of the advertising aired, and the media weight behind each ad.

During the same time period, Ragu® lost roughly 19 share points, also operating under a "traditional advertising process." While Ragu aired many executions, few were productive (Exhibit 2.22).

On the other hand, Prego *gained* share over these five years (despite the new-product activity) by having found a strong selling proposition and by continuing to refresh with productive executions (Exhibit 2.23).

Looking at the entire five-year period, Prego's advertising managed to overcome Ragu's heavier competitive spending, retailer support, and lower price (Exhibit 2.24). The estimated return-on-investment over the five-year period shows the long-term payout of Prego's process change of over 5,000 percent (Exhibit 2.25).

Campbell's Dick Nelson came to this conclusion:

"What underlies this five-year-long success story? A fundamental change in the advertising strategy and research process. Prego is the only Campbell's brand in the last five years to:

EXHIBIT 2.20

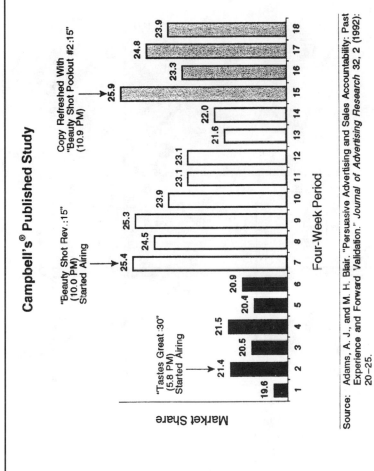

Campbell's® Published Study

"Tastes Great :30"
(5.8 PM)
Started Airing

"Beauty Shot Rev.:15"
(10.0 PM)
Started Airing

Copy Refreshed With
"Beauty Shot Poolout #2:15"
(10.9 PM)

Market Share

Four-Week Period	1	2	3	4	5	6	7	8	9	10	11	12	13	14	15	16	17	18
	19.6	21.4	20.5	21.5	20.4	20.9	25.4	24.5	25.3	23.9	23.1	23.1	21.6	22.0	25.9	23.3	24.8	23.9

Source: Adams, A. J., and M. H. Blair. "Persuasive Advertising and Sales Accountability: Past Experience and Forward Validation." *Journal of Advertising Research* 32, 2 (1992): 20–25.

EXHIBIT 2.21

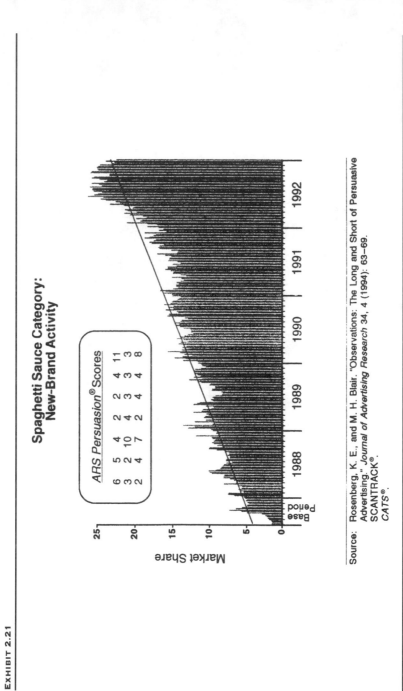

Spaghetti Sauce Category:
New-Brand Activity

Source: Rosenberg, K. E., and M. H. Blair. "Observations: The Long and Short of Persuasive Advertising." *Journal of Advertising Research 34*, 4 (1994): 63–69. SCANTRACK®. CATS®.

EXHIBIT 2.22

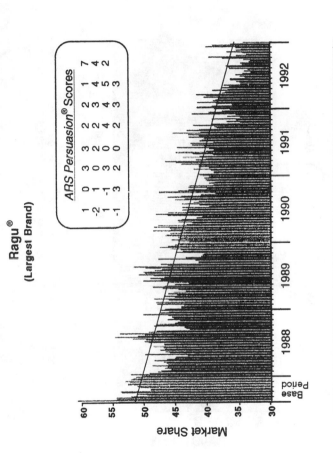

Ragu®
(Largest Brand)

ARS Persuasion® Scores

1	0	3	3	2	2	1	7
-2	1	0	2	2	3	4	4
1	-1	3	0	4	4	5	2
-1	3	2	0	2	3	3

Source: Rosenberg, K. E., and M. H. Blair. "Observations: The Long and Short of Persuasive Advertising." *Journal of Advertising Research* 34, 4 (1994): 63–69. SCANTRACK®. CATS®.

EXHIBIT 2.23

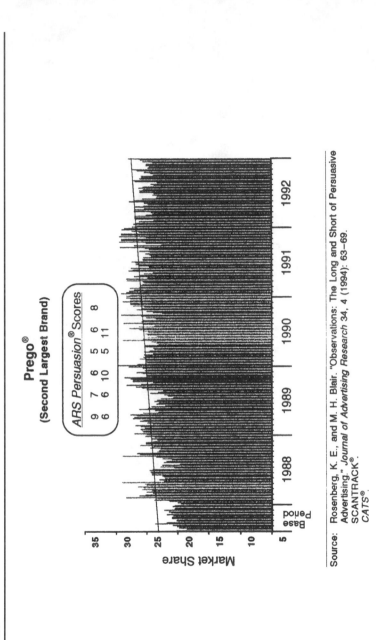

Prego®
(Second Largest Brand)

ARS Persuasion® Scores

| 9 | 7 | 6 | 5 | 6 | 8 |
| 6 | 6 | 10 | 5 | 11 | |

Source: Rosenberg, K. E., and M. H. Blair. "Observations: The Long and Short of Persuasive Advertising." Journal of Advertising Research 34, 4 (1994): 63–69. SCANTRACK®. CATS®.

EXHIBIT 2.24

Five-Year Overview
(1988–1992)

	Prego®	Ragu®
Total GRPs	15,034	20,400
Average displays	22	43
Average retailer ads	29	37
Average selling price	$1.80	$1.64
Total TV power (*PRP*® delivery)	679	448
Sales gains (units)*	+22%	-19%

* Market share increase versus base period (last 20 weeks of 1987).

Source: Rosenberg, K. E., and M. H. Blair. "Observations: The Long and Short of Persuasive Advertising." *Journal of Advertising Research* 34, 4 (1994): 63–69.

EXHIBIT 2.25

T. Q. Process — Payout Analysis
(Five-Year Prego® Case Study)

	Five-year period
Average market-share increase over baseline	4.5 points
Estimated incremental gross profit[1]	$112,500,000
Incremental cost of testing (15 more tests)	$225,000
Estimated incremental cost of production[2]	$1,875,000
Payout (ROI)	5,357%

[1] Assuming profit on incremental revenues at 50 percent.
[2] 15 commercials at $125,000 each.
Source: Rosenberg, K. E., and M. H. Blair. "Observations: The Long and Short of Persuasive Advertising." *Journal of Advertising Research* 34, 4 (1994): 63–69.

- consistently stay with the same [productive] selling proposition.
- *[ARS] Persuasion* test every poolout prior to airing.
- establish *[ARS] Persuasion* hurdles and stick to them.
- utilize *outlook* to create an awareness of when to refresh creative."

Goodyear Aquatred®

In 1991, with a change in management and the influence of CEO Stan Gault, Total Quality Management was applied to many functions within the Goodyear organization. The new management team wanted to make advertising an effective investment. Goodyear's research team and its agency, J. Walter Thompson in Detroit, began a review of ad research suppliers and agreed on *ARS Persuasion* as the best system.

The first ARS test was performed on "Tires of the Future." The introductory Aquatred ad used a few futuristic graphics, but its main focus was on Aquatred and how the tire's "advanced design channels water out of your way for dependable all-season traction, especially in the rain when you may need it most." With an *ARS Persuasion* score of 31.6 percent, the ad was predicted to be a strong driver of sales. The introduction of the "Tires of the Future :30" commercial at the end of period one resulted in large volume gains in periods two and three, and a lower rate of gain in periods four and five as the commercial became less effective due to wearout. There was a strong relationship between sales volume per store and "selling power" (or *PRP*) delivery (Exhibit 2.26).

In 1992, Goodyear began a regular program of testing advertising developed in support of its premium tire brands. The first two Aquatred ads tested used different executional approaches. "Richard on Aquatreds," a user endorsement, achieved an *ARS Persuasion* score of +6.5. The second ad, "Skiing," focused on a clear visual demonstration of the tire's performance in wet traction, and it achieved an *ARS Persuasion* score of +10.3. Since Aquatred was now an established brand, these *ARS Persuasion* scores were not as high as the score of the introductory ad but were still in the range in which single ads are expected to be effective at driving sales.

Because it was the stronger of the two ads, "Skiing" was produced as a finished ad and achieved an *ARS Persuasion* level of +8.0. These results indicated that product focus was important for the Aquatred brand.

This learning was used by Goodyear's agency to develop "Bucket," a new simple and straightforward execution that presented the Aquatred point-of-difference. Although "Bucket" did not involve expensive production costs, the commercial achieved an *ARS Persuasion*

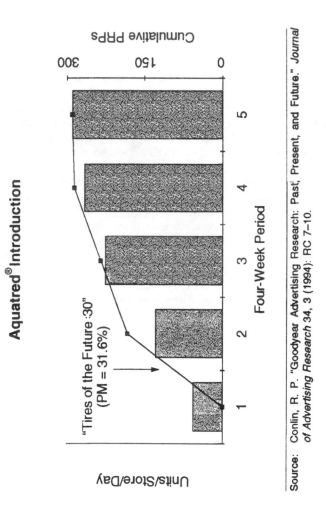

Aquatred® Introduction

"Tires of the Future :30"
(PM = 31.6%)

Cumulative PRPs

Units/Store/Day

Four-Week Period

Source: Conlin, R. P. "Goodyear Advertising Research: Past, Present, and Future." *Journal of Advertising Research* 34, 3 (1994): RC 7–10.

score of +14.6, the highest score of all ads tested in this series. Aquatred's product concept was so strong that a simple demonstration was all that was needed to achieve highly effective advertising. The introduction of "Bucket :30" and "Skiing :30" had an immediate in-market impact. As the ads continued airing, they were less and less effective over time. The relationship between advertising selling power and in-market sales effects was strong, with a correlation of .85 (Exhibit 2.27).

Goodyear's passenger-tire media budget was allocated between the Eagle® and Aquatred brands. Through *PRP* planning, this limited media budget was optimized to deliver 24 percent more selling power for the same media investment. When it became clear that Aquatred production was not sufficient to meet demand produced by the advertising, an ad rotation plan was developed that maintained the *PRP* levels and freed up approximately $800,000 in media cost (Exhibit 2.28).

Oscar Mayer Lunchables®

According to Oscar Mayer's Category Information Manager, Bill Bean: "Lunchables was brought to market by research. In fact, the Lunchables product was literally invented by the research director at Oscar Mayer at the time. And the product continues to be the best example of that philosophy."

Lunchables is a prepackaged tray of meat, cheese, and crackers. This case study is concerned with new advertising developed for the established brand in 1992. Initially, Oscar Mayer was concerned that the *ARS Persuasion* measure would not be a good indicator of ad effectiveness for the Lunchables brand. Why? First, by this time, Lunchables was a large-share product. Given its formidable position in the marketplace (a market share in the 75 to 80 percent range), it seemed unreasonable to expect a positive share shift from advertising. Second, there has been controversy in the advertising-research industry over the ability of commercials without "new news" to achieve high *ARS Persuasion* scores, and the Lunchables commercials did not introduce any new information. Also, a related controversy has challenged the ability of the *ARS Persuasion* measure to adequately measure the effectiveness of commercials with emotional appeals, and this was the path that the Lunchables advertising had taken.

Despite these research objections, Oscar Mayer tested two Lunchables commercials, "Kid Talk" and "Bad Week," in the summer of 1992. "Kid Talk" was an ad in the traditional Oscar Mayer format. It is set during lunchtime at school. The camera jumps among shots of various kids eating Lunchables and explaining why they like them: "They're fun," "I get bored with peanut butter," " 'Cause they taste good." The announcer says: "Kids love Lunchables from Oscar Mayer for all sorts of reasons: their best meats, cheeses, crisp crackers, even

EXHIBIT 2.27

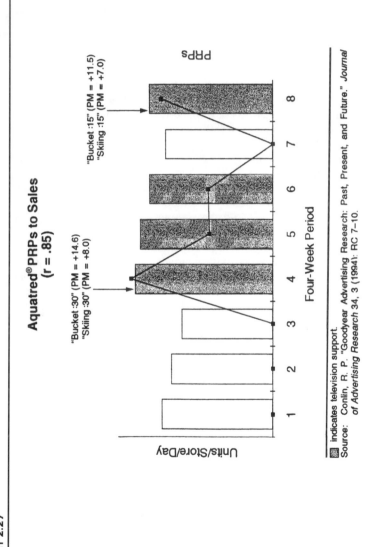

Aquatred® PRPs to Sales
(r = .85)

"Bucket :30" (PM = +14.6)
"Skiing :30" (PM = +8.0)

"Bucket :15" (PM = +11.5)
"Skiing :15" (PM = +7.0)

Units/Store/Day

PRPs

Four-Week Period

indicates television support.
Source: Conlin, R. P. "Goodyear Advertising Research: Past, Present, and Future." *Journal of Advertising Research* 34, 3 (1994): RC 7–10.

EXHIBIT 2.28

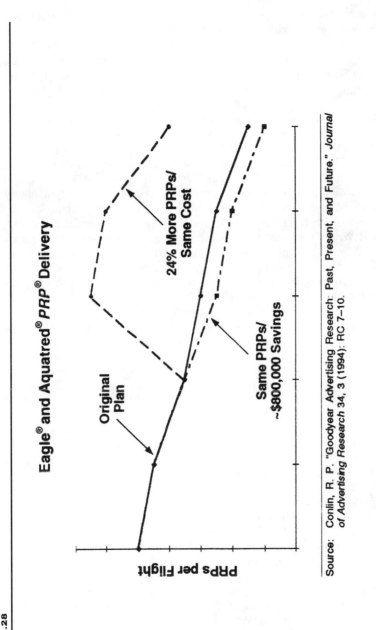

Eagle® and Aquatred® *PRP*® Delivery

PRPs per Flight

Original Plan

24% More PRPs/ Same Cost

Same PRPs/ ~$800,000 Savings

Source: Conlin, R. P. "Goodyear Advertising Research: Past, Present, and Future." *Journal of Advertising Research* 34, 3 (1994): RC 7–10.

dessert. Lunchables aren't like any other lunch. Lunchables from Oscar Mayer — for your kids, nothing but the best."

"Bad Week" was more of a departure from the traditional Oscar Mayer ad strategy. It features a boy checking his lunch each morning before he goes to school. The first four mornings are disappointing, getting responses like, "Isn't this your doggy bag from last night?" On the fifth day, he gets Lunchables and says, "Thanks, Mom!" Unlike "Kid Talk," this commercial focused more on the "thankless job" of fixing lunch each morning — and how Lunchables can make the job easier, and more appreciated.

"Kid Talk" performed poorly, with an *ARS Persuasion* score of -4.1. The second ad, "Bad Week," achieved a score of +8.3, an *ARS Persuasion* level that was significantly above "Kid Talk," significantly above the *Fair Share* degree-of-difficulty norm, and in the elastic range of sales/share responsiveness to media weight. Between the two ads, "Bad Week" was identified as the clear winner. In fact, of all established-brand ads tested by **rsc** in 1992, "Bad Week" was among the "Top Ten" relative to its *Fair Share* degree-of-difficulty benchmark of +1. According to Bean: "Bad Week generated the highest [ARS] Persuasion score in Oscar Mayer history."

Most importantly, the score meant that "Bad Week" would be expected to have significant positive impact on sales and share. When "Bad Week" hit the air, sales increased nearly three share points (Exhibit 2.29). Subsequent sales-decomposition modeling revealed that "Bad Week" accounted for 15 percent of the total Lunchables volume, the largest incremental sales increase Oscar Mayer and A.C. Nielsen had ever seen from a single ad. In conclusion, Oscar Mayer's Bean said of this experience: "We believe that the only yardstick for advertising effectiveness is sales. And the more we can know about sales *prior* to bringing an expensive ad to market, the better off we are."

Celestial Seasonings® Herbal Tea

Based on in-depth consumer-opinion research, Celestial Seasonings developed five very different selling propositions for their herbal teas, ranging from taste and health appeals to a purely emotional approach. They felt that all five propositions could be effective, but wanted to verify this hypothesis with hard evidence. *Firstep* videos were produced for each selling proposition.

ARS Persuasion testing showed that the effectiveness of the selling propositions varied widely (Exhibit 2.30). Proposition A was the strongest, with an *ARS Persuasion* score that was expected to result in measurable sales and market share impact.

Based on the results of the *Firstep* tests, Celestial challenged two different creative groups to develop advertising that enhanced the inherent sales effectiveness of the strongest selling proposition. Ad A1 used an energetic and sassy spokeswoman to highlight the selling proposi-

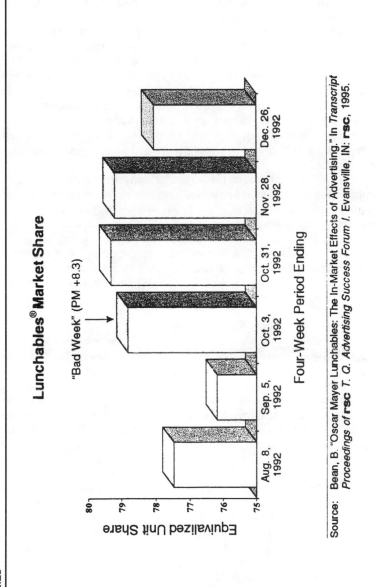

Lunchables® Market Share

"Bad Week" (PM +8.3)

Equivalized Unit Share

Four-Week Period Ending

Source: Bean, B. "Oscar Mayer Lunchables: The In-Market Effects of Advertising." In *Transcript Proceedings of rsc T. Q. Advertising Success Forum I.* Evansville, IN: **rsc**, 1995.

EXHIBIT 2.29

tion's message. She tells us that Wild Berry Zinger herbal tea "will make your tastebuds two-step but your brain won't jitterbug." This ad achieved an *ARS Persuasion* score of 12.8, indicating that the agency's execution enhanced the effectiveness of the selling proposition.

Ad A2 featured a ladder leading up to the "Celestial Moon." The ad never got around to delivering the selling proposition, and A's message ended up scoring a disappointing 3.7 (Exhibit 2.31).

Celestial aired the stronger of the two ads, experimenting with three different media weight levels. In markets in which low media weight on cable television was used, share increased about a third of a point. In key markets, cable was supplemented with spot television, and share increased more than two points. And when the spot television weight was "heavied up," share increased almost nine share points (Exhibit 2.32).

It is important to note that Celestial's advertising didn't just steal share from competitors; it helped increase sales in the herbal tea category. While tonnage for most other hot beverages was declining during this time period, herbal tea sales were up, with increases as high as 12 percent in one of the spot television markets. This is consistent with recent rsc research which indicates that "the aggregate effect of persuasive advertising in a category is an increase in *total* category volume (the more persuasive the advertising, the greater the effect)" (Ashley, 1994).

SmithKline Beecham's Citrucel® Laxative

Citrucel, a therapeutic bulk fiber laxative, was introduced in 1986. Early advertising for the brand used the slogan "It really works. Without grit." to compare Citrucel's non-gritty formula and taste to Metamucil®, the category leader. The brand met with early success based on these advantages, but over time advertising by new entries started diffusing the impact of Citrucel's positioning. Citrucel continued to advertise at a competitive spending level for a number of years with little growth. During this time, spending was converted from TV to print behind the same message, and business continued a gradual decline.

In July 1993, the Citrucel team and its agency partner, Ogilvy & Mather, developed several unique selling propositions for the Citrucel brand. When the Citrucel team began looking at alternative points of difference, they focused on Citrucel's unique active ingredient — methycellulose. Other bulk powder laxatives use psyllium, which, unlike methycellulose, can cause excess gas and bloating.

The traditional "no grit" message and the new "no gas" proposition were identified to undergo *Firstep* testing. According to Smith-Kline Beecham Senior Project Manager Ben Lipsman, "When we decided to go with *Firstep* testing we weren't sure we had any claims that would be motivating. Not only were we looking at the relative

EXHIBIT 2.30

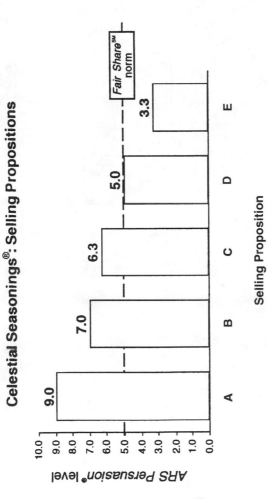

Celestial Seasonings® : Selling Propositions

Source: Mondello, M. D. "Turning Research into Return-on-Investment." In *Transcript Proceedings of the Conference Board 42nd Annual Marketing Conference*. New York, NY: The Conference Board, 1994.

EXHIBIT 2.31

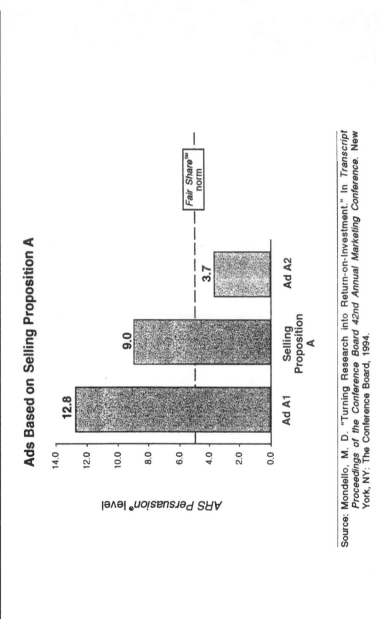

Ads Based on Selling Proposition A

Source: Mondello, M. D. "Turning Research into Return-on-Investment." In *Transcript Proceedings of the Conference Board 42nd Annual Marketing Conference.* New York, NY: The Conference Board, 1994.

EXHIBIT 2.32

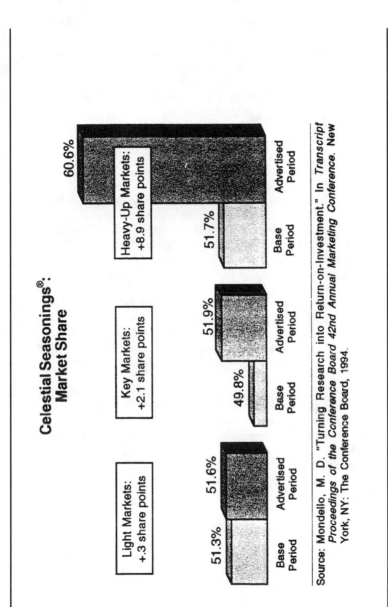

Celestial Seasonings®: Market Share

Light Markets: +.3 share points

Key Markets: +2.1 share points

Heavy-Up Markets: +8.9 share points

Source: Mondello, M. D. "Turning Research into Return-on-Investment." In *Transcript Proceedings of the Conference Board 42nd Annual Marketing Conference.* New York, NY: The Conference Board, 1994.

merits of the selling strategies, we were looking at the viability of an advertising program for the brand." *ARS Persuasion* results indicated that the alternate "no gas" proposition (with a score of +7.8) was significantly stronger than the traditional "no grit" selling idea (which achieved a score of +4.1). The "no gas" selling idea was also above SmithKline Beecham's goal (or action standard) for airing.

Using Citrucel's media plan and rsc's *outlook* model, the company determined that two executions with scores similar to that of the "no gas" *Firstep* video would be needed to see an increase in sales and share. The Ogilvy & Mather ad, "Authority Figure :30," featured a warm and empathetic spokeswoman who educates consumers about Citrucel's "effective relief without the gas." A shorter 15-second version was also produced. Both the 30- and 15-second versions duplicated the score of the "no gas" *Firstep* video.

When the ads began airing at the beginning of November 1993, share responded immediately, increasing over 70 percent from the pre-airing base period (Exhibit 2.33). The only marketing activity during this time was the airing of the two effective "Authority Figure" commercials.

Based on the initial success of Citrucel's advertising, brand management decided to spend additional media money. New executions were needed; after the initial media burst, *outlook* wearout predictions indicated that the "Authority Figure" ads would be worn into the low range of sales responsiveness to media weight and below SmithKline Beecham's off-air goal.

To save on production costs, footage from the original "Authority Figure" shoot was edited, and another 15/30-second commercial pair was produced. Both ads were highly effective, and increased emphasis on the competitive comparison helped the new 30-second version surpass the *ARS Persuasion* scores of the original "Authority Figure" spots to achieve a score of +10.6. A 40 percent increase in Citrucel's sales volume during 1994 confirms that strong advertising pulled the Citrucel brand out of its slump.

CONCLUSION

Continual improvement in advertising productivity can be achieved through an empirically based T. Q. Process that uses sales-related measurement feedback at appropriate stages in the advertising process (Exhibit 2.34). It is also critical to link the pre-market measurements of ad effectiveness to the post-market measurements of sales and share. The purpose of advertising measurement is to increase the likelihood of achieving this sales increase while showing an adequate return-on-investment for the research, production, and media dollars spent. Payout analyses (involving incremental profit over incremental research and production costs) have been calculated for the brands that have used the T. Q. Process. These analyses suggest this process is

EXHIBIT 2.33

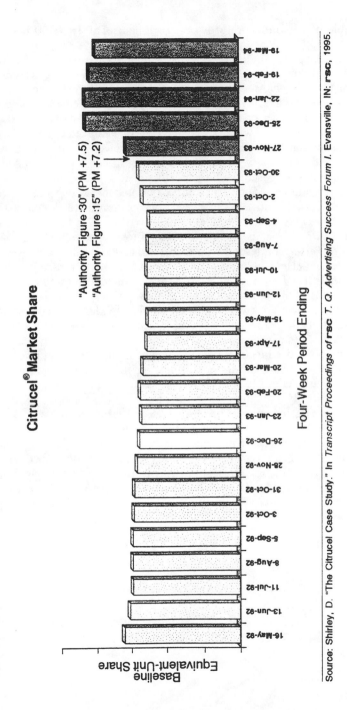

Citrucel® Market Share

"Authority Figure :30" (PM +7.5)
"Authority Figure :15" (PM +7.2)

Baseline Equivalent-Unit Share

Four-Week Period Ending

Source: Shirley, D. "The Citrucel Case Study." In *Transcript Proceedings of* rsc *T. Q. Advertising Success Forum I.* Evansville, IN: rsc, 1995.

capable of generating returns-on-investment of over 5,000 percent (Ashley, 1993).

Given these findings, advertisers may want to rethink the way their advertising budgets are allocated. At the Advertising Research Foundation's 13th Annual Conference, Irwin Gross (1967) related an advertising "parable" in which a "Madison Avenue Genie" granted an advertising manager one of two wishes: "two million dollars worth of media space and time with a campaign that is guaranteed to be average" or "one million dollars worth of space and time with a campaign that is guaranteed to be outstanding." Later in this speech, Gross concluded that "given a proposed media expenditure, it would probably pay to spend an additional 15 to 25 percent of that amount to create and screen independent alternatives — an expenditure pattern quite in contrast to current practice." Three decades later, advertisers that have embraced the T. Q. Process are beginning to follow Gross' advice; they are funding *ARS Persuasion* testing with their media budgets, thereby ensuring that media dollars will be spent only behind effective advertising.

At **rsc**'s first annual T. Q. Advertising Success Forum, Dr. Margaret H. Blair issued this call to action:

"The facts are clear, and the empirical evidence is compelling enough to bellow a resounding call to action: It's time to further the advertising renaissance, with marketing services taking ownership, establishing cross-functional teams, embracing measurement rigor and empirical knowledge, and re-engineering the media, research, and advertising functions to establish a successful continuous improvement process. Finally, to achieve success, advertisers must adopt only those measurements and applications for which there is quantitative evidence that their use will improve advertising productivity (worldwide)."

The success cases presented in this chapter have demonstrated how this T. Q. Process can be used to improve advertising effectiveness and achieve profitable growth through advertising. The marketers that adopt this type of process will likely be rewarded with healthier brands, both short-term and well into the future.

EXHIBIT 2.34

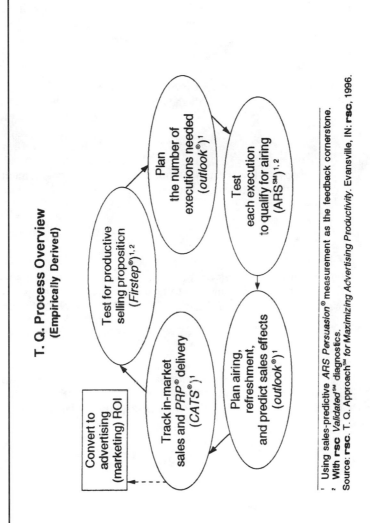

T. Q. Process Overview
(Empirically Derived)

Test for productive selling proposition (*Firstep®*)[1,2]

Plan the number of executions needed (*outlook®*)[1]

Test each execution to qualify for airing (ARS^SM)[1,2]

Plan airing, refreshment, and predict sales effects (*outlook®*)[1]

Track in-market sales and *PRP®* delivery (*CATS®*)[1]

Convert to advertising (marketing) ROI

[1] Using sales-predictive *ARS Persuasion®* measurement as the feedback cornerstone.
[2] With **rsc** *Validated*^SM diagnostics.
Source: **rsc**. T. Q. Approach^SM *for Maximizing Advertising Productivity.* Evansville, IN: **rsc**, 1996.

APPENDIX: THE PACT PRINCIPLES

In 1982, the top research professionals from several leading American advertising agencies published a paper entitled *Positioning Advertising Copy Testing: A Consensus Credo Representing the Views of Leading American Advertising Agencies.* The following principles on copy testing represent a consensus by the PACT Agencies.

Principle I

A good copy testing system provides measurements which are relevant to the objectives of the advertising.

Principle II

A good copy testing system is one which requires agreement about how the results will be used in advance of each specific test.

Principle III

A good copy testing system provides multiple measurements — because single measurements are generally inadequate to assess the performance of an advertisement.

Principle IV

A good copy testing system is based on a model of human response to communications — the reception of a stimulus, the comprehension of the stimulus and the response to the stimulus.

Principle V

A good copy testing system allows for consideration of whether the advertising stimulus should be exposed more than once.

Principle VI

A good copy testing system recognizes that the more finished a piece of copy is, the more soundly it can be evaluated and requires, as a minimum, that alternative executions be tested in the same degree of finish.

Principle VII

A good copy testing system provides controls to avoid the biasing effects of the exposure context.

Principle VIII

A good copy testing system is one that takes into account basic considerations of sample definition.

Principle IX

A good copy testing system is one that can demonstrate reliability and validity.

REFERENCES

Abraham, M.M. and L. M. Lodish. "Getting the Most Out of Advertising and Promotion." *Harvard Business Review* 68, 3 (1990): 50–60.

ASI Market Research, Inc. *Test-Retest Reliability Data: ASI Recall.* ASI Market Research, Inc.: 1991a.

——. *Test-Retest Reliability Data: ASI Tru-share.* ASI Market Research, Inc.: 1991b.

Adams, A. J., and M. H. Blair. "Persuasive Advertising and Sales Accountability: Past Experience and Forward Validation." *Journal of Advertising Research* 32, 2 (1992): 20–25.

Ashley, S. R. "How to Effectively Compete Against Private-Label Brands." In Transcript Proceedings of the 181st ESOMAR Seminar on "Building Successful Brands." Amsterdam: European Society for Opinion and Marketing Research, 1994.

——. "Measuring *[ARS] Persuasion*: Case Studies." In Transcript Proceedings of the ESOMAR Teach-In on "How to Get the Most out of Research." Amsterdam: European Society for Opinion and Marketing Research, 1993.

Bean, B. "Oscar Mayer Lunchables: The In-Market Effects of Advertising." In Transcript Proceedings of rsc T. Q. Advertising Success Forum I. Evansville, IN: rsc, 1995.

Blair, M. H. "An Emerging Renaissance in Advertising through a T. Q. Approach for Maximizing Productivity." In Transcript Proceedings of rsc T. Q. Advertising Success Forum I. Evansville, IN: rsc, 1995.

——. "An Empirical Investigation of Advertising Wearin and Wearout." *Journal of Advertising Research* 27, 6 (1987): 45–50.

——. "Maximizing the Effectiveness of Television Advertising." In Transcript Proceedings of the ESOMAR/ARF Worldwide Electronic and Broadcast Audience Research Symposium. Amsterdam: European Society for Opinion and Marketing Research, 1994a.

——. "Moving Beyond GRPs to PRPs: Another Major Challenge for the 21st Century." In Transcript Proceedings of the ARF Twelfth Annual Electronic Media Workshop. New York, NY: Advertising Research Foundation, 1993.

——. "The Role of Marketing Research in Continually Improving Advertising Productivity Worldwide." In Transcript Proceedings of the ARF Eleventh Annual Copy Research Workshop. New York, NY: Advertising Research Foundation, 1994b.

——; A. R. Kuse; D. H. Furse; and D. W. Stewart. "Advertising in a New Competitive Environment: Persuading Customers to Buy." *Business Horizons* (November-December 1987): 20–26.

——, and K. E. Rosenberg. "Convergent Findings Increase Our Understanding of How Advertising Works." *Journal of Advertising Research* 34, 3 (1994): 35–45.

Buzzell, R. D. "Predicting Short-Term Changes in Market Share as a Function of Advertising Strategy." *Journal of Marketing Research* 1, 3 (1964): 27–31.

Conlin, R. P. "Goodyear Advertising Research: Past, Present, and Future." *Journal of Advertising Research* 34, 3 (1994): RC 7–10.

Crang, D. E. "A *Global* Approach to Advertising Measurement." Presented at the ARF International/Global Research Workshop. New York, NY: Advertising Research Foundation, 1995.

Dodd, A. R., Jr. "New Study Tells TV Advertisers How Advertising Builds Sales and Share of Market." *Printers' Ink* (May 8, 1964).

Feldwick, P. "Quantitative Pre-Testing: Return of the Living Dead?" *Admap*. December 1991.

Gross, I. "Should the Advertiser Spend More on Creating Advertising?" In Transcript Proceedings of the ARF 13th Annual Conference. New York, NY: Advertising Research Foundation, 1967.

Haley, R. I., and A. L. Baldinger. "The ARF Copy Research Validity Project." *Journal of Advertising Research* 31, 2 (1991): 11–32.

Hollis, N. S. "Like It or *Not*, Liking Is *Not* Enough." *Journal of Advertising Research* 35, 5 (1995): 7–16.

—. "The Role of Creativity in Advertising and the Link with Sales." In *"Creative, but does it sell?" New Evidence*. Presented at the Millward Brown International Twenty-First Anniversary Conference, 1994.

Kelly, P. J. "The Schwerin Model: How You Can Use It to Build Your Share of Market." *Printers' Ink* (May 8, 1964).

Keil, J. M. *The Creative Mystique: How to Manage It, Nurture It, and Make It Pay*. New York, NY: John Wiley & Sons, 1985.

Klein, P. R., and M. Tainiter. "Copy Research Validation: The Advertiser's Perspective." *Journal of Advertising Research* 23, 5 (1983): 9–17.

—, and P. Tarr. "MSW AD*VANTAGE/AC-T Validation." In Transcript Proceedings of the ARF 38th Annual Conference. New York, NY: Advertising Research Foundation, 1992.

Kusc, A. R. "Measurement Tools for Ads That Sell." In Transcript Proceedings of the Eighth Annual ARF Copy Research Workshop. New York, NY: Advertising Research Foundation, 1991.

—, and D. E. Crang. "Some Universal Truths about Advertising: Conclusions from Three Major Independent Sources." Presented at the ARF Advertising and Copy Research Workshop. New York, NY: Advertising Research Foundation, 1995.

Lucas, D. B. "A Moderately Objective Overview of Copy and Commercial Tests." In *Copy Research, A Historical Retrospective*, (pp. 23–35). New York, NY: Advertising Research Foundation, 1986.

McCollum Spielman Worldwide. *AC-T Reliability and Discrimination of Primary Measures.* Great Neck, NY: McCollum/Spielman Worldwide.

McKee, M. "A North American Perspective of Japanese TQM." In Conference Board Report 1048. New York, NY: The Conference Board, 1993.

McQueen, J. "Important Learning About How Advertising Works in Stimulating Long-Term Brand Growth." In Transcript Proceedings of the ARF Marketplace Advertising Research Workshop. New York, NY: Advertising Research Foundation, 1991.

Mondello, M. D. "Turning Research into Return-on-Investment." Speech presented at the Conference Board 42nd Annual Marketing Conference. New York, NY: The Conference Board, 1994.

Murphy, M. P. "Empirical Evidence of the Effect of Advertising on Sales." Speech presented to the Professional Marketing Research Society. Toronto: 1968.

Ogilvy, D. *Ogilvy on Advertising.* New York, NY: Random House, Inc., 1983.

—, and J. Raphaelson. "Research on Advertising Techniques that Work — and Don't Work." *Harvard Business Review* 60, 4 (1982): 14–16.

The PACT Agencies. *Positioning Advertising Copy Testing: A Consensus Credo Representing the Views of Leading American Advertising Agencies.* New York, NY: The PACT Agencies, 1982.

Ray, M. L. "Introduction to the Special Section: Measurement and Marketing Research — Is the Flirtation Going to Lead to a Romance?" *Journal of Marketing Research* 16, 1 (1979): 1–5.

rsc. *Advertising Caused Awareness & Trial: ARS Predictive Validity for New Brand Advertising.* Evansville, IN: rsc, 1983.

—. *Advertising Effectiveness and the Cost of Production.* Evansville, IN: rsc, 1992a.

—. *The Effective Delivery of Advertising and Commercial Wearout: 1992 Update.* Evansville, IN: rsc, 1992b.

—. *Global ARS Reliability of ARS Persuasion and Diagnostics: 1995 Report.* Evansville, IN: rsc, 1995.

—. *Special Diagnostic Issues for the ARS Persuasion Measure.* Evansville, IN: rsc, 1992c.

—. T. Q. Approach[SM] *for Maximizing Advertising Productivity.* Evansville, IN: rsc, 1996.

—. *Understanding the Fair Share[SM] Norm.* Evansville, IN: rsc, 1984.

Rosenberg, K. E.; R. Arnold; and P. Capetta. "Heart Strings to Purse Strings: Measuring When Emotions Sell." In MSI Conference Summary of "Tears, Cheers, and Fears: The Role of Emotions in Advertising," (pp. 37–39). Cambridge, MA: Marketing Science Institute, 1991.

—, and M. H. Blair. "Observations: The Long and Short of Persuasive

Advertising." *Journal of Advertising Research* 34, 4 (1994): 63–69.

Sheth, J. N., and R. S. Sisodia. "Feeling the Heat: More Than Ever Before, Marketing Is Under Fire to Account for What It Spends." *Marketing Management* 4, 2 (Fall 1995): 8–23.

Shirley, D. "The Citrucel Case Study." In Transcript Proceedings of rsc T. Q. Advertising Success Forum I. Evansville, IN: rsc, 1995.

Walker, D. "Beyond Validation: Advertising Research for the 1990s." In Transcript Proceedings of the Seventh Annual ARF Copy Research Workshop. New York, NY: Advertising Research Foundation, 1990.

ARS Persuasion, Firstep, outlook, PRP, and *CATS* are registered marks of **rsc** THE QUALITY MEASUREMENT COMPANY.

T. Q. Process, Fair Share, **rsc** *Validated,* ARS, and ARSAR are service marks of **rsc** THE QUALITY MEASUREMENT COMPANY.

Recall Plus, Attention/Linkage Analysis, and Tru-Share are registered service marks of ASI Market Research, Inc.

APEX, Copy Effect Index, and Structured Diagnostics are service marks of ASI Market Research, Inc.

BehaviorScan and InfoScan are registered trademarks of Information Resources, Inc.

SCANTRACK is a registered trademark of the A.C. Nielsen Company.

Prego and Campbell's are registered trademarks of Campbell Soup Company.

Classico is a registered trademark of Borden, Inc.

Hunt's is a registered trademark of Hunt-Wesson, Inc.

Contadina is a registered trademark of Nestle USA, Inc.

Healthy Choice is a trademark of ConAgra, Inc.

Ragu is a registered trademark of Van Den Bergh Foods Company Consumer Products Group.

Aquatred and Eagle are registered trademarks of Goodyear Tire and Rubber Company.

Lunchables is a registered trademark of Oscar Mayer Foods Corporation.

Celestial Seasonings and Wild Berry Zinger are registered trademarks of Celestial Seasonings, Inc.

Citrucel is a registered trademark of SmithKline Beecham Consumer Healthcare.

Metamucil is a registered trademark of The Procter and Gamble Company.

The author would like to acknowledge the contribution of **rsc** THE QUALITY MEASUREMENT COMPANY in the preparation of this chapter.

Stephanie English is owner and president of The English Group, a media consulting and training firm located in the Chicago area. The English Group provides objective consulting and training to advertisers, agencies, and the media to improve the development, assessment, and management of one of the most important areas of the marketing mix: media planning and buying. The English Group offers its unique experience in both media planning and media buying in all media and combines that with case studies, pertinent examples, and the knowledge of the most recent industry developments to advise and train its clients.

Her company has worked for Ameritech, The Upjohn Company, Wrigley, New York Telephone, Association of National Advertisers, First Chicago Bank, Chicago Sun-Times, GTE, NYNEX, Lens Lab, DDB Needham, Leo Burnett, and many other advertisers, agencies, and media suppliers.

Ms. English spent two years as vice president-media director at Bozell/Minneapolis. Prior to that she served as vice president, media director at Leo Burnett USA, where she also held several other positions during her 16-year tenure.

Ms. English developed and conducts the A.N.A.'s Media Strategy Seminars. These popular seminars give hands-on experience in directing the media planning process and in evaluating and assessing media recommendations.

CHAPTER 3

MEDIA PLANNING

Media planning is an art, not a science. Despite all the research and new technologies, we are still asking ourselves basic questions—how much to spend, how many weeks should we advertise, how many weeks should there be between advertising periods and what is the optimum media mix. Media planning requires artfully applying all the information you can muster.

Media planning also requires teamwork. It cannot be done in a vacuum. It needs the attention and dedication given to all the other elements of the advertising and marketing mix. In reality, the advertiser is creating an integrated communications plan, which consists of traditional and/or new media as well as other communications, such as sales promotion, event marketing, and direct marketing.

People often ask, which comes first—the creative or the media? The ideal scenario is for both to be developed simultaneously. While this is not always possible, it is important to note that the information needs of media planning are similar to those of the creative process. Therefore, to the degree possible, it is best to plan and develop them together.

FOUR-STEP PLANNING PROCESS

Here is the first area in which teamwork is required. Whether you arc working with a full-scrvice agency, a mcdia scrvice, or an in-house media operation, teamwork and good planning are essential to an effective media plan.

Trying to do your media planning in one meeting would be short changing a very significant portion of your advertising budget. The four-step planning process (shown in Exhibit 3.1) is recommended for media planning. When followed properly, this process will arm you, the advertising or brand manager, with:

1. A media plan with accountability;
2. A process for analyzing new opportunities that arise during the advertising period;
3. A procedure for making adjustments in the plan due to budget changes.

Also this process addresses complaints many advertising managers have about media planning, complaints such as:

- "This year's plan looks like last year's plan adjusted for inflation."
- "Why doesn't the agency ever think of anything new?"
- "I wish the media plan were more creative."

This four-step process will yield a solid and viable media plan that focuses your business goals. It will also provide workable alternatives and information that allows you to make confident, informed decisions.

Overall, your role in this planning process is to:
- Provide useful information in the preplanning meeting.
- Challenge the agency and/or planner's thinking.
- Coordinate media and other communication disciplines to ensure the best possible communication plan for your brand.
- Ensure the recommended plan fulfills the objectives.
- Suggest alternate plans/strategies for consideration.
- Anticipate upper management questions and suggest information needed to answer them.

Believe it or not, good media planning starts with the advertiser, not the media department. To get a good media plan, the advertiser must become part of the solution and provide good input for the media plan development.

EXHIBIT 3.1 RECOMMENDED PROCESS FOR MEDIA PLANNING

---

4. Recommended plan

3. Media strategy meeting

2. Media objectives meeting

1. Preplanning meeting

---

1. Preplanning meeting

The first meeting in the four-step process is a preplanning meeting. The purpose of the meeting is for the *advertiser* to share marketing plans with the people who will be doing the planning. This meeting should be controlled by the advertiser, not the agency, buying service or in-house media department.

If you are working with a variety of communications disciplines (for example, sales promotions, direct marketing, event marketing), consider having them all attend the same input meeting. Since you are running this meeting, you can control the meeting site, contents and attendees. This will save you time and ensure that all hear the same information about your business and advertising goals. This also helps you coordinate with the other communications disciplines to develop a cohesive plan.

The preplanning meeting should cover the information outlined in Table 3.1.

TABLE 3.1 THE PREPLANNING MEETING

Advertiser Presents	Agency Presents	Either Party Presents (if applicable)
Marketing objectives	Brand review	Promotion plans
Marketing strategies	Advertising objectives	Research/testing plans
Explanation of planning process and timetable		Creative overview

As the agency is often a partner in the development of much of the material, you might consider having them participate in the presentation. However, the basic marketing plans for the planning period should be presented by the advertiser.

Taking an active role in the planning process is the beginning of the teamwork effort necessary to develop an effective media plan. Therefore, the preplanning meeting is crucial to setting the stage for plan development.

The preplanning meeting has three distinct advantages for the advertising manager:

1. It ensures that your business results and goals are properly communicated to the parties responsible for developing your plans.
2. It allows you access to management as well as the day-to-day workers (provided you control and encourage their attendance).
3. It initiates coordination of all communications disciplines (provided you include all of them in the preplanning meeting).

2. Media Objectives Meeting

For most advertisers, this meeting represents a departure from the way things usually have been done. In this meeting, the agency should present the media objectives necessary to accomplish the marketing goals outlined in the preplanning meeting by the advertiser.

Media objectives consist of the following information:

1. **Whom** the advertising is to reach (target).
2. **Where** the advertising is to be placed (geographical).
3. **When** the advertising is to be placed (seasonality).

The objectives should be:

A) Void of specific media usage (no flow charts)
B) Quantifiable
C) In priority order.

A) Void of Specific Media Usage (No Flow Charts)

Flow charts are inappropriate at this phase in the planning cycle, because you want objective media planning. Each year or planning period, you are faced with new business issues and goals that require a fresh media approach. If you allow discussion of media types at this point, you increase the chance of ending up with media plans that:

- Look like last year's plan adjusted for inflation;
- Overlook new or alternative approaches;
- Lack creative media solutions.

By developing objectives before strategies, you are aligning your media planning process with the creative process, as shown in Table 3.2.

TABLE 3.2 MEDIA OBJECTIVES MEETING

Creative Process	Common Media Planning Process	Recommended Media Planning Process
1. Input (analysis of product/service, competition, research)	1. Brief input meeting	1. Same input meeting as creative
2. Creative objectives often resulting in concept statements	2. Recommended media plan, including specific media vehicles and flow charts	2. Recommended media objectives
3. Review of various creative alternatives (storyboards and layouts)	3. Revised media plans necessary to address additional questions and information not raised at earlier meetings	3. Recommended media strategy meeting including recommended plan

B) Quantifiable Objectives

Quantifiable objectives are one way to provide accountability on your media expenditures. Considering the amount of money spent on media advertising, objectives written in vague language that could be used for any product or service are generally ineffective. Sample objectives are shown in Table 3.3.

It is appropriate to have ranges in your objectives. Objectives are goals, and media are not that precise. Also, you need to have a minimum of five reach points and half a frequency point for statistical difference between plans.

Achieving quantifiable media objectives is a difficult task. Often the recommended numbers are budget driven, and the budget may not necessarily be in line with the marketing tasks at hand. For major planning periods, such as annual plans or new product introductions, it might be beneficial to have the planning people develop objectives

TABLE 3.3 SAMPLE QUANTIFIABLE OBJECTIVES

VAGUE	QUANTIFIABLE
Increase awareness among target audience.	Increase brand or advertising awareness from 60-70% in first six months among women 25-54.
Reach adults 25–49, secondarily, males 25–49.	Provide a 65–80% reach of adults 25–49 with 6.5–7.5 average 4-week frequency. Secondarily reach 65–80% of males 25–49 with a 4.0–6.0 average 4-week frequency.
Advertise year-round with additional support during key promotional periods.	Provide "x" more reach, frequency, or number of weeks of advertising during specific dates.
Spend in conjunction with seasonal sales patterns.	Allocate media weight in conjunction with seasonal sales patterns.
Advertise nationally with additional support in development markets.	Provide "x" more reach, frequency, or number of weeks of advertising in development markets.
Maximize/emphasize...	Define what is meant by maximize or emphasize. Usually expressed in terms of reach and frequency or how much more than other areas.

apart from budget constraints. This should provide you with a good idea of what it will take to get the job done. Then you can decide what plan elements are most important (based on your priority order of the objectives) and affordable, given your budget.

C) Put in Priority Order

Objectives need to be ranked in priority order. Few plans today are implemented without changes. Often changes come quickly and revisions are made to the plan for expediency and without regard to their impact on the overall plan. It pays to do some advance work on what the most important objectives are, and how they should be ranked for funding. These priorities provide important direction for making changes when there are budget cuts or additions. Ideally, budget cuts should be made to the lowest priority objectives, while spending your dollars as much as possible on your highest ranked objectives. Conversely, dollars would be added to the objectives in priority order. If additional dollars became available, you can add them to the programs that rank highest. If the top priority items are fully funded, you can add dollars to the next ranked objective, etc.

The recommended media objectives need to be approved before the agency (or whoever is performing the media planning function) proceeds to media strategy development. In fact, the people involved in the ultimate decision on the media plan should sign off on these objectives. Therefore, if the media plan appropriation is approved by more senior level management than yourself, they should approve media objectives before proceeding to strategy development.

3. Media Strategy Meeting

Unless, for creative reasons, you have chosen to exclude a specific medium, all media should be evaluated at this meeting. This provides the advertising manager with valuable information to use throughout the year. It provides information on media that may not be recommended but might be considered at another time during the year. This saves time when new opportunities become available. Evaluating alternative media also helps to show the agency's thought process and thoroughness. For each medium being evaluated, the following types of information should be examined:

- Reach potential
- Frequency
- Average rating
- Composition of the medium or vehicle (audience selectivity)
- Cost per thousand (CPM) or cost per point (CPP), which is a measurement often used in buying media. CPM is the cost to purchase 1,000 impressions (exposures) in a specific target audience. CPP is the cost to purchase one rating point or one percent of a specific target audience.
- Quintile analysis (optional), which is often used to compare media, divides a given population group into five equal-size groups, ranging from heaviest to lightest amount of exposure to a medium. Groups may also be divided into tertiles (thirds), quartiles (fourths), and deciles (tenths).

Table 3.4 details what information should be examined when considering media for possible inclusion in the media plan. At this point, the specific vehicles within the medium and the absolute levels have not been determined. The key to the following analysis is that the data should be presented on the same basis for all media:

- Same target audience and geographic area
- Equal dollar volumes
- Consistent time period.

The information in Table 3.5 indicates that women 25–54 are above average users of TV-Prime, general editorial magazines and drive-time radio because their numbers are significantly above average (above 1.00) for the first and second quintiles. The data also suggest that these women are very much above average in their usage of general editorial magazines because their usage is higher for this medium than the other media for all but Quintile 5.

Quintile data should not be the sole criteria used to evaluate the appropriateness of a given medium. The inherent weakness with quin-

TABLE 3.4 CONSIDERATIONS FOR MEDIA PURCHASE

Data for Women 25-54 in the United States.
Analysis based on $1,000M per medium
4-week time period*

	TV-Prime	General Editorial Magazines	Drive-Time Radio
Reach potential	41.3%	56.6%	44.0%
Average rating	7.6	8.6	1.1
Composition	41%	36%	25%
CPM	29.96	13.27	6.62

*Source: Mediamark Research, Inc., Fall 1994 Study; 93/94 Leo Burnett Media Costs and Coverage; Leo Burnett REACH system

TABLE 3.5 A QUINTILE ANALYSIS FOR CONSIDERATION
WHEN PURCHASING MEDIA

Average Frequency Women 25-54 in U.S.; $1,000M*

	TV-Prime	General Editorial Magazines	Drive-Time Radio
Quintile 1	2.73	5.03	2.94
Quintile 2	1.77	2.68	1.67
Quintile 3	1.00	2.00	1.00
Quintile 4	1.00	1.42	1.00
Quintile 5	1.00	1.00	1.00

*Source: Mediamark Research, Inc., Fall 1994 Study; 93/94 Leo Burnett Media Costs and Coverage; Leo Burnett REACH system

tile data is that it has different measurement criteria for each medium. For example, the first quintile for television is based on people viewing an average of 38.7 half-hours per week, while the first quintile for radio is based on an average of 87 half-hours of listening per week. See Table 3.6 for details on media usage patterns by quintile.

Nevertheless, quintile information is helpful in that it does identify heavy, medium and light users of each medium. Therefore, if quintile data are evaluated, they should be used in conjunction with other data.

Once specific media have been evaluated and considered for possible inclusion, the media planning team also needs to provide a variety of alternatives for each medium, as well as alternate equal dollar media mix options. Table 3.7 details this concept for evaluating alternate television day-part mixes.

TABLE 3.6 MEDIA USAGE PATTERNS BY QUINTILE

Time Spent With Medium (Women)*

	TV-Prime (avg. # 1/2 hrs./wk.)	General Editorial Magazines (avg. # issues read/mo.)	All Radio (avg. # 1/2 hrs./wk.)
Quintile 1	38.7	28.0	87.0
Quintile 2	28.1	14.1	32.8
Quintile 3	14.6	8.9	17.6
Quintile 4	4.4	4.8	8.4
Quintile 5	0.0	0.9	0.2

*Source: Mediamark Research, Inc., Fall 1994 Study

TABLE 3.7 MEDIA AND BUDGET ALTERNATIVES

All $1,000M Plans
Women 25-54 data, total U.S.
Average 4-week data*

	Plan A 100% Prime	Plan B 75% Prime 25% Late Night	Plan C 60% Prime 40% Late Night
Reach	41.3%	43.2%	42.8%
Frequency	1.5	1.6	1.7
Total TRPs	61	68	71
CPM/CPP	$16,447	$14,706	$14,085
Gross impressions (000)	33,373	37,325	38,972
CPM	$29.96	$26.79	$25.66
# weeks of advertising	4	4	4

*Source: Mediamark Research, Inc., Fall 1994 Study; 93/94 Leo Burnett Media Costs and Coverage; Leo Burnett REACH system

TABLE 3.8 CONSIDERATIONS WHEN DETERMINING MEDIA MIX

All $1,000M Plans
Women 25–54 data, total United States
Average 4-week data*

	Plan A 100% Prime	Plan B 75% TV 25% Magazines	Plan C 60% TV 40% Radio
Reach	41.3%	48.1%	53.7%
Frequency	1.5	1.5	1.7
Total TRPs	61	73	91
CPM/CPP	$16,447	$13,699	$10,989
Gross impressions (000)	33,373	40,070	49,950
CPM	$29.96	$24.96	$20.02
# weeks of advertising	4	4	4

*Source: Mediamark Research, Inc., Fall 1994 Study; 93/94 Leo Burnett Media Costs and Coverage; Leo Burnett REACH system

Information such as that outlined in Table 3.7 needs to be provided for all media being considered. Once the best mix of vehicles within a given medium has been decided, you need to determine the best media mix. Again, this decision requires a variety of options and should include information as outlined in Table 3.8.

In the media strategy discussion, the agency or media planning unit should provide information on the pros and cons of various plan alternatives as well as a recommended plan.

In the media objectives meeting, the recommended objectives were put into priority order. Now that you have a recommended plan from the agency, the agency should also present:

- Where additional funds would be added should they become available.
- Where dollars would be cut should there be a budget decrease.

This "cut and add" feature can be an effective management tool:

- When changes in budget arise and/or
- When additional ideas/opportunities are suggested throughout the year.

This feature also provides a way to ensure that the agency's recommendations are in harmony with the marketing and media objectives. You should closely examine the "cut/add" feature in conjunction with the media objectives. The recommendations for where to add to the plan and how dollars are to be cut from the plan should be aligned

TABLE 3.9 MINIMUM NUMBER OF ALTERNATIVES FOR EACH MEDIUM

MEDIUM	REASONABLE ANALYSIS
National TV	Minimum of three alternate day-part mixes.
Spot (Local) TV	At least three day-part mix alternatives by market or by region of country.
National, wired and unwired, & Spot Radio	Three or more alternatives examining station format and another three analyzing day-part alternatives.
Magazines	Title-by-title analysis followed by minimum of three alternate plans using different magazine mixes.
Newspapers	Market-by-market and paper-by-paper analysis. One plan per market is sufficient.
Out-of-home (Billboards buses, trains, airports, arenas, etc.)	As types and usage of out-of-home varies significantly by market, analysis should be done by market and using most appropriate vehicle in each market.

with the objectives. If not, both parties need to re-examine the recommended plan.

A number of alternatives should be examined in the media strategy section. *An alternate plan is not a plan at a higher dollar level. It is another option with different media vehicles and/or mixes of media at the same dollar level as other options.* Table 3.9 defines a minimum number of alternatives to examine for each medium.

4. Recommended Media Plan

In the media strategy meeting, the agency or planning unit provides a recommended plan. If this plan requires minor revisions, another meeting may not be required. Instead, the agency could make the revisions and forward the final plan documents. If the plan that was recommended requires major revisions, you need to re-examine each party's adherence to the planning process and ask yourself why major revisions are required.

- Did you provide adequate information in the preplanning meeting?
- Was there a change in the marketing plan that was not communicated?
- Did the agency prepare media objectives that demonstrated their understanding of the marketing plan?

- Were the media objectives approved before proceeding to strategy development?
- Are the objectives in priority order and written in quantifiable terms?
- Did the agency examine all relevant media and provide a variety of plan alternatives for your review?
- Does the plan properly integrate with all the communications disciplines?

If you are diligent in following the planning process, you should be able to review a recommended media plan by the third meeting in the process. Major revisions in the recommended plan at this point are an indication that something was not communicated or understood in the preplanning or media objectives meeting. Minor revisions are to be expected and should be accommodated quickly and without another formal meeting.

As you begin to approve a recommended plan, be sure you have considered all the necessary information. Here is what you should be evaluating:

- The recommended plan should fulfill marketing and media objectives.
- Plan alternatives should be provided within media as well as a variety of media mix options.
- Reasons for media that are not recommended should also be included.
- When there is a mixture of spot (local) and non-spot (national or network) markets, be sure to examine data for each market type (spot and non-spot) separately.
- Also examine cable versus non-cable households when cable is involved.
- Think about how other communication programs can be integrated with this recommendation.
- Consider how the approval process meets with your timing for creative, development, budget approval, and other communication areas.
- Are all your questions thoroughly addressed?

TIMING

In the preplanning meeting, the advertiser is responsible for explaining the planning process and securing agreement on the dates for the subsequent meetings. Here are some recommendations with respect to timing from step to step in the four-step process. (See Table 3.10.)

The recommended timing is for major media plans. Most plans can be developed from input through final revisions in one month or less. Nevertheless, simple plans that arise from time to time during the course of a year could certainly be done in less time. However, each

TABLE 3.10 ESTIMATED TIMING FOR PLANNING

From preplanning meeting to media objectives	One week for major plans and shorter if plans are relatively simple.
From media objectives to media strategy meeting	1–3 weeks depending on complexity of media and alternatives to be examined.
From media strategy meeting to recommended media plan	If simple revisions, less than one week; if more complex revisions are necessary, the planning process was not successful.

step of the process should be followed to ensure a quality plan and to safeguard against unnecessary plan revisions, miscommunications and loss of valuable time.

Finally, your role as manager is crucial to the success of the planning process. You set the tone, the timing and the information expectations. If you are diligent, the result will be a well thought out, top-quality media plan that you can approve with confidence. In addition, the plan will provide you with the flexibility needed in today's marketplace to adjust to new business situations quickly and efficiently.

MEDIA PLANNING CHECKLIST

Exhibit 3.2 represents a summary of the media planning process in the form of a checklist for the advertising manager to use for the development of media plans.

Media planning is an art, not a science. There are no hard and fast answers or formulas. Also, don't forget that the media plan is a work in progress; as your business results and priorities change, so should your media plan. It will be easier to make adjustments to your plan if you have done your homework up front and made some decisions about the priority of your objectives. You should also look at your media plans from the standpoint of what elements are most essential and which are less important (the "cut-and-add" feature). The final plan will include good judgment and "gut" decisions. However, following a solid planning process is essential to adequately thinking through the business and making good decisions on the mix of media alternatives.

PRIMARY ELEMENT OF A MEDIA PLAN

At the end of a planning process, you will end up with reams of information that aided you and the agency in the plan development and final recommendation. Once the plan has been approved, the agency should prepare a final plan document that includes all the critical information. The primary elements of a media plan and the key information they should contain are detailed in Table 3.11.

Exhibit 3.2 Media Planning Checklist

❏ 1. Preplanning meeting

❏ 2. Media objectives meeting

❏ 3. Quantifiable media objectives

❏ 4. Media objectives in priority order

❏ 5. Approve media objectives before media strategy meeting

❏ 6. Media strategy meeting

❏ 7. All relevant media considered

❏ 8. Reasons given for media not recommended

❏ 9. Minimum of three alternate plans for each considered medium

❏ 10. Minimum of three alternate media mix options to review

❏ 11. Recommended plan

❏ 12. Establish where dollars would be cut or added should the budget change on recommended plan

❏ 13. If spot (local) media are recommended, review data for spot and non-spot markets

❏ 14. If cable TV is recommended, review data on cable and non-cable households

❏ 15. Review recommended plan to marketing objectives

❏ 16. Prepare flow chart incorporating all communication area activity onto one chart

❏ 17. Review buying strategy for recommended plan

❏ 18. Review buying guidelines for each medium to be used in recommended plan

❏ 19. Put major decision dates for plan execution onto business calendar

❏ 20. Set post-buy dates when each medium is approved for purchase

TABLE 3.11 MEDIA PLAN ELEMENTS

TOPIC	INFORMATION TO BE INCLUDED
Marketing background	A summary of the key business information provided by the advertiser in the preplanning meeting that the media planners felt most important in the development of the recommended plan.
Advertising budget summary	This clearly delineates the working media budget from other monies such as agency fees, creative, production and funds for other communications disciplines, such as direct.
Competitive review	A simple recap of the major competitive spending trends and their implications for the product/service recommended media plan. The full details should be in a separate document.
Review of prior year plan	A section that contains 1) prior year's budget summary and flow chart based on the final approved plan, 2) a budget summary and flow chart based on the plan as it was actually implemented, and 3) a short summary of the key changes that transpired from the approved to the final implemented plan. A flow chart is a graphic depiction of the plan usually done on a calendar 12-month basis showing the timing of the media and the activity levels (amount of spending, rating points, type of insertions for print and reach, and frequency data).
Media objectives & rationale	Target audience, geographical and seasonal objectives stated in quantifiable terms and placed in priority order.
Media strategy & rationale	Evaluation of all relevant media, including minimum of three plan alternatives within media and three media mix options. Also reasons why media not being used are not recommended.
Recommended plan	All plan alternatives that lead to recommended plan. Comparison of recommended plan to objectives. Include "cut-and-add" feature as well as indication of key decision dates.
Media execution strategy	Discussion of how recommended plan is to be executed, including recommended buying strategies and the basis for the pricing used to develop recommended plan costs.
Budget summary, flow chart, and exhibits	Budget summaries and flow charts prepared to meet your internal needs and specifications. If desired, include all communications disciplines on the flow chart. Exhibits could contain additional rationale and information not included elsewhere in the media plan documents.

How Media Are Bought and Sold

Understanding how media are bought and sold is an important element in managing media. Most media are negotiable, and understanding the dynamics of the media marketplace can make a major difference in your media plan costs and dollar flexibility.

First, it is important to understand the electronic media marketplace (broadcast, television, radio and cable) as it represents the lion's share of most national advertisers' media investments and serves as the barometer for the other media.

Electronic media (national and local television, including syndication, cable, and national and local radio) are negotiable. The negotiations are based on the market forces of supply and demand, which result in negotiated pricing of either cost per points (CPP) or cost per thousands (CPM) for specific target audiences. The following discussion focuses on national television, as it represents the largest dollar commitment of most advertisers and serves as a model for the other media.

The pricing used in electronic media is determined by a mixture of supply and demand.

In national television, supply is defined as 1) the number of ratings points and 2) the number of commercials available for sale. Rating points are a function of our viewing habits. As a nation, we are watching more and more television. This is seen in Table 3.12.

While the absolute hours of viewing have increased, viewing has shifted away from the three primary networks (ABC, CBS, NBC) to other program options, such as independent stations and cable, as in Table 3.13.

Different viewing patterns exist throughout the day and the year (Table 3.14). Rating levels are highest in prime time and lowest in daytime and late nighttime periods. Also, higher ratings occur during colder weather with fewer daylight hours during the first and fourth quarters.

The second part of supply is the absolute number of commercials that are created for sale. On a national and local basis, the industry self-regulates the amount of commercial inventory. For several years the American Association of Advertising Agencies (AAAA) and Association of National Advertisers, Inc., (ANA) have jointly commissioned a Television Commercial Monitoring Report, examining national and local commercial minutes, as well as other categories of nonprogram material. As detailed in Table 3.15, more commercials are scheduled in the lesser-viewed day-parts (daytime, late fringe and evening news), and fewer are scheduled in prime time.

Demand is defined as 1) the number of advertisers and 2) the rating point needs or dollars they have to invest. Demand does not necessarily follow supply; in fact, demand tends to be highest in the second and fourth quarters (Table 3.16). Second quarter commercial inventory is highest in demand. There are two reasons for this second quarter phenomenon.

TABLE 3.12 HOURS OF WEEKLY WATCHING*

YEAR	WEEKLY HOURS HOUSEHOLD USAGE
Early 1955	4:51
Early 1965	5:29
Early 1975	6:07
Early 1985	7:07
Early 1995	7:02

*Source: Nielsen Media Research

TABLE 3.13 VIEWING DATA*

Year	Network Affiliates	Independent Stations	PBS Stations	Cable
1982	72	21	3	3
1985	67	22	3	7
1990	56	27	3	22
1995	57	12	3	31

*Source: Nielsen Media Research

TABLE 3.14 TYPICAL TELEVISION VIEWING PATTERNS DURING THE YEAR

HOUSEHOLD RATINGS*

Day-Part	First Quarter	Second Quarter	Third Quarter	Fourth Quarter
Early AM	4.5	4.5	4.2	4.5
Daytime	5.1	4.8	5.1	4.9
Early News	11.7	10.2	9.6	11.4
Prime	13.8	11.7	9.6	12.9
Late Evening	4.1	4.1	4.2	4.2
Wknd. Kids	3.2	2.8	2.5	3.2

*Source: TV Dimensions '94

TABLE 3.15 WHEN MOST COMMERCIALS ARE SCHEDULED*

Day-Part/ Source	Average No. Nat'l. & Local Commercials min./hr.
Prime	10:19
Sports	10:26
Early AM	13:27
Network Evening News	14:27
Local Evening News	12:30
Daytime	14:48
Late Night	13:38
Cable	12:18 – 16:41**
Syndication	12:12 – 13:56***

*Source: AAAA/ANA '92 Television Commercial Monitoring Report; Nov. '94 data

**Range is shown for 16 cable networks

***Differs by program type. Range is across six program types representing 20 shows

TABLE 3.16 ADVERTISER DEMAND VERSUS VIEWING LEVELS

QTR.	SUPPLY (VIEWING LEVELS)	DEMAND (ADVERTISER NEEDS)	CPM
1st	Highest	Lowest	Lowest
2nd	Average	Highest	Highest
3rd	Lowest	Average	Average
4th	High	High	High

1. Several large-budget advertising categories, such as beers, fast food, automobiles and soft drinks, have increased seasonality in the second quarter. This, in turn, increases their respective demand in the second quarter.

2. For the majority of advertisers with calendar fiscal years (January-December), budgets and plans are often not set until some time later in the first quarter for second quarter implementation.

Combining the various components of supply and demand results in the following trends in quarterly pricing for electronic media.

Purchase Strategies

There are three basic purchase strategies used for purchasing electronic media:

1. Long-term or "up front"
2. Short-term or "scatter"
3. Opportunistic.

These strategies are prevalent in the purchase of national television (including syndication and cable) and radio. We will discuss them first with respect to national television and then explain the differences for other electronic media.

Long-Term or Up-Front vs. Short-Term or Scatter

Table 3.17 shows that each strategy has different time periods and is purchased at different times.

Most advertisers use a combination strategy in purchasing their television needs. The amount of long-term, short-term, and opportunistic dollars is based on advertisers' assessment of the media marketplace, as well as their corporation's needs for good pricing and dollar flexibility. (Marketing considerations play a role too, for example, new products introductions, competitive activity, etc.)

Long-term is a popular purchase strategy for most large advertisers (corporations). Compared to short-term, a long-term purchase strategy has three distinct advantages and one major difference as shown in Table 3.18.

Better Program Mix

A primary reason for making long-term buys is to secure a higher proportion of more desirable programming. Regrettably, the failure rate is very high on new programs. Therefore, many long-term advertisers try to emphasize a program mix of shows with proven track records. However, if a long-term advertiser is willing to take on more risk by purchasing a higher percentage of new or lower-rated programs, the resulting CPM would be lower than an advertiser looking for less risk in the program mix.

TABLE 3.17 COMPARISON OF STRATEGIES AND PURCHASES

STRATEGY	TIME PERIOD AND WHEN PURCHASED
Long-term	Purchased in year-long increments, usually in June or July of each year for the time period of September through August of the following year. Some multi-year deals are possible for certain day-parts and sponsorships, such as NFL football. A day-part is any of the time segments into which a broadcast day is divided — by audience composition and/or broadcast origination time (such as, for TV — daytime, early fringe, access, prime and late fringe: for radio — morning drive, mid day, afternoon drive, night or teen).
Short-term advance	Usually purchased on a quarterly basis 3–6 months in of the quarter.
Opportunistic	Purchased when the opportunities arise. See separate discussion.

TABLE 3.18 COMPARISON OF LONG-TERM VERSUS
SHORT-TERM STRATEGIES

LONG-TERM	SHORT-TERM
Better program mix	Less desirable mix
Ratings (CPM) guarantee	Guarantees are rare
20–40% better price*	20–40% higher prices*
Dollars less flexible	Dollars more flexible

*Differs significantly based on market conditions

CPM Guarantee

A major advantage of national long-term buying over short-term is the CPM guarantee. Ratings in television are volatile and given the expense of the medium (average cost of a :30 in prime time exceeds $250,000), broadcasters need to provide some guarantee to the advertiser as protection on the investment. Guarantees are usually negotiated based on a basic demographic target audience (total households, women 18–34, men 18–49, adults 25–49, etc.) and are adjusted by quarter. Therefore, the second quarter CPM guarantee would probably be the highest, and the first quarter guarantee is generally the lowest for most adult target audiences.

The guaranteed CPM is tied to rating point delivery. If a network falls short on a CPM guarantee, it will provide the advertiser with additional commercial inventory (rating points) in similar programming at no additional expense. Guarantees are made by the network by day-part. So, if an advertiser made a daytime and prime-time purchase on CBS, there would be a separate guarantee for each day-part.

In Table 3.19, for example, a buy was made against women 25–54 which fell short by 8.2 rating points. The network owes the advertiser an additional commercial or two to make up the deficiency. These no-charge units are often referred to as audience deficiency (a.d.) units or makegood units.

Rating is an estimate of the size of an audience expressed as a percentage of a given population base. Usually expressed as rating points, gross rating points (GRPs) or target rating points (TRPs).

Generally, guarantees that are not met are made good with additional inventory. However, in some cases, dollars may be refunded in lieu of additional inventory. This is more typical in cable and syndication where there are fewer program options and rating points available to cover the guarantees.

Better Price

Historically, long-term has been priced more attractively than short-term inventory by approximately 20 to 40 percent. There have been and will continue to be exceptions to this trend. During our most

TABLE 3.19 COMPARISON OF GUARANTEED VIEWERSHIP VERSUS ACTUAL

WOMEN 25–54 DATA

	Rating Points	Cost	CPM
Guaranteed	52.5	$502.3M	$18.07
Actual	44.3	$502.3M	$21.46
Index	84	100	118

recent recessionary period and particularly following the Persian Gulf crisis, there were some quarters when short-term pricing was below long-term prices. Because of the importance of the long-term market, many of the networks revised their long-term pricing to equalize long- and short-term pricing. This was most often done by giving additional inventory (rating points) to their long-term customers.

Dollar Flexibility

When the advertiser makes a long-term purchase, the terms and conditions of the buy are also negotiated. Terms and conditions gener- ally refer to the amount of firm and flexible dollars, when the flexible dollars must be finally committed (option dates), and the actual CPM guarantees.

Table 3.20 represents a hypothetical advertiser with multiple brands purchasing long-term television. The advertiser has pooled the needs of the individual brands and combined them into a $26 million long-term television budget.

TABLE 3.20 HYPOTHETICAL EXAMPLE OF LONG-TERM PURCHASING FOR MULTI-BRAND ADVERTISER

QTR.	PURCHASED $(000)	FIRM $(000)	CANCELABLE $(000)	OPT. DATE
4Q	$7,000	$7,000	$0	NA
1Q	$5,000	$5,000	$0	NA
2Q	$6,000	$3,000	$3,000	1/15
3Q	$8,000	$4,000	$4,000	4/1
Tot.	$26,000	$19,000	$7,000	

The advertiser purchased $26 million worth of commercial inventory. However, at the time of the purchase, the advertiser is only committed to the firm dollars or $19 million Generally, when long- term commitments are made, the fourth quarter dollars and all or some large portion of the first quarter dollars are firm. This is the case in the above chart. Hence, the purchased and firm dollars are the same for the fourth and first quarters and there are no cancelable dollars or option dates for those respective quarters. However, 50 percent of the second and third quarters dollars are flexible. Therefore, on or before the option date, the advertiser has the right to cancel the flexible dollars. In the case of the second quarter, on January 15th or about 45 days prior to the second quarter, the advertiser could decide that it only wants to spend $3 million and not the full $6 million as originally planned. For the third quarter, it could reduce its spending to $4 million or down $4 million from the original $8 million purchased. The amount of firm and flexible dollars and the option dates are negotiable and will differ from network to network and within day-parts. Some contracts allow the network to cancel third quarter option dollars when the advertiser exercises second quarter options.

Incidentally, it is important to note that the advertiser does not actually pay for the time any earlier with a long-term versus a short-term or opportunistic purchase strategy. In each case, the advertiser pays for the time when it is billed, which is generally after the month of service. For example, commercials that run in July are paid for in August.

It is to the buyer's advantage to secure maximum flexibility, short lead times for option dates, attractive program mixes, and attractive pricing. The sellers, however, want to increase the amount of firm dollars compared to flexible dollars and want earlier option dates than advertisers. The sellers also want greater flexibility with respect to the program mix and optimum pricing. Weighing buyer and seller goals requires very highly skilled negotiations. Table 3.21 summarizes this in visual form.

In the national television marketplace, the long-term market is

TABLE 3.21 BUYER'S AND SELLER'S GOALS

Seller's Market Higher Demand	Buyer's Market Lower Demand
Greater number of less popular or new programs in package	Greater concentration of returning to new and more desirable programs
High percentage of firm dollars	More flexible dollars
Long advance notice on option dates	Shorter notification on option dates
Higher prices (CPMs)	More attractive prices (CPMs)

the highest revenue market for the networks. Typically, 70–90 percent of the total inventories are sold on a long-term basis. The amount differs by network, syndication, and cable, and changes from year to year, depending on prevailing market conditions.

Network television is generally purchased by day-part. Cable and syndication are usually budgeted and purchased separately from network television. Network radio is purchased by network and format.

Long-term advertisers also enjoy other privileges. When there is additional unsold inventory, the networks will offer their long-term advertisers' bonus units as a gesture of good will to their best customers. When specials or other attractive program opportunities arise, they are offered to long-term advertisers first. Also, when an advertiser needs a special accommodation from the network, its status as a long-term advertiser is carefully considered by the network when responding to a special request.

Opportunistic Strategy

The opportunistic buying strategy refers to buying inventory that is unsold within a short time prior to the airing of the program. Typically, opportunities become available in programming with controversial or sensitive material or in programming that is scheduled opposite blockbuster events such as the Olympics, Super Bowl or first-run hit movies. Ratings in opportunistic programming may or may not be guaranteed. Prices are, however, very advantageous. Opportunistic pricing can be 50 percent or more less expensive than long- or short-term pricing. Lead times are very short, since purchases are made as little as one week or just hours before air time.

You need to be cautious about using the opportunistic buying strategy. It is not usually a primary strategy, because it depends upon opportunities becoming available. In a seller's market, opportunities are less prevalent than in a buyer's market.

Regardless, the opportunities are not predictable and as such, you cannot be certain to secure advertising when it is needed, or on any predictable or consistent basis. Also, opportunities require quick decisions. Most advertisers using opportunistic strategies set aside funds and have predetermined guidelines for an agency or buying unit to use should opportunities become available. Using valuable time to contact advertisers for approval of opportunities can often result in the loss of the opportunity.

Preemptibility

When you purchase network television time, it is considered sold and is not preemptible. That is, another advertiser can not come in at a later date and offer a higher price or more attractive terms and conditions for the inventory you have purchased. However, occasionally, programs are preempted due to national emergencies, presidential addresses, or sporting events running longer than planned. In those cases, the networks contact the advertiser or their respective buying agent and work out a solution for a makegood. Usually the missed inventory is made good in the same or like programming within a very short time period. You can take credit for the missed inventory, saving the money, or re-express it elsewhere.

Product Protection

When there is a break in a program for commercials, the series of commercials that are scheduled is called a commercial pod. Competitive protection within a pod depends upon the length of each commercial. When purchasing one :30 commercial on a network, the commercial is guaranteed product protection within the pod. If you purchase one :15

commercial, you have no protection within the pod. Therefore, in Commercial Pod 1 shown in Table 3.22, Brand X Auto Insurance has protection in the pod. There can be no other auto insurance, long-distance service, cheese, or fast-food commercials in the pod.

However, in Commercial Pod 2, Brand X ran one :15 stand-alone commercial and was not protected in the pod as another auto insurance advertiser, Brand Y, also has a :15 announcement in the same pod. If Brand X had used a split :30 (two-:15s scheduled separately), they would have regained their protection within the pod as in the example for Commercial Pod 3.

While more costly, purchasing a sponsorship is another way of ensuring product protection. Sponsorships generally require the purchase of more than one commercial in a program (for example, three-:30s in a half-hour program) or the purchase of multiple commercials in the same program for a 13- or 26-week cycle. Also, what constitutes a sponsorship will differ from one product category to another. For example, sponsorship of the World Series might require six-:30s per game in the domestic beer category, but only one minute (two-:30s) per game for the lawn-care category.

Sponsorship purchases include other benefits that are tailored to each advertiser. A few of the possibilities are:

1. Opening and closing billboards;
2. Trips and tickets to the event;
3. VIP hospitality services and parties;
4. Promotion of the event and your sponsorship on the same network or a sister cable network;
5. Merchandising in the form of related specialty or give-away items;
6. Additional exposure in the network's on-line service area.

Commercial Rotation

There are two things to review when discussing commercial rotation (Table 3.23).

1. Where the commercial pod will be scheduled in the program (usually numbered);
2. What position in the pod your commercial will have (usually lettered).

For most purchases that do not involve sponsorships, an advertiser will receive a fair rotation through commercial pods and positioning within the pod. Of course, in special circumstances, such as the introduction of a new commercial or product, special positioning requests can be negotiated.

Overall, the networks need to have sufficient flexibility to schedule thousands of commercials with the proper product protection and equitable rotations throughout and within the pods. If you are concerned about your rotation, have the agency or media-buying unit pro-

TABLE 3.22 EXAMPLES OF PROTECTED AND UNPROTECTED PODS

COMMERCIAL POD 1	COMMERCIAL POD 2	COMMERCIAL POD 3
:30 Auto Insurance, Brand X	:15 Auto Insurance, Brand X	:15 Auto Insurance, Brand X
:30 Long-Distance Service	:30 Long-Distance Service	:30 Long-Distance Service
:30 Cheese	:30 Cheese	:30 Cheese
:30 Fast Food	:30 Fast Food	:30 Fast Food
	:15 Auto Insurance, Brand Y	:15 Auto Insurance, Brand X

TABLE 3.23 EXAMPLES OF COMMERCIAL ROTATION

COMMERCIAL BREAK 1		COMMERCIAL BREAK 2	
Position	**Advertiser**	**Position**	**Advertiser**
1A	:30 Auto Insurance, Brand X	2A	:15 Auto Insurance, Brand X
1B	:30 Long-Distance Service	2B	:30 Long-Distance Service
1C	:30 Cheese	2C	:30 Cheese
1D	:30 Fast Food	2D	:30 Fast Food
		2E	:15 Auto Insurance, Brand Y

vide you with a report on your positioning for a specified period of time (one month or one month per quarter) on one or two networks. If there are any problems, the agency or media-buying unit can bring them to the networks' attention for explanation and resolution.

Differences Between National and Local Electronic Purchases

For the most part, the previous pages discussed electronic media on a national level with an emphasis on television. The dynamics of supply and demand and the three primary purchase strategies (long-term, short-term and opportunistic) are attributable to cable and syndicated television and national radio purchases as well. However, when it comes to local or spot purchases, there are some differences with respect to purchase strategies.

First, local electronic purchases are referred to as "spot" purchases. This means the purchase of television, radio or cable in individual markets. The media are typically referred to as spot television, spot cable and spot radio.

Spot Purchases Offer Greater Dollar Flexibility

For most advertisers, a primary benefit of spot TV, spot radio and spot cable is its dollar flexibility. The shorter lead times afforded with spot purchases (four to six weeks) make it easier to add weight to a given local market more spontaneously than long- or short-term national TV or radio.

Also, spot has flexibility once it has been purchased, a benefit not characteristic of long-term electronic purchases. In long-term spot purchases, the amounts of firm and flexible dollars are more negotiable. It is common to have long-term spot purchases with significant cancellation options of as much as 100 percent of the purchase being cancelable with two to four weeks prior notice.

Most of the inventory in local electronic media is sold on a short-term basis. Typically, buys are made four to six weeks in advance of the air date. At the time of purchase the commitment is considered firm. However, there are cancellation rights. The purchase can be canceled before start. This is usually allowed when the funds are to be re-expressed at a later date. Normally a spot purchase must run for two weeks, then the stations require two to four weeks notice for cancellation. Therefore, if you purchased an eight-week flight as shown in Exhibit 3.3, you could cancel four weeks of the commitment without incurring any penalties.

EXHIBIT 3.3 SAMPLE FLIGHT CANCELLATION OPTIONS

Week 1	Must run
Week 2	Must run
Week 3	Two-week cancellation notice given
Week 4	Second week of cancellation notice
Week 5	Can be canceled
Week 6	Can be canceled
Week 7	Can be canceled
Week 8	Can be canceled

Program Mix

The emphasis on better, lower risk and higher rated programming is less of a factor in spot purchases. Although, in some markets it ensures advertisers a presence in local news shows and local news sponsorships.

Pricing

The difference between long- and short-term prices will vary significantly from market to market for spot buys. Overall, the difference between long- and short-term pricing is less significant in spot compared to the national marketplace.

Opportunistic buys exist in all media, even on a local or spot basis. The same benefits and pitfalls that are characteristic of national opportunistic buys are also true for the local market.

Guaranteed rating points are prevalent in both national and spot long-term electronic purchases. Guarantees for short-term purchases are rare for short-term national or spot buys. The exceptions would be for special purchases, such as sporting events, award programs, and election coverage, or in a very soft or "buyer's" economy when guarantees can be negotiated for short-term commitments.

Preemptibility

Unlike national electronic media, purchases in spot or local electronic media can be preempted by higher rate advertisers. This is where considerable expertise comes into play in local buys. The buyer must assess the marketplace and pay in accordance with the marketplace. The trick is to pay a sufficient amount so that the spots run and are not preempted by higher rate advertisers.

Even the best buyers will have spots preempted from time to time. This is acceptable and in some ways a measurement of the buyer's ability not to pay too much for the inventory. Spots can be made good in another week or in another program (in the case of weekly programs) or on another day (in the case of daily programs such as local news). Excessive preemptions (more than 10–15 percent of the schedule) are not wise, since they comprise a major interruption in the general flow of the plan.

WHO OWNS THE TIME? THE ADVERTISER

Usually, the parent company owns the time, not the individual brand. Therefore, if Procter and Gamble makes a purchase in prime-time television, they can schedule any number of their products in the time slot.

The networks require ample notification (usually two weeks) in advance of the commercial date as to what product or service will be using the time. The advance notification is necessary to ensure that the proper commercials are inserted into the program, as well as to safeguard for adequate product protection within each commercial pod.

How Agency Buying Power Is Used

While the better buying services and agencies do not buy blocks of time and then allocate them to their advertiser clients, they will use the combined total dollars from all the individual client packages as leverage to negotiate with the networks. Because agencies and buying services use this buying clout as part of their media buying expertise, advertisers often think agencies can reassign time purchased for one advertiser to another. This is not the case. If one of an agency's clients wants to eliminate some of their firm television inventory and another wants to purchase television time, the agency can not simply reassign the time from one client to another. The "sale" must be taken to the networks. The networks will probably make every attempt to accommodate the agency and their mutual advertiser clients.

Requesting a "Sell-off"

Occasionally, an advertiser may have circumstances that would necessitate getting rid of network inventory that is firmly committed. This is called a "sell-off" or request for relief. This is done when the funds needed are greater than what would be eliminated by exercising option dates. This course of action should be used only when necessary.

Regardless of the marketplace, a sell-off is not guaranteed. In the case of a strong or seller's market, a sell-off request is no more ensured than when things are softer or a buyer's economy exists.

In both cases, a buyer is needed to make the sale. In the case of a strong seller's or sold-out marketplace, buyers may have already found other places to put their advertising dollars. In the case of a softer market, buyers may be scarce.

PURCHASING PRINT MEDIA

The laws of supply and demand change when buying print (newspapers and magazines) media.

Supply and Demand More Constant

The supply (rating points and circulation) is relatively constant. Nearly 80 percent of newspaper and magazine circulation is controlled by subscription. Consequently, there is not the fluctuation in circulation similar to the ups and downs in TV viewing. Yes, there are some exceptions, particularly with those magazines that have significant newsstand circulations, such as *Family Circle, Woman's Day* (over 95 percent newsstand circulation), and *People.*

In print, the amount of advertising space is adjustable. Generally, publishers like to maintain an advertising to editorial mix of anywhere from 40 to 60 percent editorial. Therefore, if a particular issue seems to be in high demand, the publisher can add advertising and editorial pages. Conversely, if the advertising demand is down, they can reduce the number of advertising and editorial pages and print a slightly smaller publication.

Opportunistic markets exist in print media through the sale of remnant space. Remnant space is any space that is unsold just prior to publication. For the most part, remnant space exists when an advertiser purchases less than the full run circulation of a magazine or newspaper (regional or zone editions). To balance the publication, the publisher needs to fill the space with advertising in all the regions. For example, if an advertiser purchased regional space in the southeast and northeast editions of a publication, the publisher would have to sell the remaining space or circulation to another advertiser. If the space cannot be paired up, it is often sold at a significant savings as remnant space.

Print Is Negotiable

In the past few years, print media, especially magazines, have become increasingly negotiable. Therefore, print can be more cumbersome and time-consuming to buy than television, as each title is negotiated. Print negotiations center on the following criteria:

* Total pages
* What issue dates
* Desired positioning and competitive separation
* Cancellation options
* Degree of merchandising and added value (less prevalent with newspaper buys).

Pages equate to dollars, which equate to leverage. Generally the more pages an advertiser (parent company) can purchase, the better the price. However, some product categories may have such large dollar amounts (automobiles, distilled spirits and cigarettes) that their dollar leverage potential is maximized, and additional discounts are difficult to achieve.

Issue dates can affect pricing. Demand for print mirrors television demand. The possible exception is the fourth quarter, which is in greater demand than second quarter because of the high volume of retail advertising in local newspapers in the fourth quarter. Negotiated prices are going to be higher in the second and fourth quarters. If an advertiser can adjust its schedule to use more first and third quarter issues, the pricing will be more attractive.

Where Ad Is Placed Is Important in Print

A large part of the negotiation in magazines revolves around the positioning (where it is placed in the publication, and what kind of editorial surrounds it), and competitive separation of the ad. Rigid positioning requirements (especially in the more competitive categories, such as distilled spirits or cosmetics) will yield higher prices. More flexible positioning needs will produce more attractive pricing. The relative importance of the position of the ad is a unique decision that needs to be made on a brand-by-brand and magazine-by-magazine basis. For some brands, positioning is paramount and felt to be worth any additional price; for others, positioning is less important than price.

Competitive separation is also an issue with many advertisers. It is common to request six, eight, or ten pages of separation from other competitors. As with the positioning requests, competitive separation requirements will affect price.

Print Has Unique Dollar Flexibility

Unlike most electronic media, national and local print purchases can be canceled. Both newspapers and magazines are cancelable up to the closing date. Closing dates are ordinarily four to six weeks prior to the on-sale date for magazines. Certain magazine categories, such as fashion, beauty, and home service, have slightly longer lead times. Daily newspapers have closing dates of one to two days. This cancelability is often a key advantage to newspapers and magazines.

However, an advertiser could negotiate for a portion of their schedule to be firm and noncancelable in print. This is similar to a long-term television buy. For example, if an advertiser planned to place 18 pages for a variety of brands in a single title, he or she might consider making nine of the pages firm and noncancelable and the other nine pages flexible or cancelable. This approach should yield better pricing from the publications.

Merchandising/Added Value

Finally, merchandising or added-value packages are commonplace in magazine negotiations today and in some newspaper negotiations as well. These added-value packages can be almost anything from a publisher's letter to key customers to tie-in exposure on related world wide web sites and shopping-mall promotions. This, too, affects price. Again, the value of the merchandising packages is unique to each advertiser. In some cases, the merchandising can act as a distinctive way to target hard-to-reach customers and extend a sales force; for other advertisers, it is cumbersome to properly administer and monitor.

Local daily newspapers are less negotiable than magazines. National advertising is still a small portion of a local newspaper's revenue at about 10 percent. In spite of this, your media department should attempt to negotiate newspaper pricing, particularly for schedules beyond a single insertion.

In fact, the industry is making an attempt to attract more national advertisers by offering a national CPM that consists of packaging local newspapers together to make a national buy. This product is called the Newspaper National Network (NNN) and is based on a price generated through a negotiated national CPM. It is a one-order, one-bill package so that the agency or advertiser does not have to individually contact the 1500+ newspapers that cooperate in the program.

FOUR BASIC WAYS TO MANAGE MEDIA FUNCTIONS

Media planning and buying require considerable skill and resources. How you manage the function depends largely upon:
- Your organizational structure
- Who and how advertising (media) decisions are made
- Your philosophy and your approach to the advertising process.

There are four basic ways to set up your media planning and buying functions:
1. Traditional full-service agency
2. Agency of record (AOR)
3. Buying service
4. In-house operation

The following discusses each of the four approaches.

1. Traditional Full-Service Agency

Traditional agencies provide a wide range of services, yet there are advantages and drawbacks to consider (Table 3.24).

2. Agency of Record (AOR)

Advertisers have an AOR to:
1. Combine individual brand budgets, creating larger corporate budgets and increasing negotiating leverage.
2. Increase corporate clout with the agency felt to have the best buying skills due to additional buying leverage with other clients.
3. Equalize pricing and market conditions across all brands.

Advertisers choose not to have an AOR when:

TABLE 3.24 ADVANTAGES AND DRAWBACKS FOR USE
OF A FULL-SERVICE AGENCY

ADVANTAGES	DRAWBACKS
• Synergy of advertising efforts from all areas: creative, research, media, etc.	• Agencies are still department-oriented. • Traditional agencies are slow to integrate other communications disciplines such as direct, event, and sales promotion.
• Very focused on individual brands. • Even though multiple brands are assigned to one agency, organization is often on per brand basis.	• Corporate efficiencies might be sacrificed. • Brand organization may not be conducive to "creative" thinking in media.
• Ease of communication — One call covers creative, media, and production.	• May require calls to several agencies to cover all brands.
• Greater accountability, since everything is in the agency's hands, no outsiders to blame for problems and/or errors.	• Focus of accountability is generally on creative function, not media efficiencies. • Media accountability is dependent upon quantifiable and measurable media objectives.

1. There are not enough brands in the corporation with synergy. AORs are most successful if brands with similar targets and media requirements can be combined to increase leverage.
2. Decisions cannot be centralized. Crossing company divisions or product groups to combine plans for a variety of brands is nearly impossible without a central decision maker.

AORs are generally assigned on a day-part or media basis. Larger advertisers often spread assignments across agencies. Decisions are based on where brands are assigned, dollar levels, and agency expertise. Hypothetical examples are shown in Tables 3.25 and 3.26.

The advantages and drawbacks to an AOR arrangement are shown in Table 3.27.

3. Media Buying Service

An independent media buying service is another way to manage the media function. By definition, a media buying service is a way of unbundling your advertising needs, instead of using a single source for everything. Years ago these services were controversial and some lacked industry-accepted business standards. However, for the most

TABLE 3.25 HYPOTHETICAL EXAMPLE OF LARGE MULTI-AGENCY ADVERTISER

Network Prime	Leo Burnett
Network Day	Grey
Network Sports	Saatchi
Cable & Syndication	DMBB

TABLE 3.26 SECOND HYPOTHETICAL EXAMPLE OF LARGE MULTI-AGENCY ADVERTISER

Network Television & Radio	Lintas
Spot TV and Radio	Grey
Magazines/ Newspapers	Saatchi

TABLE 3.27 ADVANTAGES AND DRAWBACKS
TO AN AGENCY OF RECORD (AOR)

ADVANTAGES	DRAWBACKS
• Better prices, possibly better positioning, program mix, etc.	• Smaller budget brands, especially in less competitive product categories, may not always achieve better prices through an AOR (See Exhibit 3.4.). • Price often more important than media/vehicle selection and targetability.
• Brands have greater flexibility to change plans throughout the year. • One brand can cut and another can increase without affecting pricing or availability.	• Not all brands share same target. • Not all brands share same seasonality.
• Centralized media communications for all brands.	• Burden on advertiser/brand groups to coordinate communications between creative, media planning and buying agency.
• Tighter controls and media accountability.	• Accountability often subject to competitive criticism between agency parties.

EXHIBIT 3.4 LEVERAGING A MEDIA INVESTMENT

	Budget	Discount	Category
Client A	$100,000	50%	Less competitive
Client B	$10,000,000	12%	More competitive

part this is now past, and there are a large number of reputable companies that provide excellent media buying services as well as media planning capabilities. In fact, the acceptability of media buying services is growing so much that many traditional advertising agencies are now offering their media expertise on an a la carte basis to advertisers.

4. In-House Operation

An in-house operation may be built when an advertiser handles negotiations directly, either as a purchaser or by creating its own in-house agency organization. The pros and cons of this type of arrangement are shown in Table 3.28.

TABLE 3.28 ADVANTAGES AND DRAWBACKS TO IN-HOUSE OPERATIONS

ADVANTAGES	DRAWBACKS
• Media buying and negotiating expertise, especially in spot electronic media	• Media buys may lack cohesiveness with other marketing forces, especially creative.
	• Difficult to coordinate efforts of a variety of vendors.
• Better prices, lower commissions	• Better pricing can be the result of lower quality or less targeted media purchase.
	• Better price may not hold true in post-buy analysis.
	• Need thorough understanding of post-buy reports, including full disclosure of all invoice information.

Which Method Is Best?

This is an individual decision. What works for one advertiser may be counterproductive for another. The advantages and drawbacks have different ramifications and importance for each corporation. Here are some things to think about as you assess the alternatives:

1. What is your budget size, and do your brands have synergy?
   - Multiple-brand organizations with sizable total budgets, similar media targets, and needs can often achieve excellent results with AORs.
   - Smaller-budget brands may benefit from combining them into an AOR or placing these brands strategically in agencies or services where your brand can benefit from agency clout.

2. Do you have brands, targets, and media needs that inhibit the advantages of AORs?
   - The increased cost-effectiveness associated with an in-house structure starts with the ability of the combined-brand budgets to create combined-dollar leverage.
   - If there is no central decision maker, decisions regarding the AOR or in-house operations will be severely hindered, making the arrangement unproductive. Someone needs to be empowered to make the decisions for all the brands.
   - To maximize cost-effectiveness, often a purchase decision is made that benefits a large number of the brands. However, the decision may not be "ideal" for all brands that will necessarily take part in the purchase.
   - Smaller budget brands may be usurped or forgotten due to the work load and budget dominance of one or two larger brands.
   - AOR structures require expertise at the advertiser level to evaluate the work and recommendations of AOR for all brands.
   - In-house organizational structures naturally require the greatest amount of in-house staffing and resources (Table 3.29).

TABLE 3.29 CONSIDERATIONS FOR BRINGING OPERATIONS IN-HOUSE

ADVANTAGES	DRAWBACKS
• Media may want to give better pricing to a single advertiser rather than large agency with multiple clients.	• In-house organization does not benefit from clout of total agency or AOR buying arrangement. Must create own clout. • Need staffing, resources, and expertise to justify and prove savings.
• Agency not providing media service, hence lower fee structure. • Advertiser saves on commissions.	• Do not benefit from experience of, or ideas used with, other clients within the agency. • Must develop own experience and clout with all media outlets, regardless of budget size.
• Increased confidentiality—an important consideration with highly competitive categories and increased use of AORs.	• Difficult to assess success of in-house operation based on cost, as there are no data available from other client experience. • Justification for savings can be self-fulfilling (job preservation).
• Greater brand flexibility as in-house organization can maximize ability to interchange media purchases.	• Corporate mandates take precedent over individual brand needs.

Media Buying Guidelines and Post-Buys

After the plan is done and before the buys are made, you need to articulate the parameters for making the buy or media buying guidelines. Buying guidelines describe the execution of the media strategy. Guidelines are often part of the media plan itself, but can be a separate discussion, especially prior to major media buys.

The purpose of buying guidelines is to:
1. Clarify expectations for all parties making the buy.
2. Establish parameters for negotiating the buy and using alternate strategies and executions when market conditions change.
3. Identify mechanisms for administering, monitoring, and reporting media purchases.

When using an AOR and/or media buying service, the media buying guidelines have an additional role. They foster consistency when many people are involved in the process and minimize misunderstandings of company or brand policies.

National and Local Electronic Media Guidelines

When considering national or spot television, cable or radio purchases, the areas shown in Exhibit 3.5 need to be covered in a buying guidelines document.

EXHIBIT 3.5 CONSIDERATIONS WHEN PURCHASING NATIONAL AND LOCAL ELECTRONIC MEDIA

GUIDELINE	NATIONAL TELEVISION/CABLE/RADIO CONSIDERATIONS	SPOT (LOCAL) TELEVISION/CABLE/RADIO CONSIDERATIONS
Post-buy schedule	Set post-buy due dates and information needs when approval is given to make purchases. (See separate discussion of recommended timing on post-buys.)	Same as for national.

Print Guidelines

Print guidelines should include parameters for:

- Acceptable and unacceptable positions;
- Suitable and unsuitable editorial;
- Pages of competitive separation;
- Whether the insertion date can be changed if a better position becomes available on a different day (newspaper) or in another issue (magazines);
- The circulation base and how will it be guaranteed;
- Type of merchandising or added-value sought and how performance or delivery is to be monitored.

Post-Buy Reports

A post-buy report is merely a report on how the various media buys (purchases) performed. Did they achieve the planned rating point and CPM goals? Did they achieve the desired circulation and positioning? From the perspective of the agency or media buying service, post-buys serve to monitor valuable information on actual costs and media usage (viewing/reading/listening) trends. This information can then be used for future negotiations and/or to improve and augment existing schedules.

Post-buys are also used as media management tools for assessing the abilities of individual buyers.

From the client perspective, post-buys provide a measurement of the agency's ability to assess and react to various media market conditions. They also provide an accountability measurement for media investments.

In media, and particularly in electronic media, there are three types of numeric data that are typically used in media plans, buys, and reports.
1. Goal or planned
2. Purchased (projections or estimates)
3. Achieved (post or stewardship or actual).

The goal data is the information the agency details in the media plan, flow charts, and/or buying guidelines. Purchased data is what is provided when the actual buys themselves are reported to the advertiser. This is often the report of the schedules bought by the agency. Finally, documentation of achieved audience delivery after the schedule has run is considered a post-buy report.

What to Look for in Electronic Post-Buy Reports

When the agency provides an electronic post-buy report, it should contain comparisons to goal, purchased and achieved data. Each comparison has a purpose, as shown in Exhibit 3.6.

In the post-buy report, the reasons for +/- delivery of audiences should be included. If goals are not met, details on how TRPs will be met (for example, scheduling of audience deficiency units or bonus weight) should be included. There is an industry guideline of +/- 10 percent for unguaranteed television purchases. Networks and local stations will usually work with the buyers to make good any buys that underperform the buy by more than 10 percent. Remember that both under- and overdelivery can indicate inaccurate market projections. Underdelivery means that marketing objectives tied to media delivery may not be met. Consistent overdelivery means dollars could have been shifted to other areas or saved. An explanation as to what precipitated the over- or underdelivery is important to future media evaluations, especially when projecting pricing.

EXHIBIT 3.6 POINTS TO CONSIDER IN A POST-BUY REPORT

COMPARISON	PURPOSE
Goal compared to purchased	Illustrates agency's skill at predicting the media marketplace and executing the buy based on those predictions
Purchased compared to achieved	Demonstrates the accuracy of agency projections and adequacy of agency's monitoring and maintenance mechanisms.
Goal compared to achieved	Indicates degree to which final plan met original goals and is ultimate test of agency's skill in predicting market conditions and executing media purchases

Some Common Errors Associated with Electronic Post-Buy Analyses

There are five major errors associated with electronic post-buy analyses:

1. Failure to compare to all three elements: goal, purchased, and achieved;
2. Not issued on a timely basis;
3. Exclude comparisons to costs;
4. Audience deficiency units not properly tracked;
5. Lacks discussion of corrective next steps.

1. Failure to compare to all three elements: goal, purchased, and achieved.

Many post-buy reports do not include comparisons of all three elements: goals, purchased, and achieved. Most post-buys include comparisons of purchased to achieved but not goal to purchased and goal to achieved. For thoroughness and total disclosure of information, comparisons need to be made to all three levels.

2. Not issued on a timely basis.

Post-buys are not always issued on a timely basis. Ongoing and timely monitoring is essential to enable prompt reactions to marketplace fluctuations as well as to apply post-buy learning to future media planning.

3. Exclude comparisons to costs.

Post-buys need to include comparisons on a TRP basis as well as relationship to cost either via budget or CPM. The inclusion of cost data is necessary because prices may have gone up or down during the course of the buy.

4. Audience deficiency units not properly tracked.

Audience deficiency units (a.d.s or makegoods) are often not properly tracked.

For example, deficiency units for second quarter schedules that were scheduled in the third quarter would inflate third quarter results if included in the third quarter post-buy reports. Instead, the second quarter report should be reissued with the audience deficiency units scheduled in the third quarter included in the revised report. Conversely, the third quarter report should be done with the second quarter audience deficiency units excluded for a more accurate look at the actual performance of the third quarter schedule.

At times, a unit may be given as a makegood for one day-part in a different day-part, especially in network TV. For example, a unit in prime time might be given as audience deficiency weight for sports programming. Therefore, when producing the post-buy for sports, it should include the a.d. unit that was scheduled in prime time for a complete look at the total package including a.d. weight.

5. Lacks discussion of corrective next steps.
Finally, a post-buy should include a discussion of corrective next steps. Any over- or underdelivery of the schedules needs an action plan for their impact on current schedules and future plans.

Print Post-Analysis
Post-analysis can also be done in print (magazines and newspapers), typically in two separate reports.
1. Positioning, competitive separation, and merchandising report
2. Circulation rate base report based on A.B.C. or B.P.A. audit
A.B.C. (Audit Bureau of Circulation) is an organization supported jointly by publishers, ad agencies and advertisers whose purpose is to verify the circulation statements of member magazine and newspaper publishers. Similar verification statements are provided by B.P.A. (Business Publication Audit) for business publications, trade journals and other nonpaid circulation periodicals.

In the first report, three basic areas are examined:
• Were position requests met?
• Was separation from competitors maintained?
• Was merchandising/promotion delivered?
The second report deals with whether or not the publications delivered the guaranteed circulation rate base. Examples of both report styles are detailed later in this chapter.

Recommended Post-Buy Due Dates
Exhibit 3.7 describes suggested timing of post-buy reports. When the media is approved for purchase, you should also set a date for issuing the post-buy report.

EXHIBIT 3.7 SAMPLE SCHEDULES FOR POST-BUY ANALYSES

MEDIUM	RECOMMENDED POST-BUY DUE DATE
Television, national, and local, including cable and syndication	Within two months after ratings information has been published. Network TV data are issued most frequently, and weekly or monthly reports could be issued if necessary.
Radio, national, or local	Within two months after ratings information has been published.
Print (magazines and newspapers)	CIRCULATION GUARANTEE — within two months of A.B.C. or B.P.A. report being issued. Note that the information necessary to issue these reports has significant lag times (6 to 12 months after publication).

Network TV Post-Buy Example

Network TV post-buys are generally issued on a quarterly basis. Long-term reports are issued separately from short-term. Also reports are issued by network and by day-part. However, the networks, day-parts, and long- and short-term buys can be combined for a complete picture of the actual performance of the media plan. Table 3.30 shows a post-buy with the networks and day-parts combined. On the whole, it appears as if all networks and day-parts performed well.

However, when examining the data more closely for prime time, we find that CBS did not perform up to the purchased estimates and actually some audience deficiency units are in order. The data in the previous chart includes the three levels of comparisons: goals, purchased, and achieved. However, in Table 3.31, only purchased and achieved are noted. Goals would have been made by day-part, not for each individual network.

Note: The guarantee was met on ABC and NBC. The written report accompanying these tables should detail specifics on how the CBS guarantee is going to be met.

Spot TV Post-Buy Example—Individual Market Summary

Table 3.32 details a hypothetical post-buy format for spot television; spot radio would have a similar format. However, the day-part divisions would be different.

This spot TV post-buy report is for an individual market and includes all the relevant information needed for a complete post-buy report. It has three areas of information: goal (what was planned according to the flow chart), purchased (what the buyers estimated the performance of the schedule to be when they placed the buy) and invoiced achievement (how the buy actually performed) according to rating service (Nielsen).

For managers, the most important item is the last line of the report. When comparing the results on the basis of TRPs, you want to see that the indices are all within 90 to 110. That is, the rating points delivered were within +/- 10 percent of the goal. When comparing the cost information, you want to see indices within 10 percent of the goal. Remember that a number below 100 is a positive indication. In the example in Table 3.32, the goal was for an expenditure of $5,040. The buy had an invoice achievement of $18.43 CPP or a 7-percent reduction in cost for a 93 index.

Table 3.32 is a summary sheet for one market similar to a report issued from any agency or buying service using the Donovan or a similar media system. There is a variety of media computer systems for tracking, monitoring, reporting, billing and paying media purchases. Donovan is probably the most popular of these. Additional detail is

TABLE 3.30 POST-BUY WITH NETWORKS AND DAY-PARTS COMBINED

		WOMEN 25-54		
	$(000)	CPM	(000)	TRPS
PRIME				
Goal	1420.0	19.75	71,900	135.0
Purchased	1418.6	19.51	72,702	137.5
Achieved	1418.6	17.29	82,052	155.3
Index				
vs. Goal	99	87	114	115
vs. Purchased	100	89	112	113
DAY				
Goal	170.0	6.54	26,000	50.0
Purchased	166.8	6.20	26,881	50.9
Achieved	166.8	5.85	28,465	53.9
Index				
vs. Goal	98	89	109	108
vs. Purchased	100	95	106	106
TOTAL				
Goal	1595.0	16.29	97,900	185.0
Purchased	1585.4	15.92	99,583	188.4
Achieved	1585.4	14.35	110,517	209.2
Index				
vs. Goal	99	88	113	113
vs. Purchased	100	90	111	111

TABLE 3.31 SAMPLE REPORT SHOWING INDIVIDUAL NETWORK DETAIL
FOR PRIME TIME PURCHASES DEPICTED IN TABLE 3.30

		WOMEN 25-54		
	$(000)	CPM	(000)	TRPS
ABC				
Purchased	386.7	19.24	20,099	38.0
Achieved	386.7	14.11	27,398	51.9
Index	100	73	136	137
CBS				
Purchased	502.3	18.07	27,751	52.5
Achieved	502.3	21.46	23,431	44.3
Index	100	118	84	84
NBC				
Purchased	529.6	21.27	24,852	47.0
Achieved	529.6	16.97	31,223	59.1
Index	100	79	126	126
TOTAL				
Goal	1420.0	19.75	71,900	135.0
Purchased	1418.6	19.51	72,702	137.5
Achieved	1418.6	17.29	82,052	155.3
Index				
vs. Goal	99	87	114	115
vs. Purchased	100	89	112	113

TABLE 3.32 SUMMARY SHEET ISSUED BY AN AGENCY OR BUYING SERVICE

DAY-PART	GOAL			PURCHASED					INVOICED ACHIEVEMENT						
	TRPs	$	CPP	TRPs	GOAL INDEX	$	INDEX	CPP	TRPs	INDEX	PURCH INDEX	$	GOAL INDEX	PURCH INDEX	CPP
DAY-30	100	2,000		96		1,800		18.75	89		93	1,700		94	19.10
ELY-30	100	2,000		102		1,950		19.12	122		120	1,950		100	15.98
ACC-30	0	0		40		900		22.50	36		90	900		100	25.00
WKD-30	40	1,040		7		150		21.43	8		114	150		100	18.75
BUD-30	240	5,040	21.00												
TOTAL-30	240	5,040	21.00	245	102	4,800	95	19.59	255	106	104	4,700	93	98	18.43

TABLE 3.33 BRAND MANAGER'S SPOT TV POST BUY SUMMARY SHEET

MARKET	GOAL TRPs	PURCHASED TRPs	ACTUAL TRPs	INDEX TO GOAL	INDEX TO PURCHASED	CPP GOAL	CPP PURCHASED	CPP ACHIEVED
Albany	675	690	735	109	107	76	74.35	69.80
Champaign	675	682	682	101	100	42	41.57	41.57
Columbus	675	680	674	99	99	137	135.99	137.20
Detroit	675	677	687	102	102	292	291.14	286.90
Flint	675	682	687	102	101	53	52.46	50.46
Grand Rapids	675	690	709	105	103	88	86.09	91.38
Harrisburg	675	675	650	96	96	103	103.00	96.56
Indianapolis	675	700	720	107	103	158	152.36	153.45
Kansas City	675	683	695	103	102	131	129.47	129.09
Pittsburgh	675	678	685	101	101	185	184.18	178.39
Rochester	675	692	700	104	101	73	71.21	72.78
St. Louis	675	680	677	100	100	144	142.94	147.27
Washington, D. C.	675	690	660	98	96	384	375.65	376.20
Total	675	685	689	102	101	1866	1838.76	1828.08

available by day-part, program, and station for each market. This greater level of detail is usually not necessary for most advertising managers.

Spot TV Post-Buy Example — All-Market Summary

A manager might not need all of the detail in Table 3.32 for each market. However, a summary report, such as Table 3.33, would be valuable. What is important is that the key data, TRPs and CPM or budget, are compared on a three-level basis; goal, purchased, and actual (achieved) for all markets, not just a bottom-line summary for all markets combined. Again, when reviewing spot TV post-buys such as those summarized in Table 3.32 you should look for purchases to perform within +/- 10 percent of the goals and purchases.

Print Circulation Post-Buy Example

Table 3.34 is the format for a circulation rate base post-buy in print. Typically, deficiency in circulation would be discussed in a cover letter. Usually deficiencies are made good in print through a prorated reduction in price on the next scheduled insertion. However, if no insertions are scheduled, a check for the appropriate sum could be issued.

In Table 3.34 note that the guarantee type is noted by publication. Each publication has a different policy for meeting circulation guarantees. An issue-specific guarantee means that the publisher will guarantee the circulation for each specific issue. A six- or twelve-month guarantee means that the publisher will guarantee the average monthly circulation based on a six- or twelve-month average. In addition to seeing if the circulation guarantees are met, you should make note of the circulation trends of each magazine. Significant upward trends are signals of a publication's vitality, but are also indications of possible future rate increases. Conversely, downward trends indicate that the publication may have lost popularity with its reader base and should be examined carefully when considering future insertions.

Print Positioning Post-Buy Example

The first report that can be issued for print purchases is a positioning report (Table 3.35) that details how the ads were positioned in the publication compared to position requests or guarantees and how the separation from competitors was maintained. When examining competitive separations, note the nearest competitor in front as well as behind your ad. As with other post-buy reports, indicated action is an important element in the report or the corresponding cover letter.

MEDIA PLANNING — SOME FINAL THOUGHTS

As noted earlier, media planning is an art, not a science. Yes, there are lots of numbers to analyze. However, it is not the numbers or the computers that develop the plans. People do. The best plans come from people who are well-versed and involved in your business. Invite the creative people to the media meetings and vice versa. You will be surprised at the good ideas that can come from their involvement.

Give your media plan the same attention — and respect — that you do to other advertising elements, such as promotion and creative. Develop some good planning disciplines. Hold yourself and the people doing the plans accountable for results, results based on quantifiable objectives and strategies that evolve from examining a myriad of alternatives. Don't merely judge the merits of your media plan on the basis of CPM and TRPs but rather on the amount of reach and/or frequency necessary to achieve the TRP levels.

Finally, do your best to understand how media are purchased. Meet with a media salesperson. Magazine salespeople call on advertisers all the time. Meet with them and learn about their business the way they are trying to learn about yours. Ask a television, radio, or cable salesperson to call on you. Share an idea with them. Ask them questions. You will probably learn something and be able to apply it to your brand.

TABLE 3.34 GUARANTEE BY PUBLICATION

Publication	Guar. Type*	Brand	Issue Date	Guar. Rate Base	Actual Delivery	+/- (000)	%
Better Homes & Gardens	12-MO	Cookie	10/90	8,000	8,174	174	2.2
		Snack	11/90	8,000	8,058	58	0.7
Family Circle	IS	Snack	8/90	5,250	5,322	72	1.4
		Cookie	10/16	5,250	5,375	125	2.4
		Cake	11/27	5,250	6,354	104	2.0
Good Housekeeping	IS	Cookie	9/90	5,000	5,049	49	1.0
		Snack	10/90	5,000	5,036	36	0.7
		Cake	11/90	5,000	5,100	110	2.2
		Snack	9/90	5,000	5,049	49	1.0
Ladies Home Journal	IS	Cookie	8/90	5,000	4,945	-55	-1.1
		Snack	9/90	5,000	5,039	39	0.8
		Cake	10/90	5,000	4,944	-56	-1.1
McCall's	IS	Cake	12/90	5,000	5,008	8	0.2
Redbook	IS	Cake	12/90	3,800	3,853	53	1.4
		Muffin	12/90	3,800	3,853	53	1.4
Woman's Day	6-MO	Cookie	7/90	4,600	4,059	-541	-11.8

*IS = Issue-specific, 6-MO = 6-month average, 12-MO = 12-month average.

Note: Data based on July-December 1990, ABC White Statements

TABLE 3.35 POST-BUY REPORT ON PRINT PURCHASES

Publication/ Brand/ Issue	Request	Actual	Nearest Competitor Forward	Nearest Competitor Backward	Indicated Action
Better Homes & Gardens COOKIE 10/90	Opp. low-fat edit.	Right pg. opp. full pg. of food edit.	Brand X 6 pgs. forward opp. 1/2-page ad and nonfood edit.	Brand W 12 pgs. back on left opp. decorating edit.	None; no low-fat edit. in this issue.
Family Circle COOKIE 10/16	Opp. fitness edit. or low-fat edit.	Left pg. opp. diet edit. and 1/3-col. ad for seasonings	Brand Y 10 pgs. forward opp. full pg. of food edit.	Brand Z 20 pgs. back on rt. pg. opp. full pg. of low-fat edit.	Stress need for opposite full pg. of edit. as priority, followed by type of edit. desired.
Good Housekeeping SNACK 10/90	Opp. fitness or low-fat edit.	Right pg. opp. full pg. of gourmet cooking edit, not low-fat.	Brand Y 4 pgs. forward on right pg. opp. full pg. of low-fat edit.	Brand Z 6 pgs. back on left pg. opp. full pg. of low-fat edit.	Seeking compensation for lack of competitive separation of 6–10 pages. Want better editorial compatibility; will take left pg.
Ladies Home Journal CAKE 10/90	Opp. table of contents or low-fat edit., must be opp. full pg. of edit.	Opp. TOC and 1/3-col. ad for cosmetic.	NA	Brand Z 10 pgs. forward opp. 1/2-pg. ad and nondiet edit.	None; were advised of 1/3-col. ad next to TOC and approved position.

This chapter is taken from material in the Sales Promotion Handbook *published by Dartnell.*

CHAPTER 4

SALES PROMOTION TECHNIQUES

PROMOTION COMES OF AGE

Strictly speaking, a promotion is the use of a price-off or value-added offer or incentive for the purpose of influencing purchasing behavior. Promotion marketing is the systematic use of such incentives to achieve specific sales and marketing objectives. Promotion works best in concert with, but differs from, conventional advertising in the sense that its goal is not to create a perception or polish an image, but to get the consumer to do what the marketer wants.

Promotional devices range from money-saving coupons and rebates in price-off programs to premiums, prizes, and product samples in value-added campaigns. A promotional offer can be communicated through advertisement in conventional media, such as magazines, newspapers, radio, and TV, but it is more commonly delivered through alternative media, such as newspaper inserts, co-op and solo direct mail, point-of-purchase displays, or on the outside or inside of the package itself. Promotion differs from advertising, too, in that the promotional device — for example, a coupon or rebate — can serve as its own response mechanism and can be traced back or used to "track" actual sales.

THE ORIGINS OF PROMOTION

As a marketing technique, promotion has been around as long as advertising. The prize at the bottom of the Cracker Jack box, for example, has sold tons of caramelized popcorn for that company's owners for more than 75 years. Donnelley Marketing was distributing Ivory Soap door-to-door for Procter & Gamble in the 1920s. Bubble gum makers have been packing trading cards with their product at the very least since World War II. And children were saving their Wheaties box tops to send in for Captain Midnight decoder rings more than half a century ago.

The difference between then and now is that we call such premium offers, trial generators, pantry loaders, and continuity programs "promotional techniques" and apply them to a vast array of products.

Until the 1970s, promotion practitioners regarded their work more as a sideline to advertising than as an industry unto itself. That was when service and supplier companies began to grow, and opportunities opened up for people who could combine consumer marketing expertise with a working knowledge of such things as product sampling, retail merchandising, point-of-purchase advertising, premium sourcing and fulfillment, direct marketing, audiovisual production, and specialty printing.

Seeing this, a number of brand, product, and promotion managers left corporate life to start their own promotion marketing agencies. Among the pioneers were Ralph A. Glendinning, founder in 1959 of Glendinning Associates, based in Westport, Connecticut. A few years later came the so-called "Chicago School" of promotion, with namesake agencies founded by Bud Frankel (Frankel & Company, 1962), William A. Robinson (now Robinson & Maites, founded in 1991), and Lee Flaherty (Flair Communications, founded in 1964).

In the 1970s, a number of service companies, including Comart Aniforms (now Comart/KLP) in New York, Einson Freeman in New Jersey, and Connecticut Consulting Group/Ted Colangelo Associates (now Clarion Communications, a unit of D'Arcy, Masius, Benton & Bowles) set a trend by offering client companies strategic consultation as well as program execution.

Suddenly these and other companies that had been slide houses, display makers, direct marketers, and field service contractors found themselves acting as full-service promotion agencies. Without calling it that, of course, they were offering corporate marketers their considerable expertise in the business of behavior modification.

WHAT PROMOTION ISN'T

Despite its emergence as a marketing discipline, many different notions persist as to what promotion really is. In Hollywood, for example, the term refers to movie publicity; in broadcasting, it means on-air plugs for TV and radio programs; in the auto industry, promotion is still what they call sales literature and dealership display materials. Ad agencies continue to confuse it with the procurement of "trinkets and trash," or premiums and ad specialties. Worst of all is the Wall Street label of "promoter" as someone who profits by buying, driving up the price, and then bailing out of cheap or worthless stock before others can do the same.

WHAT PROMOTION IS

Practitioners view promotion marketing as a discipline because the offer-response-reward sequence can take place over time, and it comprises a wide variety of techniques. The essential characteristics of a promotion are (1) the creative concept or offer, (2) the vehicle or system for delivering it, and (3) the fulfillment of the reward promised in the concept or offer.

Contrasted with advertising, where the "creative" concept is the communication of an idea or image, the creative concept in promotion is the idea or proposition that gets the consumer to act. The concept of promotion as a behavioral rather than a communications medium was stated succinctly in an ad for Donnelley Marketing's co-op coupon program that ran in *Advertising Age* several years ago. "Advertising May Change Her Mind," the ad declared, "But Carol Wright Will Change Her Behavior."

The "creative concept in a continuity program for a brand of barbecue charcoal, for example, could be the offer, over time and perhaps on a self-liquidating basis, of a cook's apron, a chef's hat, a mitt, and several outdoor cooking utensils in return for a specific number of purchases. While the theme and look of the campaign would carry through in ads, coupons, display materials, and merchandise, the "promotion creative" concept would be neither the message nor the image projected, but the proposition for participants to acquire the ensemble by behaving in a certain way, that is, buying and continuing to buy the charcoal.

A number of delivery systems—direct-mail co-op, newspaper insert, point-of-purchase display, in-store coupon, in-pack flyer—would be suitable for such a promotion. The choice would depend primarily on the availability of funds, of course, but also on the likelihood of a successful response based on what is known about the brand's usage profile, buyer demographics, market share, and the potential for meaningful trade support in the territory to be covered.

The truly effective promotion generally aims at one, sometimes two, clearly defined specific brand objectives. To name a few:

- the generation of new product trial and repurchase;
- the protection of market share in the face of a competitive threat;
- brand purchase continuity over a period of time;
- "pantry loading," or the temporary removal of users from the marketplace;
- a build-up of consumer traffic at retail;
- an increase in trade support at a critical time period or season.

This chapter covers a range of promotional techniques that may be very useful to "get the word out" about your products or services. It is not a detailed account of any single technique, but rather an introduction into the variety of promotion strategies.

If you're at a smaller company, you may find yourself handling promotion as part of the advertising mix. At larger companies, where promotion and advertising are handled in different groups, you as an advertising professional need to know about the strategies, because they impact your advertising efforts.

SAMPLING

Your people have invented the next best product. It's passed all the in-house and consumer tests. You've got a dynamite ad campaign, decent distribution, and excellent packaging. The new product goes on the shelves. And what happens now? What motivates customers to switch from their old brand or to try a whole new product that they didn't even know they needed?

New products require the consumer to "risk" the price of the product to try it out. Sampling is a very effective way to get customers to "test" a new product, without risking their own money. Consumers are notoriously slow to take that risk. Sampling gets new products into the hands of potential buyers.

"Use it..." "Taste it..." "Try it out..." These promises may be implied or explicitly stated, but the most important element is inherent in the sampling process: You the consumer have nothing to lose.

Marketers have fine-tuned the art of sampling. Here are some of the techniques that are used today.

Sampling at or near the Point of Purchase

Sampling can be carried out in, near, or away from, the actual point of purchase. This distinction may seem simple, yet it is important. Products that can be "experienced on the spot," at the point of purchase, can be immediately converted into a revenue sale. This allows the sampling effort to be executed as a total "event," fully involving the distribution channel in the process of quickly building up both trade and consumer franchises.

Sampling conducted away from the point of purchase is more akin to the "sale in the mind" effect attributed to advertising. The more time that elapses after sampling the product before the actual opportunity of buying the product in the store presents itself, the more likely the occurrence of "interference" — ranging from competitive efforts to simple forgetfulness — which will negatively impact the initial intent of buying the product sampled.

Further, when an account implements a sampling program in its stores, it is safe to assume that the product is in distribution (in at least the account's stores) facilitating the conversion of customers sampled to actual users/purchasers. This may not be the case when the product is sampled away from the point of purchase where gaps in distribution may have a further negative impact on the customer's intent to buy.

Often, manufacturers (primarily, their local sales organizations) will insist on fielding and managing the execution of in-store sampling programs in their sales areas through services that are available locally. Given the hodgepodge of services operating in each market, and the fact that different accounts or stores will allow access to different services, one can end up using 20 or more in-store sampling companies in one single market.

This makes for the rather formidable task of calling on each local sales office to recruit, train, assign, monitor, and process reports on the work done on each sampling program fielded. Further, one must order supplies and equipment; arrange for their timely delivery and transshipment, where needed; and determine whether the product used in sampling is to be warehoused and delivered to stores, according to schedule, or purchased in-store. The local sales offices also must store and distribute coupons, when they are used, to the individual demonstrators under secure conditions and, finally, provide a paymaster function, carefully evaluating all documentation submitted on both time and expenditures.

Since most in-store sampling programs are still executed locally under the conditions described above, one must query the logic of continuing these practices, given the costs involved. Many argue, with obvious justification, that, in today's competitive environment, salespeople have their hands full properly servicing their own accounts. Diverting their efforts and attention to the handling of sampling programs — a task which, if it is to be done well, is highly time-intensive — is neither desirable nor cost-efficient.

The alternative, assigning in-store sampling programs to national companies that provide top-to-bottom management and performance accountability across the board, is becoming increasingly prevalent.

Personal Sampling away from the Point of Purchase

Products in high-penetration categories in wide distribution benefit from intensive sampling, reaching large numbers of people as cost-efficiently as possible. Conversely, niche products directed to targeted consumer segments require tailored sampling approaches that are specifically relevant to both usage and purchase of these products.

High-traffic sampling that depends on reaching large numbers of potential consumers over short periods of time is indicated when the product sampled fits in broadly based usage categories, thus minimizing the potential waste inherent in handing out samples to people who are not likely to use them.

Sampling in high-cluster areas (such as shopping centers and commuter stations) and at special events (such as county and state fairs) enables companies to generate immediate, large-scale trial. In years past, cigarette companies used to sample heavily on street corners in downtown locations. Given their shrinking user base, this is less prevalent today. However, companies that manufacture food products (such as candy, beverages, and those that do not require special preparation or storing conditions) continue to include high-traffic sampling in their plans.

Up to this point, we have talked about in-hand, person-to-person sampling efforts. This form of sampling allows for several levels of selectivity:

- *Locational selectivity* — Sampling is executed selectively in areas that meet the specific potential user profiles, whether classified by area of the country, urban vs. suburban locations, ethnic clusters, and so forth.
- *Visual selectivity* — This allows samplers to visually identify

the people who are to be offered the specific samples. (Samplers can visually separate males from females; the young from the old; or bald people from people with hair.)

- *Verbal selectivity* — The ultimate selectivity level in which people can be queried about their likelihood of using the sampled product; that is, their having a dishwasher in their home or owning a dog or cat.

Sampling by Mail

A great deal of sampling is conducted today by mail. Its ease of execution, coupled with its potential reach of every single dwelling across the country, makes it attractive, although not necessarily economical, particularly in a marketing environment that mandates increasingly narrow targeting.

Much of the sampling by mail goes third class. This is primarily "occupant" mailing that delivers samples to current residents in dwellings in the geographical areas included in the distribution plan. There are no time imperatives to the delivery of samples sent by third-class mail. While first-class mail has overall priority, samples sent third class may linger for a long time in local post offices. When they add up to a lot of undelivered units, the local post office may decide to "lighten the mail" and donate them to a local county hospital, for example, for distribution to its needier patients. That, of course, may not have been the intent of the company whose samples they were.

First-class mailings are often used in preference to third-class mailings when specific recipients have been identified and addressed. By law, the post office must return to the sender mail that cannot be delivered, or forward it if the addressee has moved away and filed a forwarding address. While this is deemed positive, some companies continue to use third class, as they find that the additional benefits inherent in first class do not justify the additional costs involved. These include the incremental cost of buying and processing specific target mailing lists available from various compilers who specialize in this field.

In-Home Sampling

While mail samples are delivered by the U.S. Postal Service, in-home sampling (often referred to as "door-to-door" sampling) is carried out by special crews who work out of delivery vans.

At one time, door-to-door sampling was quite prevalent, particularly when heavier samples were distributed. In recent years, this form of sampling has declined significantly; only a few companies continue to use it to any substantial degree.

While it enables one to pinpoint distribution to specific clusters of homes, and does not impose the same size limitations that one must keep in mind when sampling by mail, door-to-door sampling raises questions of its own:

1. How is the sample delivered? The "ring-and-leave" approach in which the sample is left — usually in a polybag hung on the doorknob — after the deliverer rings the bell to alert those inside the dwelling, is the way most sampling takes place.
2. The safety concerns when samples are distributed by the "ring-and-leave" approach increase significantly, since samples left unattended can be pilfered, tampered with, and misused by minors.
3. The same questions regarding the inclusiveness of the sampling plan, when sampling by mail, apply here, as well.

COUPONING

The two main sources for coupons are manufacturers and retailers. Most manufacturers are generally happy with "direct to the consumer" couponing results but are exploring new avenues and added-value ideas. Retailers are still looking to see how they can make the most of coupons, and are increasing their own in-ad couponing as well.

As couponing matures, manufacturers and couponing service firms alike are viewing this as a time to make the tool more efficient and to generally improve the state of the couponing art.

Definition and Strategic Use

Coupons, simply stated, are certificates that offer the consumer a stated value, for instance, cents-off or free product, when presented to the appropriate vendor accompanying the appropriate purchase. It is easy to see why coupons, with their obvious immediate value and savings, are the one promotional technique that has dominated the last two decades.

Coupons have many advantages. First, couponing to consumers helps ensure that savings are passed directly to the consumers. Trade allowances paid to the retailer, often to encourage price discounting, may or may not ever filter down into savings to the user. Second, while the consumer receives the benefit of a cost savings, this is perceived as a temporary special offer rather than a price reduction, which would have greater ramifications if removed. Third, coupons can create traffic for retailers, especially when retailers capitalize on this promotional device by doubling or tripling the coupon redemption value at their own expense.

Couponing is not, of course, without problems. Foremost, couponing has become so popular and widespread that the enormous number of coupons in circulation create "coupon clutter," resulting in falling coupon redemption rates. Coupon clutter also increases the potential for misuse and abuse through coupon fraud and misredemption.

Furthermore, some allege that couponing is often used as a life support mechanism for weaker brands, while redemption for established brands occurs primarily from loyal users and thus rarely generates incremental business from new users, as it was intended.

Because coupons can be distributed via many different avenues, from mass distribution with free-standing inserts (FSIs) in newspapers or magazine advertising to more targeted delivery via the package itself or through direct mailings to the home, coupons offer flexibility in accomplishing a variety of common promotional goals. The most common objectives for using couponing follow.

Couponing for Trial and Awareness. Coupons are particularly efficient at generating trial of new products or line extensions of current brands.

Couponing for Repeat Purchase. While trial is often a first goal of couponing, converting trial users to regular users is also a key couponing task.

Couponing to Trade Consumers Up. The specific terms of a coupon deal can be designed to manipulate users into buying larger quantities of a product or particular brand flavors, sizes, or forms if that is the goal.

Couponing for Competitive Pressure. Couponing can be used with respect to the competition as either a defensive tactic or as an offensive move. By discounting one brand to users of competing brands, coupons entice those competitive users to buy the couponed brand instead.

Couponing can also defend a brand by offering current users coupons toward continued purchase or "loading" current users up with product through a cents-off promotion for multiple brand purchases. Coupons keep current users using and ward off competitive switching.

Couponing to Encourage Retail Distribution and Support. Since manufacturers' coupons are paid for and distributed by the manufacturer in most cases and must be redeemed within a retail store, couponing benefits the retailer with very little out-of-pocket cost. This can help to gain trade support and secure product distribution.

Couponing to Move Out-of-Balance Inventories. When inventories are at higher-than-desired levels, by either manufacturer or retailer terms, couponing can act as a catalyst to trigger interest and pull the product through the distribution channels.

Couponing to Target Different Markets. Coupons can be strategically placed within particular media aimed at key audiences or targeted directly to particular consumers on a list.

Couponing to Cushion Price Increases. Coupons offering enough of a discount to offset the increase in price can temporarily cushion the sting of the higher price until the time when consumers become accustomed to the higher price levels.

Couponing as an Add-On to Other Promotional Efforts. Often, couponing will be used in conjunction with refunds or sweepstakes to increase participation (and purchase).

Tactical Variations of a Coupon Deal

A coupon promotion can be designed to offer deals or savings in many different forms. In reality, most coupon offers exhibit a combination of the following characteristics and can become quite complex and thereby difficult to classify.

1. **Cents-Off.** The product to be purchased is offered at a certain cents or dollar amount off the regular price for a specified time frame.
2. **Free.** A free product is given upon redemption.
3. **Buy One, Get One Free (BOGO).** With the purchase of a product at the regular price, a second is given free.
4. **Time Release.** Several cents-off coupons are positioned together with different expiration dates, encouraging repeat usage over time.
5. **Multiple Purchase.** The coupon offer applies only when more than one unit of the product is purchased.
6. **Self-Destruct.** Two or more coupons are printed over each other in an overlap manner so that in order to redeem one, the other is destroyed.
7. **Personalized.** The coupon is personalized by geographic location or store and is redeemable accordingly.
8. **Cross-Ruff.** A coupon for one product is obtained with the purchase of another, unrelated product.
9. **Related Sale.** A coupon received from the purchase of one product applies to another product, which is related in some way to the purchased product.
10. **Sweepstakes Entry.** The redeemed coupon becomes an entry into a sweepstakes promotion.

Coupon Distribution Methods

FSI couponing accounted for 77 percent of all coupons distributed in 1991, while all other distribution channels combined account for less than one in four coupons delivered. Given the sheer absolute numbers of coupons, every distribution channel contributes substantially to couponing's success and some, like targeted direct mail couponing, are becoming more popular.

Direct Mail. Direct mail distribution uses the U.S. Postal Service to deliver coupons to mailboxes of consumers. Direct mail couponing achieves the highest redemption rates of any media or mailed couponing, primarily due to its more targeted distribution. Couponing that is mailed can be either solo or co-op. A solo coupon promotion would consist of coupon(s) for a single company or brand. A co-op coupon promotion includes coupons for a combination of brands usually from different companies. Clearly the co-op route is more efficient and cost effective but there are some limitations to co-ops in terms of their potential pinpoint delivery to very specific list criteria or competitive users.

In-Store or Central Location. Coupons are often distributed in the store where the items can be purchased or in high-traffic locations such as malls, shopping centers, and street corners.

Print Media Delivered Coupons. Advertising in newspapers with run-of-press (ROP) coupons or free-standing inserts (FSIs) and including coupons in magazine advertising constitute the primary print media used for delivery. Also in this category are print ads that offer consumers coupons if they send in their name and address or call an 800 or 900 number.

In-Pack and On-Pack Coupons. In- or on-pack couponing is an ideal strategy for encouraging repeat purchase of a given brand and holding current users. It is a relatively inexpensive distribution method in comparison to other methods, without the same misredemption potential of media-delivered coupons.

Retailer In-Ad Coupons. In-ad coupons are manufacturers' coupons that are distributed via retailers' advertising and/or mailings. In-ad coupons can be for a single or multiple purchase. They are generally very limited in time, with typical expiration dates of one or two weeks. The average face value for in-ads also tends to be much higher than that for other coupon methods. In-ad coupons are, in a way, another form of trade promotion because they stimulate product sales for a specific retail account.

Coupon Redemption Rates

Through the later half of the 1980s and into the 1990s, redemption rates have declined and flattened. This is probably due in part to the clutter of more coupons across more product categories, along with the increasing saturation of competitive couponing within a given product category.

Redemption rates vary depending on a number of product and coupon characteristics, including face value, product category and competitive activity within the category, area of the country, coupon delivery method, audience characteristics such as brand loyalty, and the design and appeal of the coupon advertising itself. Listed in Table 4.1 are average redemption rates in 1990 and 1991 for the overall grocery category by delivery method, provided through NCH Promotion Services.

As discussed in the previous section, the highest redemption rates occur for in- and on-pack delivery methods in which coupons are selectively targeted to users of the product in conjunction with purchase or use of the product. In-store handout couponing and direct mail delivery offer relatively high redemptions as well. The lowest redemptions occur for print media delivery, which usually requires more effort on the part of consumers to cut or clip the coupon.

TABLE 4.1 AVERAGE COUPON REDEMPTION RATES

Delivery Method	1990	1991
Instant on-pack	35.0%	32.5%
In-pack	12.5	12.3
On-pack	10.8	9.2
Cross-ruff on-pack	4.1	4.9
Cross-ruff in-pack	3.1	3.4
Handout couponing	4.1	4.9
Direct mail	4.7	4.3
FSI	2.5	2.4
Sunday magazine supplements	1.5	1.6
Newspaper ROP	1.5	1.5
Magazine tip-in	1.5	1.3
Magazine on-page	1.2	1.2

PREMIUMS, REFUNDS, AND PROMOTION FULFILLMENT

The most concise definition of the term *incentive marketing* appeared in *Incentives in Marketing* written by George Meredith and Robert P. Fried and published by the Association of Incentive Marketing (formerly National Premium Sales Executives, Inc.). Fried and Meredith describe incentive marketing as "a promotional device that induces purchase or performance on the part of a consumer, salesperson, or dealer through the offer of tangible reward in the form of merchandise or travel." The only addition to this definition in today's marketplace would be to include "employees" to the list of those induced.

Premiums and merchandise incentives are used for the following objectives:

Consumer incentives:
- Attract attention at the point-of-sale
- Sample new users
- Boost repeat sales
- Enhance consumer goodwill
- Obtain higher advertising readership
- Provide sales with a talking point
- Encourage store display usage
- Increase overall sales volume

Types of Premiums and Promotions

Each type of merchandise incentive promotion has its advantages and disadvantages. When planning promotions involving merchandise, the advantages and disadvantages must be weighed carefully. For planning purposes, the following is a recap of these plus/minus elements for the major incentive promotion types.

Trade and sales incentives:
- Introduce new or improved products
- Pull slow-moving or line extensions through the system
- Increase the customer base
- Reinforce consumer promotions
- Offset competitive promotions/introductions
- Boost sale/dealer morale
- Obtain sales display
- Increase productivity
- Increase overall sales volume/market share

Premium/merchandise incentives cannot make up for a product that is inferior in quality or does not do what it has been advertised to do. Nor can these incentives substitute for inadequate advertising or a poorly trained or inferior sales staff, or change negative consumer attitudes. Consumers can be motivated to buy and try a new product or service or to retry an improved version of the product or service, but if that product does not perform as advertised or the "new, improved" version is not really improved, no amount of incentive promotion will induce consumers to continued purchases.

Types of Premiums and Promotions

Mail-in Premiums — Self-Liquidators, Partial Self-Liquidators, and Free-in-the-Mail Offers. Oftentimes, premiums are acquired through the mail. The premium may be offered free to the consumer responding to the promotion, or it may be purchased by the consumer — usually at less than the expected retail price. A self-liquidating premium is one for which any direct cost associated with the premium, including mailing or handling charges, is paid up front by the respondent. For instance, the incentive to the consumer consists of receiving a desirable premium item at the same low wholesale price at which the promoter can buy it. Therefore, the consumer receives a good value at very little cost to the promoter.

Frequent Buyer/User and Continuity Plans. Frequent user programs have been in existence for many years and fall into a number of categories. A differentiating factor here is that, in order to encourage continuity of use/purchase, customers must save up to acquire a premium. By redeeming product proofs of purchase, game pieces, or savings stamps the consumer can "buy" a premium, often selecting from a variety of options offered at different price levels.

Direct Premiums — In-Pack, On-Pack, and Near-Packs. Direct premiums are those directly received by the consumer upon purchase of a product by virtue of being packaged or sold with the premium.

In-pack and on-pack incentives are either packaged in or on the product being promoted. The most widely recognized in-pack offer is the one that has been used to promote the sale of Cracker Jacks for more than 50 years. Cereal companies are major users of in-pack offers.

A near-pack incentive is usually shipped separately from the product being promoted and is displayed directly adjacent to the product. Fast-food restaurants also use this type of promotion to promote add-on sales — for example, buy a burger and a carbonated beverage and get a special, decorated glass free. These promotions usually have a number of differently designed glasses to encourage continuity of purchase.

Container Pack Incentives. Specialty container packs have been used for many years. One of the most successful container pack promotions was offered by General Foods on their Maxwell House coffee brand. Maxwell House packed its coffee in a decorated glass coffee carafe, which was given to consumers at no additional cost. This program generated tremendous sales increases in Maxwell House coffee and provided consumers with an ongoing reminder of the brand. Glassware incentives have also been used for years on jam and jelly products.

Account Openers. Account openers have been used by many companies to encourage their current and new consumers to purchase an item on time or, in the case of financial institutions, to open a new type of account or to secure a loan or certificate of deposit. The direct mail industry utilizes these incentives to encourage consumers to purchase or try an item of merchandise of much greater value. In the event the consumer wishes to return the trial item for credit or refund, the incentive item may be retained as a reward for the trial.

Business Gifts. Business gifts are rewards given to stockholders, customers, business friends, and employees as an expression of appreciation for performance, loyalty, or friendship. The federal government limits the dollar amount that can be paid for such rewards. While there are some minor advantages and disadvantages to this type of incentive, the major purpose is a gesture of friendship.

Employee Awards. Incentives used to reward employees for safety, quality control, attendance, productivity performance, longevity, or suggestions fall into the employee awards category. Most employers use one or more of the motivational techniques to reward employees for predetermined performance levels. There have been substantiated reports of employee lost-time accidents being reduced by more than 50 percent as a result of safety award programs. It is a normal practice to present these incentive awards at special luncheons and dinners to honor those who have achieved the level of excellence required to earn an award. This recognition can also encourage teamwork and is an employee morale builder.

Dealer Incentives. Dealer incentive merchandise sales accounted for more than $2 billion of the almost $13 billion of incentive sales in 1991. Dealer or trade incentive programs are structured to reward these customers for purchasing, displaying, and selling products and services. The program can be a "short-term" offer built around a single item — for example, purchase a predetermined quantity of product, put up a display detailing the consumer offer, and keep the consumer incentive item affixed to the display when the program is completed. Alternatively, these programs could be very detailed "long-term" offers promoting continuity of purchase and requiring accumulation of points redeemable for high-cost merchandise and/or travel displayed in very high-quality, four-color, comprehensive catalogs with custom-designed covers and promotional literature. There are also "step" catalogs offering a variety of items at various point levels that are used for this type of incentive, as well as offering executive gifts.

Sales Incentives. Sales incentives provide a reward for achievement performance of a predetermined sales goal during a defined time period. The length of the program varies from very short-term events, often referred to as "spurt" programs, to programs that last the entire year. These programs can be designed to motivate a salesperson to sell a particular product or service, a product line, or multiple lines or services.

Many believe that a salary or commission should be sufficient motivation to perform to the utmost ability, but the use of sales incentives has proven that sales forces can be motivated to achieve sales goals far in excess of forecasted levels. The drive to make the extra sales call or push the promoted line or service to "win" the sales contest or award has resulted in sales increases of more than 100 percent of the projected goal.

Cash, merchandise, and travel are the most popular awards. Some sales incentive programs offer a wide selection of gifts, and this merchandise is pictured in a catalog from which winners may select awards based on the points or credits they have earned as a result of their sales efforts. Other programs offer exotic travel destinations for all winners who have achieved or surpassed their sales goal. Successful sales incentive programs are structured so that even the top goals are within reach of all participants. If goals are set at levels that are not achievable, a negative reaction could result.

SWEEPSTAKES, GAMES, AND CONTESTS

Sweepstakes, games, and contests are among the hottest sales promotion techniques today. There are several reasons for this popularity. Certainly, one of the best is that a lot of people, in a lot of fields, have learned how to use them effectively.

It is important to understand the terms *sweepstakes, games,* and *contests.* A sweepstakes is a prize promotion in which winners are selected by chance. These promotions are regulated primarily by federal and state lottery laws, which declare that a lottery is an illegal promotion. A lottery is any promotion that contains these three elements: prize, chance, and consideration (purchase).

So, how can the states run lotteries? They pass legislation authorizing their own lotteries.

Private-sector marketers avoid the lottery restriction by eliminating the element of consideration. Authorities have agreed to allow sponsors to request proof-of-purchase with sweepstakes entries, as long as consumers are given the alternative of not submitting proof-of-purchase. In most cases, the acceptable alternative is a plain 3" x 5" piece of paper with the brand name handwritten on it.

All forms of sweepstakes, including the instant winner games that utilize some form of concealment device, fall under the same laws and guidelines. All these programs, no matter how complex or how steep the odds, are random-chance events.

A contest, like a sweepstakes or lottery, is a prize promotion. However, in a contest, prizes are awarded not on random chance but on the basis of a test of skill or personal talent. A contest can require a recipe, a photograph, a jingle, or an essay as a test of skill. The winners in such a program are not picked randomly. All contest entries must be opened and screened, and the judging proceeds according to a weighted set of criteria that are made known to all entrants as part of the contest rules.

Because the element of chance is not present in contests, they are not subject to the same restrictions that govern sweepstakes. In a contest, consideration, or purchase of a product, may be required for entry in many categories. Because skill is involved, contests logically generate far fewer entries than sweepstakes. In fact, in terms of entries, industry observers say sweepstakes will generate anywhere from four to 10 times more entries than contests. Because a contest will generate only a fraction of the entries generated by a sweepstakes, many marketers waive any purchase requirement in a contest, even though such a requirement is legal. The idea is to present as few obstacles to entry as possible.

Sweepstakes Promotion Formats

Few marketers are aware of the many types of sweepstakes, games, and contests. There are no fewer than five sweepstakes formats plus three types of games.

First is the *Standard Sweepstakes* in which a consumer receives an entry in some print media or at the point-of-sale and is instructed to mail it in to a specific post office box or deposit it in a handy ballot box. The drawing to select winners is conducted at some specified later date.

Yes, this is the old workhorse program we've all known since sweepstakes began. But, given the right product, the right prize structure, and the right advertising support, this type of program can grab attention and deliver readers. It is why so many more marketers are using sweepstakes today.

Second is the *Multiple-Entry Sweepstakes* in which each prize is literally a separate sweepstakes by itself. So, in order to be eligible to win any of the prizes in this type of program, a separate entry is required for each prize. This type of format greatly multiplies consumer involvement in the advertising and, not incidentally, mushrooms the number of entries received.

The multiple-entry sweepstakes is clearly an ideal way to focus on or enhance the importance of a specific number. For Benson & Hedges 100s, which used the format for many years, that number is obviously 100 — 100 individual sweepstakes, supporting a top 100mm brand.

The *Programmed-Learning Sweepstakes* uses a technique that's popular in elementary education. It's like an exercise in conditioning. As a prerequisite to entering, we require the consumer to read the ad and give us back key copy points or information.

The *Qualified-Entry Sweepstakes* is similar to programmed learning except that the information needed to qualify the entry is not presented in the advertising: The consumer must guess the answer from clues or solve a puzzle, for example. Involvement here is at a maximum. Increasingly, marketers are using toll-free or 900-number telephone systems to provide clues or information to qualify entries.

One of the hottest sweepstakes techniques today is the *Automatic-Entry* format where a store coupon in an ad doubles as a sweepstakes entry. When the consumer redeems the coupon with the name and address information filled in, he or she is automatically entered in the sweepstakes without the need for mailing in the entry or adding extra postage. The result? Incremental entries. In fact, we estimate that automatic-entry coupons will hype coupon redemption rates by as much as 25 percent.

Interactive telephone programs also offer an automatic-entry mechanism for consumers. By calling an 800 or 900 telephone number featured in advertising, consumers may also enter a sweepstakes.

Three Types of Games

Games represent the most powerful sweepstakes formats to create traffic and sales. The *Matching Instant Winner Game* literally steers consumers into stores. That's because one key element of a matching game is an ad that contains a matching symbol the consumer has to take to the store to find out if and what he or she has won. In fact, the headline often says, "You May Have Already Won — ."

In matching games, where it is difficult to set up displays, the UPC number, which is on every package, may be used as the matching element.

Collect-and-Win Games are often used in conjunction with instant winner games, but they can stand alone, as well. In this format, consumers get a game piece or symbol that represents a piece of a picture or part of a name or phrase. By getting enough game pieces to spell the name or complete the picture, the consumer can win a prize. Generally, one or more of the individual collect-and-win phrases or symbols is a rare game piece, limited to the total number of prizes available.

Instant Winner Games are self-contained and self-judging random-chance promotions. Consumers receive a game card requiring one or more scratch-offs or peel-offs to reveal a prize message, or instructions to enter a "second-chance" random drawing, or to save for a collect-and-win prize. New technologies include interactive games in which cards are scanned by readers with a voice message announcing a win or "Sorry, Try Again" message, or even devices that heat or cool the cards to reveal a hidden message.

Contests Fall Into Basic Types

A contest requires a demonstration of skill or personal trait on the part of the entrant, who mails the entry to a post office box or deposits it in an on-premise container. The contest, therefore, has remained a basically static type of promotional program.

This does not mean that there is no purpose for contest programs. In recipe contests, marketers are trying to appeal to heavy users and tap the creative genius of the American homemaker. Winning recipes may appear on product labels, in printed ads, in TV commercials, or in recipe booklets. In photo contests, winning entries may provide visual elements for a continuing series of advertisements. An essay contest winner may be recruited as a corporate spokesperson for the brand or service.

Marketers who equate promotion success with sales may select contests over sweepstakes simply because proof-of-purchase can be required. However, contests will generate only a fraction of the entries generated by a sweepstakes. If a sweepstakes entry blank asks for either an actual or a facsimile proof-of-purchase, the number of actual proofs-of-purchase will probably far exceed the number generated by a contest identically exposed and advertised to the target audience, simply because the sweepstakes generates so many more total entries.

Planning for Sweepstakes, Games, and Contests

1. **Determine the objectives.** Before you can know whether a sweepstakes, game, or contest will do the job, you must analyze the reasons for the promotion and determine what you expect it to achieve. For example, you must decide whether the problem is sales or distribution and whether the promotion is to cover a single product or the full line.

2. **Establish the markets.** The next step is to determine whether the promotion is to be national or regional and to establish the audience at which the sweepstakes will be aimed. Both these factors will affect the ad media and the prizes.

3. **Assign responsibilities.** Decide who will be responsible for each facet of the promotion and who will do the planning and create the sweepstakes idea and mechanics. Specify what your ad agency will be responsible for and who will handle the sweepstakes and post-sweepstakes details. Decide whether to use the services of a sweepstakes planning organization. Sweepstakes specialists can create sweepstakes ideas; develop the mechanics; draft the rules; receive, process, and store entries; judge the winners; arrange for the prizes; and handle all details and correspondence in connection with the prizes, including supervising their delivery. The important thing is to use every available source of assistance to carefully plan and administer the promotion.

4. **Develop the theme.** The sweepstakes idea or theme must be integrated with your objectives so that your product will not suffer from being subordinated to the sweepstakes itself.

   Another approach is to spotlight a specific product feature or benefit and build the sweepstakes theme around it. As noted, Benson & Hedges 100s cigarettes focused on the length of the product in its sweepstakes.

   Another effective way of integrating a sweepstakes and the product is to make the product an integral part of the grand prize, as Sunkist did recently with a "Win a Carload of Oranges" sweepstakes.

5. **Determine the entry mechanics.** Should the promotion be a sweepstakes or a skill contest? If getting a lot of entries is important, then a sweepstakes is best. On the other hand, if you want to be able to require a proof-of-purchase with every entry, you'll have to go with a skill contest. As we've seen, that doesn't mean you're limited to the old "25-words-or-less" format. There are jingle-writing contests, photography contests, and the ever-popular recipe contests. Bear in mind, too, that a clever entry device can sometimes greatly enhance the promotion.

The entry mechanics should spell out the duration of the promotion and the conditions covering participation and judging. In a skill contest, it's especially important to make certain that you establish measurable, judgeable criteria. Most important, keep the sweepstakes and the rules as simple as possible.

6. **Check the regulations.** Although there's some confusion in this area, sweepstakes are perfectly legal. It's lotteries that are illegal for use in connection with consumer goods and services. There are federal, state, and local lottery laws, as well as Federal Trade Commission regulations, that must be adhered to. And several states now require that sweepstakes be registered and reported. Just make sure that you, your attorney, or your sweepstakes planning firm is up on the latest statutes governing games of chance.

7. **Select the prizes.** The prizes are the heart of any sweepstakes, contest, or game. They should be appropriate for the audience and the time of the year, and they should tie in with the theme. Offer as many prizes as possible so that people will feel they have a better chance of winning. For the supplementary prizes, a variety of merchandise is preferable to cash. Merchandise is more interesting and significant than a small cash award.

8. **Estimate the costs.** Early in the planning stage, firm up estimates of the cost of advertising, production, sales promotion and display materials, prizes, handling, and judging.

9. **Plan the advertising.** If you're going to have a promotion, promote it. Be prepared to devote both print space and airtime to the sweepstakes. Use the same media you have used all along. Keep the layouts simple and feature the prizes prominently; they are the carrots you are dangling before your audience.

10. **Get the sales force fired up.** Whether you have your own sales force or you sell through brokers, jobbers, distributors, or dealers, the task is still the same: to convince them that the sweepstakes is a sales tool designed to make their jobs easier and help them write more business. The sweepstakes gives them a change of pace, another reason for asking for a display or an order.

11. **Sell the trade.** Dealer cooperation is essential. Sometimes it's the reason for the whole promotion. Get dealers excited about the impact the promotion will have on consumers and the traffic it will pull into their stores. Set up a trade sweepstakes to run simultaneously with the consumer sweepstakes; this will give dealers an added incentive to cooperate.

12. **Plan the publicity.** Back up the advertising with publicity. Frequently, the sweepstakes idea or the fact that you are running a sweepstakes is news. Send trade publications a publicity story

spelling out the details. When it's over, send releases to every prizewinner's hometown paper. Then follow up with "how-we-did-it" articles.

13. **Arrange for judging the winners.** Whether you're running a sweepstakes or a skill contest, the safest thing is to have the judging done by a professional organization. You want to make certain that the winners are selected fairly and impartially; so leave the judging to the experts.

14. **Check the major winners.** Conduct a background check on the major prize winners to ascertain that the entries are their own work and that there is no question about their entries or their eligibility as winners. The judging agency usually will handle this for you.

15. **Announce the winners.** Once the sweepstakes is over, see that the judging is done as quickly as possible and that the winners are announced promptly. You must also send a list of winners to anyone who requests it.

16. **Deliver the prizes.** Nothing creates more ill will than a disappointed prize winner. Delivery of the prizes should therefore be handled quickly and smoothly.

17. **Analyze the results.** The most important criteria are as follows: Did the sweepstakes achieve its objectives? How did the sweepstakes affect sales? Did it succeed in getting all the displays you wanted? What did the sales force think of the promotion?

Budgeting for Sweepstakes, Games, and Contests

As has been noted, a critical benefit of a prize promotion is the fixed-cost nature of the event. The fact that there are no major open-ended liabilities in a sweepstakes or contest makes this type of promotion affordable to marketers for whom an elaborate program of coupons, samples, or refund offers may be too costly. At the other end of the spectrum, a sweepstakes may be ideal for brands in product categories with such high volume and purchase frequency that a coupon drop or refund offer will result in a redemption rate so high that the promotion becomes a victim of its own success, blowing budgets through the roof.

Many sweepstakes and contest programs are overlaid with coupon offers for the sponsoring brand. This has the function of encouraging purchase of the product in association with the sweepstakes and of utilizing media delivery of a sweepstakes or contest ad to provide a direct price incentive to the consumer. In such combination programs, the cost of the add-on promotion device must be budgeted separately from the sweepstakes or contest event itself, and the marketer must use all the data available in planning for the coupon response.

The costs of the sweepstakes or contest event can be grouped as follows:

1. **Advertising and point-of-purchase costs** in a prize promotion are no different from those in any other type of promotion, and the result of a greater expenditure on media advertising is also the same. Strong, extensive national advertising and a major drive to get the store materials up will result in a much stronger program, whether it's a coupon drop or a sweepstakes. Television and radio support will also increase awareness of the program and add somewhat to the entry rate, but at an increased cost.

2. **Prizes** in a sweepstakes or contest are the great variable. We have long since crossed the $1 million threshold in private-sector prize promotions. The various state lotteries have yielded cash prize jackpots of $50–$60 million or more, and this has had an impact on prize promotion planning.

3. **Administration and judging costs** depend on such factors as the complexity of the program mechanics, special printing involved in concealed-device instant winner games, the need to visit printing or packaging plants to supervise the production and distribution of instant winner game cards and packages, prize fulfillment, and special tabular analyses of entrants. For planning purposes, marketers may estimate that the administrative cost of a typical prize promotion, exclusive of any special printing, will range from $7,000 to $25,000.

CONTINUITY PROMOTIONS

Frequency or continuity programs are one of several basic sales promotion techniques that form an integral part of the marketing arsenal available to use in today's marketing mix. These are promotions whereby customers are rewarded in some manner for repeated or frequent purchase or use of a product or service. The parameters of the promotion may vary, but the intent is the same—to encourage purchase loyalty, continuity, and frequency. Today, all indications appear to point to frequent "buyer" programs as one of the most important promotion forms available to consumer marketing.

To continue from a solid conceptual foundation, a definition is needed:

> To identify, maintain, and increase yield from the best customers through a long-term, interactive, value-added relationship that encourages our target audience to continually utilize or purchase the services and products we offer.

The benefits of frequency programs include the ability to break through the clutter of a crowded marketplace and bring customers in to shop at a store, fly on a particular airline, stay at a given hotel, rent cars, or purchase a branded product or service. Once a customer has purchased a product or service, the programs can also be an effective method of ensuring that the customer stays loyal and that he or she comes back week after week. Perhaps most important, frequency programs can be a powerful defensive strategy to counteract competitive activities — a key benefit in an age of product parity, intensified competition, and eroding brand equities. Frequency programs can go a long way toward building a wall around customers to keep the competition out and customers in.

Types of Frequency Programs

1. *Continuity Programs.* A continuity program is a self-liquidating or profit-making plan, most often used by supermarkets, in which a set of related items is offered. For instance, the consumer could get a different item each week for a given time in return for purchase or use. Supermarkets may offer dishes, flatware, cutlery, glasses, or encyclopedias. Today, these types of programs are used by quick-service restaurant establishments as well, where a continuing line of toys is offered each week to be collected. The programs encourage regular repeat visits.

2. *Frequency Programs.* A frequency program is a tracking program of purchases by a given consumer of a particular product, with a reward, usually free goods or services of the same nature as what was tracked or purchased. These programs are customized by the sponsor. Frequency programs are most often used by airlines, hotels, and name-brand products, such as canned goods.

3. *Trading Stamp Program.* Stamp programs were created long before the term *frequency program* was developed or implemented. In this instance, stamps are collected in conjunction with use or purchase and redeemed for merchandise. Stamp programs were most often used by gas stations and supermarkets because they built strong loyalty for an individual store, bringing the customer back repeatedly. Trading stamp popularity spread usage from store to store until the stamps lost their power to set apart any individual store. Now, due to the popularity of frequency programs in general, trading stamps are enjoying renewed interest as a continuity vehicle.

4. *Sweepstakes Continuity.* This kind of continuity program works by collecting the parts to build a slogan, picture, or other device. Much like a jigsaw puzzle, each game ticket is obtained by making a visit or purchase or writing to the sponsor.

Advantages of Frequency Programs

The advantages of using a frequency-type promotion are many. Frequency programs can achieve some or all of the following:

- Increase frequency of purchases of goods or services
- Increase frequency of store visits, where applicable
- Create a purchase habit that continues after the promotion period is over
- Provide a database of participant buying behavior
- Are easy to measure and track effectiveness

One of the side benefits of creating a promotion to induce short-term continuity of purchase is that these programs can also create a purchase habit that continues after the promotion has ended.

A very important advantage of most frequency programs is the extraordinary database that can be obtained. Properly maintained, it contains the buying or usage habits of consumers over time. Information gained from the program can actually become an additional source of revenue through the sale of mailing lists, information, purchasing habits, interests, and other data to providers of noncompetitive services. In many cases they also provide data that can be used to target new products and offer a reason for both former customers, as well as new prospects, to purchase.

Disadvantages of Frequency Programs

The disadvantages of frequency programs are as follows:

- May have a limited appeal
- May have difficulty in getting trade support due to the long-term nature of programs
- Opportunities exist for misredemption, barter, or reselling
- May create an IOU for the sponsor that can have detrimental effects on total dollar allocations (reserves) needed to address the building of obligation to participants
- May be difficult to alter
- May be difficult to terminate
- May be more costly to administer than estimated
- May be easy for competitors to duplicate and improve
- Possible rewards may be given to customers who did not alter their purchase habits, but were rewarded anyway
- Customers may anticipate program and collect proofs-of-purchase before announcement, to hold for later redemption. This is especially effective in label savings' programs such as school computers, for which high levels of collectibility are required.

A frequency program can suffer from limited appeal if the consumer doesn't perceive that the added value of the reward is high enough. It can also be difficult to obtain trade support because, by their nature, frequency programs are long term and there can be a substantial difference between a sponsor's interest and the retailer's. It could be a major mistake to assume that retailers or distributors will participate in the program unless their needs were considered in its development.

Frequency programs can also, unfortunately, have a high potential for abuse. The opportunities for misredemption, bartering, and reselling can be significant. Airline frequent flier programs have found this to be an especially difficult problem to overcome.

Careful administrative planning is essential to the successful frequency marketing program. Costs can get out of hand if the program grows more quickly than anticipated and there's a poorly designed system in place to handle it.

POINT-OF-PURCHASE

How does one define point-of-purchase advertising? As the name itself suggests, point-of-purchase is advertising where the sales transactions occur. Point-of-purchase advertising dominates the moment at which all the elements of a sale converge — namely, the buyer, the seller, the money, and the product. Point-of-purchase advertising assumes countless forms and employs myriad materials, but it always is directed toward one very important objective: to communicate sales and marketing messages at the moment purchasing decisions are being made.

Types of Point-of-Purchase

To develop a manageable working understanding of P-O-P displays, it is useful to categorize them by (1) length of time they are to be used, (2) location in which they are to be used, and (3) their marketing function.

1. **Time.** A P-O-P program is considered permanent if its materials are durable and its intended period of use is six months or longer. Anything less is considered a temporary or semipermanent display. These guidelines were established by the Point-of-Purchase Advertising Institute, which administers an annual awards contest for both permanent and semipermanent displays. Obviously, the type of material used and method of manufacture greatly affects a program's potential for permanence. So development of a P-O-P program requires the planner to determine first the desired length of use.

   A study by Nielsen Marketing Research, reported in *P-O-P Times*, provided an affirmative answer to the question: Are semipermanent displays worth the extra expense? Nielsen conducted research on behalf of a packaged drink manufacturer that supported the argument that higher-quality displays generally are worth the extra associated costs. While both types of displays are of comparable effectiveness, the semipermanents have a bottom-line edge because more retailers accept them and they stay up longer.

2. **Location.** Every square inch of a retail environment represents an opportunity for P-O-P advertising. Just where the advertising ought to be positioned for maximum result is a central issue when planning P-O-P programs, because location tremendously influences performance. Designing P-O-P to fit a specific location can increase its effectiveness. Another Nielsen study, reported by *P-O-P Times*, showed that displays for a snack product located in the front, rear, and lobby of a store generated up to twice the volume of displays in other locations. The manufacturer also discovered that "substantial differences in responsiveness" to specific display locations differed brand by brand and region to region.

   The ability of marketers to make informed recommendations to retailers concerning the strongest sales-building display locations for their brands is greatly enhanced by scanner data generated at the checkout counter. Applying such information is crucial for marketers in today's retail environment, where the trade is increasingly tightfisted about how nationally advertised brands are presented at the point-of-purchase. Marketers must be prepared to prove that a retailer's category-wide profits will improve if their brand is given special exposure in a prime retail location. Some retailers, aware of the ability of displays to increase sales, now design their stores to maximize the potential of display space. Such was not the case 10 or 20 years ago.

3. **Function.** What P-O-P advertising can accomplish at retail falls into a variety of broad categories:
   - *Merchandisers* generally are designed to hold the product being advertised and are meant to create a specific "home" for the product apart from standard store shelving. Examples include permanent racks that hold candy, overhead racks for cigarettes typically found at the checkout counter, and pallet displays. Temporary units known as prepacks consist of the shipping cartons themselves, turned inside-out to become a display unit.
   - *Signage* reinforces a product, company name, or an advertised theme. It can also simply inform the consumer of various product benefits. For example, an outdoor sign might be used to tell a consumer that a certain brand or category of goods or services is available. Indoors, signs can help alert consumers to the availability of a product and influence the sale.
   - *Glorifiers* make the product stand out to the consumer in stark contrast to other products. Glorifiers almost always hold the product in some way, by placing it on a pedestal or otherwise surrounding it with an attention-getting device.

- *Organizers* help the retailer control inventory or help the consumer make a selection more easily.
- *Shelf space* has itself become something of a de facto point-of-purchase advertising medium. Faced with decreasingly available space for traditional displays (and only temporary access to such opportunities), many manufacturers are cleverly enhancing the advertising value of the shelf itself through more effective product packaging and merchandising concepts, such as "shelf-talkers" that extend from the shelf without interfering with consumer access to the products.
- *New media* include shopping-cart "billboards," in-store sound systems, digital signage, interactive video kiosks, and even television sets at checkout lanes.

P-O-P Integration

Integrating P-O-P advertising with a brand's image advertising campaign and coordinating the program with both the advertiser's sales supports and the retailer makes fundamental good sense. A recent study by Information Resource, Inc. showed that when P-O-P reinforces an advertising message, sales increase for that product 128.2 percent over P-O-P that does not underscore the ad.

Integration, however, should not be considered the end-all and be-all of marketing into the 21st century. Another study, this one by Nielsen Marketing Research conducted exclusively for *P-O-P Times*, showed that displays generated significant sales increases by themselves, without any accompanying promotional or advertising support. The research study analyzed scanner data across 26 product categories in 323 markets over a two-year period, and found that display-only promotions consistently improved sales in every instance. The average percentage increase in sales for stand-alone P-O-P advertisements ranged from 57 percent in Tampa and Miami to 108 percent in Milwaukee, and from 33 percent for salad dressing and beer to 177 percent for dishwasher liquid.

Although the power of P-O-P is uniformly evident in this research, it is also clear that P-O-P effectiveness can vary by product category and region. This underlines the imperative for marketers today to fully understand the dynamics of P-O-P advertising relative to the specific, market-by-market conditions that affect the fortunes of brands. When developing a P-O-P program, one must also consider the manner of distribution. Will the program be installed by the advertiser's sales force, by independent reps, or by the retailer's own staff? Such considerations must be factored in when designing the program.

The decline of small, "mom and pop" retailers and the consolidation of retail chains throughout the country has given the retailer a strong voice in the in-store marketing environment. P-O-P advertisers must consider whether the retailer will accept a particular P-O-P program—even before thinking about whether a consumer will respond to it. Many retailers today have their own facility planners who dictate the type of display material they will allow in their stores. Displays may be required to conform to customized gondolas and may be restricted in terms of color, height, size, or location.

Managing the P-O-P Function

The P-O-P industry is comprised of a diverse group of individuals and organizations that design, manufacture, or subcontract P-O-P advertising materials.

Advertisers typically see the industry as comprised of three types of suppliers:

1. Factories that specialize only in production of a specific type of display, such as wire or corrugated;
2. Agency/Factories that specialize in production of one or more of the display's components and subcontract the rest to produce finished displays; and
3. Agencies, that do not own a manufacturing plant but design and then subcontract production of the finished displays.

The category of supplier the advertiser uses obviously depends on the nature of the project at hand. Sometimes an advertiser knows in advance the type of material best suited to produce the planned display and will select a supplier based on its ability to deliver a display constructed of that material. Because of the rapid advance of new materials and technologies, however, advertisers increasingly are keeping options open because a new material or production process might significantly reduce costs or improve the durability of the display.

Creativity and P-O-P

"Cutting through the visual clutter" is an overused phrase in point-of-purchase, but it holds true; the job of a creative P-O-P is indeed to cut through that visual clutter and stand out.

The two key design principles of point-of-purchase advertising are especially challenging, but if followed, they help the creative process:

1. Keep the design simple, using symbols and not words wherever possible; and
2. Make the product the "star," not the display. David Ogilvy said it very well: "Make the product itself the hero of your advertising." Never lose sight of the fact that it is the *product* you are selling, not the display.

And, as in any creative endeavor, distance yourself from what you think you know to be true. One of the most common, creativity-stunting misconceptions is that point-of-purchase displays are a few steps short of a commodity. Nothing could be further from the truth.

Creativity in point-of-purchase advertising first demands an understanding that effective P-O-P amid the cluttered retail environment requires *ownable* ideas. Generic, off-the-rack solutions are nearly always inadequate and are unnecessary given the wide choice of materials with which to work, as detailed in this chapter's section on "Types of P-O-P."

Following are four open-ended "rules" for opening the door to creativity in point-of-purchase advertising, including some examples of especially creative P-O-P programs.

1. **Be visual.** Anyone who walks into a supermarket and sees a floor display shaped like a giant Dixie Cup knows immediately what is being sold. Putting freezer tape in a freezer makes the same statement, as does displaying champagne in an outsized champagne bottle replica.

2. **Involve the consumer.** As discussed, store help today is scarce to nonexistent. Every time you can involve the consumer, therefore, you are closer to closing a sale.

3. **Provide information.** While big, bold images are great for capturing attention, the job of good P-O-P sometimes is simply to merchandise information in a new and better way.

4. **Enhance the brand.** Building a brand's image does not necessarily mean translating its advertising campaign into an in-store setting. Displays that project moods, taste, prestige, glamour, and excitement are also ably communicated at the point-of-purchase.

Creativity in point-of-purchase advertising takes many forms and can make a giant difference. A profit-driven creative approach can reduce the cost of producing or shipping P-O-P displays or programs. Creative construction can make it easier for a retailer to set up and, thereby, increase usage. Creative design can more effectively communicate to the consumer in the retail environment.

If it isn't creative, it doesn't sell. To bring out the best creative effort, both the buyer and creator of P-O-P must join together and get to know each other and each other's business. Then, within their respective organizations, others must be allowed to *dare* to approach point-of-purchase advertising in a fresh, new way. There is always a better way to do something, but we must be challenged to find it. And when that fresh, new approach is found, we must have the courage of our convictions to do what we believe will work.

Of course, all this is risky. You may strike out, but you will also hit some home runs rather than a few safe singles. So take risks. And above all, have fun. Without fun, creativity at point-of-purchase is only an academic exercise.

DATABASE MARKETING

Database marketing is the promotion of products or services customer by customer, by means of an information source. The information source is the database. The database provides the information necessary to customize the communication to meet the needs and desires of the individual customer. Currently, the communication vehicles used in database marketing are the mail, interactive point-of-sale, and interactive telecommunication services.

As with all business endeavors, the purpose of a marketing database is to positively impact the financial performance of a company. There are three fundamental strategies to achieve this.

1. *Acquisition of New Customers.* New customers come in two types. The first is a customer that is new to your product or category. Given the penetration of most products and services these days, this target may only be a marketing opportunity for truly new categories of products and services. The second group, the competitor's customers, is an opportunity for a much larger group of companies. Both types of new customers can be part of a database. The decision about who to include on the database is made during the planning stage of the database.

2. *Retention of Current Customers.* The airlines' frequent flier and hotels' frequent stayer programs are excellent examples of proactive retention programs. Using a database of all the flights and visits, the travel industry is able to fashion programs based on past behavior. For example, if a traveler normally takes a flight to Kansas City every month, an early warning system might alert the marketing and promotion team when two months go by without a trip. The airline or hotel has the ability to send a personalized message to the individuals offering a special perk on the next trip if she returns a satisfaction survey for previous trips. The program identifies if there is a problem and also provides an incentive to make sure the valued traveler is not flying on a competitive airline.

   Another example of retention programs is reactive programs. The Tylenol product tampering scare of several years ago was dealt with very effectively by McNeil Consumer Products. The damage control plan would have been even stronger if a database of Tylenol users had been available. Imagine a letter sent within a matter of days to loyal Tylenol consumers explaining the extent of the product tampering, describing the steps the company was taking, and delivering a coupon to ensure the loyalty of this important group. A private, direct channel of communication to customers without a news media filter through a database would be invaluable.

3. *Maximization of Customer Contribution.* Imagine being able to tailor a promotion based on past behavior in your product or

service category. A continuity program could be designed that would cause even the heaviest customer to make an incremental purchase. The information on the database can provide the foundation for programs to promote cross-selling of other products, trading up to a more expensive line, and increasing your share of purchases from a customer. An industry that employs a customer maximization strategy is financial services. These programs leverage the information available at an individual level to ensure your company receives the maximum purchases possible. The only way to truly maximize the volume and profits of a company is customer by customer, matching programs and incentives to individual customer behavior and potential.

Building a Marketing Database

As with any successful endeavor, you plan before you build. The process of building a database is comprised of seven phases.

1. *Needs Assessment*. In the first phase, you determine the objectives for the database. Thorough planning with an eye to the future is required when establishing the objectives for the database. Key areas that the objectives should cover are audience or target, expectations for the database (financial and marketing), who will be using the database, and the degree of interaction required. The objectives drive who will populate your database, what data structure you will use, how much it will cost, and who can access it.

2. *Function Analysis*. This phase of the database building process focuses on what the database has to do from a technical standpoint to meet your objectives. The answers to the questions during this phase will aid in determining which software and hardware are required.

3. *Internal vs. External*. Once the needs assessment and function analysis are completed, the question of where and how to house the data must be answered. When making the decision, it is important to consider two options. Housing the base internally will require additional head count, training, software, and potentially hardware. If the marketing department will have access to the database, you will also need a group to support these users. Any and all additional costs associated with housing the database internally should be compared to outsourcing the database. Outsourcing the database provides several benefits. First, you will be able to access the knowledge of people who have years of experience in this area. Second, you will be a number-one priority even at month's close. Third, you will be able to choose a company that can provide one or all of the services required to implement database marketing.

4. *Gather Data.* Now that you have determined the information that should be included in the database, the source(s) of the data should be identified. Internal sources should be evaluated first due to their cost-effectiveness. The sources that are usually maintained internally are billing and inventory systems, customer service, panel or advisory boards, and mailing lists.

5. *Clean Data.* The information for your database will come most likely from multiple sources. Prior to loading the information into the database, several steps are required to "clean" the data. The first step is to place the data from the multiple sources in the same format. The name and address will be placed in the same fields, and the additional data will be given the same specific locations in each customer record. Next, the customer names and addresses will be sent through a piece of software that standardizes the addresses according to U.S. Postal Service guidelines and corrects or adds zip codes and zip-plus-four. These changes increase the deliverability of any mailings from the database.

The next step is to eliminate duplicates. Duplicates can occur during data entry or are the result of a customer responding to more than one stimuli. When an exact duplicate has been identified, one of the records is deleted. The final step in cleaning the data is the updating of the addresses. With more than 20 percent of all households moving every year, some of your customers will no longer be at the address contained in your information. By using the National Change of Address (NCOA), a service of the U.S. Postal Service, the addresses can be updated electronically. The source of NCOA is the change of address card you fill out to notify your mail carrier of your move.

6. *Database Design.* The first five phases provide the input for this phase. The architecture, hardware, functions, and information requirements shape the design of the database. In this phase, the actual detailed database design is completed. The design may encompass the writing of a customized database architecture or merely the customization of a licensed or off-the-shelf software package. Tests of all functions occur during this phase. Modifications are made as necessary to meet the processing and marketing objectives.

7. *Database Building.* During this phase the information is loaded into the database. Final tests are conducted prior to the system's being released. Any further modifications are made during this time.

8. *Maintenance.* The value of a database is determined by two factors — the information contained on the database and the accessibility of the information. Information and accessibility are of equal importance.

For the information to be truly valuable, it must reflect the current environment. To maintain current information, the ongoing database marketing plan should include two methods for updating information. The first involves two of the processes described in the data cleaning phase of the database build. Addresses should be updated at a minimum on an annual basis. To supplement NCOA, you should consider requesting address corrections on all mailings. The cost of address corrections should be evaluated against the benefit. Addresses will need to be updated to meet changes in postal areas, such as zip codes and carrier routes.

The population of your database is not static. You will be adding and deleting members. Information will be updated through response to programs. The second area of maintenance accomplishes this through what are most commonly called adds and updates. An add is the process of adding new customers to the database. An update is the process of updating some part of an already existing customer record.

In an add, all steps of the cleaning process should be undertaken. This process is similar to preparing the original names, addresses, and information for the database. You will need to make sure the "new" customer is not already on the database, a duplicate, and the data will need to be normalized to fit the database structure.

In an update, you are adding some information to an already existing customer record. The first step is to prepare the information for insertion in the database. If it is an address change, the address will need to be standardized to meet postal standards. If the information is sales, demographic, or lifestyle, the codes will need to be reviewed to determine if they match those already on the database. The second step is to locate the current record on the database and append or change the appropriate information.

Another type of update is aging. This update involves information based on time. For example, if age is a critical factor in your targeting, you would want to update a customer's age annually. Another example is recency, the time since a past purchase. To be able to update your customer information, you need a source for that information. The sales information can be captured through coupon response, rebates, refunds, or sales transactions. The competitive set, demographic, and lifestyle data may require what is called a rescreen. A rescreen involves a questionnaire or screener that is completed by the customer answering such questions as brands purchased on a regular basis, brands used most often, frequency of purchase, and demographics/pyschographics. The timing of the rescreens is dictated by how dynamic your business environment is and how critical these variables are to the performance of the database.

CO-OP ADVERTISING

Cooperative or co-op advertising is the sharing of advertising costs between mutually interested businesses, usually retailers and their suppliers.

To understand co-op's role in advertising and its importance in the sale of goods and services, you must examine those elements that make up a co-op advertising program and the motivation behind them, beginning with the manufacturer-retailer relationship. Most co-op dollars are spent within this vertical chain of production, distribution, and sales. The vertical co-op chain starts when a manufacturer establishes a program, either at the retail or wholesale level, to support local advertising and sales promotion by offering to pay part, or even all, of the cost. As part of this support, the manufacturer also may provide material for use in the retailer's advertising or sales promotion programs. The co-op support is not unconditional. There are usually extensive rules with the co-op offer to be sure that the retailer or wholesaler actually advertises or promotes the manufacturer's products.

A manufacturer's conventional advertising is a responsibility of its advertising department. Media used, timing, and content are under complete control. The manufacturer's co-op advertising is under the control of a customer, the retailer, who usually decides on timing, media used, and advertising content, within the restrictions of the manufacturer's co-op policy. In addition, the retailer's advertising will usually have a feature lacking in the manufacturer's advertising: price and where to buy.

Manufacturers who run conventional advertising campaigns in the mass media (television, radio, newspapers, magazines) are pre-selling to create demand. Their intent is to make customers go to retail stores to look for the advertised products. Such advertising does not identify specific places where the products are sold and gives pricing only in the familiar "suggested retail" form. Manufacturers' advertising may also be intended to create consumer demand so retailers will want to sell the advertised products.

Since co-op advertising runs at the level where products are being sold, its intent is to attract customers into specific stores by identifying products with prices and a retail location. Those products have already been purchased by the retail store, and may or may not have been "presold" by the manufacturers' advertising.

Co-op and the Law

When a manufacturer offers co-op funds or assistance to a retailer, our unique antitrust laws become involved. Those laws started with the Sherman Act of 1890, a move to break up the cartels and trusts that controlled the economy of that period. There were loopholes in the Sherman Act that were closed by the Clayton Act of 1914. But the Clayton Act overlooked one very large loophole: advertising and promotional allowances. During the 1920s big retailers used that loophole to gain price advantages from their suppliers and stifle competition from smaller stores. The worst offenders in this area were the grocery chains, with the A&P being the most aggressive and visible offender. In 1936 the Robinson-Patman Act passed, specifically prohibiting discriminatory practices when using promotional allowances in the sale of commodities in interstate commerce. The laws do not apply to intrastate commerce or to the sale of anything but commodities. Those three pieces of legislation are known as our "antitrust laws." They are intended to prevent discriminatory pricing and price fixing and to maintain open and competitive free trade. Since the provision of co-op money for advertising and promotion reduces advertising and promotion expense, it affects the price at which a product sells at retail. That is why the antitrust laws regulate co-op advertising and all promotional allowances.

In 1969, a landmark ruling by the U.S. Supreme Court ordered the Federal Trade Commission to lay down guidelines for the use of advertising and promotional allowances. Those guidelines, known as the "Meyer Guides," define the rules of co-op advertising. Anyone involved in the use of co-op and promotional allowances should have a copy of these guides, which can be obtained from the Federal Trade Commission.

As a result of the antitrust laws and the court decision, co-op advertising and promotional allowances are almost universal in our marketing system. The laws have helped in assuring that co-op funds are available to all retail outlets that sell products whose manufacturers offer co-op and in making that co-op proportionally equal to the co-op given to other competing retail customers. In other free market economies, where there are no such laws, co-op is still offered on an arbitrary and unfair basis.

Manufacturers' Use of Co-op

A general insight into exactly why manufacturers use co-op is demonstrated by the following list of the reasons they give when asked about the purpose of their co-op programs:

- Building sales for the most profitable product line
- Supporting the most profitable product line
- Building sales for a weaker product line
- Introducing a new product
- Meeting competitors' efforts
- Leveling out peaks and valleys of demand by timing of program
- Acceding to requests of retailers, wholesalers, distributors, and others
- Building sales in a particular region
- Heightening brand awareness

- Controlling local ad content
- Stretching advertising budgets

Most suppliers offering co-op do so for one or more of these specific reasons. On the average, however, fewer than half have systems in place with which to measure the effectiveness of their co-op programs in accomplishing their stated goals.

Retailer Goals in Co-op Advertising

Here are some statements often made by retailers when asked how they feel about co-op advertising:

Co-op is too much trouble. I wouldn't use it if it weren't for the money.

I love it!

Co-op is a curse; stores are too dependent on the money, advertising only the merchandise that comes with the largest number of co-op dollars.

Viewpoints as divergent as these are not uncommon when talking about co-op to anyone in retailing. The first opinion, however, reflects the essence of co-op at the retailer level — money to fund advertising. The use of that money may be as variable as the world of retailing itself, but it forms part of the two basic reasons why most retailers want co-op: getting money to fund advertising and to extend store promotion budgets and getting help with the creation and expansion of store advertising programs. Within those two frameworks — funding and promotional assistance — co-op must fit the basic needs of retail advertising. These common goals include the following:

1. Creative and timely advertising programs that will enhance the image of the stores involved and bring customer traffic into those stores.
2. Advertising of products that are needed and wanted in the store's market area at prices that are competitive and attractive to consumers.
3. Linking of stores to brand name products, frequently through advertising and promotional programs that coincide with national or regional promotions on the part of the vendors.

Except to exclusive dealerships, brand recognition is least important to the retailer. Good retail advertising is structured on offering merchandise that people want to buy, not on co-op dollars. Retailers who carry a variety of merchandise may find it impossible to use all the co-op available from their many suppliers, choosing to advertise only products they feel will produce traffic in their stores.

The Wholesaler's Place in the Co-op Chain

In the vertical chain of co-op advertising that links the manufacturer to the retailer, there is quite frequently a middleman: the wholesaler or distributor. The presence of the wholesaler can have varying degrees of influence on the co-op arrangement, depending on the way in which a manufacturer establishes a co-op program.

Wholesalers and distributors, when handling a particular product line, may have exclusive sales territories. Some manufacturers may also sell their products directly to larger retailers within their distributors' sales territories. In other cases, the types of products sold may not lend themselves to exclusive distributorships and are available to the market through several wholesalers with overlapping sales territories. These different methods of distribution influence how co-op advertising reaches the retailer by way of a wholesaler.

PRODUCT LICENSING AND TIE-INS

Both retail licensing (the purchase of the rights to a legally protected name, logo, design, or likeness for use on an item to be sold for profit) and promotional tie-ins (licensing agreements for an advertising or promotional use) have grown exponentially over the last decade. Retail sales of licensed products in North America, for example, have tripled from a total of $20.6 billion in 1982 to $62.2 billion in 1992, according to figures compiled by *The Licensing Letter.* Since 1990, growth has leveled off; the market for licensed products has matured after close to 15 years of enormous growth. In addition, a recession adversely affected retailing in the early 1990s.

Still, a $60 billion-plus business is significant, and product licensing has become recognized as an effective way for an owner of a legally protected name, graphic, or likeness (a property) to earn significant revenue. A manufacturer who associates with a particular property (the licensee) stands to increase awareness of its products without having to build a brand from scratch. Simply being linked with a licensed property is not in itself enough to guarantee increased sales, of course. But licensing, as part of a total marketing strategy, can be a successful sales tool if the fit between product and property is a logical one.

Product Licensing

The main players of any licensing agreement are the *licensor* (the property owner) and the *licensee* (the purchaser of the rights to the property). The *property* is the trademarked or copyrighted entity, be it a character, design, name, logo, sports league or team, event, or likeness. In some cases, a *licensing agent* will also be involved. The agent acts on behalf of the licensor in seeking appropriate licensees, negotiating contracts, and overseeing the licensing program. *Manufacturers' representatives* sometimes act on behalf of licensees in seeking appropriate licensed properties for their products.

The types of properties licensed out for other products fall into 10 major categories:

- **Art**, which includes copyrighted designs and fine art for use on a wide range of products;
- **Celebrities and estates**, which include the likenesses and names of famous people such as James Dean, Marilyn Monroe, Laurel & Hardy, and many others;
- **Designer names**, particularly in fashion and home furnishings, such as Gloria Vanderbilt, Ralph Lauren, Donna Karan, and Bob Timberlake;
- **Entertainment and character properties**, which comprise films, television, classic cartoon characters, and comic book superheroes;
- **Music and musical artists**, including Elvis Presley, New Kids On The Block, and the Grateful Dead;
- **Nonprofit organizations**, such as the World Wildlife Fund and other environmental groups, relief organizations including CARE, medical research and money-raising organizations;
- **Publishing**, which includes book characters such as Waldo from the *Where's Waldo?* series, or Babar the elephant, as well as magazines (*Playboy, Cosmopolitan*) and book titles (*The Baby-Sitter's Club*);
- **Sports**, incorporating all four major leagues and colleges, as well as other sports entities such as the Olympics, NASCAR auto racing, soccer, wrestling, and so forth;
- **Trademarks and corporate brands**, from all areas, especially apparel brands (J.G. Hook), footwear (Converse), automotive trademarks (Jeep, Harley-Davidson), and food and beverage brands (Betty Crocker, Coca-Cola, Budweiser); and
- **Toys and games**, that license out into other products, such as Barbie, LEGO, G.I. Joe, Transformers, Hot Wheels, and videogame characters such as Super Mario Brothers and Sonic the Hedgehog.

Many manufacturing companies find that both licensing in (that is, purchasing rights to a property for one of their products) and licensing out (selling the rights to their own properties) fit into their strategy; thus, they act as licensors and licensees. For example, the toy manufacturer Mattel oversees licensing programs based on its own properties, Barbie and Hot Wheels, extending to apparel, accessories, and many other products. Meanwhile, they also manufacture toys under license from other companies, such as plush toys based on Walt Disney animated films, fashion dolls based on the television show *Beverly Hills 90210,* and Nickelodeon brand games and activity toys.

Promotional Tie-ins

A promotional tie-in is typically a licensing agreement for the use of a property that is promotional in nature (as opposed to permitting the creation of a product for sale). Consequently, since there is no sales figure upon which to base a royalty, the core element of payment is a flat fee, with other additional costs added on as applicable. The cost structures of certain tie-ins can become quite complicated, depending on the nature of the promotion, and in many cases the amount of the flat fee itself is hidden among all the other elements of payment.

A tie-in can be as simple as the use of a character in a print ad. On the other hand, it can be as complicated as a multi-tier, multi-partner promotion involving premiums, advertising in various channels, rebates, packaged goods promotions, sweepstakes and contests involving mail-ins, and interactive phone technology — all targeting both consumers and the trade (retailers or distributors). Tie-ins can involve sports personalities and events, nonprofit entities, or entertainment properties. Timing is variable as well; a film tie-in, for example, can coincide with theatrical release, video release, or subsequent broadcast and cable airings.

For licensors, tie-ins serve the purpose of generating awareness for their properties, thus advertising the event or entity itself (as well as related products made by licensees, if any). Tie-ins also enable the property to become known in channels where it would normally not be advertised. Filmgoers traditionally become aware of new films through print or broadcast advertising or through in-theater trailers, for example, but a tie-in allows the message to get to the consumer in other outlets, such as grocery stores and fast food restaurants. Last, but certainly not least, tie-ins are lucrative for licensors. The income earned through tie-ins can be as important a factor for them as the marketing benefits, depending on the property.

Virtually any sales promotion technique can be used in a tie-in with a nonprofit, sports, or entertainment entity. The main element of the tie-in is the licensed property, so the promotion will focus on that. A major use for the property itself is using its likeness or logo in advertising — for example, television, print, newspaper inserts — or on packaging. In addition, personal appearances by a film or sports star or a costumed character at retail outlets, local promotional events, press functions, and so forth, are also often included as tie-in components. And contest prizes can involve meeting key personalities associated with the property, seeing behind-the-scenes action such as a locker room or film set, or attending an event such as a film opening, a concert, or a sports event.

Simply associating with a popular property is not enough to effectively differentiate a product or brand from its competitors; thought and creativity need to go into tie-ins and product licensing relationships in order to make them successful. Rather than an automatic way to sell merchandise, licensing and tie-ins are now recognized as effective marketing tools, used in conjunction with the rest of a company's marketing strategy.

As a result, not only "hit" properties are used for tie-ins and licensing. The fit between the property and its licensees and tie-in partners is more important than the overall popularity of the property. There are times when companies will successfully tie in with the high-profile "hits"—they still generate excitement and widespread, short-term awareness. But different companies have different marketing needs, and there are many properties out there that can fit the bill, depending on a marketer's specific goals.

Licensing and tie-ins should be part of a company's overall marketing strategy, not the only facet of that strategy. Risks should be minimized as much as possible (although marketers should be aware that most licensing and tie-in deals are inherently risky). And all properties should be considered — not just the obvious hot entertainment properties, but smaller properties, long-term classics, trademarks, nonprofits, sports outside of the major sports leagues, and so forth.

Flexibility and trust among the partners are key to a successful relationship. Those two elements—as well as open communication among all players—will help allow the creation of a unique tie-in, will minimize risks, and will enable the partners to adapt to unforeseen contingencies.

EVENT MARKETING— IT'S NOT THE EVENT THAT MATTERS

Event marketing is not really a new idea. Rather, it is the updated use of very sound marketing and promotional disciplines that have been molded to fit today's marketplace. To really understand why events have become such a successful promotional tool, consider what they offer:

- An exciting, memorable, often entertaining environment, exclusively available to the sponsor and free from competitive clutter and distractions;
- A completely captive and receptive audience, who is often quite demographically homogeneous and thus desirable from a targeting point of view;
- An opportunity to satisfy all the key players in the marketing arena, including the consumer, the trade, and the media, simply by capitalizing on and leveraging the event's popularity; and
- A tool that can enhance a brand's image and shift some marketing clout and power back into the hands of the manufacturer once again.

Events offer what no other medium today can, and in many respects, events offer the best of what radio, television, and advertising used to offer, only in today's marketplace.

What Is an Event?

The fundamental notion behind an event sponsorship is that a sponsor/marketer associates with an event property — entertainers, sports, Olympics, Superbowl, etc. — and "trades off" on the popularity of that event to fulfill its marketing objectives. Sponsownership™, a concept trademarked in the early 1980s, is a sponsorship that is owned by the sponsor. This ownership not only allows sponsors/marketers to utilize and leverage the event to achieve their marketing objectives, it also allows them to take in revenues generated by the event itself (ticket sales, merchandise sales). It allows marketers to build and control their own events for years to come, thus building equity and longevity into their own marketing programs. Because of their effectiveness and profitability, sponsownerships are sure to become the marketing avenue of choice for sponsors over the next few years.

It all starts with the marketer's/sponsor's objectives. Because event marketing is multidimensional, it can simultaneously deliver multiple objectives. Therefore, all objectives must be identified. For example, what objectives might event marketing accomplish for a laundry detergent?

- Trial and incremental sales
- Trade support, displays, features, promotional pricing, incremental case orders
- Reaching women ages 25 to 49
- Key selling or competitive timing
- Brand image and awareness
- Publicity
- Easy sell-in for the sales force
- Sales force enthusiasm
- Trade relations building
- Cost-effectiveness
- Easy/turnkey execution

Once marketers/sponsors have carefully identified all the objectives they wish to achieve, the criteria by which the success of the program are measured must be determined. While some may question whether event marketing results are, in fact, measurable, the reality is that events provide more measurable results than most other advertising media and promotion techniques.

The key and "soul" to successful event marketing is to remember the following: *Marketers achieve their objectives through event marketing by achieving the objectives of others. Marketers' success depends on influencing the trade, the consumer, their sales force, and the media to do their bidding.* No other medium has the direct ability to allow all who are important to a marketer's goals to achieve those goals simultaneously. Therefore, after identifying the objectives (manufacturer/sponsor), you must look at the objectives of the other players who will be affected by the event promotion.

This diagram may also be expanded to include other "players" (depending on the manufacturer/sponsor) such as franchisees, bottlers, promoters, and brokers.

Executing an Event

Execution is the most important element in event marketing and probably in every other marketing venture. A big idea is just that, an idea. To bring it to life and to make it work takes flawless execution and implementation.

To properly execute a successful event marketing program takes a lot of experience, much planning, proven systems for implementation, and the realization that it's not the obvious things that will get in the way of success. Rather, the small, almost unknown or unseen elements will cause an event to falter.

To be a successful event marketer, agency, or sponsor takes a talent for execution that cannot be taught anywhere. Successful execution takes experience, an unbelievable amount of diplomacy, and an ability to respond quickly to unforeseen problems when they occur. All the planning and focus on detail are critical, but so is the ability to react and to react quickly.

Measurement

Not only can an event's success be measured, but also the results can be measured better and more accurately than with almost any other medium today. Since the exact promotional periods of the event promotion are known, event success can be directly measured:

By Account:
- Case sales
- Display penetration
- Shipments
- Features
- Price reductions
- Post-event surveys

By Intangibles:
- Image/awareness
- Product positioning
- Trade relationship building
- Field enthusiasm

By Media:
- PR (conversion)
- Leveraged (affidavits)

By Consumer:
- Scanner detail
- Redemption
- Nielsen (market share)
- Exit polls/intercepts

There also exist "bonuses" to event marketing that are harder to measure directly but are certainly part of its success. These bonuses/elements include:

- **Trade relationship building** — especially after a successful program with a fun personal backstage party visit
- **Sales force morale** — giving them the upper hand for once and making them feel good about their jobs
- **Brand imaging and awareness** — through the multitudes of media and promotions and the association with the event or star

One event can deliver all of the above; it is doubtful that a television commercial could do the same.

SPECIALTY PROMOTIONS

When Ohio newspaper publisher Jasper Meek found in 1880 that revenues from printing ads on schoolbook bags and horse blankets were enough to successfully operate a stand-alone business, he drew numerous imitators and, in effect, launched what has since become a $5.5 billion industry.

In the early days, the ad-imprinted merchandise — usually made of cloth, paper, wood, glass, or leather — was thought of as "reminder" or "goodwill" advertising. Those functions are still important. However, the inventory of applications has proliferated enormously.

Under the "promotional products" umbrella we find ad specialties, business gifts, premiums, awards, prizes, and commemoratives. The fact that an item, such as a desk paperweight, can be used as any of these promotional products, tempts one to ignore some significant distinctions.

Ad specialties are always imprinted with an advertiser's identification or message, and they are given free.

Business gifts are also given free. They cost more than some ad specialties, and normally they don't carry an imprint. Nowadays, however, there seem to be more business gifts with the donor's logo subtly inscribed.

Premiums are the true incentives because the receiver needs to do something to get them. Sometimes imprinted, but usually not, premiums are distinguished from ad specialties by the fact that they are earned by making a purchase, a deposit (in a bank), or a financial contribution.

Awards, too, are earned by performance or simply by hanging onto the job long enough to be honored for retiring gracefully.

Strengths and Weaknesses

Ad specialties are a perfect way to keep a company's name in front of its prospects, provided, of course, that an item has been selected that is useful to the prospect and is likely to be retained. The ability to give a company a continuous presence with buyers is an important attribute of ad specialties, but there are other advantages as well, such as the following:

- **Long-lasting exposure** that produces high recall.
- **Targetability** to narrowly defined audiences.
- **Budget flexibility**
- **Goodwill**
- **Unobtrusiveness**
- **Compatibility with other media**

Tactics

Skillful promotional products distributors are as much tacticians as they are purveyors of imprinted merchandise. They often use tactics related either to the product itself or to the psychology of consumer behavior. Designed to motivate or excite, these tactics are many and varied.

- **Contingent fulfillment.** Here the target audience receives part of an ad specialty — maybe a pair of sunglass lenses without the frames or a single glove. They get the other part — the one that makes the item work or completes a pair — only when they respond in the manner the marketer desires.
- **Peer approval.** A helmet adorned with performance decals does more than give a football lineman an opportunity to crow about the number of running backs he's leveled. Such symbols motivate teammates to earn their own insignia that infer they belong in the company of star performers. So, too, awards and other recognition devices drive salespeople to either show them who's best or at least justify their position on the payroll.
- **Status conferral.** A riverfront restaurant in Virginia offers ID cards to its best customers, making them feel special, which they are. Flashing the cards to the maitre d', they get preferred seating and don't have to bother with long waiting lines. They also receive T-shirts, sunglasses, and other ad specialties from waiters serving their tables. Club privileges are much sweeter when they create envy.
- **Curiosity arousal.** Arousing curiosity goes beyond mere teasing. The target audience needs to ask, "What is it?," and be willing to find out. For instance, a bank in Spokane, Washington, scheduled a grand opening for a new branch. Prospective depositors were mailed an unrecognizable plastic disk and were told they could find out what it

was — and get the part that made it a useful appliance — by attending the open house. Several hundred did, and they found out that the mailed enticement was the top to a tape dispenser.

• **Collector appeal.** From antiques to baseball cards, the pervasiveness of collector mania is evident in the number of newspaper columns, magazines, and trading shows devoted to this special interest. There is a marketing parallel, too. One National Basketball Association team provides an example. As an attendance builder, a set of coins was struck with likenesses of the team players. For many fans, the first one they were given was sufficient bait to draw them to the next dozen or so home games to acquire the complete set.

• **Influencing the influencers.** Perhaps no group influences purchase decisions more than children, a perception that led to placing the first premium in a cereal box. Promotional products formed the enticement of the "Kids Go HoJo Fan Club" campaign in which children, ages 3 to 12, of guests at any Howard Johnson property received free "fun packs." The contents included imprinted crayons, coloring/activity books, decals, and postcards. And tactics that work with children can also work with adults.

• **Authentication.** In this case, the specially crafted promotional product becomes attention-getting memorabilia because it is actually a piece of the real thing. For its "Dodger Diamond Dust" campaign tying into the 25th anniversary of Dodger Stadium, a cable TV service scooped up dirt from the L.A. team's infield and it authenticated, poly-bagged, and packaged the dirt in collectible cans. An accompanying romance curl described the inaugural day in 1962 when "the dust of a freshly groomed diamond was kicked up for the first time." To add excitement, genuine diamonds were inserted in randomly selected cans.

TRADE PROMOTION

The practice of offering rewards in order to induce specific kinds of actions by the distribution channel for a packaged goods product is generally known as trade marketing or trade promotion. The practice has evolved over the past quarter-century into an extremely important class of marketing tool.

If your responsibilities are in sales planning, sales promotion, or brand management, you'll want to know how to employ trade marketing for maximum effectiveness in both the short and long term. Your success will probably depend upon it. Because trade marketing has become such a large portion of most marketers' budgets, the amount of time spent planning, discussing, and defining trade marketing programs has mushroomed.

The Techniques of Trade Marketing: Purchase Incentives

There are two primary classes of trade marketing techniques: purchase incentives and performance allowances.

Purchase incentives are all of the forms of payment offered to the distributors of packaged goods products, which are designed to cause initial purchase, restocking, or increased inventory of the product. The following are among the purchase incentive techniques of trade marketing:
1. Slotting allowances
2. Off-invoice purchase allowances
3. Dating
4. Free goods

This class of techniques has seen explosive growth in recent years. It's this class in which the shift in power from marketer to retailer has been so strongly reflected. Retailers collectively have been extremely successful in obtaining ever growing amounts and forms of purchase incentives.

To illustrate the dramatic shift, one of America's largest and most successful food marketers has seen an overall net shift in marketing spending from 30 percent trade/70 percent consumer focus 20 years ago, to 70 percent trade/30 percent consumer focus currently.

Performance Allowances

Performance allowances are all of the forms of payment offered to distributors of a product, which are designed to induce an action by the distributor that increases the rate of sale of the product to the final consumer. Key activities that occur in the distribution channel and positively affect the rate of sale of a product to the consumer include the following:
1. Temporary price reduction
2. Second location or off-shelf display
3. Expanded shelf space
4. Demonstrating or sampling product in store
5. Advertising the product under the store's name to the consumer

Marketers typically offer performance allowances to induce some or all of these activities on their products. These specific types of performance allowances include the following:
1. Price reduction allowance
2. Display/merchandising allowance
3. Advertising allowance
4. Count/recount allowance

A marketer wishing to use performance allowances has many hurdles to overcome. First and foremost, retailers generally resist billback offers because too much administrative time is used qualifying and collecting and because they want additional flexibility. Second, retailers have the benefit of the balance of power to use to enforce more favorable terms, and that enables the request for less restrictive kinds of offers to have more clout. Third, the marketer's own sales force resists performance allowances because of the extra time it takes to administer the contracts and because of the retailer resistance, which limits their success.

The fact that marketers still do use performance allowance offers indicates how much value comes from giving them, in spite of all these difficulties. A general rule today is that the program for which performance allowances are offered should be an exceptionally strong one with obvious retailer benefits to offset the negatives of the offer.

The Dilemma

Here is the dilemma you will face if you're considering what type of trade marketing effort to propose for your products. Carefully constructed trade marketing efforts, which are executed with precision and discipline, usually meet or exceed objectives. That's good, right? Initially yes, but the dilemma is how to meet or exceed those results in the next quarter or annual period.

This dilemma exists and becomes increasingly bigger over time because of the following rationale. Since trade marketing by itself primarily attracts consumers by means of the positive effects of extra in-store merchandising and sale pricing, most marketers find it is impossible to meet or exceed the sales volume of the first trade marketing program without repeating the trade marketing offer that fueled the earlier success.

In fact, since most trade marketing efforts of equal value do slightly less well the second time around, the temptation is to enrich the program to achieve sales goals. At this point, the marketer is well along on a path to marketing that is increasingly weighted toward trade marketing. This is the exact path that most packaged goods marketers have followed over the past 15 years.

The Better Way

The better way is to utilize trade marketing as part of a balanced overall program of marketing, with sufficient funding for brand franchise-building activities — for example, brand-equity-focused advertising, trial-generating consumer promotion, product innovation. This is easy to say, but it's very hard to do, especially if you're already spending heavily on trade marketing.

A number of leading packaged goods marketers today are embarking on an effort to alter the balance to a more favorable consumer-to-trade ratio by significantly reducing the overall level of allowances and at the same time reducing the everyday cost of the product to the retailer and the consumer.

This effort has acquired a name: EDLP (everyday low pricing) or value-pricing. This effort has quickly drawn much media attention and significant retailer resistance. Retailers are very concerned about seeing a major revenue source reduced, and trade marketing funds are a major revenue source. In fact, the trade marketing expenditures of the top two packaged goods marketers, Kraft General Foods and Procter & Gamble, recently exceeded the total profits of the 40 largest food chains.

What will it take to make the reinvestment in brand-building consumer marketing — that marketers need — and at the same time, address the retailers' need for building customer loyalty and traffic and for maintaining high levels and advertising awareness of their stores? It will take a concerted effort by marketers to create and implement programs that:

1. Reach consumers with brand-building messages,
2. Identify individual retailers and their special merchandising,
3. Do both at the same time.

The best news is that this type of approach has been tried with major success by a few leading marketers. This is how it's been done.

First, the marketer decides how best to attract the consumer to his product with positioning and consumer benefits, traditional advertising tools. Then, the marketer creates and runs the advertising for the consumer to see. But rather than creating the advertising and then placing it in the traditional manner, the marketer goes to the retailer, shows the advertising and shows how it will look with each retailer integrated into the advertising. The marketer obtains the retailer's commitment to specially merchandise the product at a time of the retailer's choosing, and then the marketer schedules advertising to run that tells the consumer both about the product and about the retailer's special merchandising in the same ad.

The marketer does this for each retailer on a proportionately equal basis. The net result is a total amount of advertising that is effective in achieving share of voice for the product. In addition, all of the advertising directs the consumer to a specific retailer who has special merchandising on the product at that time; consequently, advertising and merchandising work together to generate incremental results for both the marketer and the retailer.

Since the advertising is brand-benefit based, it attracts consumers who are interested in the product because of its benefits, not because it is cheap. Since the advertising is also retailer-specific, it attracts the consumer to a store with strong brand visibility for the product. So the retailer who provides special merchandising gets extra sales with less emphasis on deep-cut pricing.

For the marketer, the best news is that dollars previously deployed for wasteful levels of couponing and/or too-frequent trade deals can now be rechanneled to reward both the retailer and the marketer with significantly higher sales and better long-term prospects.

A major additional benefit is that marketers can create and implement brand-reinforcing consumer promotion programs, which will provide big sales volume increases at the same time. This is possible because the program is advertised with effective message, reach, and frequency to the target audience, and with the news of which specific retailer has special merchandising of the event.

CONCLUSION

Promotion is an important part of the marketing mix for most companies. As an advertising professional, you may find yourself running events, coordinating in-store sampling, or dealing with coupons. These are just some of the techniques to get product into the hands of potential customers. Used effectively, you'll find promotion and advertising create a synergy that moves product through the marketing pipeline at hyperspeed.

REFERENCES

Chapter 4, Sales Promotion Techniques includes material provided by the following authors.

Origins of Promotion
Kerry Smith
Editor and Publisher, *PROMO Magazine*

Sampling
Dan Ailloni-Charas
Chairman and CEO, Stratmar Systems

Couponing
Tamara Brezen Block,
President, Block Research, Inc.

Premiums, Refunds, and Promotion Fulfillment
Don Roux
President and CEO, Roux Marketing Services, Inc.

Sweepstakes, Games, and Contests
Don Jagoda
President, Don Jagoda Associates

Continuity Promotions
James Feldman
President, James Feldman Associates

Direct Response
Larry Tucker
President, Larry Tucker, Inc.

Database Marketing
Connie Kennedy
Vice President, Targetbase Marketing

Co-Op Advertising
Neil L. Fraser
President, Fraser Advertising

Product Licensing and Tie-Ins
Karen Raugust
Editor, *The Licensing Letter*

Event Marketing — It's Not the Event that Matters
Paul Stanley
President and Creative Director, PS Productions, Inc.

Specialty Promotions
Richard G. Ebel
Director of Marketing Communications
Promotional Products Association International (PPAI)

Trade Promotion
James Kunze
Executive Vice President and General Manager
J. Brown Advertising

Robert Cannell is an associate professor in the School of Communication at Roosevelt University in Chicago where he has taught integrated marketing communications in a graduate program since 1994.

Before teaching, he worked in advertising as a copywriter and creative director, including 19 years at the Marsteller agency. Following that, he was senior vice president and chief creative officer with the Stern Walters/Earle Ludgin agency; and has headed his own creative services and consulting firm, Robert Cannell, Inc., since 1985.

He has developed campaigns for a variety of clients, including Sears, Roebuck & Co.; Spiegel; Lanier Business Products; Fort Howard Paper; Ameritech Yellow Pages; National Safety Council; National Association of Realtors; and the American Hospital Association.

Cannell's work has been recognized with a number of creative awards, including CLIO, ADDY, EFFIE, and BPAA PRO COMM. In addition, he has served as a judge on a number of awards programs.

Chapter 5

PERSUASIVE COPYWRITING
GETTING YOUR WORDS WORTH

Lemonade: 10¢. Real good for thirsty people.

As a kid, did you ever sell cold drinks on a sweltering summer day? Or did you ever say 389 times: "Would you like to buy some candy? It's for our Little League team"?

You didn't realize it at the time but that's when you discovered copywriting. It is, after all, simply composing the right thoughts and words to deliver a persuasive message.

When those few words, however, go on billboards, into television commercials, or onto the pages of slick magazines, we elevate the importance of the copywriter's craft. Words such as Nike's "Just Do It" or United's "Fly The Friendly Skies" go to market with millions of dollars behind them. Those three or four words, and how they are "packaged" as communications, carry huge responsibility in the battles being fought for brand image and share of market.

But most advertising copy is not served up as slogans on 30-second national TV spots or the glossy pages of *People* magazine. Consider the countless words of copy in all the catalogs we receive, brochures from banks; flyers from fast food eateries; mailers, coupons, premiums, posters, and packaging; all the way to refrigerator magnets and bumper stickers.

Marketing's appetite for sales-winning copy, in all media forms, is insatiable and will continue to grow with burgeoning global markets and growing demand for goods and services.

That's good news for copywriters. But more does not equate to more effective advertising. What makes advertising copy effective? Why do some messages get talked about and trigger action while others simply float past us like so many wisps on the wind?

FOR A HAPPY ENDING, BEGIN WITH SMART STRATEGY

A copywriter's first concern, together with others on the marketing team, is to set the right strategy. Here's a suggested planning outline for setting creative strategy:

1. Product Description (What is the uniqueness or advantage?)
2. Personality (What human traits could be used to describe the product?)
3. Prospect Definition (Who are the best prospects? And why?)
4. Competition (Whom will you take business from? Or what behavior will you change?)
5. Obstacle to the Sale (Why will prospects *not* want to buy? The resistance factor.)
6. Message Objective (Convince prospects that...)

7. Reward (What end benefit will customers feel from using the product?)

Remember these seven ingredients in the recipe for creative strategy and you will have a valuable checklist to work with before you start writing. Take a closer look at each issue:

Defining the Product and Its Personality

First comes product information. What are the essential facts? What uniqueness does the product offer? What need does it fulfill? How is it positioned? SnackWell's Cookies are fat-free (or reduced-fat). Volvos are designed for safety. Timberland boots survive the challenging elements.

Ask another important question: What personality should your product (or company) project to prospective buyers?

Financial marketers, for example, want to convey images of stability and security. Athletic shoes ride the coattails of athlete celebrities, with messages emulating the stars' confidence, determination, boldness, and, sometimes, irreverence.

Cake-mix marketers traditionally relate the product to strong images of moms, kitchens, and childhood memories such as licking the bowl. And fast-food chains connect to the enjoyable experience of eating out with friends and family.

> *"Our best work has always begun with a marketing solution, not a creative solution. The ads flowed from the strategy, not the strategy from the ads."*
>
> — Jay Chiat,
> co-founder of Chiat/Day
> advertising agency[1]

Defining Your Target

How about target audience or prospect definition? Who are the best prospects for the product and why are these particular people more likely to buy? Leading brands of beer direct their messages toward the largest beer-drinking market segment, blue-collar men. Graphic designers are top prospects for Apple Computer because Macintosh offers perceived advantages in graphics applications. Luxury cars, lawn care services, and mutual fund investments are targeted to prospects living in high-income zip codes.

Next, never overlook, or underestimate, the competition. Whom will you be taking business away from? Or, what behavior in prospects do you seek to change?

A market is like a pie to be divided. There is only so much to share. What portion will you get? If the market is static (no growth) you can only gain share by taking from others. If the market is expanding, you can win the incremental growth while competitors remain static.

If your product creates a new market, your objective will be to change behavior. For instance, the first facsimile machines changed behavior when users switched from mail and messenger services to communicating by fax.

"Good copy means hard work. I am not a facile writer. Writing that really communicates requires piercing insights into the heads and minds of your audience. Getting those insights is even harder than writing."
— Peter Geer,
co-founder of Geer DuBois, Inc.
advertising agency[1]

Overcoming Obstacles

In public service campaigns, ads strive to change potentially harmful behavior such as drunk driving, smoking, or neglecting health check-ups (see Timberland/City Year public service ad, Exhibit 5.1).

What is the obstacle to the sale of your product? Or the behavior change you seek? You cannot simply assume that presenting the facts will compel the target audience to take action. Potential buyers have to be convinced, their resistance worn down, their loyalties to others put aside. A carefully identified obstacle leads to a well-focused message objective.

Prospects for Chivas Regal Scotch might resist the premium price. In that case the message objective might read: Convince Scotch drinkers that Chivas Regal smoothness and flavor transcend concerns for economy. Or this: Convince holiday shoppers that giving Chivas Regal as a gift makes the recipient feel highly valued and appreciated.

Vacationers targeted by a cruise line might resist simply because they fear being too confined on a ship. Message objective: Persuade vacationers that the on-board dining rooms, casinos, health clubs, and open decks make your cruise ship a spacious resort at sea with many options for fun and relaxation.

"Content is critical—the wrong message to the right person obviously won't work. But content alone isn't enough. You wouldn't write a love letter in the same tone and style as a letter to your uncle. Different products and audiences demand different styles. Tone and style can create a personality that will reach, touch and move your readers.... Effective copy is simple, but not simplistic: intelligent but not obtuse; interesting but not frivolous.... Positioning lines? Slogans in new clothes; narcissism in print. They seldom speak to customer needs."
—James J. Johnston,
co-founder of Jim Johnston Advertising
and the Johnston & Johnston Group[1]

EXHIBIT 5.1 TIMBERLAND/CITY YEAR (MAGAZINE AD)

Using its product in a figurative sense, Timberland takes its social responsibility seriously on behalf of City Year, the urban peace corps. The big-type headline commands the reader to act, leaving no doubt about message intent.

Setting a Reward

And finally: What Reward (end benefit) should the user of your product feel from using it? The range of human emotions presents many options that can be incorporated into your message. The right emotion gives persuasive power far beyond the basic presentation of facts. It is emotion that motivates behavior.

In a well-publicized example from the automotive category, General Motors' Saturn advertising has communicated a special kind of bonding Saturn drivers feel with their cars and the company itself — a sense of loyalty that motivated thousands of Saturn owners to drive to an owners' rally held at the company's headquarters in Tennessee in the summer of 1994.

Apparel marketers want us to feel "cool" wearing Levi's, "successful" wearing Liz Claiborne, "daring" wearing Calvin Klein.

> *"How you dress your sales force is very important.*
> *So is how you dress your advertising. We call that*
> *tone and mood."*
> — Bill Backer,
> co-founder of Backer & Spielvogel
> advertising agency[1]

In the down-to-earth world of business-to-business marketing, Microsoft wants customers to feel a sense of confidence gained from using its Windows 95 software. Caterpillar wants its customers for earth-moving machines to feel satisfaction from high productivity.

Product, Personality, Prospect, Competition, Obstacle, Message Objective, Reward. The copywriter who understands how these seven points connect, like pieces in a puzzle, will know what questions to ask before starting to write.

HOW COPYWRITING DIFFERS FROM WRITING

Journalists write. Novelists write. Poets write. Yet many of them would find it difficult, or at least challenging, to write an effective advertisement.

An advertisement, first of all, is defined by a limited and specific amount of space and time. The copy typically occupies a fraction of a page for a typical magazine ad. Thirty seconds for the most common TV spot. Six words or less for a powerful billboard. And because of these rigid constraints, the advertising copywriter must think and write in succinct ideas and language.

Copywriting serves the business world. So the writer must think as a marketer. Copywriters start with a mountain of information about the marketing situation: the product, the prospect, behaviors and attitudes, the competition; and in that mountain must find a few golden nuggets of information. Ultimately, an advertising idea comes down to one simple, but insightful, point.

THE PURPOSE OF THE HEADLINE

In print advertising, the headline carries a heavy responsibility. Headline purposes include:

- *To issue a command.* Exhibit 5.1.
- *To deliver news.* Exhibit 5.2.
- *To offer information.* Exhibit 5.3.
- *To select the audience.* Exhibit 5.4.
- *To make a promise.* Exhibit 5.14.
- *To intrigue the reader.* Exhibit 5.15.

But headlines don't work in isolation, they work together with pictures. Consider each of the above headline examples by itself; then, for comparison, find the ad reproduced here in this chapter. The conclusion is obvious. It is words and pictures working together for powerful and immediate impact that defines the craft of copywriting. Words alone do not often persuade.

> *"Headlines make ads work. The best headlines appeal to people's self-interest, or give news.... Simple words are powerful words. Even the best-educated people don't resent simple words. But they're the only words many people understand.... Once I changed the word 'repair' to 'fix' and the ad pulled 20% more.... Fact-packed messages carry a wallop. Don't be afraid of long copy. If your ad is interesting, people will be hungry for all the copy you can give them. If the ad is dull, short copy won't save it.... Don't save your best benefit until last. Start with it, so you'll have a better chance of keeping your reader with you."*
>
> —John Caples,
> Copywriters Hall of Fame
> and Advertising Hall of Fame[1]

COPY AND ART MUST WORK TOGETHER

Copy is clearly just one component of the message. The total visual presentation might include photography or cinematography, illustration, typography, calligraphy, graphic design. In broadcast media, there is also the audio track: voices, actors, singers, music, sound effects.

In addition, message perception is influenced by media environment: newspapers, magazines, television, radio, posters, catalogs. Each has its own characteristics and special credibility for its audience.

It is through the complete message — words, pictures, sounds, media — that advertising captures the attention, involves the audience, and, we hope, gets remembered. But it is effective copywriting that gets the audience to take action.

EXHIBIT 5.2 WILLIAMS-SONOMA
(DIRECT MARKETING CATALOG, SAMPLE PAGE)

CHUCK WILLIAMS

A New Kitchen Color: European Blue

Did you know that the color blue is probably the most popular color in our lives? We often favor blue in our clothing, and blue is certainly a popular color for the kitchen. Blue and white kitchen towels have always outsold any other color combination. For the past few years we have been featuring dark green as a color accent for the kitchen, but now we feel it is time to feature blue. The blue that we have chosen is a European shade of blue, a shade especially favored in Holland, Germany, France and Sweden. As in nature, it goes well with all of the primary colors and with most of the secondary colors. Our emphasis at this time is on coordinating the color of electric appliances used in the kitchen. All too often our kitchen appliances look ill at ease in their surroundings. But lined up on the counter as they are apt to be for convenience, it is very attractive when they match each other. Colored appliances are a splendid way to add style and cheer to the kitchen, too. The blue appliances you see on these pages are only available through Williams-Sonoma. In addition to these, you also will find other housewares items in this catalog in the same shade of blue.

Our Guarantee
For 39 years, we have offered America's cooks a select range of fine products. If you are not completely satisfied with your purchase, please return the item for an exchange or refund.

KitchenAid Mixers
The KitchenAid mixer made its debut in 1919. A machine for home use, engineered like a powerful commercial mixer, it remains the leader in electric stand mixers. Ten-speed solid-state controls provide the right power for any task; unique planetary action ensures more thorough mixing because the beater not only spins, but rotates around the bowl. With its 325W of continuous power, the heavy-duty KSM5 (shown) has a 5-qt. bowl raised and lowered by a lever; the 300W, model KSM90 has a 4½-qt. bowl that locks to the base. Both models come with a flat beater, dough hook, wire whip and stainless steel bowl. The new European blue finish shown here is exclusive to Williams-Sonoma. Made in the USA. Blue, Black or White.
KSM5 (shown), 13¼" x 10¼" x 16¼". #61-979047 **$269.00**
KSM90, 14" x 8½" x 13¾". #61-979039 **$219.00**

Krups Toasters
The many features of Krups toasters expand the range of morning offerings. The two extra-long slots have built-in guides that automatically adjust to any width of bread, bagel halves and English muffins. A defrost feature thaws frozen breads and pastries before toasting, while a reheat setting warms toast. The four-slice toaster will heat only one slot if that's all that's needed. The housing is stay-cool plastic with a removable crumb tray and a quartz heating element for uniform browning. Blue or White.
Four-Slice Toaster (shown), 15½" x 6½" x 7" high. #61-979021 **$60.00**
Two-Slice Toaster, 15½" x 4" x 7" high. #61-979013 **$45.00**

Company founder, Chuck Williams, opens the catalog with some newsy tips. Product description, such as "engineered like a powerful commercial mixer," adds conviction to product specification copy.

EXHIBIT 5.3 MIDMICHIGAN REGIONAL MEDICAL CENTER
(NEWSPAPER AD)

No Wonder Your Neck Hurts.

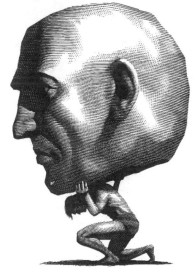

After all, your head weighs twenty pounds. And your neck is susceptible to all sorts of injuries, excess tension, poor posture and various wear and tear.

Come to our free "What's giving you a pain in the neck?" seminar at the Towsley Auditorium on Monday, November 25 at 7 p.m., featuring Neurosurgeons M. Gueramy M.D. and Victor Sonnino M.D., as well as Occupational Therapist Pamela Gifford.

To preregister, call the MidMichigan Health Line at 839-3199 (Midland), 1-800-999-3199 (outside Midland).

MIDMICHIGAN
REGIONAL MEDICAL CENTER
NEUROSCIENCE INSTITUTE
4005 Orchard Drive, Midland, Michigan

Dramatic problem/solution copy attracts neck-pain sufferers to a seminar. Copy adds credibility by including names of participating physicians. Agency: The Sturm Communications Group, Chicago.

EXHIBIT 5.4 IRV'S MEN'S STORE (NEWSPAPER AD)

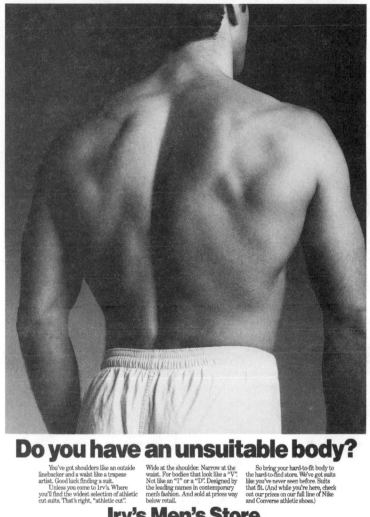

Do you have an unsuitable body?

You've got shoulders like an outside linebacker and a waist like a trapeze artist. Good luck finding a suit.
Unless you come to Irv's. Where you'll find the widest selection of athletic cut suits. That's right, "athletic cut".

Wide at the shoulder. Narrow at the waist. For bodies that look like a "V". Not like an "I" or a "D". Designed by the leading names in contemporary men's fashion. And sold at prices way below retail.

So bring your hard-to-fit body to the hard-to-find store. We've got suits like you've never seen before. Suits that fit. (And while you're here, check out our prices on our full line of Nike and Converse athletic shoes.)

Irv's Men's Store.
Inconveniently located (but there's nothing inconvenient about saving money).
Chicago, 2841 N. Laramie, 286-7293. Prospect Heights, 610 Milwaukee Avenue, 459-8060. Darien, 7511 Lemont Road, 910-1333.

This question headline selects the target audience — men with hard-to-fit bodies. The tagline adds low-price positioning and a clever ploy about locations. Agency: Lou Beres & Associates, Inc., Chicago. Executive Creative Director: Earl Weingarden.

"Art and copy aren't mutually exclusive. An art director should be something of a writer, and a writer something of an art director. I think it's simpler to visualize the ad and write it, although many don't agree."

— Hal Riney,
founder of Hal Riney & Partners[1]

WHERE DO GOOD IDEAS COME FROM?

We all have ideas. Go to any brainstorming meeting and you will find someone filling a blackboard or a flip-chart with ideas.

The issue for copywriters is how to have ideas that are original and relevant to the marketing problem. Then, how to implement them. As someone has said: The only good ad is the one that's running.

"Good ads take one of two approaches: an exercise in persuasive logic you can't ignore. Or an exercise in charm so likable you want to buy the product or service. Remember good isn't great. Great ads are made of superb logic and great charm. The idea is to create ads that make people say, 'Wow, I love that ad!' It's not easy. But that's what we try to do."

— Mike Sloan,
founder of Mike Sloan, Inc.
advertising agency[1]

There are several commonly accepted models for the idea-generating creative process. One came from James Webb Young of the Young & Rubicam advertising agency in a concise little book titled *A Technique for Producing Ideas.*[2]

Young's model is based on a four-step process: Preparation, Incubation, Illumination and Verification. The model is credited to Graham Wallas, author of a 1926 book titled, *The Art of Thought.*[3]

The following is adapted from Young's book:

THE CREATIVE PROCESS
How Ideas Are Born

A. Gather input
  1. Specific knowledge
  2. General knowledge
B. Digest the information
  1. Examine the facts
  2. Ask questions
  3. Contemplate "the puzzle"
  4. Accept partial solutions

C. Stop thinking about it
 1. Send "the puzzle" to your subconscious
 2. Seek unrelated mental stimulation
D. BAM! The idea comes to you
E. Shape the idea
 1. Share it with others and listen to them
 2. Refine it, test it, implement it

Specific knowledge refers to the product and marketing information relevant to the project; general knowledge to the creative person's personal life experiences.

Accepting partial solutions suggests that as part of the information-digesting process we naturally begin to hatch ideas. They will likely be unpolished ideas at this point, but we should accept them nevertheless, if only to hang on to them for further review.

The step we often ignore is: Stop thinking about it. In the rush to meet deadlines and promises to the boss or the client, it is all too easy to push for immediate ideation. Taking shortcuts might yield good results sometimes. But more often, true creativity requires a gestation period. As we often say, "Let's sleep on it." Good advice.

Finally, after the idea has struck like lightning, BAM!, it is critical that it be shared and evaluated in the cold light of day; then, carefully fine-tuned. Be careful, though; ideas are fragile and easily crushed by committees and generally low-risk behavior.[3]

> *"If I'm trying to sell you something, I have several options. I can yell at you and hope that you break down and buy the product. Or I can make your experience worthwhile by entertaining you. There has to be a reward — information, a smile, something that compensates for the time you spend with the message. That's a major part of the craft, a key part of the assignment."*
>
> — Stan Richards,
> founder of The Richards Group
> advertising agency[1]

THE COPYWRITER'S CRAFTY TECHNIQUES

As in any specialized field there are tricks of the trade, many of which copywriters use without even consciously realizing it.

Association

Many advertising ideas are built upon thought connections or associations. It is one of the most common creative problem-solving techniques, linking a product feature or benefit with some familiar reference. Simile, analogy and metaphor are with us in our daily lives when we use expressions such as: chip off the old block, solid as a rock, in a heartbeat. Associations are useful tools for the copywriter because they connect unfamiliar things with the familiar.

In the Frech U.S.A. ad, Exhibit 5.5, the copywriter has associated the reader's beliefs about German automobile engineering (the familiar) with the product, a high-speed die-casting machine (the less familiar).

We use celebrity endorsers and presenters to associate their success and popularity with a company or product. Gatorade, Exhibit 5.6, associates with professional athletes in its positioning as a sports drink. Shure Microphones, Exhibit 5.7, associates with a well-known musician and uses copy written in the language of a hip music audience.

We use metaphors to overcome complexity in our message by associating with simple concepts and symbols. Prudential Insurance associates with the solid imagery of the Rock of Gibraltar. Merrill-Lynch built an association with the bull, saying "We're bullish on America."

Positioning

This marketing term, made popular by Al Ries and Jack Trout in their book, *Positioning: The Battle for Your Mind*, directs the copywriter to differentiate his or her product from the competition in a meaningful way.[4]

Positioning refers to the niche the marketer occupies in the minds of consumers. Ries and Trout's guidelines to positioning include being first and being right.

Being first means you're new, the first one to say or show something (not necessarily the first one to have something). Being right means that your strategy is on target, resonating with the audience as being truthful and relevant. Avis positioned itself with, "We're only No. 2. We try harder."; Seven-Up with "The Uncola ."[5]

Preemptive Claim

In this technique the message makes an assertion of superiority, thereby preempting an advantage before any competitor claims it. This can work very effectively when there is a new or awakening market where competitive advertising is generic or nonexistent. Gatorade, for example, preempted a position over soft drinks by creating the sports drink category when it was first introduced. Timex preempted a durability advantage with its many survival stories about Timex watches. As their spokesman used to say: "Takes a licking, keeps on ticking."

Unique Selling Proposition

Coined as the USP by the Ted Bates agency in the 1950s, this copy strategy makes a superiority claim based on some unique physical

EXHIBIT 5.5 FRECH U.S.A. (BUSINESS PUBLICATION AD)

The latest marvel of German engineering doesn't have alloy wheels, a turbocharger or aerodynamic styling.

But boy can this baby move.

The new DAK 800 cold chamber diecasting machine. Another first from FRECH. The cycle times are faster. The ECOPRESS injection unit delivers more precise injection and operates at a blazing speed of 10 meters per second. And world-reknowned quality and reliability maximizes uptime when casting aluminum and tough-to-cast magnesium. You can select cold chamber machines from 100-1000 US tons locking force. All available with the Rauch magnesium dosing furnace. So get rolling. Call 1-800-FRECH-NA. And discover the faster diecaster.

FRECH®
U.S.A.
Ahead in Diecasting Technology

Industrial marketers do well to add some human interest copy to their product messages. Here, the oblique reference to German auto engineering links attributes of speed and high quality with the DAK 800 cold-chamber diecasting machine. Agency: Davis Harrison Dion, Chicago. Creative Director: Doug Davis.

EXHIBIT 5.6 QUAKER OATS COMPANY — GATORADE
(30-SECOND TELEVISION)

Quaker Oats Company
"Through The Years-Visuals" :30 TV

1. (MUSIC: UNDER THROUGHOUT)
CHUCKIE VO: I think something...

2. just got into me as a kid.

3. (MUSIC)

4. I set up this triathlon in my
backyard.

5. You know, wading pool, tricycles.

6. But we barely get going, and
these kids are falling out for nap.

7. I mean no, NO ability to pace
themselves.

8. (MUSIC)

9. CHUCKIE: Now my life is one
big sport.

10. (MUSIC)

11. Runnin', bikin', swimmin',
mountain bikin'...

12. guzzling Gatorade...

13. and sleepin'.

14. Basically everything my
guidance counsler was afraid of.

15. Life is a sport. Drink it up.

Bayer Bess Vanderwarker 1995

Gatorade's association with sports has led to many spots with leading athletes like this one featuring professional triathlete, Chuckie V. With a flashback concept, the tongue-in-cheek copy tracks Chuckie and Gatorade since his childhood. Agency: Bayer Bess Vanderwarker, Chicago. Reprinted by permission of Stokley-Van Camp, Inc.

EXHIBIT 5.7 SHURE BROTHERS, INC., EVANSTON, IL (MAGAZINE AD)

Speak the language of your customers and your copy will tune in quickly to their needs, wants, emotions. Shure uses a music celebrity and copy targeting a hip audience for its microphones. Agency: Jack Levy Associates, Chicago. Creative Supervisor: William Hagerup.

feature or benefit. M&M candy "Melts in your mouth, not in your hands," for example, states a unique benefit resulting from a physical attribute. Listerine Antiseptic "Kills germs that cause bad breath, plaque, and the gum infection, gingivitis."

Brand Image

In some product categories psychological differentiation is more important than a product's physical attributes. The Marlboro Man, the Gerber Baby, Aunt Jemima and Absolut vodka are a few who have staked out psychological territory, packing tremendous power as brand equity.

Compelling Words

Certain words have added value in advertising: FREE, NEW, and REAL to name a few. When a product is new, you don't want to miss the opportunity to use the NEW word because the product won't be new for long. FREE, almost always used in all caps to make sure readers see it, attracts like a magnet. But don't use it indiscriminately; a transparent come-on for something of little value can backfire on the advertiser's integrity.

> *"First I go right to the merchandise; feel it, wear it, eat it, know it. Second, I try to write an ad so it sounds as if I'm talking to somebody—talking to one person. A friend. An intelligent friend. Telling her what I want her to know about the product. I try to be very specific, very informative—and very interesting."*
>
> — Reva Korda,
> former Creative Head of
> Ogilvy & Mather advertising agency[1]

Many packaged goods claims for "Improved" products or "Real" ingredients, such as "Real natural fruit juices," are monitored and regulated by the Federal Trade Commission. (See the discussion on legal issues with advertising copy later in this chapter.)

Resonance

Here the copywriter attempts to tap into the stored experiences of prospects with relevant connections. The technique works well with many products, but particularly those with high social significance. A television commercial for a dandruff control shampoo brings up the critical first impressions when dating. A warm family scene going through old photos reminds us to buy more film. The Little League team going out for hamburgers makes heroes of dads and the familiar fast-food franchise.

Involvement

Publishers' Clearing House asks you in their direct response mailing to tear out a stamp and place it on the order form. They have engaged you in the specific action step of placing an order. That is involvement.

When a sweepstakes promotion tells you to take the game piece to a retailer's store to see if you have won, that is involvement. And, when a public service announcement on television asks you to call a 900 number to voice your opinion, that is involvement.

"I don't think you can let style get in the way of the message. Intrusive headlines, provocative visuals, they're terrific. But only if they don't blur the real message you want people to get. The best print advertising seems to the reader to have no style; it's simply an intelligent, believable presentation of the facts."
— Lois Korey,
former creative leader at
Needham Harper & Steers Advertising[1]

Fear

Less ominous than it sounds, a fear strategy simply implies that if one does not use the marketer's product, he or she will face some undesirable consequences. Health and beauty products such as toothpaste, mouthwash, and body soaps typically base their creative efforts on fear. Fear of cavities. Fear of social embarrassment. Fear of not getting a date.

The television commercial for First Alert smoke detectors and fire extinguishers (Exhibit 5.8) clearly uses the fear approach when the spokesman says, "Stupid little kitchen fires that take out people's houses."

Humor

Who doesn't enjoy a commercial that makes you smile, chuckle, or even guffaw? Copywriters love the opportunity to write something cleverly funny; or, in some cases, to work with celebrity humorists such as Johnathan Winters, Jerry Seinfeld, or Whoopi Goldberg.

A few writers with exceptional talent for humor have been highly successful with independent production companies specializing mostly in radio commercials. Stan Freburg, Dick Orkin, Bert Berdis, and Alan Barzman are among the best at writing and delivering effectively funny radio spots. If the humor fits the marketing situation (never make fun of the product), if it is truly funny and well-produced with capable talent, it can generate excellent results.

Much advertising, while not belly-laugh funny, is simply fun. It has extra entertainment value to get attention, to get talked about, and to be remembered.

EXHIBIT 5.8 BRK ELECTRONICS, (30-SECOND TELEVISION)

First Alert®
A WARNING AND A WEAPON™
"FIREFIGHTER" :30

FIREFIGHTER: I see it over and over.

Stupid little kitchen fires that take out people's houses.

Fires where they lose everything.

Fires where not everybody got out.

What I don't see, I don't see why you're sitting in a house without a fire extinguisher.

FIREFIGHTER VO: You got a smoke detector? Great.

But you gotta get a fire extinguisher, too.

AVO: Smoke detectors and fire extinguishers from First Alert. A warning . . . and a weapon.

FIREFIGHTER: You have a fire . . . what are you gonna say? They cost too much? I was too busy?

A real smoke-eating firefighter talks candidly about "stupid little kitchen fires that take out people's houses." Very dramatic fear technique. Very believable. Agency: LOIS/USA, Chicago. Executive Creative Director: Mickey Brazeal. © 1992 BRK Electronics, Inc.

Can a small advertiser with a limited budget use humor effectively? The Mini-Moves example (Exhibit 5.9) shows what can be done without celebrity talent and a lavish budget. This start-up company uses postcards to make business contacts, and the copywriter has given the cards just enough fun to stick out in the mail and get attention.[6]

Facts Are Not Enough

In a heralded speech before the American Association of Advertising Agencies in 1980, creative leader William Bernbach told the industry that "Facts Are Not Enough."

The co-founder of the Doyle, Dane, Bernbach agency led the creative revolution of the 1960s with campaigns for Volkswagen, Avis, and many more. He strongly believed advertising without an emotional dimension was dull and doomed to failure. A small sampling from that speech:

> *"Yes, it is insight into human nature that is the key to a communicator's skill. For, whereas, the writer is concerned with what he puts into his writing, the communicator is concerned not just with what he puts into a piece of writing but with what the reader gets out of it. He therefore becomes a student of how people read or listen.*
>
> *He learns that most readers come away from their reading not with a clear, precise detailed registration of its contents on their minds, but rather with a vague, misty idea which was formed as much by the pace, the proportions, the music of the writings as by the literal words themselves.*
>
> *He learns that the reader reads with his ego, his emotions, with his prejudices, his urges and his aspirations. And that he plots with his brains to rationalize the facts until they become the tools of his desires."*
>
> — William Bernbach,
> co-founder of Doyle Dane Bernbach
> International, Inc.[7]

HOW COPYWRITING DIFFERS FROM MEDIUM TO MEDIUM

A good copywriter has the versatility to write for all media, but most have preferences that bring out their particular writing strengths.

Television

Television is powerful because it combines audio and video for double-sensory penetration. Therefore, television copywriters must be

EXHIBIT 5.9 MINI-MOVES
(BUSINESS-TO-BUSINESS DIRECT MAIL POSTCARD SERIES)

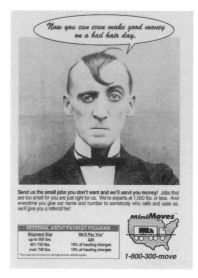

Humorous balloon captions over zany stock photos separate these postcards from ordinary-looking business mail. Inexpensive and effective. Agency: Bayer Bess Vanderwarker, Chicago. Creative Director: Noël Weimer, Chicago.

very strong visual thinkers. They should be good at writing storytelling narratives and lively dialog.

It also helps if they contribute ideas in a team effort with art directors, film directors, casting directors, and others. It is important to understand television production, simply because the creative concept comes with a price tag for production. A simple commercial to be produced at the local cable TV station must have an equally simple production concept. No marching bands or location footage from 12 time zones away.

For television and radio scripts, keep in mind that 75 words is considered the maximum for a 30-second script—that is, if you are writing "wall-to-wall" words. Commercial producers always advise shorter scripts, allowing time for pauses, music, and other effects.

Jingle writing for broadcast is a more specialized copy skill, often most comfortable for writers who also have musical talent. Collaboration between writer and composer generally requires some give and take over the words. A copywriter who can handle simple poetry usually feels comfortable writing lyrics for jingles. Some music producers prefer that you give them only a copy theme line and let them take it from there.

Radio

Radio commercials can vary from the low-budget, announcer-read script to the most elaborate multi-voice scenario with sound effects, music, and singers. Good writers of radio advertising have the ability to paint pictures with words. Because it is the one totally aural medium, radio is often referred to as the "theater of the mind."

The radio script for St. Paul Federal Bank for Savings (Exhibit 5.10) demonstrates an inexpensive two-voice format, the announcer interacting with a befuddled would-be homeowner. The scenario hits home with many typical folks. They're afraid to take on a mortgage, not feeling too confident about their job security. A serious subject treated with breezy light humor.

Newspaper

Since newspaper is the primary retail medium, much newspaper advertising is oriented to quick-hitting, product-for-sale kinds of messages. Grocery chains, department stores, tire dealers, and a host of other retailers dominate most newspapers. Health-care providers have become another sizeable category.

The environment is cluttered and competitive like a street bazaar and often he who shouts loudest wins. Direct wording that selects the target audience and delivers the message quickly is often the right style for the task. Color is not as readily available, placing more of the burden for attention on bold typography, strong illustrations and special borders.

EXHIBIT 5.10 ST. PAUL FEDERAL BANK FOR SAVINGS (60-SECOND RADIO)

SCRIPT/COPY

Bayer Bess Vanderwarker

CLIENT ·	ST. PAUL FEDERAL	DATE ·	3/7/94	PAGE · 1	OF · 1
PRODUCT ·	ST. PAUL FEDERAL	DRAFT# ·	8 MM/jw	LENGTH · :50	
JOB # ·	RA94889	COMM'L CODE ·	XXAC6387		
TITLE ·	"WHAT IF..."		AS RECORDED		

RADIO ☑
PRINT ☐

ANNCR: Ever find yourself thinkin': What if I bought a house?

MAN: What if I bought a house? A house? What about my job? What about those funny looks my boss Mr. McCorkle's been giving me huh? What if he's trying to tell me something? What if he's trying to say don't go buyin' a house or anything? What if he gives me one big, funny look and then he actually says it: Pack up your stuff. Clean out your desk. Hang up your company softball jersey, mister. What then? What if I had a house? What if I had a mortgage?

ANNCR: Hey, calm down. St. Paul Federal can help. Because now new home buyers who sign up for our hassle free mortgages can get mortgage unemployment coverage at no cost for the first year. That way, if you lose your job within the first year of owning your home, your mortgage payment will be covered for up to 6 months.

MAN: I bought a house! What if I have a party! What if McCorkle shows up? Nah, he hates me.

ANNCR: Call St. Paul Federal Bank For Savings. 1-800-321-BANK. Or, stop by one of our 50 branches, including all Omni Superstore locations. Mortgage unemployment coverage is provided by Balboa Insurance Company, Irvine, California. St. Paul is an equal housing lender. Certain restrictions and exclusions may apply.

Bayer Bess Vanderwarker
225 North Michigan Avenue
Chicago, Illinois 60601
312 · 861 · 3800

Sometimes referred to as "the theater of the mind," radio gives the copywriter solo creative freedom (no art director involved). This spot, for example, creates a worrisome character we can all relate to and resolves his problem with a "hassle-free" mortgage. Agency: Bayer Bess Vanderwarker, Chicago. Copywriter: Noël Weimer, Chicago.

The newspaper ad for MidMichigan Regional Medical Center (Exhibit 5.3) is an excellent example of strong black-and-white illustration that makes the message stand out in the busy newspaper environment.

> *"When you tell the truth, when you're straight and direct with the reader, there's some shock involved, simply because the stock answer is to tiptoe around the truth. But that's good, because you need to jolt people with your advertising. Nobody has the time to try and figure out what you're trying to say, so you need to be direct. Most great advertising is direct. That's how people talk. That's the style they read. That's what sells products or services or ideas."*
> — Jerry Della Femina,
> founder of Della Femina, Travisano & Partners
> advertising agency[1]

Magazine

Consumer magazines are read at a more leisurely pace, with greater appreciation of longer articles, enticing color photographs, and the subtleties of advertising creativity. For the copywriter, magazine ads are a showcase of best efforts, those ads that look especially good in a professional's portfolio.

Writer and art director teams put their heads together over stunning ad concepts, beautiful photos or illustrations, and elegant typography where each word, each space, has been considered in crafting the total effect.

Direct Response

Direct response copy can be found in all media, print ads, direct mail, catalogs, TV infomercials, and most recently, the Internet. Print ads for record clubs, books, and collectibles demonstrate the classic long-copy, very persuasive writing style pioneered in the days when patent medicine and mail order underwear were sold to rural America.

Direct mail experts cite the importance of the envelope copy that must entice the recipient to open it, the cover letter that must make an emotional one-to-one connection between the writer and reader, and the offer — the critical invitation to product trial.

> *"Nothing beats getting out of your office, going out and trying to sell the product in person. Do that and you'll gain insights that'll help you sell in print. And you'll write in language people understand and respond to."*
> — Bob Stone,
> co-founder of Stone & Adler direct marketing agency,
> member of the Direct Marketing Hall of Fame[1]

Catalog

Direct-response catalogs have proliferated in recent years, showing us styles from the price-hype, copy-crammed computer catalogs to the slick and sophisticated apparel and housewares offerings.

Taking examples from the upscale mail, Williams-Sonoma (Exhibit 5.2) presents its goodies and gadgets for the kitchen with inviting copy that tells the reader enough, but not too much. J. Peterman's copy for The Niven Blazer (Exhibit 5.11) takes copywriting to lofty new heights with clever association techniques and name-dropping snootiness woven through their pages with aplomb. Great fun for the reader and the writer.

Out-of-Home Media

This media category typically includes outdoor billboards, transit posters on buses and train stations, kiosks, and point-of-purchase displays.

The creative emphasis is highly visual with very few words, sometimes no more than the advertiser's signature. Recognizing that either the medium (a bus, for example), or the audience (a commuter or shopper) is on the move, you have only seconds to communicate. Because of this, posters and billboards are typically used as a reinforcing medium rather than a primary media vehicle.

Whatever the product or message objective, the admonition to writers is "simplify."

Business-to-Business

The famous ad for McGraw-Hill (Exhibit 5.12), states the case emphatically for business publication advertising. The ad has been running for four decades and its message never wears out.

There are more than five thousand business publications in the United States and many more thousands of copywriters toiling at ads for business-to-business marketers. From the latest computer mouse pad to a multi-million-dollar jet aircraft, there's a story to be told, a product to be sold. Business publications provide essential job-related information to their readers, and the readers are seeking products and services that will fit the needs of their company.

The challenge for writers of business-to-business advertising is to be specific and factual with business products, but at the same time bring human interest into the message. The Dayton electric motor ad (Exhibit 5.13), for example, humanizes a homely, dirt-covered motor by saying it "looks beautiful to the guy who hasn't had to replace it in the last seven years."

Seaquist Dispensing (Exhibit 5.14) deftly presents its superiority claim by taking a gentle swipe at its brag-and-boast competitors. The style of the writing makes the message more engaging, more believable.

Motorola (Exhibit 5.15) doesn't merely blurt out that its cellular

EXHIBIT 5.11 THE J. PETERMAN COMPANY (APPAREL CATALOG)

British Unflappability.
(The Niven Blazer.)

Some men can emerge from a smoking bomb crater looking incredibly relaxed, even elegant.

Are they born that way?

Some actually are.

Others are just lucky enough to be wearing a navy blue Blazer at the time.

A good navy blue Blazer confers upon a man the propriety of a blue suit and the unstuffiness of an easy-fitting jacket. All at the same time.

Blazers give you the gift of looking right. With flannels, cords, khakis, jeans. With ties, with T-shirts. But you already knew that. In fact, you probably already own one or two. Why, then, this Blazer?

Because this is the Blazer of Niven and Grant. Of O'Toole and Howard and Bond. It is: classic, chic, cocky, comfortable, casual, cool, charismatic, clean-lined, and altogether unflappable.

100% worsted wool. Antiqued brass buttons (2 in front, 4 on each sleeve). 3-3/4" lapels. 10 1/2" deep center vent and slightly suppressed waist complete the rakish silhouette. 2 inside chest pockets. Fully lined. Flapped patch pockets. Two darts in front enhance drape and fit. Is that you in the mirror? It is.

Men's even sizes: 38 through 48, Regular; 40 through 48, Long.

Color: H.M.S. Navy Blue.

Niven Blazer. Regular (N⁰. 38B1052); Long (N⁰. 38B1053). Price: $173.

WWII pants.

Exactly the pants to wear with a blue blazer.

WWII pants. 100% cotton cravat twill. Washable. 6 suspender buttons. Button pocket. Plain front (no pleats).

Color: Khaki.

Men's even sizes: 30 through 46. Free hemming (max.: 36") or cuffing (max.: 33").

WWII Pants (N⁰. 38B1084). Price: $47.

Clearly targeting a sophisticated buyer, copy for "The Niven Blazer" creates an aura of very, very British correctness. The 120-page catalog is as much fun to read as a clever short story.

EXHIBIT 5.12 THE McGRAW-HILL COMPANIES' MAGAZINES
(BUSINESS PUBLICATION AD)

The McGraw·Hill Companies

" I don't know who you are.
I don't know your company.
I don't know your company's product.
I don't know what your company stands for.
I don't know your company's customers.
I don't know your company's record.
I don't know your company's reputation.
Now–what was it you wanted to sell me?"

MORAL: Sales start **before** your salesperson calls–with business publication advertising.

THE McGRAW-HILL COMPANIES' MAGAZINES
BUSINESS • PROFESSIONAL • TECHNICAL

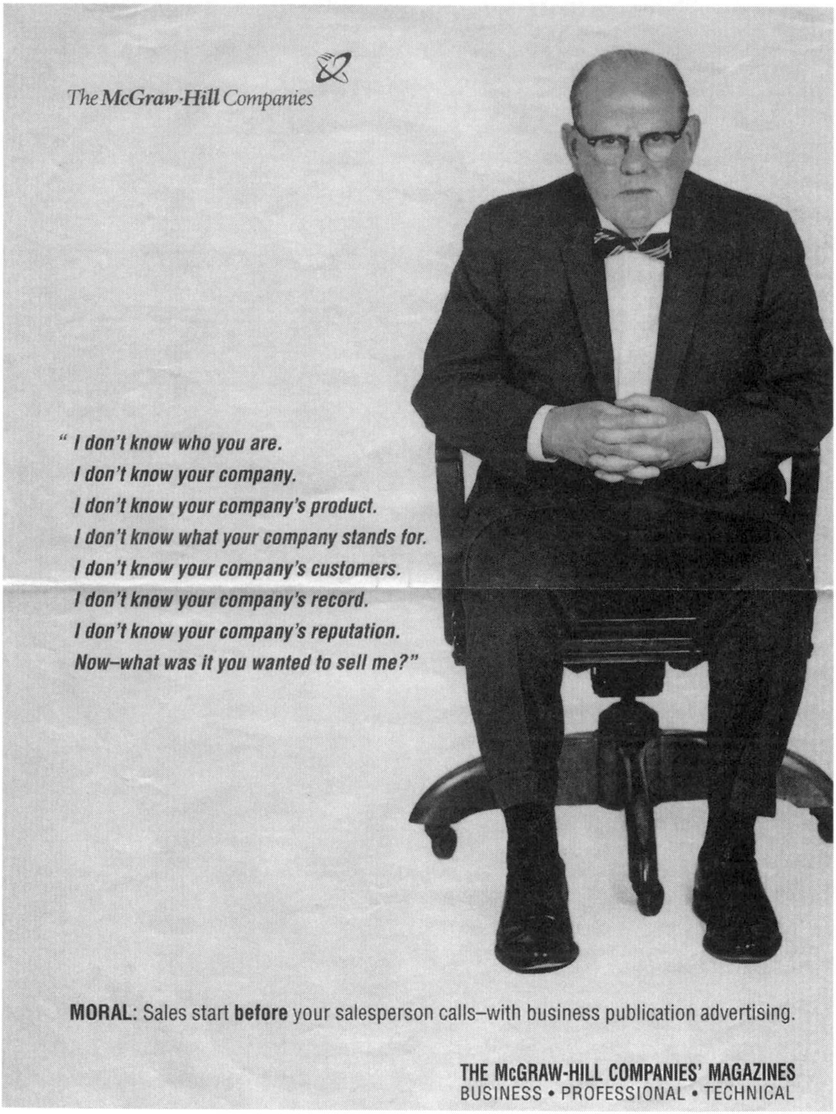

A golden oldie, this ad promoting business publication advertising first appeared in the 1950s and is still running today. Brief, easy to read, yet very meaningful. Truly timeless. © The McGraw-Hill Companies, Inc. Reprinted with permission of The McGraw-Hill Companies, Inc.

EXHIBIT 5.13 W. W. GRAINGER, INC. — DAYTON ELECTRIC MOTORS
(BUSINESS PUBLICATION AD)

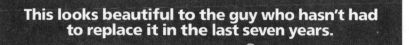

This looks beautiful to the guy who hasn't had to replace it in the last seven years.

This 7 year old Dayton ▶
40 HP motor mixes chemicals
50-60 hours a week at a
Michigan detergent plant.

How so? Every Dayton® integral horsepower motor is built better than it has to be. Engineered to outlast the best motor it'll ever replace. Why bother?

Well, we never know where it'll be used. Like this 40 HP motor used on an industrial mixer. It's the same one used to move products on a conveyer. So we design it for the tougher job. And build it to exceed the industry average.

All 1,500 of our motors up to 250 HP exceed industry standards for performance. Before making it into the Dayton lineup, they undergo rigorous computer performance testing and field evaluations.

And you'll find the exact Dayton motor you need as close as your nearest Grainger branch. Home of the complete line of Dayton motors as well as all the other durable Dayton products. Including air compressors, blowers and generators. All built to exceed the industry average. Beautiful.

Dayton®

©1993 W.W. Grainger, Inc.

By calling a homely product beautiful, Dayton shocks us into paying attention to their reliability message. Photo caption gives credibility to the story. © 1993 W. W. Grainger, Inc. Reprinted with permission.

EXHIBIT 5.14 SEAQUIST DISPENSING (BUSINESS PUBLICATION AD)

Taking a humorous swipe at the brag-and-boast competition, this copy announces concrete evidence of Seaquist's quality leadership. Notice how the closing copy line ("...as the others keep on talking.") ties back to the headline. Agency: Semel/Kaye & Co., Northbrook, Illinois.

EXHIBIT 5.15 MOTOROLA, INC. (MAGAZINE AD)

Forty-one firefighters couldn't put it out.

Baked. Drenched. Tested to the extreme. A Motorola cellular phone stands tough in the face of torture. Just ask Danielle Behe, whose phone came back from the ashes of a three-alarm fire. Motorola. The best-selling, most preferred cellular phones in the world.

Testimonial reflects actual event. 1-800-331-6456 ® and Motorola are trademarks of Motorola, Inc. ©1994 Motorola, Inc.

(M) **MOTOROLA**

Using its heritage of wireless radio leadership, Motorola connects World War II product reliability to its cellular phones of today. Engaging headline leads in to brief copy. © 1994, Motorola, Inc. Reproduced with permission from Motorola, Inc.

phones are reliable; it relates that message in an interesting story about the product's forerunner, a Motorola wireless radio used in World War II.

In business marketing it is also critical to understand that buying is a team function. Purchasing agents, office managers, design engineers, plant managers, financial vice-presidents—many people, with many different buying criteria—get involved in decision-making.

NAMES, THEME LINES, TAGLINES, SLOGANS

All marketers want to be remembered, and there is no doubt that the right words and phrases stick like velcro in our minds. Hollywood has always known, for example, that names created for its stars add box-office appeal.

While many successful and familiar companies have plain vanilla names—Campbell's, Ford, Stanley, Anderson—today's start-up business will most likely want a name with more of a memory hook. Company names that define the marketer's business have tremendous equity, such as Burger King, Computerland, Masterlock, Whirlpool, and Skil. Then there are names that are simply distinctive: Crate and Barrel, Stolichnaya, Hammacher Schlemmer, Orville Redenbacher.

Memorability comes from repeated exposure as well as from uniqueness. But uniqueness will certainly accelerate awareness for a new company or product.

Healthy Choice, for example, is a functional brand name that arrived at the right time to emphasize lower fat content and calories.

Copywriters often get to name products. The assignment can be a wonderful opportunity, but also a very formidable task. In some product categories, so many names are already taken that it seems next to impossible.

The major automakers, for example, have been known to trademark many more names than they need simply to preempt them from competitors and to have some in reserve. Some would postulate that the Edsel failed as a car model back in 1958 because the name sounded un-carlike, as opposed to other successful Ford brands such as Mustang and Taurus.

How about theme lines or slogans? Chances are, you know the marketers who use these lines:

"The Dependability People"

"Fly the Friendly Skies"

"We try harder."

"I Love What You Do for Me"

"… the Place with the Helpful Hardware Man"

"We bring good things to life."

As with names, slogans gain memorability from repeated exposure over years, often decades, in multi-million-dollar campaigns. Lines set to music as jingles have particularly potent mind-sticking quality.

The power of such themes prompts many marketers to believe a theme line is the answer to their prayers, that some magical and instant success will come of it. Consequently, copywriters spend thousands of hours writing lines, and more lines, and more lines in search of another "Just Do It."

Mere words, however, do not make marketing magic. Maytag, United Air Lines, Avis, Toyota, Ace Hardware, and General Electric (see above list) had established products and proven marketing programs before they had memorable slogans. The successful slogans, as part of well-executed and well-financed advertising campaigns, can be credited with taking these marketers to new levels of awareness.

LEGAL ISSUES WITH ADVERTISING COPY

Copywriters must also take caution and be aware of what they can't say. Advertising faces restrictions set up by government agencies, including the Federal Trade Commission, the Food and Drug Administration, the Federal Communications Commission, the U.S. Postal Service, the Securities and Exchange Commission, and the Alcohol and Tax Division of the Internal Revenue Service. It faces additional restrictions from state and local agencies as well as from the media running the ads.

The advertising industry itself established the National Advertising Review Board (NARB) to apply pressure against agencies and advertisers to get misleading ads out of circulation and off the air. In addition, the National Association of Broadcasters publishes guidelines for television and radio copy.[8]

Television scripts, particularly for national commercials, usually must be cleared by the appropriate networks or stations before they are recorded and aired. Questions regarding product claims and comparative advertising must be resolved with documented substantiation. In print media, most publications write into their contract terms that they have the right to reject ads they deem to be inappropriate.

Product categories often requiring legal mandatories in the copy include food and beverage, banking and financial investments, and pharmaceuticals. Liquor and tobacco products are limited in that they cannot advertise in U.S. broadcast media.

THE RIGHT WORD

Words are always in abundant supply. But only a few of them belong in your message.

As a writer, you're expected to have a good vocabulary, but even more important is the ability to reach for the right words at the right time.

William A. Marsteller, founder of Marsteller Inc., was an advertising leader with an appreciation for language. In 1971, he wrote a piece that began as a memo to the employees of his agency, later became a full-page newspaper ad for the agency, and eventually became the title and lead chapter of an anthology he authored. Here is an excerpt:

THE WONDERFUL WORLD OF WORDS

Human beings come in all sizes, a variety of colors, in different ages, and with unique, complex and changing personalities.

So do words.

There are tall, skinny words and short, fat ones, and strong ones and weak ones, and boy words and girl words and so on.

For instance, title, lattice, latitude, lily, tattle, Illinois, and intellect are all lean and lanky. While these words get their height partly out of "t's" and "l's" and "i's," other words are tall and skinny without a lot of ascenders and descenders. Take for example, Abraham, peninsula, and ellipsis, all tall.

Here are some nice short-fat words: hog, yogurt, bomb, pot, bonbon, acne, plump, sop, and slobber.

Sometimes a word gets its size from what it means, but of course sometimes it's just how the word sounds. Acne is a short-fat word even though pimple, with which it is associated, is a puny word.

There's a difference between tall-skinny words and puny words. Totter is out-and-out puny, while teeter is more just slender. Tea, tepid, stool, and weary are puny.

Puny words are not the same as feminine words. Feminine words are such as tissue, slipper, cute, squeamish, peek, flutter, gauze, and cumulus. Masculine words are like bourbon, rupture, oak, cartel, steak, and socks. Words can mean the same thing and be of the opposite sex. Naked is masculine, but nude is feminine....

There is a point to all of this.

Ours is a business of imagination. We are employed to make faceless companies personable, to make useful products desirable, to clarify ideas, to create friendships in the mass for our employers.

We have great power to do these things. We have power through art and photography and graphics and typography and all the visual elements that are part of the finished advertisement or the published publicity release.

And these are great powers. Often it is true that one picture is worth ten thousand words.

But not necessarily worth one word.

The right word.[9]

A Summary of Tips for Aspiring Copywriters

1. *Be clear before clever.* Cleverness can work for you or against you. Sometimes it slows down the communication process. Most people won't take time to figure out the copywriter's inside joke or convoluted play on words. So try your ideas on others first to make sure they work. In a flash.

2. *Keep asking what's in it for the prospect.* If your message doesn't quickly get to a benefit, or a promise, or a "hook" that will hold attention, you've lost the opportunity.

3. *Simplify.* The best ideas are the quickest and easiest. Keep stripping away extraneous elements and let the single, simple idea shine by itself.

4. *When stuck, just start writing.* Writers all have blocks occasionally. When it happens to you, don't tighten up and get frustrated. Start writing and keep going until something special happens.

5. *Study the media.* Read the magazines or newspapers where your ad will run. Watch the television programs. Listen to the radio stations. You will gain insight into the minds of your audience and be able to strike responsive chords with your writing.

6. *Read your writing aloud.* Read to someone else, or even just to yourself. Listen for slow spots, for advertising cliches, for sentences that are too long, for foggy logic.

7. *Learn to edit.* Put verbs in active voice where the verb takes a direct object: Rosemarie cooked sauerkraut. Not passive voice: The sauerkraut was cooked by Rosemarie — in which case the object is turned into the subject. Add impactful adjectives. Change straight, dull wording to colorful, sometimes surprising language. And simplify.

8. *Be inquisitive.* Don't just accept the direction you are given. Be skeptical. Ask plenty of questions. Talk to customers and prospects; find out why they would resist buying the product. Dig for meaningful facts or hidden benefits.

9. *Have sources of inspiration.* To get yourself going with effective writing, read your favorite writers, publications, and some award-winning ads. Immerse yourself in great art or photography. Talk to people you find very believable.

10. *Be collaborative.* Writers usually work in teams with artists. Get your partner involved early. Turn off the phones and kick ideas around. Don't be negative about any ideas in the early stages. And remember that good artists write some of the best headlines; good writers think up some of the strongest visuals.

11. *Listen for ad ideas.* When you're in meetings, talking with others about the product, almost anywhere, anytime — listen for ideas. Some of the best copy comes out of everyday conversation with the people around you.

12. *Review competitive ads.* Before you begin writing, study the competitors' messages. What is their strategy? How can you top them? Remember, you're trying to win business away from the other guys.

13. *Defend your work, but don't be stubborn.* When you present an idea to a group, and nobody responds, move on. They're telling you kindly that there must be something better.

> *"I can't teach you to write. Neither can anyone else. You learn to write by writing. You write dozens, even hundreds, of headlines for each ad. You write, rewrite and, again, rewrite the body copy. You make sure you've found the right idea, and that it comes right out of the product. You make sure it relates to the people you want to buy the product."*
>
> — Al Hampel,
> former creative leader of
> Benton & Bowles advertising agency[1]

REFERENCES

1. *The Wall Street Journal* © 1993 Dow Jones & Company, Inc. All rights reserved. Reprinted by permission of Dow Jones & Company, Inc., which has not participated in the preparation of this book.

2. James Webb Young, *A Technique for Producing Ideas* (Chicago: Advertising Publications, Inc., 1962).

3. Graham Wallas, *The Art of Thought* (London, Jonathon Cape, Ltd, 1926).

4. Al Ries and Jack Trout, *Positioning: The Battle for Your Mind* (New York: Warner Brothers Books, 1981).

5. James L. Marra, *Advertising Creativity: Techniques for Generating Ideas* (Englewood Cliffs, NJ: Prentice-Hall, Inc., 1990).

6. Terrance A. Shimp, *Promotion Management and Marketing Communications*, 3rd ed. (Orlando: The Dryden Press, Harcourt Brace Jovanovich, 1994).

7. William A. Bernbach. From a speech titled, "Facts Are Not Enough," delivered to the American Association of Advertising Agencies national convention, 1980.

8. Roy Paul Nelson, *The Design of Advertising* (Dubuque, Iowa: WCB Brown and Benchmark, 1994).

9. William A. Marsteller, "The Wonderful World of Words," Memorandum to the employees of Marsteller, Inc., 1971.

Arthur Congdon is founder and president of Congdon & Company LLC, consultants in visual communications, in Greenwich, Connecticut.

Congdon has been designing effective and highly visible graphics for major U.S. and international corporations for more than 20 years. His portfolio includes advertising and print communications, identity programs, and packaging for a wide range of business entities, including Bacardi-Martini USA, BBC Worldwide/Americas, Budget Rent a Car, CBS, the Guggenheim Museum, Pepsi-Cola, Safeco Insurance, the United Nations, and the United States Government.

As an expert in the design field, Mr. Congdon has held senior executive positions with the Guggenheim Museum in New York (design director), with Sandgren & Murtha in New York (vice president and design director), with Lippincott & Margulies (vice president and executive creative director) and Congdon Macdonald and Shear in New York (chairman and managing partner).

Mr. Congdon holds a BFA degree in Advertising Design from Boston University, an MFA degree in Graphic Design from Yale University and is a member of the American Institute of Graphic Arts and other professional design organizations. He has taught design and photography at Yale University and has received numerous awards for his work in visual communications.

CHAPTER 6

DESIGNING TO OPTIMIZE
THE ADVERTISING MESSAGE

The degree to which an ad communicates its intended message to its intended audiences is the measure of its success.

The steps to get to that result—from creative thinking to sound strategy to concise copy—lead you to the integral stage of advertising design. Now is when it all comes together as the "face" you present to your buyers. Your goal, as advertising manager, is to find that next great idea that captures that attention of your audience.

No one can tell you what the next great ad should look like. However, this chapter describes the processes and techniques you need to design effective ads, to facilitate communication with ad designers, and to provide you with some guidelines for understanding and evaluating ads.

YESTERDAY'S GREAT ADS ARE NOT TOMORROW'S

Some designers are more than willing to provide step-by-step "recipes" for the creation of an effective advertising design. Following one of these recipes and mixing the graphic ingredients on the list as directed would, in all probability, lead to a serviceable ad design. Following the formula again would, similarly and predictably, lead to another ad design looking very much like the first. And so on and so forth.

Herein lies the flaw in the "formula" approach! Once a chocolate cake (from the recipe, of course) always a chocolate cake! After only three lessons you too can play Mozart! Build your dreamhouse with easy-to-follow plans! Learn to paint like the Old Masters! But very quickly you'd find your chocolate cake getting stale, your Mozart uninspired, your dreamhouse unfulfilling, your paintings predictable and unsatisfying.

To be truly effective, an ad must be fresh. Advertising design is a "living" discipline. Like great art, it is a mirror of its times. Like great art, it must successfully communicate an idea or concept to specific audiences, using contemporary media and communications conventions in a unique way. As times change, ideas and concepts change, audiences change, and media and conventions change, so advertising design must change as well.

WHAT "ADS" ARE WE TALKING ABOUT, ANYWAY?

This chapter deals with print ads for the most part. These are black-and-white or color ads that appear in magazines or newspapers. However, the processes, techniques, and evaluation principles for print advertising can be applied to other media as well (for example, bill-boards, transit posters, direct mail flyers, magazine and newspaper inserts, even Internet web sites).

WHAT IS GOOD ADVERTISING DESIGN?

Advertising design is the process of creating, selecting, modifying, and organizing graphic elements on a surface to communicate a predetermined editorial message (generally the selling of a product, service, or idea) to a target audience based upon a specific marketing strategy. (That's not *all* advertising design, it's just *good* advertising design!)

In successful advertising design, all of the elements work together to ensure the desired communication ... to implement the desired strategy, to support the brand character, to declare the "unique selling proposition," to make The Promise. (See the first chapter on Strategy.) Advertising design is not effective when the elements fail to work to implement the strategy. True, an ad may be beautiful, or it may display some exciting, punchy graphics, or it may feature completely original typography. But if it doesn't enhance or reveal the message through its graphics, those graphics are wrong and the ad is not a good one.

THE ADVERTISING "DESIGNER"

Effective advertising is usually the product of teamwork between design professionals, which include graphic artists, illustrators, and photographers, and nondesigners, which include corporate ad managers, agency account executives, copywriters, and market researchers. These talents work together, each bringing unique conceptual, technical, and experiential knowledge to the ad-development effort. In some cases, individuals play multiple roles either by inclination, by training, or by both.

But this is a creative process. So while respecting talent and training, relax a little about job descriptions. The final result will be a whole greater than the parts (and generally greater than one contributor, alone). So it's important to optimize the early stages of the creative process by setting aside strict role definitions. Remember: in addition to the role proclaimed on each team member's business card, each team member is a person, a thinker, an observer, a body of experience, a participant in contemporary life, and a consumer.

Welcome a headline written by a designer; encourage a copy-writer to suggest photo subjects; and solicit other nondesigners (including yourself) to offer design opinions. Keep your eyes open for fresh ideas ... cross the boundaries ... stretch some minds ... and take risks. The reward is in the risks.

THE AD DESIGN "PROCESS"

There is a commonly used procedure for the design of effective advertising. It leads from initial exploration and discovery, through evaluation and refinement, to a final design. Here are the usual steps in that process. It is important to remember this is not a linear process; backtracking occurs frequently on this path. You'll find it necessary to move back and forth between steps to revisit, reinterpret, or revise ideas along the way. The process is a dynamic one, and should be, to produce the best result.

Strategy/Message Development
Determining the "Destination"

This is the stage at which the broad ad strategy is articulated and primary ad message or messages are defined. Ad designs will be judged on how they support the strategy and communicate the message(s).

Strategy/message development should always be the first step in the process of ad design. The step may or may not involve the corporate ad manager. And it may or may not involve the ad agency's graphic designers. It is important to note, however, that the designer's exploratory efforts can only bear fruit when a clear advertising strategy exists and a clear message is defined before the start of graphic exploration. Since all elements of an ad, graphics, text and other, should work to support a specific strategic message, the absence of such a message means the absence of a conceptual (and graphic) destination for the designer.

The strategy/message may also have an expression in words. If so, having a specific headline or headline idea will also help to define the designer's ultimate destination. Again, since the creative process is a "joint venture," do not be surprised to have headline concepts or even actual words come from a designer. Concepts grow out of the process of graphic exploration.

Regardless of how the strategy/message is developed, it is important that designers and the other members of the creative team meet to discuss it. It is not uncommon for the germ of a brilliant advertising campaign design to have its beginning at one of these "kick-off" sessions.

Thumbnails
Generating Many Different Ideas

This is the initial design exploration process. Doing thumbnails actually means looking for ad ideas, thinking of ad visuals/concepts, recording them in a quick and efficient manner, and moving on to more ideas.

Thumbnails are not used for client presentations. And regardless of how solid the underlying idea, thumbnails should be graphically sketchy, unrefined, and numerous (hundreds are not uncommon). The purpose of thumbnails is to depict the large elements (graphics and text) in the simplest manner. They can be produced by traditional methods (marker or pencil on paper), on computers, or in any other way that facilitates the quick generation and recording of ideas. They can be in color or black-and-white. In all cases, they constitute the first step to the realization of an ad. It is important not to spend too much time on an individual thumbnail, since the objective is to develop a broad range of ideas. Refinement comes later.

Designers should approach the thumbnail phase aggressively, enthusiastically, and with an open mind. In many instances, the real thumbnail exploration begins when the usual store of ideas for a particular ad is used up and the designer is "forced" to take the voyage of discovery into uncharted territory.

A designer should fully expect to generate a fair share of "bad" designs (unworkable, inappropriate, or weak designs) during the exploratory process. It is important to realize, however, that "bad" designs as well as good designs can provide understanding of and direction to the project. Designers must evaluate each new idea, learn from it, and use this insight on the next thumbnail. They must strive for the appropriate, but also risk the unorthodox, the "far out," the unexpected, the outrageous, the clever, the humorous, the startling, and the ridiculous. They must "ideate" to their limits and then beyond. Developing a broad range of ad alternatives at the thumbnail stage will significantly improve the opportunities for a great final ad.

Note: Sometimes designers encounter "designer's block," rendering them unable to advance in the exploration process. Here are two techniques for overcoming this curse.

1. Have designers develop thumbnail ideas against the clock. Suggest that a new idea be developed every 30 seconds during a 10-minute period, placing emphasis on changing conceptual direction frequently to generate the most unique ideas.

2. Pair designers and have each alternately build on the idea of the other. In other words, Designer A sketches an idea, Designer B extends or modifies that idea and sketches another, Designer A takes that design and gives it a twist. Lots of bad ideas come out of such exercises but some good ones do too, and "designer's block" usually disappears.

The process continues with an evaluation of the thumbnails. This evaluation may be undertaken by the designer or with the agency team members. The thumbnail ideas and concepts should be judged in terms of how effectively they support the strategy, how well they might communicate the intended message, and whether the graphics seem strong and memorable. The most promising ideas are then selected for further development.

Roughs
Rendering the Most Promising Ideas for Further Evaluation

Roughs are full size, and sometimes full-color, renderings of the ad which are intended to demonstrate the core idea/concept for the ad and to accurately indicate all major visual elements, including headline type, photography, company logos, product images, and other graphics. In the absence of an actual photo or illustration of a required subject, "stand-ins" are frequently used to indicate the style or content of the final image. Body copy is simulated using parallel, horizontal marker strokes or "dummy" copy ("nonsense" words set in the proper type style and size).

Although these renderings are called "roughs," they may look very finished. Roughs were traditionally produced by agency illustrators, specially trained for the task, using felt-tipped markers on layout paper. Times have changed. Now roughs are frequently produced by designers on computers. As a consequence of this technological boost, roughs can look, in every way, just like finished ads. Don't let a flashy, realistic-looking rough dazzle and blind you in your evaluation of it. Roughs must be approached as communications that are still only partially formed, still steps away from finalization, still awaiting improvement. It is sometimes helpful to view the computer as merely a very expensive and very powerful 50-pound "pencil," a device to put human thoughts and ideas on paper.

To evaluate roughs, consider how effectively they support the strategy, how well they communicate the intended message, how arresting and memorable they are, and how visually exciting. (See "Evaluating Ads.") One or more of the ad concepts should then be selected for further refinement.

Comps
Producing Realistic-Looking Ads for Judging the Best Ideas

"Comps" is short for "comprehensives." This is the stage at which the most promising design ideas are refined and rendered in a form that looks just like the final ad. The resulting comps are then evaluated by the account team and client. Even executives unable to visualize anything should be able to "read" a comp.

The best ad ideas are then thought out, distilled, refined, adjusted, and rendered as comps for presentation. Comps are created to duplicate the intended final look of the ads. They show, wherever possible, the actual components of the finished ad, including the following:

- Headline copy, using actual wording in the intended type style or styles;
- Pictorial elements with product photos, models, and illustrations; and
- Text copy (set as it will appear).

It is these comprehensives that you, as advertising manager and your associates on the client side, will view, evaluate, and accept or reject. It is in the best interests of the advertising creative team, therefore, to eliminate as many graphic "unknowns" as possible from these comps. Many people are not able to visualize as well as designers and feel insecure when asked to "complete the picture." Keep this in mind if you're called upon to present to senior management at your company. Insecurity of any kind is not usually a stepping-stone to success for an ad.

Based upon an evaluation of these comprehensives, the final look of the ad or campaign will be confirmed.

Mechanicals

Preparing the Best Ad for Printing

At this stage, the final ad is prepared for reproduction. All of the graphic and technical activities undertaken and decisions made during this step lead to an interpretation of the ad in print that duplicates the approved comp.

With final management or client approval of the ad design, which may include legal, regulatory, governmental, association or other approvals, the mechanical is produced. A mechanical is the vehicle that will "carry" the approved ad to print.

Traditionally, mechanicals were prepared on boards (they used to be called "keylines" or "pasteups") with numerous vellum or acetate overlays, each overlay containing a part of the final ad image. Each part could then be manipulated individually by professionals in various printing disciplines to optimize the final reproduction of the ad.

Today, mechanicals are prepared on the computer and the layers are electronic. In both cases, the layers can be likened to a sandwich with an ingredient (for example, type or pictorial element) on each layer. Each layer is separate and distinct for ease of handling, but when combined and eaten (seen), the sandwich (ad) ingredients blend together to form a single, special taste (communication).

Large agencies employ professionals specially trained in and dedicated to the art of mechanical preparation. In small agencies, the designer may perform the task. In any event, the key to producing a good mechanical is:

a) knowing the opportunities and limitations of the chosen reproduction method;

b) fully understanding the "look" which is to be achieved; and

c) having the ability to manipulate many complex and varied graphic elements with a high degree of precision.

A good mechanical will mean a good ad. A bad mechanical can mean bad (and sometimes costly) "surprises."

As an ad manager, you may or may not be asked to approve a final mechanical on behalf of your company. It is important to remember to make any last-minute changes at the mechanical stage. Changes at the next stage, called the proofing stage, become complex and expensive.

Proofs

A Preview of the Printed Ad

The proof is a full-size, full-color reproduction of the final ad made prior to printing. It is produced from the mechanicals and is the final point at which changes can be made.

Proofs come in many forms and most are provided either by printers or pre-press specialty firms. The most accurate proof is a "press proof," which is made using the actual printing films and printing process that will be used for the final print run. Other kinds of proofs are available with a descending scale of reproduction fidelity and cost.

For the most part, small color and other adjustments can easily be made at the proof stage. Although larger changes can also be made, for example, moving elements around or changing copy, they are expensive to execute at this stage.

TALKING "DESIGN"

The successful execution of the processes outlined above requires meetings and other communications between designers, team members, and you, the ad manager. During these meetings, ad designs will be viewed, discussed, and evaluated to select and refine the most promising candidates and, ultimately, approve a "winner."

Understanding is an important part of such communications. In fact, communication without understanding is no communication at all. To intelligently discuss the design of an ad, and facilitate mutual understanding, it is helpful if everyone shares the same "dictionary" of graphics concepts and terms.

Not unexpectedly, many design terms were created by designers ("picture people" not "word people"). It is possible for a nondesigner, like you, to struggle through a conversation with a "creative," and make some headway communicating, using a nondesigner's vocabulary. But who needs the frustration?! Remove a communications barrier: talk the talk. You can eliminate a bad graphic idea quicker if you employ sharp, precise graphics terminology such as, "That distressed font is so packed the descenders bleed into the dingbats. It's a kern for the worse!"

To make communication easier for everyone involved, a glossary of terms is provided at the end of this chapter (Appendix A), along with a visual glossary to highlight some of the more important concepts (Appendix B).

If you have need of more detail, other definitions, or would simply like to delve further into design minutiae (much is available and much is very interesting), take a designer to lunch and pick his or her brain.

THE "STUFF" OF WHICH ADS ARE MADE

Type

The informational "voice" of the message of an ad usually resides in words set in type in the headline copy and body copy. The organization and arrangement of these reading elements of an ad is called typography. Readability is the key to good typography in advertising.

Readability was an important objective of the early type designers, as can be seen by the fact that their designs are still widely used today. Many of these typefaces bear their proud designers' names, for example, Garamond, Bodoni, and Caslon. For these artisans, designing and producing a font was a lengthy and difficult process, requiring a great deal of thought and experimentation along the way. Clearly, to produce an unreadable typeface was a waste of time.

Today, there are thousands of typefaces available to the advertising designer, each possessing its own unique character. The advent of the computer adds a new dimension to these thousands of typefaces. Not only can you set type using the computer, you can manipulate, stretch, condense, italicize, and even distort it fairly easily. In fact, using sophisticated but inexpensive software, such as Fontographer®, anyone can design a typeface. Unusual and quirky typefaces designed on the computer have narrowed the gap between "type" and "picture" to such a degree that type and picture have, in many cases, become one. Unfortunately, readability has sometimes been lost in the process.

Pictorial Images

The range of visual images that can be used in contemporary advertising is virtually limitless. "Pictorial images" can include photos, illustrations, symbols, logos, shapes, and other graphic elements. Type, which is a graphic element as well as a reading element, may be part of the image. You may also find yourself evaluating figurative (literal) or abstract creations; images produced by "hand," camera, or computer; or something that has been solarized, silhouetted, screened, morphed, filtered, anti-aliased, distressed, feathered, blurred, distorted, squeezed, roughened, tweaked, cloned, pixelated, scaled, or rotated beyond recognition.

This extensive range of images and interpretations of images contributes to the richness of contemporary advertising. Once again employing computer "magic," it is possible to radically alter the character, mood, and impact of an image by changing its background, colors, scale, proportions, and even seamlessly inserting elements from other sources. A giant tube of toothpaste can become a part of the New

York City skyline, scoops of ice cream dips can be stripes, polka dots, and plaids, and golfers can putt on the moon.

Clearly, the way in which an image is interpreted graphically has become as important as the image itself. But wielding the computer "wand" in the cause of advertising design brings with it new responsibilities. As Mickey Mouse discovered in *Fantasia*, it is risky to let the power of magic sweep you away!

Color

There is nothing more difficult to discuss, use, or control with precision than color. In the film *Mr. Blandings Builds His Dream House* (a film known to people who are old enough to call mechanicals "pasteups"), you can see a classic confirmation. Envisioning the color for the living room, Myrna Loy tells her housepainter, "I want it to be a soft green. Not as blue-green as a robin's egg, but not as yellow-green as daffodil buds. Now the only sample I could get is a little too yellow, but don't go to the other extreme and get it too blue. It should just be a sort of grayish, yellow-green." Enough said.

Fortunately, a system called the Pantone® Matching System has come to the rescue in the color specification department. Thousands of individual colors have been printed, using strict controls, on little color swatches and each has been assigned a unique number, called the Pantone number. A designer can pick up a Pantone Color Specifier book, find just the right color, and specify that number to another designer or printer a million miles away. That person looks up the number in his or her copy of the Pantone Color Specifier book, finds the swatch, and sees the same, precise color. Pantone color control tools continue to multiply with specification books and swatches for metallic colors, "hot" colors, tints of colors, and Pantone colors translated into standard printing inks (CMYK). Designers tend to gravitate to this comprehensive system when specifying colors. You should also own a Pantone Color Specifier book.

Using color, however, is a subtle, personal, and complex issue. Color doesn't merely "sit" on the surface of the paper, it is alive. You may have heard that warm colors "advance" and cool colors "recede," that pale blue is "soothing," and that bright red is "agitating." Nice. Joseph Albers, the father of modern color theory and color interaction also demonstrated, for example, that a single color can be both red and green at the same time and that colors can interact to visually "contract" or "expand" an image! Coupled with the fact that colors printed on glossy surfaces look "brighter" than colors printed on matte surfaces and that the look of a color changes as the character of the light falling on it changes ... well, enough said. The best way to evaluate color is to look at it. Make sure you do this when using color in advertising. And don't be afraid to say "It looks too blue!"

Relationships

The relative positioning and emphasis of type, other graphic elements and color on an ad page determines the "look" of the ad. Considerations are many and include such issues as large elements vs. small elements; sharply defined images vs. blurred images; color images vs. black-and-white images; single images vs. many images (repetition or pattern); balance (a static, firm look) vs. imbalance (a dynamic sometimes tension-creating look); organized images vs. "random" images (a great design challenge!); dark images vs. light images, the images themselves vs. the spaces around the images ("white" space or "negative" space); proportions of all elements; the visual "axis" (spine) of the ad; and directing the eye.

There are other relationships as well that pertain to the medium in which the ad will appear. Although these are generally out of the designer's control, they are worth considering. These include the size and shape of the page(s) on which the ad will appear; whether the ad is to be a solitary ad or in the company of others on a page; whether the ad is designed to be a single presentation or part of a larger series of ads; whether the ad is to be used in one medium (for example, a single magazine) or in many; or the placement of the ad in a publication (for example, an inside front cover or right-hand page).

There is no single relationship that makes an ad a success, but there are many relationships that can make an ad a failure. The best ad look is a unified one, where all elements, including the background, words, type, graphics, and color, work together to communicate one clear and strong message. The whole is greater than the sum.

Reproduction

The printing method that will be used for the ad is also a factor to consider when designing ads. It is important to know what process or processes will be employed so you are aware of the opportunities and limitations the process represents.

For example, an ad that is being designed for use in a newspaper, which generally means black-and-white only; coarse printing screen; irregular, matte paper surface; and poor ink coverage, requires a different design mindset than an ad for a full-color, glossy fashion magazine with its smooth paper surface, fine printing screen, and good ink coverage. Clearly, the printing method at the end of the process can and should drive design decisions at the beginning of the process.

"RULES" TO FOLLOW TO DESIGN GOOD ADS

There are some general design rules that can lead to an effective ad design. Follow them, but don't marry them. A talented designer might "violate" one of these rules and, in the process, create a more effective communication. Rules should never replace sound judgment, so don't automatically dismiss the act and, therefore, the ad. Challenge the designer to support his or her decision; it may be right. The art of advertising design has been advanced this way before, and it will be again.

1. **Create a graphic that embodies the intended message.** This is the ultimate challenge for the ad designer, deciding upon the visual that will do the most to advance the strategy of the ad. In many cases, this means that the designer must exercise restraint.

2. **Develop a distinctive look for your ad.** Success in this arena requires knowledge of what's out there. Know the competition, and make your ad stand out. If your competitors all wear gray suits, consider a red suit. If they all wear red suits, consider a gray suit. A gray ad in a gray environment will get as lost as a red ad in a red environment. Anything can be made to stand out from the crowd.

3. **Control the reading pattern.** In Western cultures, we read from left to right and from top to bottom. A lifetime of conditioning and reinforcement causes us to use this pattern as a "default" reading pattern unless otherwise directed. In an ad, it is always desirable to control the reading pattern of the viewer. This is done by creating strong type and other graphic elements as "landmarks" to guide the viewer along a predetermined path through the ad. This path leads to understanding and action.

4. **Select readable typefaces.** If it is important for a viewer to read a line of type, make it easy for that to happen by selecting a readable typeface. Contorted, extreme typefaces may be "in," but if they don't communicate their underlying words, they should be "out." Doubt about readability can be resolved without a lot of sophisticated and expensive testing. Just expose the set copy line to your mail carrier and ask for a quick read aloud.

5. **Avoid long lines of text.** Generally, lines longer than an alphabet and a half (39 characters) are difficult for a reader to follow and difficult to find the way back to the beginning of the next text line. Breaking one wide column into two or more narrower columns is one way to avoid this problem.

6. **Consider the advantages of upper and lower case letters.** A combination of upper and lower case letters will have greater readability than all upper case letters. The ascenders, descenders, and other shape variations of lower case letters make their silhouettes more unique and easier to interpret by the eye. Consider these benefits when designing an ad.

7. **Use small text type with care.** Pay careful attention to the readability of text in small sizes. Most reproduction methods screen the graphics. This breaks up all images, including type, into small dots. These dots can erode the design of small letterforms and compromise readability. When in doubt, use a larger size text type.

8. **Exercise caution when using reverse type.** Light type on a dark background is generally more difficult to read than dark type on a light background. The lighter forms visually "expand," changing the familiar relationships between and within letters. It is best to enlarge letters or increase the spacing between the letters in reverse type. Again, test your setting on the mail carrier, if you're in doubt.

9. **Avoid complex backgrounds for type.** Placing type over photographs or illustrations, over backgrounds that are textured or complex, or over backgrounds that contain frequent color or tone changes can make type very difficult to read. Move the text, enlarge the text, or simplify the background to assure readability.

10. **Avoid using too many graphic "tricks" in one ad.** Dazzling the reader with an overabundance of graphic tricks can obscure the message of the ad. Keep such interpretations to a minimum. Use them sparingly and then only to enhance the message.

11. **Consider using some of the "tried and true" ad design methods.** Here are some techniques for developing creative ad graphics that can be traced back to the Ancient Masters. Again, any and all should be used in the service of the strategy/message.
    - Creation (invent an innovative ad visual)
    - Exhumation ("resurrect" an old visual for your new ad)
    - Contrast (juxtapose unlike visuals to highlight differences)
    - Humor (present visuals to evoke amusement or laughter)
    - Shock (select visuals that are unexpected, surprising)
    - Sloth (provide an "incomplete" visual for the viewer to complete)
    - Covetousness ("adjust" or enhance a familiar visual)
    - Gluttony (fill the ad with lots of pieces of visual "stuff")

EVALUATING AD DESIGNS

If you can select a "good-looking" suit for yourself, if you can buy a car that everyone thinks is "way cool," then you're as qualified as the next person to participate in an ad design review meeting. In fact you're more qualified, because, besides obvious taste, you have the divining rod of ad evaluation, you have the strategy, the message. Remember, the message is the meaning, the measure, the magic, the magnet, the mother, the master, the matchmaker, the melody, the monarch ... the money!

As you review an ad design, here are some questions to consider.
- Is the ad strong? (Are the intended message and product or service absolutely clear?)
- Is the ad interesting? (Will it capture the viewer's interest? Will it merit a second look?)

- Is the ad effective? (Will it evoke the desired response?)
- Is the ad unique? (Does it have its own special personality?)
- Is the ad memorable? (Will the consumer retain the desired information?)
- Is the ad extendable? (Can it work as a series, if required?)
- Is the ad flexible? (Can it be effectively "reshaped" for other formats, if required?)
- Do all of the graphic elements work together to communicate the desired message?
- Are there any unnecessary or superfluous graphics that obscure the message? If so, which elements should be removed, replaced, refined, or reworked?

SOME LAST "REMEMBRANCES"

- Remember, the value of an ad is not measured by the beauty of its visual forms and colors, which may be very pleasant, but in the way it sells products or services or ideas. The idea must always prevail. The idea must always drive the design effort.
- Remember that the look of an ad and the message of an ad will be perceived as one (whether good or bad). The viewer will not separate the two.
- Remember, the ad must have a strong visual or editorial "hook" to stop and engage the viewer. This will cause the viewer to become more involved with the ad and may result in a more thorough reading of it.
- Remember to be aware of your audience/viewers and what they will and will not understand or respond to. Always look at a new ad design as if you possessed no knowledge of the product or service. See if you get the message.
- Remember that some people can't visualize. Comps should be finished enough to be understood by the viewer least able to visualize.
- Remember, also, that a comp can be painstakingly prepared to look like an "as printed" ad and can look spectacular. Don't let spectacular-looking comps anesthetize your critical brain.
- Remember that type is a pictorial (graphic) element as well as an editorial element and must "work" as hard, visually, as the other graphic elements.
- Remember, every part of the page is important in the design, even parts that contain no graphic elements. "White" or "empty" space can provide a needed frame of inactivity around graphic elements requiring emphasis.
- Remember, changes and adjustments are a necessary part of every ad development process. Changes are least expensive to make at the early stages and become more expensive as the

process proceeds. Changes at the proof stage are most expensive. An ineffective ad costs the most!

- Remember, there are usually many graphic ways to depict a given editorial concept; keep an open mind. Innovative solutions may not feel "comfortable" at first. Give them a chance.
- Remember to remove as many communications barriers from the ad evaluation process as possible. Pictures are pictures and words are words; they are not the same. If words could *precisely* describe pictures (ad graphics, in this case), we probably wouldn't need pictures. But we do need pictures. And even though a picture may equal 1,000 words, it's nearly impossible to find the 1,000 words that can even begin to equal a great ad design!

BRING ME THE GOOD STUFF!

You will find some very successful ads on the following pages. Try evaluating these ads against the measures described on the previous pages. Imagine the satisfaction the design team felt when they "discovered" each unique graphic solution, and try to find that satisfaction with your ads.

If all else fails, invoke the council of a wise, old designer: "If you can't make it good, make it big. If you can't make it big, make it red."

EXHIBIT 6.1

Client: The Absolut Company
Agency: TBWA/Chiat Day Advertising, Inc., New York, NY
Creative Director: Eric McClellan
Art and Copy Directors: Dan Braun & Bart Slomkowski
Production Manager: Peter Oppenheim

Absolut Country of Sweden Vodka & logo, Absolut, Absolut bottle design and Absolut calligraphy are trademarks owned by V&S Vin Sprit AB.

EXHIBIT 6.2

Client: The Absolut Company
Agency: TBWA/Chiat Day Advertising, Inc., New York, NY
Creative Director: Eric McClellan
Art and Copy Directors: Alix Botwin
Production Manager: Peter Oppenheim

Absolut Country of Sweden Vodka & logo, Absolut, Absolut bottle design and
Absolut calligraphy are trademarks owned by V&S Vin Sprit AB.

EXHIBIT 6.3

Client: The Absolut Company
Agency: TBWA/Chiat Day Advertising, Inc., New York, NY
Creative Director: Eric McClellan
Art and Copy Directors: Dan Braun & Bart Slomkowski
Production Manager: Peter Oppenheim

Absolut Country of Sweden Vodka & logo, Absolut, Absolut bottle design and
Absolut calligraphy are trademarks owned by V&S Vin Sprit AB.

EXHIBIT 6.4

Client: Utah Symphony
Agency: Williams & Rockwood, Salt Lake City, UT
Creative Director: Scott Rockwood
Art Director: David Carter
Copywriter: Harold Einstein
Illustrator: Clint Hansen
Production Manager: Sue George
Account Manager: David J. Cole

EXHIBIT 6.5

Client: Utah Symphony
Agency: Williams & Rockwood, Salt Lake City, UT
Creative Director: Scott Rockwood
Art Director: David Carter
Copywriter: Harold Einstein
Illustrator: Clint Hansen
Production Manager: Sue George
Account Manager: David J. Cole

EXHIBIT 6.6

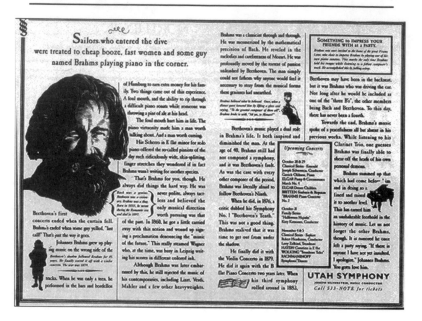

Client: Utah Symphony
Agency: Williams & Rockwood, Salt Lake City, UT
Creative Director: Scott Rockwood
Art Director: David Carter
Copywriter: Harold Einstein
Illustrator: Clint Hansen
Production Manager: Sue George
Account Manager: David J. Cole

EXHIBIT 6.7

Client: BBC Worldwide/Americas
Agency: Congdon & Company LLC, Greenwich, CT
Aegis International, Greenwich, CT
Art Director: Arthur Congdon
Copywriter: David Bushko
Production: Rob Penner

EXHIBIT 6.8

Client: National Geographic
Agency: Arnold Advertising, McLean, VA
Creative Director: Jim Kinsley
Art Director: Nora Jaster
Copywriter: Francis Sullivan
Production: Myles Marlow

EXHIBIT 6.9

Client: National Geographic
Agency: Arnold Advertising, McLean, VA
Creative Director: Jim Kinsley
Art Director: Nora Jaster
Copywriter: Francis Sullivan
Production: Myles Marlow

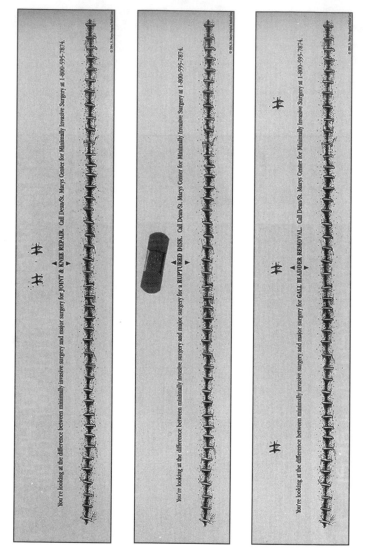

Client: Dean Medical Center and
St. Mary's Hospital Medical Center, Madison, WI
Agency: The Hiebing Group, Inc., Madison, WI
Creative Director: Barry Callen
Art Director: Bob Martin
Writer: Barry Callen

EXHIBIT 6.13

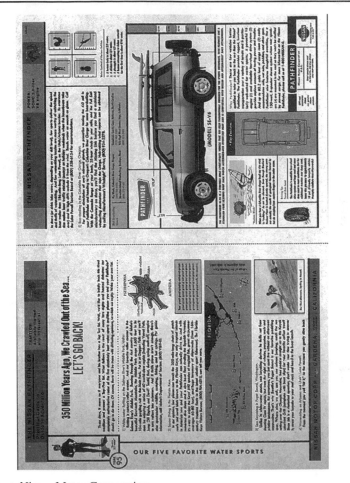

Client: Nissan Motor Corporation
Agency: Chiat/Day Inc. Advertising, Venice, CA
Creative Directors: Rob Siltanen and Yvonne Smith
Account Manager: Stephanie Stephens
Copywriter: Eric Grunbaum
Art Director: Craig Tanimoto
Production Artist: Charles Anderson Design
Production Manager: Madeline Bailey
Photographer: Shawn Michienzi, RIPSHAW inc.
Designer: Charles Anderson Design

Copyright Nissan (1996). Nissan, Pathfinder, and the Nissan logo are registered trademarks of Nissan.

EXHIBIT 6.14

Client: Nissan Motor Corporation
Agency: Chiat/Day Inc. Advertising, Venice, CA
Creative Directors: Rob Siltanen and Yvonne Smith
Account Manager: Stephanie Stephens
Copywriter: Eric Grunbaum
Art Director: Craig Tanimoto
Production Artist: Charles Anderson Design
Production Manager: Madeline Bailey
Photographer: Shawn Michienzi, RIPSHAW inc.
Designer: Charles Anderson Design

This glossary is oriented to the nondesigner. On the left is a list of design concepts/things expressed in plain English. Any of these terms may enter a conversation on advertising graphics. Each concept/thing is followed by a precise designer talk word or words. The glossary covers the most broadly used concepts and terms. By keeping this glossary at the ready, you'll a) significantly increase your understanding of what's going on at design meetings, b) effortlessly transform your brilliant suggestions into the official graphic designer "code," and c) impress the hell out of everyone.

Plain English	Designer talk
A set of letters, numbers and punctuation in one design and size.	Font
The large letters in type (capital letters).	Upper case
The small letters in type (not the large letters).	Lower case
The part of a lower case letter that sticks up, as in "b."	Ascender
The part of a lower case letter that hangs down, as in "p."	Descender
Letters with little "feet" at the top and bottom.	Serif
Letters without those little "feet."	Sans Serif
Letters that don't slant (they stand up straight).	Roman
Letters that slant (to the right).	Italic
Letters that look squeezed horizontally.	Condensed
Letters that look stretched horizontally.	Extended
Letters that are fat (or "fat-ish").	Boldface
Letters that are thin (or "thin-ish").	Lightface
Letters that look a little like handwriting.	Script
Letters designed to look chipped, scratched or damaged (yup!).	Distressed
Letters that you can hardly read (but some look very pretty).	Decorative
Odd little geometric or pictorial characters appearing with type.	Dingbats
Big type (for the BIG ideas).	Headline type
Small type (for supporting copy).	Body type
Lines of type that line up evenly on the left.	Flush left
Lines of type that line up evenly on the right.	Flush right
Lines of type that line up evenly on both sides.	Justified
A unit of measure for typesetting, approximately 1/6".	Pica
A unit of measure (really little) for type, approximately 1/72".	Point
The distance between lines of type (measured in points).	Leading
To move two letters closer together (to get rid of "ugly" space).	Kern
To add space between letters in a word.	Letterspace
To remove space between letters in a word.	Pack
The name of a company or product in a special design.	Logotype (logo)
A drawing or sketch of a proposed ad.	Layout

A place where you can buy photos and illustrations to use.	Stock house
Art that someone else created and which you can reproduce.	Swipe
Another term for mechanical used by some old folks.	Pasteup
To make one image change into another.	Morph
Color (red, green).	Hue
Color darkness or lightness (dark red, light red).	Tone
One color gradually changing to another color or tone across a surface.	Blend
A color specification system used by many designers and printers.	Pantone®
A dull paper finish.	Matte
A shiny paper finish.	Glossy
All ad elements, on a board or in electronic form, ready for the printer.	Mechanical
Printing process for most magazines and newspapers.	Offset lithography
Printing process for very large print quantities.	Gravure
The shift during normal working hours at a printing plant.	Day
The shift after normal working hours at a printing plant.	Night
The shift between midnight and early morning at a printing plant.	Graveyard
To convert a continuous tone image into small dots for printing.	Screen
A screened photograph or illustration printed in one color.	Halftone
A one-color photograph or illustration printed in two colors.	Duotone
A printed image with edges that gradually fade to unprinted paper.	Vignette
Stamping a 3D image into paper in color using ink or foil.	Embossing
Stamping a 3D image into paper without using color.	Blind embossing
The seam between two facing pages in a publication.	Gutter
Overlap of two images or an image extending to the edge of the page.	Bleed
Printing simulating all colors using only four process ink colors.	Process printing
The four process ink colors: cyan, magenta, yellow, and black.	CMYK
A print of an ad that shows how the ad will look when reproduced.	Proof
A full-color ad proof printed using a 3M photomechanical process.	Matchprint™
A full-color ad proof printed on a printing press.	Press proof
A print of a one-color ad that can be used like a mechanical.	Slick
What you see is what you get!	WYSIWYG ("wiz-ee-wig")

C = Cyan or a special blue; M = Magenta or a special red; Y = Yellow; and K = Black

APPENDIX B — A VISUAL GLOSSARY OF DESIGNER TERMS

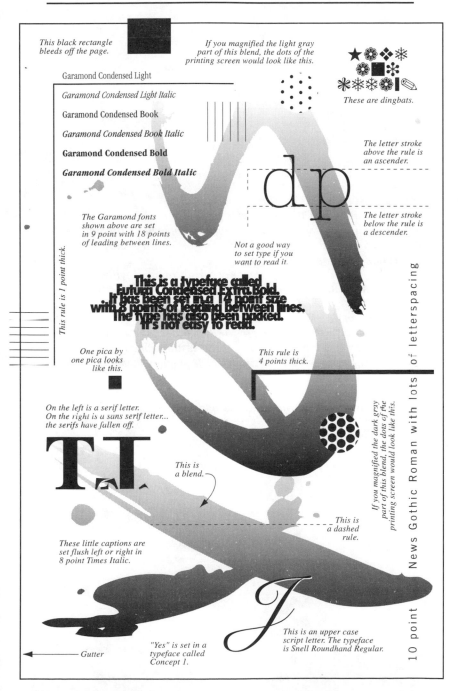

This black rectangle bleeds off the page.

If you magnified the light gray part of this blend, the dots of the printing screen would look like this.

These are dingbats.

Garamond Condensed Light

Garamond Condensed Light Italic

Garamond Condensed Book

Garamond Condensed Book Italic

Garamond Condensed Bold

Garamond Condensed Bold Italic

The letter stroke above the rule is an ascender.

dp

The Garamond fonts shown above are set in 9 point with 18 points of leading between lines.

The letter stroke below the rule is a descender.

Not a good way to set type if you want to read it.

This rule is 1 point thick.

This is a typeface called Futura Condensed Extra Bold. It has been set in a 14 point size with 8 points of leading between lines. The type has also been packed. It's not easy to read.

One pica by one pica looks like this.

This rule is 4 points thick.

News Gothic Roman with lots of letterspacing

On the left is a serif letter. On the right is a sans serif letter... the serifs have fallen off.

T T

This is a blend.

This is a dashed rule.

If you magnified the dark grey part of this blend, the dots of the printing screen would look like this.

These little captions are set flush left or right in 8 point Times Italic.

10 point

Gutter

"Yes" is set in a typeface called Concept 1.

This is an upper case script letter. The typeface is Snell Roundhand Regular.

Sheri Bretan is the senior vice president of Behavioral Analysis, Inc., (BAI) a full-service research company located in Tarrytown, New York, where she develops and assesses marketing and advertising strategies for major corporations.

She has extensive experience working for and with advertising agencies. At Benton & Bowles, she held a variety of positions, culminating as manager of the Creative Guidance Unit, the division responsible for all concept development and advertising testing for the agency. She then served as research director for Ted Bates/NY, where she wrote handbooks on new product development, testing rough versus finished productions, and assessing alternate copy testing methodologies.

Ronnee Fried is a principal at Brown, Koff, Fried, in New York City. This company provides tactical and strategic research for major advertisers and agencies.

She honed her research skills while working at key research companies, including the Data Development and Decision Center, and has worked on several ground-breaking research projects.

CHAPTER 7

MEASUREMENT

A sound advertising campaign begins with a marketing strategy. With that strategy in mind, you can create and finalize your campaign. Furthermore, within the context of that strategy, you can decide your campaign budget and plan your media strategy. Those decisions generally are made during the process illustrated in Exhibit 7.1.

Having done and implemented this, you now need to know whether all of your hard work is paying off. That means measurements, and that is what this chapter is about.

WHY SHOULD YOU WANT TO MEASURE?

Since the late 1890s, people have questioned the value of spending money on advertising. In what has become a cliché within the advertising community, John Wanamaker has been quoted as saying, "I know half of my advertising budget is wasted, I just don't know which half."

In today's environment, the question is even more critical. Marketing's window of opportunity is becoming narrower and narrower. Most companies want to launch products successfully, see the impact of their marketing strategy, and obtain a return on their promotion and advertising far faster than ever before. Any spending is scrutinized more critically. Pressure to produce near-term profits is mounting as it becomes more expensive to enter a category and/or maintain brands. Proving the value of any marketing expenditure is essential.

In many corporate environments, measurement is a given. How else will the choices made be evaluated and refined? Further, there is implicit recognition that sound management requires accountability. Corporations that have ongoing evaluative programs know that such programs provide far more value than mere report cards of past performance.

In other corporations, however (usually those in which the marketing function and/or consumer-directed marketing is newer), advertising, let alone advertising measurement, may be viewed with considerable skepticism. In fact, an American Business Press survey of senior business-to-business advertising executives reported by Robert Anderson indicated that half of these top executives didn't know whether or not their advertising was working.[1]

The ultimate issue is accountability. Without measurement of some form, you are open to a much more subjective assessment of your decisions. And, how do you know which of the many variables in your marketing plan are working hardest for you? Which should you adjust?

EXHIBIT 7.1 RESEARCH IS AN INTEGRAL PART
OF STRATEGIC DEVELOPMENT

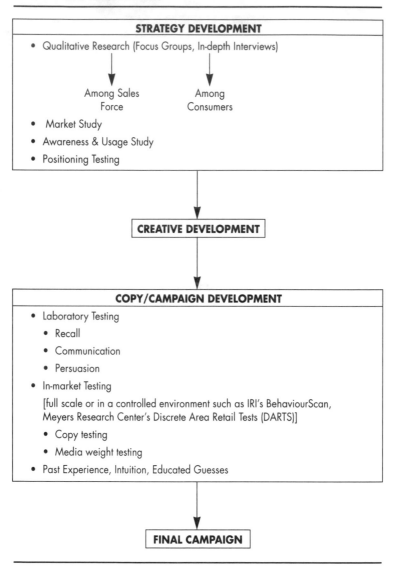

STRATEGY DEVELOPMENT

- Qualitative Research (Focus Groups, In-depth Interviews)

    Among Sales   Among
    Force   Consumers

- Market Study
- Awareness & Usage Study
- Positioning Testing

CREATIVE DEVELOPMENT

COPY/CAMPAIGN DEVELOPMENT

- Laboratory Testing
  - Recall
  - Communication
  - Persuasion
- In-market Testing
  [full scale or in a controlled environment such as IRI's BehaviourScan, Meyers Research Center's Discrete Area Retail Tests (DARTS)]
  - Copy testing
  - Media weight testing
- Past Experience, Intuition, Educated Guesses

FINAL CAMPAIGN

Without a structured measurement system, your "sense" of how well the campaign is doing cannot yield the insights commonly provided by a structured program. For example:

- Your sales are going up, but are you maximizing the potential gain?
- Your sales are increasing, but are you reaching all facets of your target?
- You're attracting new users, but are you turning off your current franchise?
- Is your strategic message being heard clearly?
- Are there ways of tweaking the campaign to enhance it?
- Is the media placement hitting your target?

Even if you aren't challenged in these ways, you may face more general questions as to whether or not you have, in fact, made the right choices, and if those choices will continue to be correct as your market situation changes and/or time passes.

What Is Ahead?

Measurement, when applied to the effectiveness of advertising campaigns, might seem to focus on a straightforward issue: How well are we doing?

But the reality is that selecting the appropriate measurement program and, within that, selecting the appropriate measures to assess the effectiveness of a campaign can be quite complex and require a good deal of up-front discussion and consideration.

One of the critical questions to address early is: "What do you want to measure?" To resolve this issue, you *must* have a clear definition of your campaign objectives — beyond the obvious goal of generating (incremental) sales.

The assumption here is that the strategic objectives have been previously articulated, agreed upon and, importantly, that the creative development and media plan are a reflection of these objectives.

While we will discuss these and other issues in greater detail later, we want to emphasize that the goal is to measure what the advertising is trying to accomplish — that is:

- Is the intended message being clearly communicated?
- Is the *targeted* audience hearing it?
- Is the target audience responding/being affected as desired?

The measurements required to answer these questions can take many forms. This chapter will address your major alternatives for answering the question, "How well is the advertising working?" Many might think the way to answer is obvious: "Did sales go up?" Or, a more sophisticated version might be, "Did sales go up enough, incrementally, to at least cover the cost of developing and placing the advertising?" Thus, at first blush, you might think that looking at sales data,

either on a within-company basis or, better yet, from a category perspective might be sufficient. After all, "If my sales went up, then my
advertising must be working. Why do I need consumer research?"

There is more to measuring advertising campaign effectiveness
than sales alone. While sales data are critical, there is very strong
incremental value to examine *both* sales and consumer-based data to
assess the effectiveness of a campaign.

Neither type of data provides a full picture of the campaign's
effectiveness. Only by addressing effectiveness from both sales and
consumer-based perspectives can you fully understand how and *why*
your campaign is succeeding or not.

But, "sales data" and "consumer-based data" are broad constructs. As shown in Exhibit 7.2, each type can be observed/gathered in
a variety of ways.

Within this framework, this chapter will address:
1. The importance of measurement objectives;
2. Sources of measurement;
3. Measurement options — alternative approaches to collecting
   data;
4. Understanding key measures used in tracking programs;
5. Issues to consider when commissioning a tracking study.

EXHIBIT 7.2 DATA-GATHERING OPTIONS

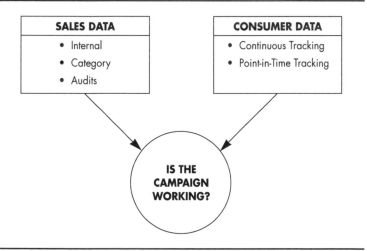

THE IMPORTANCE OF MEASUREMENT OBJECTIVES

To *effectively* evaluate your campaign, you need to define specific objectives for the evaluation. These objectives must be predicated upon your marketing and advertising strategy. As indicated earlier, the ultimate purpose of most marketing efforts is to increase sales. (There are a few exceptions: for example, to slow the rate of decline of a brand or category.)

However, in too many instances, advertising campaigns are developed solely to increase business without articulating specific intermediary goals (that is, a road map of how to get there). Campaigns developed without such intermediary goals are difficult to measure.

Some intermediary goals may be:

- to attract new users to the category;
- to attract retrial among lapsed users;
- to increase brand loyalty;
- to increase frequency of purchase among the current franchise;
- to encourage new uses of a product;
- to address a new target audience;
- to differentiate a product in a category with little differentiation;
- to introduce a new product or line extension;
- to reposition a brand.

This list is neither mutually exclusive nor exhaustive; there may be overlapping goals. But once the goals have been articulated, a measurement plan can be developed.

Specific learning or research objectives will evolve from a clear understanding of the advertising goals:

- Are sales increasing ...
  - — beyond what might have happened anyway?
  - — as much as they might have been?
- From which brands are we getting our business?
- What types of customers are we ...
  - — adding to our franchise?
  - — getting more business from?
  - — losing?
  - — reaching through the media plan (providing the opportunity to see your campaign)?
- In what (new) ways, if any, is our product being used?
- Is our product cannibalizing another product of ours?
- What imagery is being conveyed/how are consumers perceiving our brand and its benefits?

SOURCES OF MEASUREMENT

As indicated in Exhibit 7.2, there are two sources of information:

- Sales-based data;
- Consumer-based data.

To assume a direct correlation between sales increases and advertising effectiveness can be misleading: if sales are up, you might say, "Great! Keep going." But which aspects of the program should you emphasize or discontinue? How do you know that you've reached maximum potential? If cost cutting is required, what part of your program could be dropped with the least impact?

If sales are not as expected, sales data cannot tell you if the problem was with the advertising or with other parts of the marketing program (for example, promotions, in-store placement, distribution, competitive activity, etc.). Even if you were to assume that it *must be* the advertising, reading of sales data alone cannot answer questions such as:

- Was the message correct?
- Were the desired changes in beliefs about the brand effected?
- Was the audience right?
- Was the media weight sufficient to break through the clutter of competitive "voices"?
- Was the selected media appropriate for the desired target? Did the target have the opportunity to see/hear the advertising?

It is through the convergence of the sales and consumer-based data that the strongest evaluations and decisions are made.

In short each channel measures different aspects of a campaign. What should you expect to learn from each type of data?

Key Learning from Sales-Based Research

On an overall basis, the first indication of effectiveness is any change in actual sales between the pre- and post-advertising period. This is most simply learned by analyzing your internal sales data to identify any difference in units or dollars between the two periods. This difference is the gross measure, with more refined sales data providing additional input and guidance. Incremental sales, from pre- to postadvertising campaign is always good news, but it does not tell you enough. More in-depth learning opportunities exist.

As Exhibit 7.3 indicates, well-constructed sales analyses can get you far beyond the question of whether total sales have gone up or down since implementation of the advertising campaign. Ordering sales analyses which allow you to collect data by needed SKUs, distribution channel, and so on, are critical when the goals of your campaign require information from these sources.

Analysis of this information allows you to address issues such as:

By SKU
- Has the advertising helped generate greater movement for the desired "flavor/form/size?"
- Has the featured "flavor/form/size" expanded the total brand's sales or has it cannibalized from your other SKUs?

EXHIBIT 7.3 TYPES OF SALES-BASED ANALYSES

SKU	CHANNEL	EXTERNAL VARIABLES
•Main Brand vs. Sub-lines	•Type of Outlet	•Regionality
•Package Size	•Size of Outlet	•Seasonality
•Form	•Specific Chain/Unit	•Competitive Activity
•Flavor/Fragrance		•Sales Force Strength

- Is the strongest growth curve generated by less profitable forms?

There are ancillary benefits of SKU-based analysis. For example, in cases where the parent brand is NOT the focus of the tested campaign, you can determine whether it is benefitting from the line extension's efforts. (This is called a halo effect.)

By Distribution Channel
- Is there a weakness in sales in a specific type of outlet? Do you need to adjust your media strategy by boosting your co-op advertising for a specific channel?
- Focused analyses can also identify situations such as: while your campaign has generated stronger sales in most outlets, results in one chain are disappointing. Is that vendor adequately supporting your brand with shelf positioning, end-aisle displays, and other in-store promotions? Do you need to adjust your relationship with that vendor? Only analysis at the outlet level can identify this sort of problem, whether it is advertising-related or not.

By "External" Variables
- Is there a softness in sales in a specific region? Does this reflect a heightened or different competitive picture? Is additional spending required ("heavy-up" advertising) to defend the brand against competitors' heavier spending/other marketing activity in that region? Is another strategic message needed against a new competitor?
- Sales data indicate different results by season. Is there a need for a change of execution more relevant to each season's needs?
- Should you continue to advertise in the "off-season"? If no one else is advertising, should you consider contraseasonal advertising (that is, advertising in seasons when consumption of your category is traditionally weak)? As an example, beer consumption is heavily weighted to summer months. Traditionally, advertisers have done relatively little advertising in the winter months. To ease some of that sales seasonality, some advertisers have begun advertising during the winter (contraseasonally).

- As a side benefit, you may learn, for example, that sales in a given region are particularly strong. If all other variables are consistent, it may be that the sales force in that region is doing something unique/special. Do you need to review, retrain, or inform the balance of your sales force based on the stronger region's approach(es)?

Key Learning from Consumer-Based Data

Given this exhaustive list of information you can obtain from sales data, you may well be asking, "Why do I need anything else?" Simply stated, because consumer-based data provide the why's (or the diagnostic learning) that are not available from sales-based data. Through consumer data you have the opportunity to understand and assess the details of what happened, so you can (ideally) repeat your successes, build on them, and refine your advertising and/or media strategy, if needed.

How does consumer data help to do this? Exhibit 7.4 begins to answer this.

EXHIBIT 7.4 THE TYPES OF QUESTIONS THAT CONSUMER-BASED RESEARCH CAN ANSWER

THE ISSUE		THE RESEARCH CONSTRUCT
Who has seen/heard the advertising?	⟶	Stopping Power
What have they heard?	⟶	Strategic Message Communication
What impressions/images do they now hold regarding brand and/or category?	⟶	Belief Structure
Who is purchasing and/or using and how?	⟶	Behavioral Impact

While these topics sound good, what are the practical applications of learning about each? Exhibit 7.5 is a checklist of questions you may be asking (or have been asked) about a campaign.

Each issue relevant to your marketing situation can be examined among various demographic and behavioral consumer segments including:
- Current users;
- Lapsed users;
- Those who have never used;
- Heavier users;
- Desired demographic target.

EXHIBIT 7.5 CHECKLIST TO ASK ABOUT AN ADVERTISING PROGRAM

STOPPING POWER

- Is your campaign breaking through the clutter? What percent of your target audience
  a) is able to remember your brand product name?
  b) claims to have seen the advertising?
  c) recognizes your brand/product?

- At what point does the campaign begin to lose its power or wear out?

- If you have chosen a noncontinuous advertising schedule, either "flighting" the advertising (a pattern of months with and then without advertising) or "blinking" (an on-off pattern with shorter periods of advertising and not advertising), then
  a) how much loss occurs between each on/off period or flight?
  b) how long does it take to recoup? Should you tighten up the period between flights (assuming you can afford to do so)?
  c) can you actually lengthen the period between flights?

STRATEGIC MESSAGE COMMUNICATION

- Which, if any, of the intended messages are being heard?

- Are they being heard properly? Is there misinterpretation of your messages?

- Is the advertising clear?

BELIEF STRUCTURE

- Have the strategic messages been translated into stronger/changed attitudes or beliefs about the category? Your product/brand? Its ability to deliver desired benefits?

- Has the advertising changed/reinforced overall feelings about the product/brand and its appropriateness for the target?

- Does the campaign differentiate the product/brand from its competition?

- Is the competition perceived as delivering key benefits better/more attuned to current needs?

- Have perceptions of the product/brand softened? Does the campaign need refreshing?

BEHAVIORAL IMPACT

- Has the advertising increased your product/brand's presence within the consideration set?
  a) Is the product/brand now considered when it hadn't been previously?
  b) Has the product/brand taken a more primary role in consumers' consideration sets?

- Is there greater loyalty to the product/brand?

- Is the increase in sales a function of new users or of more use by the "same" set of consumers?

- Has there been the desired change in how the product/brand is used?

Using Consumer Data to Assess Media Plans

By examining consumers' claimed media habits in relation to the executed media plan, another dimension can be added to your learning. As an example, let's assume there is low claimed recall of your advertising. Is it because your target didn't have the opportunity to be exposed (for example, not in magazines he/she reads) or is it that the advertising itself just didn't break through the clutter? Exhibit 7.6 indicates how that question can be answered.

Exhibit 7.6A shows that recall is not what had been hoped for. But, by examining the level of recall *within* various consumer segments, we learn that recall is not uniformly weak (Exhibit 7.6B). In fact, in Segment A recall is quite satisfactory, while in Segment B it is not. If we look further at the data, we can see that media exposure, too, is not uniform (Exhibit 7.6C). In fact, recall is highest among those with the highest media exposure.

Thus, you could conclude that, *if* they saw the advertising, Segment B would remember it. This tells you to look more critically at the media plan, rather than at the campaign itself.

By examining the "who" as well as the "what," you gain a clearer view of your problem and can make better decisions about how to solve it.

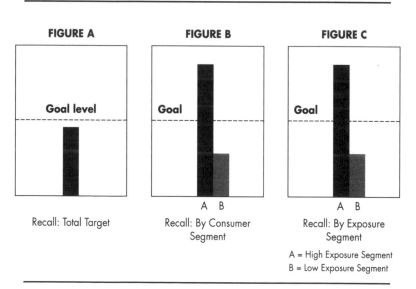

FIGURE A — Recall: Total Target

FIGURE B — Recall: By Consumer Segment

FIGURE C — Recall: By Exposure Segment

A = High Exposure Segment
B = Low Exposure Segment

Some Types of Sales Data

There are a number of types of sales data available. Which you choose depends on whether you are going to measure from a company-based perspective only or look at competitive brands as well (category-based perspective). While the former means setting up ways of monitoring sales internally, the latter usually requires purchasing "outside" information.

Relying on internal sales data is, by far, the simplest and least costly option. The odds are strong that there are already mechanisms in place to "count" how many units of a given item have been shipped and the dollar value. (In categories where returns are an issue, these counts are surely collected as shipped and not returned.) Depending on the nature of the sales analyses you desire (refer to Exhibit 7.3 for examples), you may need to adjust the way these counts are made — but in all but the rarest of instances, the general "counting" is already in place.

However, these counts give you a narrow view of the world. Internal sales data, by definition, only tell you what's happening in your company. But your advertising efforts are not operating in a vacuum. To more effectively understand the impact of your advertising program on the customer, you should look at what's happening to the category as a whole. If your sales are up, is it a function of the advertising or, for example, is the entire category's sales up due to weather?

It is a cliché by now to say that numbers can lie; the goal of setting up an evaluation system is to keep you from being misled. In this context, working with category sales data is a good starting point for avoiding erroneous conclusions.

There are literally dozens of sources of category-based sales data. The choices depend primarily on the (main) channels of distribution for your product. If, for example, the majority of your category's sales are through supermarkets, drugstores, or mass merchandisers — outlets that are well penetrated by scanners — you can probably work with one of the two major distributors of scanner-collected data: Information Resources, Inc. (IRI) or A.C. Nielsen. These companies can provide a range of detail, depending upon your needs, your budget, and your specific category.

If you cannot depend on this kind of collection method, other options are available, often depending on the product category. There are syndicated service providers (these vary widely, depending on the category) who offer:

- Analysis of warehouse withdrawals;
- Storage for audit data;
- Household panel purchasing data;

- Business inventory assessment audits;
- Industry newsletters.

For any given category, these data may be available on a syndicated basis — that is, the measurements are ongoing; all you need to do is "buy into" the service — or, you may need to develop customized approaches unique to your category through independent research organizations.

The options are category-dependent and are, therefore, too numerous to mention. The specific service(s) available for a given category can best be identified by talking with your industry's trade associations. (Note: There are some industries where general, category-wide data can be obtained free of charge from trade sources or newsletters, for example. However, to get quality and/or detailed information, you usually must purchase it.)

Whichever category-based route is indicated for you, the rule is quite simple: have consistent collection and sampling methods. This is mandatory so that shifts in data from period to period are not a function of the collection or sampling methods themselves.

Since most companies do some sort of sales analysis — at minimum, of internal-based data — the remainder of this discussion will focus on the complementary avenue of consumer data.

Consumer-Based Data

There are several alternative approaches to investigating effectiveness based on consumer-derived data, but it is all based on tracking consumers' knowledge. By and large, advertising tracking research is conducted on a customized basis through studies designed for and purchased by individual client corporations.

Since this work is ordinarily customized, we will explore conceptual issues in greater detail. In this way, you will be better prepared to decide what is needed given your specific situation. Broadly speaking, these alternative approaches fall into two primary categories:

Point-in-Time Tracking. Point-in-time tracking studies take a pulse of the marketplace at specified intervals throughout the year. The number of these intervals (or "waves") reflects both research budget levels and the media plan.

Continuous Tracking. Interviewing for continuous tracking studies is conducted year round. The number of reporting periods depends on budget and timing of business decisions. (It is better to read a reliably sized sample quarterly than a less reliable sample size monthly.)

An advertising tracking study — be it point-in-time or continuous — normally measures consumers' awareness, usage, and attitudes toward your brand and key competitive brands *over time*. In addition, media habits and shopping/usage behavior may be included. Demography is always included. Typically, these studies are conducted over the telephone among the specified target audience (for example, heads of household, 18–54 years of age, who use the category; Human Resource directors in companies with revenues greater than $1 million).

The most inclusive approach to tracking is the continuous one. Although it can be more costly, it provides the greatest range of learning as well as the greatest range of analytic flexibility. What does continuous tracking offer that point-in-time does not?

1. Continuous tracking data are less impacted by non-campaign-related variables. Continuous tracking collects data throughout the year. (Depending upon budget, target group, and the issues being addressed, interviewing may be conducted daily, semiweekly, weekly, or on some other consistent schedule.) This permits some extraneous variables to be "smoothed out" over the course of the analytic period. But what are some of these variables that might impact your ability to interpret results?

Marketing Variables
- Heavy promotion;
- A new competitor;
- Increased advertising spending by competition;
- Defensive campaign response by competitor.

Environmental Variables
- Weather;
- Adverse publicity for the category or your brand;
- Distribution failures/extreme out-of-stock situations.

2. Continuous tracking is more flexible than the point-in-time approach. Since you are measuring on an ongoing basis, the data collected are not simply a function of *your* specific media plan. Continuous tracking reflects *your* marketing program and that of your key competitors as well.

Typically, the schedule for point-in-time tracking waves is determined based on your own media plan. Interviewing periods, for example, are selected on the basis of when your advertising flights begin and end. As a result, you have gathered a vision of the category through the filter of your own media plan. With a continuous tracking program, you view the category less subjectively: you have the benefit of learning from the successes and failures of your competition, too.

As an ancillary benefit, specific time periods reflecting special circumstances can be tabulated at any time (assuming there is sufficient sample size for stable reading). Thus, a short national campaign or promotion, terminating mid-September, can be quickly evaluated using, for example, September 15 to October 15 data. Prior month's data are used as a benchmark.

3. Continuous tracking of recall, attitudes, and behavioral response to your advertising allows you to better understand consumers' response curves within your category. How quickly can a brand be integrated into the consideration set? (That set represents the group of brands from which consumers select their purchase, either because they are apparent to the consumer or because something in the marketing has suggested that these brands more readily fulfill current needs.) How quickly does recall and/or attitudinal fall-off take place once advertising is off-air? How quickly can you anticipate attitudinal changes? Responses to questions such as these can help shape your next media plan. Yet, they cannot be addressed in a point-in-time setting, since that setting doesn't let you see the actual ebb and flow of purchasing over time.

4. Continuous tracking offers the opportunity to address/ investigate consumer response to unplanned-for issues as they arise, rather than attempting to cope after the fact. As an example, a strike by your factory workers is generating a lot of press about your company. As part of your ongoing tracking study, you can add questions to assess consumer awareness of and reaction to the event. If you want a particularly quick read, you can increase the number of interviews being conducted that week or month. And, because you have the ability to "cut" the data by any time frame, you can evaluate any change that may have occurred from the exact point in time the press began. You can assess potential impact on your franchise and quickly develop defensive strategies, if needed, without waiting for your next wave of tracking to come in, and without conducting additional research.

5. Continuous tracking provides time and dollar efficiencies when you want to evaluate additional marketing variables. Let's suppose that the campaign has been successful. Now you wish to test a promotional overlay in a particular region. Previously collected data from that region can serve as the benchmark against which this new marketing activity can be judged. How? By conducting additional or "augment" interviews in a particular region once the promotion is in place. This permits you to build up to a sufficiently stable base size and provides insight into the impact of the promotion on consumers. If payout levels are not reached, you know why.

The major advantage of point-in time tracking, however, is a powerful one — in almost all circumstances it is less costly. Given that it is of no value to conduct continuous tracking with an insufficient sample size, it is certainly far better to field a point-in-time tracking program than to conduct a poor continuous study or no tracking program at all. If budget dictates, it's better to choose a point-in-time tracking program (even with few data collection periods) than no program at all.

Undertaking a Tracking Program

The foundation of traditional tracking studies is a questionnaire. An example is shown in Appendix A at the end of this chapter.

This example is designed to help you more easily visualize key points that are covered in the following sections. Most, but not all, of the alternative measures mentioned have been included. The idea is to give you a *sense* of what your questionnaire will look like.

The traditional demographic measures, including age, income, family size, or, for business-to-business products, company billings and number of employees, have been omitted since they are fairly standard throughout the industry and will vary by product category and target.

The Screening Questionnaire — the first part of the questionnaire which is dedicated to qualifying eligible respondents and terminating those who do not qualify for your interview — has also been omitted because it is so category/brand/objective specific.

The "grid" portions of this example questionnaire, which include questions 1 through 12, 14, and 15, are shorter than usual. The brand list (left-hand side) usually contains more than three brands (Brands A to C on the questionnaire). It usually includes as many brands in the category as possible so that most responses to unaided brand questions are covered. The "Other (SPECIFY)" will catch those brands not prelisted. The aided questions, however, usually include fewer brands — your brand, leading brands, and key competitors. The asterisks next to the brand list tell the interviewer which of the brands to include when administering the aided questions.

UNDERSTANDING KEY MEASURES
USED IN TRACKING PROGRAMS

Traditional tracking studies — whether continuous or point-in-time — always address the key topics:

- Stopping Power,
- Strategic Message Communication,
- Belief Structure, and
- Behavioral Impact.

The specific measures taken and questions asked may vary, depending upon the marketing issues, category, or brand development.

We will address each of the key measures in a tracking study individually. For some concrete examples of each measure, we have indicated the question number in the example questionnaire (Appendix A).

Stopping Power

Brand awareness questions are always asked (Exhibit 7.7).

Brand Name Recall

This is also known as unaided brand awareness, brand saliency or top-of-mind brand awareness. It may include recording the first brand mentioned separately.

This may be *the* key brand awareness measure *if* the brand is well established and *if* the brand name is well known by the vast majority of the target. Thus, the critical issue on the awareness dimension will be

EXHIBIT 7.7 WAYS TO TRACK STOPPING POWER

THE ISSUE	THE RESEARCH MEASURE	AN EXAMPLE OF THE QUESTION*
Stopping Power	• Brand Awareness	
	– Brand name recall (unaided brand awareness)	#1, 2
	– Brand name recognition (aided brand awareness)	#8
	– Package Recognition (association of package description with brand name or familiarity with package)	#7a, b
	• Advertising Awareness	
	– Unaided	#3
	– Aided	#11
	– Execution prompted	#16c
	• Proven & Related Recall	Analytical Constructs derived from #16a

*See Appendix A for example questionnaire.

"For what proportion of the target is the brand highly salient?"

Further, research has indicated that there is a strong correlation between top-of-mind awareness and the probability of being used/purchased.[2]

Brand Name Recognition

This is also known as aided brand awareness. In analysis, it is always combined with brand name (unaided) recall to yield a measure of Total Brand Recall.

For new brands, brands in low involvement categories, and brands with relatively weaker shares of market, this is typically *the* key brand awareness measure.

Package Recognition

Brand name recall and recognition are always included in a tracking study. Less frequently used, but sometimes very valuable, package recognition is appropriate for shelf-displayed products where a consumer may recognize the product on sight but not by name. For example, a consumer may not know the brand name of baking soda. However, the consumer does recognize the yellow box with the white and red circle. This recognition indicates another level of brand awareness.

Advertising awareness questions should be included in tracking research. While these measures, by title, purport to tell you what proportion of your target has seen the advertising, the reality is that these are measures of *claimed* awareness. Other measures based on advertising playback or recall come closer to identifying the proportion of your target that has *actually* seen the advertising.

These awareness questions can help put into perspective the potential impact that the advertising is having relative to that of competitors and over time.

Unaided Advertising Awareness

As in Brand Name Recall, this is considered a more salient measure than Total Advertising Awareness, which is the combination of unaided and aided awareness.

Unaided awareness refers to the brands the respondent mentions when asked what brands within the category he or she remembers seeing advertised. The only prompt is on a category level (what cars? fast food restaurants? hammers?). If a respondent doesn't mention a studied brand on an unaided level, the researcher prompts the respondent with an aid to memory such as "Do you remember seeing any advertising for Cadillac? Lexus? Infiniti?"

Aided Advertising Awareness

This is a brand-name prompt rather than a category prompt as used in the unaided measures. For example, consumers are prompted with the name "Tide" rather than the category, laundry detergent. It, too, is always reported as part of Total Advertising Awareness.

Execution-Prompted Awareness

Advertising awareness, both unaided and aided, is critical in an advertising tracking study. Execution-prompted awareness is not universally used but can be helpful in a number of situations, including:

- When share of voice is low, the execution may have been seen but not very frequently. This measure identifies additional consumers who, in fact, have seen the execution.
- When a product has a long history of advertising — particularly within the context of an ongoing campaign — or the manufacturer's name is so well known that the consumer assumes that he or she *must* have seen advertising recently (for example, IBM), execution prompting can identify overstated claimed ad awareness levels by having the respondent think about specific elements of execution within the campaign. If the respondent doesn't remember the elements, one can reasonably assume the claimed awareness is exaggerated.

Proven and Related Recall

These are not actual measures but they deserve mention. Proven and related recall are analytical constructs derived from the open-ended advertising playback measure to be discussed in the next section.

The advertising playback question simply asks respondents to describe in their own words the advertising that they claim to have seen. Responses to that question are classified (or coded) into categories of those who, based on their commentary:

1. We know must have seen the advertising (**Proven Recall**).
2. We think we must have seen the advertising, but we cannot be sure since they play back general ideas but nothing specific (**Related Recall**).
3. Those who, while claiming to have seen the advertising, cannot demonstrate it, yet say nothing wrong (**Non-Related Recall**).
4. Those who claim to have seen the brand's advertising but have confused it with that of another brand (**Incorrect Recall**).

Strategic Message Communication

Advertising Playback

The advertising playback measure will almost always be included (Exhibit 7.8). These data are derived from an open-ended question asking for a description of everything the respondent remembers seeing or hearing in the advertising. The key use of this question is to assess the degree to which the intended strategic message is *voluntarily* played back, along with the advertising's executional details.

Tagline Association with Brand Name

Often a campaign will have a tagline, which is designed to provide a summary of the key strategic message(s) or a quick mnemonic for the brand. We cannot assume that consumers will play it back when asked to talk about what they remember seeing or hearing. Yet, it can play a valuable role in supporting a brand. Thus, as an addendum to volunteered ad playback, you can ask your audience to identify the brands supported by various taglines.

Typically, if the measure is used, the taglines of all key players in the category are investigated.

Perceptions of Delivery of Key Benefits

One of the ways of assessing the strength of communication of your message is to determine the extent to which your target *believes* your brand can do what you have promised. Issues such as these are best addressed through a series of ratings of your brand on benefit and or image statements.

Typically, scaled responses to a set of statements (attributes) are obtained (for example, the extent to which you agree/disagree that the brand ... or the extent to which the statement describes the brand).

EXHIBIT 7.8 DETERMINING IF THE STRATEGIC MESSAGE
IS GETTING THROUGH

THE ISSUE	THE RESEARCH MEASURE	AN EXAMPLE OF THE QUESTION*
Strategic Message Communication	• Advertising Playback	#16a, b
	• Tagline Association with Brand Name	#17
	• Perceptions of Delivery of Key Benefits	#19

*See Appendix A for example questionnaire.

EXHIBIT 7.9 DELVING INTO IMPACT OF ADVERTISING
ON BELIEF STRUCTURE

THE ISSUE	THE RESEARCH MEASURE	AN EXAMPLE OF THE QUESTION*
Belief Structure	• Overall Attitudes Toward the Brand	
	– Overall Rating	#18c, d
	– Purchase Intent	#18a, b
	– Perceived Uniqueness, etc.	
	• Product Perceptions	#19

*See Appendix A for example questionnaire.

Belief Structure

Overall Attitudes Toward the Brand

There are quite a few overall attitude measures that may be included (Exhibit 7.9). At least one, if not more, should always be included.

Among the more common measures used are:

- Overall rating;
- Perceived uniqueness;
- Purchase intention/Likelihood/Frequency of use.

It is important to recognize that these are attitudinal measures. The purchase intention question is not a predictor of sales but a relative measure (for example, over time and versus competitive brands).

Product Perceptions

An important part of the tracking program is assessing the impact of a campaign on the target's beliefs about your brand. It is especially important to measure the campaign's ability to convince your audience that your brand can deliver these benefits as well if not better than can the competition.

By asking respondents what they believe about your brand and, at the very least, one competitor, you can track changes in consumers' beliefs or perceptions of your brand in the context of the "category." This type of analysis also allows identification of possible weaknesses in image that need to be addressed in future campaign and/or executional development.

If this seems familiar, it's because these same attribute ratings are the basis for determining the extent to which key strategic messages have been integrated and translated into beliefs about the brand (see Exhibit 7.8). This means you can use the same questions to test both the message and the belief structure.

The distinction is in the nature of the analytic approach taken to the data. When addressing the extent to which the strategic message has been communicated, we look only at responses to our brand — identifying which beliefs are most strongly held. When attempting to understand our brand's image and position within the context of the category, we compare our ratings to those of our competitors.

Behavioral Impact

When framing behavioral measures, it is important to be sensitive to the differences between use and purchase measures (Exhibit 7.10). You should consider both the category in which you are operating and the goals of the advertising campaign when deciding whether to track one or both.

Framing the measures in a "usage" context is more appropriate for products with long purchase cycles as well as in categories where multiple brands tend to be kept on hand and selected on some rotating or situation-specific basis.

EXHIBIT 7.10 LOOKING AT THE EFFECT OF ADVERTISING ON BEHAVIOR

THE ISSUE	THE RESEARCH MEASURE	AN EXAMPLE OF THE QUESTION*
Behavioral Impact	• Use/Purchase Experience	
	– Brands...	
	– Ever Bought	#9
	– Bought Recently	#4, 10
	– Bought Last	#12
	– Bought Time Before Last	#14
	– Used Most Often	#6
	• Consideration Set	
	– Brands Would Consider	#15
	– Brands Would Not Consider	#15
	• Frequency of Consumption	#13
	• Uses/Intended Uses	

*See Appendix A for example questionnaire.

Framing the measures in a "purchase" context works better for some categories, including impulse purchases, high-ticket items, and durables.

Whichever measures are selected, keep the learning goal in mind: how deeply has the advertising affected behavior over time?

ISSUES TO CONSIDER WHEN COMMISSIONING A TRACKING STUDY

In a perfect world, you now know everything there is to know about evaluating your advertising campaign. You have a clear set of specific objectives that the campaign is intended to accomplish. You have set in motion a procedure to obtain the most appropriate pre- and post sales data that your budget allows, and you are ready to begin the process of putting your tracking program into place.

Tracking studies are virtually always commissioned to an outside, independent research organization. Since the cost of tracking programs is substantial, in most cases more than one organization is asked to bid on the project.

The initial information you provide to research companies should include background information on the marketing situation of your brand and competition. Data about the number of brands in the category, your brand's share, the nature of your "new" advertising and marketing efforts, competitive activity (where available), as examples, help the research company better understand the environment to be studied. It is also valuable to provide information about the types of business decisions you would like to make with the help of the tracking data. And, of course, the research company needs to know about the planned advertising campaign — its objectives, target audience, type of media, media weights/flights, and so on.

With this information in hand, the organizations may pose a number of questions. As you answer these questions, research organizations will, in turn, identify and explain the issues specific to designing a tracking program most appropriate for your brand. Thus, you will be privy to the way in which they are thinking. These dialogues have added value as well. They provide:

- a basis for a much deeper understanding of the recommendations of *other* research organizations with which you speak;
- a guide to help you determine which research organizations are most thorough in considering the situation of your particular brand or category versus having an "all tracking research is the same" mentality;
- a sense of whom you would best be able to work with — that is, do you have a rapport with your potential contact? (You may have frequent contact with the organization as you proceed. Thus, rapport is a key issue.)

Each firm may make different recommendations. We encourage you to ask each firm to explain why they recommend or reject any particular technique or approach suggested by another firm. In this manner, you can begin to develop a real feel for the advantages and disadvantages of each design alternative.

Question each organization as to who will be your daily contact person and what that person's position is within the organization. In some research organizations, tracking studies, once "sold," are turned over to a middle-level project director with perhaps 4–5 years of experience, rather than being handled by a senior member of the firm as in other organizations. As an advertising manager, it is probably best to work with an organization structured so that you work with a senior-level person.

The remainder of this section is devoted to reviewing some of the issues with which you and the research organization will be grappling as the tracking program is designed. These are usually discussed in the context of "specifications" for the project. Exhibit 7.11 contains a list of specifications that must be nailed down when designing (and, importantly, prior to costing) a custom tracking program.

Whichever approach and whatever decisions are ultimately made, it is of paramount importance that all of the details are handled

EXHIBIT 7.11 RESEARCH PROJECT SPECIFICATION CHECKLIST

- Method of Interview: Telephone .... ❑

                                  Mall Intercept .... ❑

                                  Mail .... ❑

- Description of eligible respondents in the survey sample _____

    _____

    _____

- % of population qualifying for interview (anticipated incidence): _____

    Number of Interviews Per Wave: _____

    Quota Groups for Analytic Segments: _____

    _____

- Scheduling: CONTINUOUS: .... ❑ POINT IN TIME: .... ❑

                                  ↓   ↓

                            Daily: .... ❑ Wave Frequency: _____

                            Weekly: .... ❑ Wave Dates: _____

                            Bimonthly: .... ❑

                            Other (Specify) .... ❑ _____

                            _____

                            _____

    Date advertising will begin: _____

- Interview length: # Minutes _____

- Geography: National .... ❑

                            Top 20 markets .... ❑

                            Sales Regions (Define) .... ❑

                            _____

- Sampling Issues:

    If consumer survey: Random Digit Dialing .... ❑

                              Other (Specify) .... ❑

                            _____

                            _____

Continued on next page

EXHIBIT 7.11 CONTINUED

If Business to Business
Survey:

        Ratio of Names ____ to 1

        Sample List source provided by:

        Client ....❏

        Other List Source...................❏

            Specify: _____

        Research Co. Purchases. ....❏

        Anticipated # records available:_____

- Additional Considerations:

- How frequently you want data reported (for continuous tracking)?

        Monthly: ....❏

        Quarterly: ....❏

        Semi-Annually:.......................❏

        Annually ....❏

- Deliverables: Data Only (tabs/disk)..............❏

                      Analytic Report ....❏

- Number of brands for which advertising playback and benefit delivery rating data will be collected: _____

consistently over time and across waves. Otherwise, if shifts in data are observed, you won't know if they are attributable to the marketing issue(s) being studied or to the research process itself.

While you might not know the answers to all of these questions initially, you will be able to address them as you work with the research organization. That company will help you decide which options make most sense in your specific situation. Further, the organization can, and should, discuss the ramifications of the choices you make.

The following are some of the key specification points for a survey and primary issues related to each.

Method of Interview

Almost all advertising tracking programs are conducted by telephone. This method provides the greatest potential for reliable data and consistency over time, with both cost and time efficiencies.

If your target is extremely costly to reach (for example, chief executives of Fortune 500 companies) and your budget is very limited, you might consider a mail survey. However, there are a number of downsides to consider before making that choice. First, the data collected will be somewhat less reliable due to the greater potential for response bias, both in terms of potential respondent bias and question order bias.

Respondent bias in mail surveys can impact the integrity of your data in a number of ways. One concern is that only a small portion of those to whom you send the survey actually completes it. You must always be concerned if those who chose to return the survey represent the full population to whom it was sent. Further, there is a lack of control regarding who, in fact, fills out the questionnaire. If, for example, the CEO is the target, did he or she actually fill it out or was an assistant who may not have the knowledge or background required to do so.

In mail surveys, there also are limitations that arise from potential question order bias. On the telephone, responses are top-of-mind thoughts. Question order is carefully designed, recognizing the potential for earlier questions to impact results of later ones. In a mail survey, respondents have the opportunity to review the entire questionnaire before completing it or to retrace their steps and change responses based on information gleaned from subsequent questions.

For advertising tracking studies this can be particularly problematic. How, for example, can we accurately measure unaided brand or advertising awareness if the respondent can look down a list and see the brand name? Further, it is very difficult to gather strong data from nonstructured or "open-ended" questions because there is no interviewer present to probe superficial responses.

The analyst cannot control these possible effects. In survey research, we strive to control as many variables as we can. Mail surveys don't allow as much control as do, for example, phone surveys.

Personal interviews are rarely used for tracking programs

because it is very difficult to maintain strong sampling consistency from wave to wave. However it has been done, if the target and budget dictate it, discuss this option with the research organization.

With all this said, if possible, use a telephone methodology and cut corners as necessary, using, for example, a smaller sample size or a shorter interview.

Nature and Size of Sample

Determining the target for interviewing is quite straightforward: you interview the predetermined target for the advertising. However, this may not be your media target. Typically, media targets cannot be finely tuned. They are almost always articulated solely in terms of demographics, as that is how media are selected and purchased. However, the advertising (and, thereby, the interviewing) target may be defined behaviorally or attitudinally.

Consider this scenario: The media-defined target is "females, 25–49 years of age, in households with $50,000+ income." But this is actually a surrogate for your true target—women with an interest in high-end sports equipment. Your advertising tracking sample should represent women with an interest in high-end sports equipment.

Sometimes advertising is written against a somewhat more intangible target. Consider, for example, a salad dressing that you make yourself, using packaged herbs and spices. The target audience is women who are willing to put a bit more of themselves into their dinner preparation. That target will be reflected in the content and tonality of the advertising, but it may not be part of the media plan. Advertising can't be bought against intangibles.

Your tracking study can and should reflect both the advertising and, if differently articulated, the media target. When developing the tracking study, both need to be considered. Ideally, when developing the sampling design, age and income should also be included to fairly assess the results against the media target.

With this in mind, you can next consider study incidence. Incidence is the proportion of those contacted for interview who meet the qualification (eligibility) requirements. Out of every 100 people you speak with, how many fit the requirements? It is a critical factor in determining the cost of the survey. If you don't know the precise incidence of your advertising target, make a best guess based on census data and any sales data you may have on hand. Category penetration data are collected by a number of syndicated research services (Mediamark Research and Simmons, as examples) but there is typically a subscription fee required. If you are estimating, ask the research organization to give you bids based on two or three reasonable guesses of the incidence, so that you have an idea of the potential range of costs you might incur up front.

The total number of interviews to conduct per wave is another of the most critical factors influencing cost. In the ideal world, the more interviews you can afford to do, the better. In the real world, sample size needs to be considered in light of what you want to know, and the confidence level and margin of error you are willing to work with.

The following are among the most important analytic issues to consider when thinking about sample size:

- **What margin of error are you willing to work with?** There is always error around any given number. How much are you willing to or can you afford to have?

Your research firm can help you calculate the sample size required to yield responses accurate to +/- x percent. Note that small increments in sample size will not affect the margin of error very much. Typically, one might anticipate working in the range of +/- 7 percent. If you anticipate less movement than that, you may want to boost your sample size to reduce the margin of error.

- **How many brands do you need rated?** To better understand the meaning of any shifts in your brand's ratings over time, imagery ratings for one or more key competitors should be collected. Working with your research company, you can isolate those brands that will provide the best competitive context in which to assess your brand's performance within your budget.

- **What portion of the sample can rate each of these brands?** Only those aware of a brand (either on an unaided or aided basis) can possibly rate it. But, depending on the situation/goals of the campaign, you and your researchers may decide that imagery shifts are important only among those who have ever used the brand or used it in the recent past.

You must make a "best guess" of what portion of the sample will be able to rate the key brands so you can be sure that a reliable ("stable") base of respondents can answer the questions from wave to wave. Companies use different criteria to judge what is a stable base, but most fall in the 100 respondents range.

Scheduling

Go out of your way to begin the program with a benchmark wave. The benchmark (sometimes called a "prewave") should be conducted as close to start of advertising as possible. However, interviewing must be completed *before* launch of the advertising.

Why is a benchmark so important? Research is truly a relative science. The benchmark shows you where the brand was before the campaign began. "The nature of the response to any given advertising effort depends on where on the particular curve you start. In fact, only entirely new products are likely to start from zero on the response curve. This means that in assessing the impact of advertising it is important to know the starting point."[3] A benchmark wave provides a point against which to compare post advertising data. Without it, it is virtually impossible to measure the true impact of the campaign. (Without a benchmark it is still possible to measure the effect of the campaign across each postadvertising interviewing period. However, the full impact of the campaign cannot be assessed.)

Within the context of continuous tracking, the specific interviewing schedule can best be determined by the research organization. The key is that *consistency must rule*. If, for example, the decision is to interview three days a week across a six-month period, you must interview the same three days each week, at the same hours each week, and complete the same number of interviews during each interviewing period.

If you've chosen point-in-time tracking, the usual method is to begin the postwave(s) after a flight (if flighting). If budget considerations restrict the number of postwaves possible, select a schedule based on common sense with respect to your media plan. If, for example, you are running four two-month flights with a month's hiatus between each flight, you might schedule interviewing to start at the beginning of the second and fourth hiatus periods. If advertising is scheduled throughout (most) of the year, evenly spaced waves of interviewing (quarterly, semiannually) are the norm.

Geography

The goal is to interview, proportionately, in region(s) in which your media are placed or, minimally, in a way that represents your total geography. (Clearly, if your brand is marketed only in metro areas, there is no reason to interview outside of metro areas.)

Sampling Issues

If your advertising target is fairly broad (for example, female heads of household with specific demographic requirements who purchase toothpaste), the best choice is a computer-generated random digit dial (RDD) sample. An RDD sample selects telephone numbers from the desired geography on a random basis. These types of samples ensure that every telephone number, whether listed or not, has an equal chance of being dialed. This eliminates potential sampling error. Properly used, RDDs provide probability samples — the Gold Standard for sampling — for whatever geography you require. While RDDs were once prohibitively expensive, they are no longer.

Because they are representative of your geography and use only existing telephone exchanges with the last four digits of the number randomized, unlisted households will be included. (This is increasingly important as more and more residences are unlisted.) An ancillary benefit of RDD samples is that there are fewer nonproductive dialings, because the sample generated is limited to working telephone exchanges.

When your target is more narrow, it may be possible to purchase lists of your target (or something close to it). While often these lists are not as representative as RDD samples, the cost benefit may outweigh the reduction. Suppliers such as Survey Sampling, MetroMail, and Zeller can be useful in isolating potential lists for your use. Using alternative list sources is far preferable to not tracking. There is, however, considerable variation in the quality of lists available for purchase. Ask your research firm for its experience with the lists under consideration.

If your target is businesses, you will be using a list. You may be able to generate a fully representative list of the target/category, or you may have to purchase one. Companies such as Survey Sampling, Dun & Bradstreet, and American Business Lists can be useful. Your trade organization may also be a good list source.

Once you have a representative list of the target in hand, the goal is to assure that no bias is introduced into your survey because of the way in which the listed target is sampled. The research company you are working with will create a randomized sampling pattern for working through the data. This typically involves creating replicates within the sample and then creating randomized starting points to determine where dialings should begin. The replicates help ensure that the entire potential sample can be worked through, and that you don't interview only from the "top" of the list. Nothing can destroy a well-laid-out tracking program more than a poor sampling design.

Many more names will be needed than the final number of completed interviews. The ratios vary, depending on the category, audience, nature of the list, etc., but they can range from 8:1 to upwards of 15:1. In small universes, the total size of the list you acquire may impact the number of interviews you can complete; you cannot assume 200 interviews will be completed if there are only 300 names on the list!

Frequency of Reporting the Data

In point-in-time tracking, data are reported following each wave of data collection.

With continuous tracking there are more options, based primarily on sample size, budget, and business requirements. It would be wasteful to tabulate more frequently than sample size permits — there is little reason to report data that may be unstable due to small sample size. However, it is often possible to report some "global" measures (that is, those answered by everyone such as brand and advertising awareness) more frequently than for more specific measures (advertising playback that is answered only by those claiming to have seen the advertising).

END PIECE

Having settled on the study goals, specifications, and analytic approaches, you can now sit back and wait for the data to be reported. Then, you can bask in the glory or look for ways to refine your advertising campaign for the next round.

REFERENCES

1. Robert F. Lauterborn. "How to Know If Your Advertising is Working." *Journal of Advertising Research* 25, 1 (1985): RC 9–11.

2. Prakash Nedungadi. "Recall and Consumer Consideration Sets: Influencing Choice Without Altering Brand Evaluations." *Journal of Consumer Research* 17, 4 (1990): 263–76.

3. David W. Stewart. "Measures, Methods, and Models in Advertising Research." *Journal of Advertising Research* 29, 3 (1989): 54–60.

SUGGESTIONS FOR FURTHER READING

Aaker, David A., and Kumar, and George S. Day. *Marketing Research* 5th ed. (New York: John Wiley & Sons, Inc. 1995).

Advertising Tracking Studies. Transcript Proceedings, July 31–August 1, 1984. New York: Advertising Research Foundation, 1984.

Dittus, Edward C., and Marty Koop. "Advertising Accountability in the 1990s: Moving From Guesswork and Gut Feelings." *Journal of Advertising Research* 30, 6 (1990, 1991): RC 7–12.

Kress, George. *Marketing Research*, 3rd ed. (Englewood Cliffs, NJ: Prentice Hall, 1988).

Percy, Larry, and John R. Rossiter. "A Model of Brand Awareness and Brand Attitude Advertising Strategies." *Psychology & Marketing* 9, 4 (1992): 263–74.

Schreiber, Robert J., and Valentine Appel. "Advertising Evaluation Using Surrogate Measures for Sales." *Journal of Advertising Research* 30, 6 (1990, 1991): 27–31.

Wansink, Brian, and Michael L. Ray. "Estimating an Advertisement's Impact on One's Consumption of a Brand." *Journal of Advertising Research* 32, (May/June 1992): 9–16.

Woodside, Arch G. "Measuring Advertising Effectiveness in Destination Marketing Strategies." *Journal of Travel Research* XXIX, 2 (1990): 3–8.

Zufryden, Fred S. "Prod II: A Model for Predicting from Tracking Studies." *Journal of Advertising Research* 25, 2 (1985): 45–51.

WIDGET TRACKING STUDY: MAIN QUESTIONNAIRE

1. I'd like to talk to you for a few minutes about widgets. When you think of widgets, what brand comes to mind first? (DO NOT READ LIST. RECORD ONE ANSWER ON GRID UNDER Q.1 "FIRST MENTION.")

2. What other brands come to mind? (DO NOT READ LIST. RECORD ANSWERS ON GRID UNDER Q.2 "OTHER MENTIONS.")

3. For which brands of widgets have you seen any advertising recently? (DO NOT READ LIST. RECORD ON GRID UNDER Q.3.)

4. And what brands of widgets have you purchased in the past ____ days? (DO NOT READ LIST. RECORD ON GRID UNDER Q.4.) Note: Timeframe is category (purchase-cycle) specific.

5. Please tell me all the other brands of widgets you have ever purchased. (DO NOT READ LIST. RECORD ANSWERS ON GRID UNDER Q.5.) What other brands have you purchased?

   (ASK Q.6 IF MORE THAN ONE BRAND MENTIONED IN Q.4 and 5.)

6. Including all the brands of widgets that you may use, which one brand do you use most often? (DO NOT READ LIST. RECORD ON GRID UNDER Q.6.)

7a. There is a brand of widgets which comes in a gray box with a large maroon stripe and maroon lettering. Have you seen this brand of widget?

   Yes 1 (CONTINUE)
   No 2 (SKIP TO Q.8)

7b. Which, if any, of the following brands is sold in this box? (READ LIST. RECORD ON GRID UNDER Q.7b)

8. Have you ever heard of... (READ *'D BRANDS NOT MENTIONED IN Q.1-6, 7b. RECORD ON GRID UNDER Q.8.)

   (ASK Q.9 FOR EACH *'D BRAND NOT MENTIONED IN Q.4-5.)

9. Have you ever purchased (READ *'D BRANDS NOT MENTIONED IN Q.4-5. RECORD ON GRID UNDER Q.9.)

   (ASK Q.10 FOR EACH *'D BRAND MENTIONED IN Q.5 AND 9 AND NOT MENTIONED IN Q.4.)

10. During the past ____ days have you purchased (MENTION BRAND)? (RECORD ON GRID UNDER Q.10.) Note: Timeframe is category (purchase-cycle) specific.

(ASK Q.11 FOR EACH *'D BRAND MENTIONED IN Q'S 1, 2, 4, 5, 7b-10, BUT NOT MENTIONED IN Q.3.)

11. Have you seen or heard any advertising for (MENTION BRAND) recently? (RECORD ON GRID UNDER Q.11.)

	Q.1	Q.2	Q.3	Q.4	Q.5	Q.6	Q.7b	Q.8	Q.9	Q.10	Q.11
	Unaided Brand Awareness										
	First Mention	Other Mentions	Unaided Advertising Awareness	Unaided Purchase Past __ Days	Unaided Ever Purchased	Use Most Often	Package Recognition	Aided Brand Awareness	Ever Purchased	Aided Past __ Days	Aided
Advertising Awareness											
Brand A	1	1	1	1	1	1	1				
* Your Brand	2	2	2	2	2	2	2	2	2	2	2
* Brand C, etc.	3	3	3	3	3	3	3	3	3	3	3
Other (SPECIFY:)		1		1	1	1	1				
None/Don't Know	x	x	x	x	x	x	x				

12. Which one brand did you purchase last?

(RECORD ONE RESPONSE UNDER Q.12 BELOW)

13. About how long ago was that?

(DO NOT READ LIST. CIRCLE ONE RESPONSE.)

Less than one month ago   1
One to two months ago   2
Three to four months ago   3
Five to six months ago   4
More than six months ago   5

(NOTE: THE PRE-LISTED RESPONSE CHOICES SHOULD REFLECT THE TEST CATEGORY'S PURCHASE CYCLE.)

14. And what brand did you buy the time before that? (RECORD UNDER Q.14 BELOW)

15. Which brands, if any, would you not consider purchasing? (RECORD AS MANY AS APPROPRIATE UNDER Q.15 BELOW.)

	Q.12 Purchased Last	Q.14 Purchased Time Before Last	Q.15 Wouldn't Consider
Brand A	1	1	1
*Your Brand	2	2	2
*Brand C, etc.	3	3	3
Other (SPECIFY:)			
None/Don't Know	1	2	1 / 2

(ASK Q.16a IF AWARE OF ADVERTISING FOR (YOUR BRAND) IN Q's 3 OR 11. OTHERWISE SKIP TO Q.16b.)

16a. Please tell me everything you remember about the advertising you saw or heard in the advertising for (YOUR BRAND). (PROBE FOR SPECIFICS.) What specifically did it say or show? What else do you remember seeing or hearing in the advertising for (YOUR BRAND)?

(ASK Q.16b IF AWARE OF ADVERTISING FOR (BRAND C) IN Q's 3 OR 11. OTHERWISE SKIP TO Q.16c.)

16b. Please tell me everything you remember about the advertising you saw, read, or heard for (BRAND C). (PROBE FOR SPECIFICS.) What specifically did it say or show? What else do you remember seeing or hearing in the advertising for (BRAND C)?

_____

_____

_____

_____

[ASK EVERYONE]

16c. You may have mentioned this, but there is an ad for Category A with (READ AD DESCRIPTION). Do you remember seeing this particular ad?

Yes   1
No   2

17. I'm going to read a few slogans to you. As I read each one, please tell me which brand you think of when you hear the slogan (READ X'D ITEM)? (REPEAT UNTIL ALL ARE ASKED)

Start With   Brand

( ) Tagline A.............   _____

( ) Tagline B.............   _____

( ) Tagline C ....   _____

CHECK Q's 1-11:

- *IF "YOUR BRAND" AND "BRAND C" CIRCLED, ASK Q'S 18a-d.*
- *IF "YOUR BRAND" CIRCLED BUT NOT "BRAND C," ASK Q'S 18a AND c. THEN SKIP TO Q.19.*
- *IF "BRAND C" CIRCLED BUT NOT "YOUR BRAND," ASK Q'S 18b AND d. THEN SKIP TO Q.19.*
- *IF NEITHER CIRCLED, SKIP TO Q.19.*

18. We're asking different people about different brands. For the next few questions, we'd like to talk with you about [PAUSE]: SAY EITHER/BOTH BRAND(S).

18a. I'd like to know how likely you would be to purchase (YOUR BRAND) the next time you were going to buy widgets. Would you say you... (READ LIST)?

Definitely would purchase it 5
Probably would purchase it. 4
Might or might not purchase it. 3
Probably would not purchase it. 2
or, Definitely would not purchase it 1

18b. I'd like to know how likely you would be to purchase (BRAND C) *the next time* you were going to buy Category A. Would you say you... (READ LIST)?

Definitely would purchase it 5
Probably would purchase it. 4
Might or might not purchase it. 3
Probably would not purchase it. 2
or, Definitely would not purchase it 1

18c. Overall, how do you feel about (YOUR BRAND)? Do you think it is... (READ LIST)?

Excellent. 5
Very good 4
Good. 3
Fair 2
or, Poor 1

18d. Overall, how do you feel about (BRAND C)? Do you think it is ... (READ LIST)?

Excellent. 5
Very good 4
Good. 3
Fair 2
or, Poor 1

(ASK Q.19 ABOUT EACH BRAND BELOW WHICH RESPONDENT IS AWARE OF IN Q'S 1-11. START WITH "X" TO DETERMINE WHICH BRAND TO ASK ABOUT FIRST.)

19. Now I'd like to ask your opinion about (READ BRAND). In order to do this I will read you some specific statements. As I read each one, please tell me how much you agree or disagree that the statement describes (READ BRAND). To tell me how you feel, please use a scale of 1 to 5 where "5" means you agree completely, and "1" means you disagree completely. Of course you may use any number between 1 and 5.

Even if you may not have tried (READ BRAND), please answer based on anything you have seen or heard or feel about it. There are no right or wrong answers, we are only interested in your *impressions*.

Let's start with (READ X'D STATEMENT). What number between 1 and 5, where "5" means agree completely, and "1" means disagree completely, would you give (READ BRAND) for (REPEAT STATEMENT)? (RECORD ON GRID BELOW.) Now how about... (ASK EACH STATEMENT FOR THE FIRST BRAND BEFORE GOING ON TO THE NEXT BRAND. REPEAT SCALE AS OFTEN AS NECESSARY.)

START WITH:

START WITH:	YOUR BRAND ( )					BRAND C ( )					BRAND D ( )				
	Agree Completely				Disagree Completely	Agree Completely				Disagree Completely	Agree Completely				Disagree Completely
( ) Is easy to use	5	4	3	2	1	5	4	3	2	1	5	4	3	2	1
( ) Is compact	5	4	3	2	1	5	4	3	2	1	5	4	3	2	1
( ) Is a good value for the money	5	4	3	2	1	5	4	3	2	1	5	4	3	2	1
( ) Made by a reputable manufacturer	5	4	3	2	1	5	4	3	2	1	5	4	3	2	1

CLASSIFICATION SECTION: Additional background and demographic questions appropriate to your category which are needed for analytic purposes.

Thank you very much for your cooperation. (CONFIRM NAME, ADDRESS, ETC.)

TIME ENDED _____ LENGTH OF INTERVIEW _____

"As a CASRO member, we subscribe to the Code of Standards for Survey Research established by the Council of American Survey Research Organizations."

Bill Foley is president of his own consulting firm, William F. Foley & Associates, in Pelham, NY, where his clients include Dentsu, Young & Rubicam, BBDO Worldwide, BDDP, Publi-Graphics, and McCann-Erickson Worldwide.

He has worked in advertising for more than thirty years. After earning an M.B.A. from University of Chicago's Graduate School of Business, he was national retail advertising supervisor for Montgomery Ward. In sequence, he became a copywriter for Needham, Harper & Steers; account supervisor for Frank C. Nahser, Inc.; research director for Marsteller Advertising; and head of training worldwide for Young & Rubicam Advertising. In addition, Foley has taught marketing and advertising courses at Chicago City Junior College, Manhattan College, and New York University, and has published extensively.

CHAPTER 8

COMMUNICATING THE VALUE
OF ADVERTISING

Some day you will be asked to explain how advertising contributes to the success of your brands or your organization. Let's consider how to respond to senior managers, marketing and salespeople, financial managers, the trade, and employees, starting at the top of the organization chart.

Senior managers are usually concerned about three areas: tracking the results, understanding the creative rationale, and controlling the investment. Somehow, these three nagging issues never seem to get settled, but it's your job to try.

QUESTION 1: RESULTS VERSUS VALUE

The first question may be stated in a variety of ways: What is it getting us? What are the results of our advertising? What is it doing for the brand?

You could reply with hard data: sales reports, increases in share of market, favorable reports from consumer tracking or other research. But also consider soft data, such as qualitative information, verbatim comments from consumers who saw ads, letters from customers, call reports from salespeople, and sometimes even what competitors say. This scattered feedback may give you insights into how the advertising is working or what its indirect effects are. For example, the publicity and visibility of a national campaign can motivate dealers to put up your point-of-sale displays or start co-op advertising in local markets.

In other words, multiple measures of what a campaign is doing for you will give you and management a higher degree of confidence than a single research report.

QUESTION 2: CREATIVE STRATEGY VERSUS GOALS

Depending on the manager, you may hear something like this: "Why run this campaign?" Be brief with your answer. For example, "It satisfies our objectives." Then demonstrate how and why the campaign will get people to try your brand or use it more often. You might say, "It works." And then show how the advertising stops the consumer and connects with his or her emotions. Note that this might be expressed as a simple judgment more than logic or data, for example, "Our consumers have never seen anything like this before in the category and, therefore, are very likely to pay attention to our message." Or you could point out, "It has legs." This means that it works in other media. For example, the theme might lend itself to special events, publicity, trade promotions, what salespeople say to customers, employee communications, and more.

You have a partner in your advertising agency; it knows how to sell a new campaign. Typical agency presentation structure begins with strategy, starting from business problem or opportunity, objectives, competitive frame, positioning, targeted consumers, and message. It then goes on to the creative idea with rationale and the execution, followed by media and budget. (Although some say it is better to talk the idea first, then show the ads, and finally explain how the campaign is strategically sound, providing a more natural way for managers to evaluate a new campaign idea.)

Agencies often do their best campaign presenting when pursuing new business. BBDO won the Apple Computer account from Chiat/Day by structuring their presentation in this manner: Marketing situation, strategy, positioning, creative theme ("The power to be your best"); the results demonstrate its versatility in the home, business, and education markets. As Apple's then CEO John Scully said after awarding BBDO the business, "The best advertising reaches deep inside the product [brand] and finds its soul ... as a theme line it said everything we were trying to become."[1] In other words, it sells Apple today and builds an emotional bond with the consumer for tomorrow.

When asked what it takes to sell a campaign to client management, most agency people will tell you, "You'd better have an idea you are willing to fight for." Sometimes it is the passion and belief in the campaign that gets someone to buy it.

Some chief executive officers look at this kind of decision as a big one and require time for deliberation. Others, pressed by other problems, delegate the decision. In the latter case, the CEO will look to you for expertise and an opinion.

Your senior manager has to see how the creative strategy fits into his or her world. That means you need to do several things:

1. Give a clear reason why it works;
2. Help the executive think and feel like the reader or viewer and then react to the campaign first as the consumer;
3. Provide a selling idea that is original, persuasive, and extends to other forms of communication;
4. Show that it satisfies the objective and the strategy;
5. Align the campaign with the brand's equity and long-term growth.

QUESTION 3: COST VERSUS POTENTIAL REWARD

A third question a senior executive might ask is: "Why are you requesting more money?" How do you persuade him or her to spend more on advertising? A tough question.

Usually, there is a problem or opportunity that has led you to propose increased spending. There could be any number of situations:

- With inflation and competitive pressures, spending the same as the previous year is usually equivalent to losing share of voice in the category or standing still. As a general rule, historically, the aggressive advertisers have increased share of market, assuming strong media strategies and cost efficiencies.

- Study the marketing history and forecast. Is the category evolving in a way that favors your campaign's positioning? And is your brand's share of voice big enough to win a bigger share against the competition? Is this the right time to increase the budget?
- If you know that your strategy and creative idea are working, then you may have a good argument for spending more on advertising.

One study of 3,000 U.S. households tracked supermarket purchases among consumers. The conclusions were clear:

"The key to advertising productivity on established brands is to identify when a piece of copy is working and then spend heavily behind it. Companies should make a basic, long-term commitment to TV advertising, but spend the money unevenly: more when the message is working and less when it is not. Implementation of this concept raises two issues: (1) Changes in the budgeting process for marketing funds, perhaps establishing a reserve to heavy-up periods, and (2) How to determine when the message is working."[2]

A new product launch may be tied to systemic change in the corporation, not just the new product itself. When Kirin launched Ichiban Shibori ("first squeeze") in Japan in 1990, it reversed its declining share of the beer market and became the market leader again. But its success also came from fortuitous timing. The introduction coincided with a total corporate reorganization — new management, new logo, and more.

Therefore, one campaign for a product can contribute to growth of other products, or a campaign can be reinforced or supported when timing connects to major corporate changes.

Regional or other segmentation opportunities may call for increased spending against targets that will be more responsive to advertising in the coming year or connected to your new campaign.

Look for changes or combinations of changes in market dynamics. Some media experts recommend increasing media spending for new or growing products or when consumers are happy with your product and repeatedly buy it, but your penetration of the market is below average.

How long has the campaign been running? Advertising campaigns tend to decrease in effectiveness; therefore, there is a need for new execution, increased media weight, or media phasing. Increased clutter and fragmentation of media may mean trying bold, new uses of media vehicles.

If you are selling an increased media budget, you may want to arm yourself with a battery of competitive ads and media schedules, analyzing each and its probable effects on the target group. Or you could demonstrate behaviorally how repeated exposure to your commercials helps viewers learn about your brand. Playing out the scenario of the increased budget and how it will work may help the senior manager see and understand what he or she is approving.

You may also want to "get outside the box." Look for creative alternatives to spending. Be open to fresh, unusual, creative approaches that challenge the reader, listener, or viewer.

There is a point of diminishing returns, where little or no sales increase is seen despite greater advertising spending. But companies that spend more on their corporate image or brand usually dominate the market. The Profit Impact of Market Strategy (PIMS) study,[3] which was conducted by the Strategic Planning Institute of Cambridge, Massachusetts, looked at the advertising practices of 700 companies from 1970 to 1986. The PIMS study, the first of its kind, is generally recognized as an impartial longitudinal study. The results suggest that businesses with higher advertising-to-sales ratios gained greater shares of market. (See Exhibit 8.1.)

Similarly, companies with advertising budgets higher than their leading competitors tend to have superior perceived quality in the marketplace and higher returns on investment.

UNDERSTANDING THE SENIOR MANAGER

Senior executives differ widely by type of business, education, and personal experience. What to say begins with understanding who he or she is as a person, realizing that the engineering mind works slightly different from the mind of a lawyer or a chief financial officer. One looks for alternatives; the other for proof and reason why.

Some commonsense rules: If your decision maker is analytical, make your presentation logical. If this person is orderly and precise, make it neatly structured. If it is a power person, open with group discussion.

Begin by asking yourself, "What are the senior manager's priorities?" Advertising is usually not one of them. Interrupt a CEO suddenly and chances are one of these topics was on his mind: current price of the company's stock shares (not yesterday, but ten minutes ago), profits (are they on target this week or month?), Wall Street (are we a buy or hold among the analysts?), growth (is our momentum still going forward), shareholders (are they happy or in revolt?), competitive threats (how much do we really know?), achieving business goals (are all those reports I see real numbers?), acquisitions, etc.

So far, advertising is not on this agenda or top of mind. So how can you fit what is going on in this person's life? If you say, "advertising," what springs to mind? The precise dollar budget. So what does this person want to know?

EXHIBIT 8.1 ADVERTISING AFFECTS MARKET SHARE

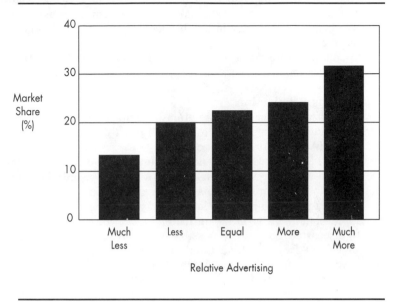

Relative Advertising

Some company presidents are calling today for accountability or proof that their advertising really works. Does it make a cost-effective contribution to the selling process or to corporate objectives? This is a fair question, but one that is difficult to answer.

The central problem, according to one management consultant is: "Many advertisers have general communication objectives, such as increasing or maintaining awareness, but set quantitative targets all the same. The image or positioning of a product tends to be driven by how management would like the brand to be perceived or by its heritage, rather than by an understanding of the links between positioning, the resulting perceptions, and their impact on the behavior of distinct segments. The need to adapt positioning to the differing needs of individual segments is often acknowledged, but rarely acted upon."[4]

Objectives need to be specific, single-minded (not multiple goals), and written for each segment.

INCREASING YOUR EFFECTIVENESS

What is an advertising or marketing communications manager to do? One approach is to make the marketing and advertising planning process more disciplined, define market segments, and set specific, measurable objectives for each segment linked to the incremental contribution that advertising can make. And get management to agree to these. The chapter on strategy in this handbook provides tools to help with this process.

In addition, here are a few ideas for improving your situation with the CEO or top manager.

Build a Strong Relationship

Do you have a one-to-one relationship, either informal access when you need it or a regular meeting more than once a year? Advertising (like R&D or quality control) is at the core of the company's business. Some CEOs won't admit it, but they would like to be more involved with their advertising. (A few may even believe they are advertising experts, according to this author's experience.)

This is a person-to-person relationship issue; the communicating will happen naturally. But in taking the initiative, you should be prepared to discuss any number of possible questions or issues that may interest the CEO. Be ready, for example, to address advertising-to-sales ratios in your industry and others, feedback from competitors' advertising, trends, and forecasts. Broaden your reading list to include *Harvard Business Review*, *Fortune*, *The Wall Street Journal*, *Barrons*, and business publications that cover your industry. You may even want to send the CEO an occasional article that discusses advertising issues relevant to your company.

Reach for books that put you on the same mental playing field. You will know you are there when the CEO begins to see you understand his or her world. Then the CEO will ask for your opinion.

Prepare a Stewardship Report

This is a traditional, formal, but sometimes effective technique. The term "steward" is defined as a person morally responsible for the careful use of money, time, talents, or other resources, especially with respect to the needs of a community or group.

The Stewardship Report is an accountability presentation, comparing sales volume, share of market, brand power or equity, media spending, postbuy analysis, advertising campaign evaluation, and results. It is not a performance review of the agency, but an assessment of current and future marketing communications, including advertising. Your ad agency would be flattered to help you write and stage this important meeting. Initiating it will identify you as a take-charge kind of manager. Suggestion: If and when you do it, use plain business English, not "adspeak." Avoid words like "impact," "dissolve," "effective frequency," etc.

Review Feedback from Consumers

The CEO gets reports, sees numbers and charts, listens to technical explanations, and lives with uncertainty. Almost all the feedback on advertising is hearsay and unreliable.

Putting faces and voices on the feedback is generally more valuable than ad recall scores. Seeing and hearing what your ads mean to people gives the CEO another view of what is happening in the marketplace. Videotaped interviews, focus groups, or comments from consumer panels can show what people are taking away from your campaign. Second-hand reports from salespeople and the trade about consumer reactions to advertising are encouraging to see, but need to be examined closely.

Now we will turn to others who may become your audience for the value of advertising: marketing managers, sales managers, financial directors, employees, and people outside the organization.

TALKING TO THE MARKETING MANAGER

Marketing, brand, and product managers are interested in many of the same issues as senior managers, but they are probably your most jaded audience. Consider how many times they have been exposed to this topic.

We asked some managers in several industries how they would answer this question: "How do you measure the value of advertising?" Their responses may give you some useful perspective.

Automobiles: Ghafoor Rawtaer, managing director of Borneo Motors in Singapore, says he wants to know the following: "How well is my advertising dollar being spent? Does the message get through? What is the impact on my sales this year? Will the advertising help my brand's positioning? I can measure sales promotion immediately by store traffic, if the offer is a good one. How do you propose to measure the advertising to prove its value? You are ultimately driven to the voice of the consumer." [5]

Business Services: Eavesdrop on Paul Walker, Asia/Pacific marketing director at Andersen Consulting in Singapore, and you might hear him discuss how a management and information technology consultant firm markets itself:

"Planning is done by individual key account, including the positioning, opportunities, and the desired relationship at each of these important clients. If the advertising does not support our effort with these accounts, it is not worth doing. This approach ensures advertising will connect with prospects." [6]

By focusing on what is in the minds of its clients, Andersen keeps its advertising on target and does not allow it to stray or drift away from its communications objectives.

Marketing: Laura McCorvie, a partner with the CSC Weston

Group, Wilton, Connecticut, takes a branding point of view: "First, think of the value of advertising from a consumer perspective. Branding simplifies choices for the consumer, giving someone confidence to repeatedly buy a brand because he or she knows what to expect. Investing in building confidence among consumers is what drives the economic value of brand or a business. That explains why a company like Coca-Cola is worth far more than its syrup formula and Kraft is more valuable than cheese factories. Brands have economic value because they have strong meanings and recognition among consumers."[7]

Does your company have a policy or point of view about brand equity? (Some do; surprisingly, many don't.) Who in your organization is responsible for brand building and brand equity? Who is in charge? In companies with strong brands it is the marketing manager or a brand equity manager; in others it is the CEO, a communications coordinator or a committee. But you can play a responsible role in helping manage the brand equity. While branding has become a hot topic in marketing and in many companies, there are still major corporations that have not yet determined what their brands represent. You can make a contribution by asking questions and initiating action toward a new brand equity program.

Responding to Marketing Issues

Depending on how strong a role advertising plays in the sale of your products, marketing people may place a greater or lesser value on advertising. But because of the wide scope of the marketing and brand management jobs themselves (new products, pricing, distribution, sales, marketing research), advertising may appear as a small item on their agendas. Therefore, it may be necessary to keep in mind a few principles of how advertising is helpful in marketing:

- Advertising is fast (to prepare and use), controllable (message, media), competitive (opportunity, for example, to dominate a medium), strategic or tactical (national, regional, or local; or seasonal).

- Advertising is a powerful force to differentiate a brand. When strategically used, advertising can change people's attitudes, perceptions, or beliefs about a brand so that people want the brand. Sometimes, even a parity product, which is a product physically similar to the other brands, can command a premium price and dominant market share even in a mature category. Baby powder is plain talc (soft, white, foliated mineral, magnesium silicate, which you might have trouble distinguishing from a private label talcum powder on your skin. Several decades of advertising, including "...a feeling you never outgrow" in the last decade, by Johnson & Johnson, have convinced mothers that its baby powder is different and better than all other brands. You will find this is what mothers believe almost everywhere you travel in the world.

- Advertising defines the personality of the brand and the company. It captures the true spirit of the brand, the cumulative emotional essence of its heritage and communications (name, logotype, package, slogans, etc.) over time, and people's feelings about the brand. In simple terms it is sincerity (like Kodak or Hallmark), excitement (like Benetton or Absolut), competence (like IBM or CNN), ruggedness (like Marlboro) that is expressed, usually nonverbally, in the tonality of the advertising.

- Advertising shows what the brand wants to stand for, its brand essence, but research is needed to identify exactly how to express this in words. This could be the beginning of a policy on managing brand equity and strengthening the strategic direction of your advertising.

- Advertising would be missed. What happens if you stop advertising? This might actually be discussed if profits are down or a recession or slowdown in sales becomes the rationale for cuts across the board.

Here are some facts from previous recessions: Businesses that increased advertising spending in a recession (when only 25% of them became aggressive spenders) gained an average of 1.5 points of market share vs. 0.63 for all businesses. (Source: The Strategic Planning Institute, 1989.) Another study of six recession periods and 133 companies points to greater increases in sales and net income than for those which cut back their advertising. (Source: American Business Press.) Japanese companies invest in manufacturing and advertising during a recession, generally the opposite of western companies. (Source: *The New York Times*, January 1, 1991.) Textbook case: Kellogg's advertised its brands during the Great Depression; Post did not. Post has never caught up with Kellogg's dominance in the category.

It might be a good idea to keep and update a file called "Stop Advertising" for immediate reference if someone suggests cutting your budget or interrupting a successful campaign's media schedule.

Learning from the Big Campaigns

Just as the practice of law is based on court decisions described in cases, good advertising practice follows the rules of the market. Look at ads; study the great campaigns of the past and what happened. Advertising and marketing professionals can learn from examining the dynamics of advertising ideas, consumer behavior, and results in the marketplace. If you can separate the facts from the hype, you can become a valuable resource on what really works in advertising.

So let's go to school on some big campaigns, why they worked, and how they might be relevant to marketing people.

If your product or service has a *unique claim or promise* that people want, this may become the center point of the advertising campaign. Consider the following strong claims:

Success Story 1:
The first ad for Ivory Soap appeared on December 21, 1882, making it the longest-running soap advertising claim in the world. The ad used only a line drawing of two hands cutting a bar of the soap in half with a string to illustrate its message:
> The "Ivory" is a Laundry Soap, with all the fine qualities of a choice Toilet Soap, and is 99 44/100 percent pure ... The Ivory Soap will "float." TRY IT. SOLD EVERYWHERE.

The ad is still delivering profitable sales for Procter & Gamble, which is a lesson in consistency in positioning.

Success Story 2:
Dove Soap print advertising includes this headline and short copy: "*End a dry spell.* Dove® contains 1/4 moisturizing cream. It won't dry your face like soap." This strong claim was introduced in 1957 and is still effective.

Success Story 3:
Duracell Batteries gives the consumer a reason to buy the brand. "They last 6 times as long" is a powerful message to consumers.
Often, the job of the advertising manager is to fight for the strongest possible claim, based on the ability to document its authenticity, and then to advise senior managers on which is the best claim.
Dramatizing the claim is the job of your advertising agency, but you play a part in asking for the most creativity and giving clear direction in the briefing.

The Impact of Visuals
Remember that visuals are more powerful than words when you are reviewing a layout or storyboard. Consumers see visuals first in a print ad; they stop (or don't) in a split-second. With a TV commercial, you win them or lose them in the first few seconds.
Consider these two print campaigns:
Johnson & Johnson has grown its share of the baby products market while expanding the adult usage. Most of the advertising was print, featuring one simple concept (very few words) combined with art direction and photography that elicits an emotional response.
Absolut Vodka was a tiny, unknown, premium brand selling 12,000 cases a year in the U.S. in 1980. A new print ad campaign became an instant success, using quirky headlines like, "Absolut perfection" or "Absolut L.A." with only a humorous illustration of the bot-

tle and no copy. By the early 1990s, Absolut was selling close to 3 million cases each year. Absolut repositioned its vodka as the fashionable drink for hip young people.

Challenging the Customer

"Challenge" ads can sometimes be very effective. Here are a few winners:

Do you remember the traveler in the TV commercial whose wallet or purse was lost and who should have taken his or her American Express travelers checks? Voice-over narration, provided by actor Karl Malden, warned, "Don't leave home without 'em"? This is a persuasive and memorable bid for product usage.

Polaroid used demonstrations to capture consumers' attention. The announcer identified the new Polaroid Land Camera, took a picture, then explained how it worked as the audience waited in suspense to see if the photo would really show up. In an extreme close-up, the photograph developed and came into focus, literally right before your eyes. The audience applauded every time. Taking such a risk and putting suspense into sixty seconds challenged the announcer to do it right, and the viewer to verify a breakthrough new product in action.

Lee Iacocca, CEO of Chrysler, helped bring his company back from near bankruptcy with his challenge to Americans, "If you can find a better car, buy it." Using the president as spokesperson is an old idea, but this one was surprising and credible, and it worked. (Later, after a bigger success than anticipated, Mr. Iacocca complained about "wasting two days of my time shooting that commercial," raising the question about how well some CEOs really understand advertising.)

Making an Emotional Argument Work

For some categories, brand personality, imagery, and emotional arguments work better than rational arguments.

Michelin Tires uses one or two babies sitting or in action inside an automobile tire. The visual in print or broadcast is powerful, and the copy builds on that: "Some things in life are more important ... because so much is riding on your tires." In a category of old claims and buyer confusion, Michelin simplifies the case for paying a premium for safety without a lot of unnecessary words and claims.

The Marlboro cowboy relaunched a brand and made it the world's leading cigarette and a big profit maker. After a few years, Philip Morris tried a different campaign. Sales dropped, and the company returned to the cowboy. The moral is: Stay with a winning campaign. "Marlboro Country" is more than forty years old and still going strong.

In the early 1980s, Levi's 501 Jeans and the entire category were in trouble in Europe. Young people believed that jeans had gone out of fashion and were for older people. Levi Strauss relaunched the brand as the classic jean, targeting 15-to-19-year-olds. The highly charged, emotional TV commercials used new releases of American tunes to reinforce the message. The result: sales more than doubled.

Benetton's theme, "United Colors of Benetton," has helped build a small Italian clothing company into a worldwide network, from a low-end producer to a fashionable brand sold on the Ginza, as well as the best shopping boulevards elsewhere. The print ads moved from simple photos of children a few years ago to hot social issues, causing much controversy. But Benetton has successfully courted young people and identified with their values, which are basically the same in most countries.

Using Nostalgia as a Motif

Nostalgia or returning to the past can be effective. Knowing that music can be a language, Ford revitalized its Mercury brand with a launch of the new Sable using music from the fifties in an unusual series of commercials, emotionally connecting with the target audience of young buyers. Other brands like Chiquita, Ovaltine, and Campbell's Soup have brought back old advertising ideas that worked well. As one creative director explains:

"Refreshing people's warm memories by resurrecting a successful old campaign cuts through the clutter and instantly telegraphs fundamental values about a brand that people have deeply rooted in their psyches."[8]

In the 1960s Maxwell House Coffee was known as "Good to the last drop." But the sound of bubbling, percolating coffee was so memorable that it was reintroduced in the 1990s.

Believing What You Say

Can you make the advertising become something that people believe in? If employees and salespeople bear witness to the truth of the advertising, customers want to buy. If retailers, customers, and others believe in the brand, esteem — and value — go up, up, up.

Avis is the classic case.

(Headline:)   Avis is only No. 2
in rent-a-cars.
So why go with us?

(Copy:)   We try harder. (When you're not the
biggest, you have to.)

Research advised not to run the ads. Nobody liked them at the agency or the company. But a few people believed that if the employees could change or improve the service, it would be a big promise. And it was. The rest is history.

Ingersoll-Rand's Pump Division stopped advertising to begin an intensive internal quality-control program with employees. Three new promises or challenges then could be made in new ads, like delivering parts on time or cutting the price in half. The new promises were competitive, highly believable, and achieved new sales objectives.

Intel is the number one maker of microprocessors with a 75-percent market share. It prevents manufacturers from using competitors' microprocessors by calling attention to what's inside the computer. Ads urge computer buyers to ask if the machine has "Intel inside." Every Intel customer (except IBM) includes this slogan prominently in all their computer ads and packaging; Intel worldwide sales rose 63 percent in the first year of "Intel inside." Most computer users do not even know what a microchip is, but they prefer "Intel inside."

Picking a Winner

Great campaigns are easy to discuss in hindsight. They are not easy to identify when seen for the first time. The first Marlboro print ad showed a cowboy with a headline that announced, "New from Philip Morris...." Not too inspiring, yet, the campaign succeeded. Some said the great Volkswagen ads of the 1960s were negative advertising. Headlines such as "Lemon," "Ugly is only skin deep," and "Think small" are hardly favorable for a small, low-priced foreign car when Americans favored big cars. But the ads created interest, recognition...and sales.

Several new effective campaigns, including the advertising for Heineken Beer in the United Kingdom ("Refreshes the parts [of the body] other beers cannot reach"), failed miserably in pretesting. The later success supports many experts' opinions that emotions are almost impossible to test.

"There are many ways to be right and wrong about a campaign," according to Paul Best, a European creative consultant. "You only understand a campaign and where it can go after the first ad when you will have gotten feedback from the marketplace."[9]

The lesson for managers is that there are no rules for good advertising. (Goodbye, checklists!) Once you understand how advertising works, you develop your own principles for making decisions. Which is why your marketing manager should now look to you for help.

HELPING SALES MANAGERS UNDERSTAND
THE VALUE OF ADVERTISING

Sales managers have probably seen more advertising presentations than any agency account executive. The entire sales force will be a tough audience. Consider the truisms they hear again and again:

- A good product sells itself.
- Advertising reduces the cost of selling.
- Advertising is salesmanship in print.

They see advertising get more credit than selling, live with some wins as well as rejection and complaints from some customers, and have their sales quotas increased each year by management (rationalized as "stretch goals"). And they have seen or heard every selling promise under the sun. Now, what was that you wanted to say to the sales manager?

There are three things you can do to turn cynicism into synergy.

1. Do your homework. Understand how the customer buys and the steps in the buying cycle (who gets involved, how long it takes from selling to buying to usage, exactly where the organization's salespeople fit in).

2. Get to know salespeople's attitudes toward the brand, its quality and service support, and how they talk about the advertising to their customers.

3. Understand the exact role of advertising in the selling process. Are you trying to generate sales leads, make customers feel confident, evaluate the brand?

Ask the sales manager to interpret what you have learned to get some perspective. Now you've got a context or a common ground for a dialog with the sales manager in which you can both agree on the value of advertising.

The types of questions you can ask are simple.

• What are the steps in a sale, starting at the point when the customers (or end users) realize they need and want our product (or service)?

• How complex is the sale?

• How long does the process take?

A quick way to get all the questions answered is to ask the sales manager to tell a success story; then listen. This open-ended question is easy to answer, reveals more than you would ever have asked, and gives you a transition to follow-up questions to elicit information and reveal his or her attitudes toward advertising.

If the sales manager is convinced of the value of advertising, he or she will become one of your supporters in decision-making, fighting for budget dollars you will need.

You should try to get the sales manager to agree on some basic premises about the relationship between selling and advertising. Here are a few possible approaches:

Show a Strategic Connection of Advertising to Selling.

Back to basics. For example, what is the role of your advertising? (It is seldom "awareness"; all advertising increases awareness.) Does it put your brand on their shopping list? Is it getting people into the showroom to see the car and talk with a salesperson? These are precise statements of the role or objective of the advertising. Few marketing or advertising professionals are this specific. A sales manager will usually appreciate this attention and look at the value of advertising in a new way, visualizing its contribution to the sale. And it might be worthwhile for you to read a book about advertising strategy.[10]

Explain How the Creative Concept Influences the Consumer.
The way advertising works may sound simple, but, amazingly, even some ad agency people do not have an up-to-date explanation of the process. For example, your TV commercial shows new ways to prepare Jello®. New ideas in food preparation rank high in attentiveness among women and are also the easiest excuse to try the brand again. You might say the ad gives the homemaker "permission" to buy Jello®, an old product, to be used in a new way. This strategy could be persuasive for a Kraft General Foods salesperson to make a sales presentation to a chain store buyer, calling on distributors, or even training new sales representatives.

Become a Teacher.
Offer training, for example, a short workshop or self-teaching notebook for sales and marketing people to learn more about the value of advertising, which you could write, together with the sales manager. Use the company's brands and real ads so every salesperson can talk (and listen) more knowledgeably with customers and key accounts.

Suggestions for projects:

a) The advertising success book. Create a three-ring binder with just a few pages (new ads, new budget figures) explaining the A-B-C's of advertising, showing customers reading magazines and watching TV, and telling how many see and hear your ads/TV commercials/radio spots (this data should be available from your advertising agency); illustrations of ads, briefly explaining the selling proposition; showing how the selling idea is used by salespeople and integrated into other promotions; quoting satisfied customers who talk about the brand, using words from ads. The binder can be given to new employees who join sales and marketing departments and updated annually.

b) Speech or miniworkshop on advertising. Put together a slide presentation or video that any manager can show new employees, customers, retailers, distributors, visitors, etc. Include your brand (logo, product) and its competitive superiority features and benefits. Explain why people need or want this product and a description of who they are (demographic, lifestyle, and product usage profile). Demonstrate what a salesperson says to a customer and what an ad says to the customer. Include sample ads and/or television commercials (in printed form). Use illustrations and brief numbers of media. Highlight the results of last year's campaign.

c) An "ad idea" file. Maintain a file of articles and news about advertising, success of your brand(s), your industry — anything that will educate sales and marketing people. Use these selectively to send with personal notes to people. If you have a lot, distribute them as attachments to your "news" memo every month (only if people are interested in receiving these). Keeping people up to date opens relationships and gives you topics of conversation when you meet with them.

d) Competitive reviews. Sales and marketing people are always envious of the competition and sometimes suspect their advertising is better than yours. Have your ad agency collect all competitive advertising. Sit down with your marketing and sales manager quarterly or annually and analyze what is working. Then conduct "competitive seminars" with sales and marketing people to report on the competitors' strategies and selling ideas, media, and what you have heard by way of results. If this is an open-discussion type of meeting, you will learn as much or more than they do.

Multiply the Sales Message; Help the Sales Force.

How can you translate advertising into something that sales can say or show customers? Talk to salespeople first; their words will inspire you; then your sales kits will be real, paraphrasing your advertising so customers find it interesting and persuasive.[11]

Dramatize the Value of Advertising to the Sales Force.

This is an opportunity for creative thinking. Sales forces have heard the same old pitch year after year from the advertising or marketing communications department. What is "creative" about an advertising presentation or a new campaign? Consider these three examples:

1) Appliances. David Mattingly, chairman of Mattingly & Partners, a large advertising agency in Australia, tells this story:

"Ten years ago we were appointed to handle the advertising for Dishlex Dishwashing Machines. We decided to use Australia's premier women's fashion designer, Prue Acton, as presenter for the brand. Prue is young and attractive; a "big name" within and outside the fashion world. Prue was an expected spokeswoman from the consumer's point of view.

We launched the new campaign to the Dishlex sales force at their annual sales conference. It received a very positive response. Point-of-sale featured Prue Acton in life-size cut-out figures to dominate the appliance dealer's showroom and tie in with the advertising.

The highlight of our presentation was Prue herself on stage talking to the sales force. She said how delighted she was to be representing such a good brand as Dishlex and would help them sell it to retailers. Any salesperson who sold twenty or more units to a retailer in the next thirty days could bring a guest to a private dinner and fashion show of the latest Prue Acton styles. If the salesperson or guest liked any of the merchandise, he or she could buy it at half price.

This linked the sales force to the customer, to Prue Acton, to the brand. The campaign was a huge success and is still recalled today by the consumer, sales force, and the trade." [12]

2) Industrial plate steel. Your author conducted an image-tracking study for Lukens Steel Company years ago and presented it to the CEO. The results showed a great improvement attributable to the advertising campaign. Together, we decided the results might be too good to be believed by some of the sales force. Why? Salespeople usually hear complaints from current customers and alibis from prospective customers, not good news.

The president really wanted to present the true, favorable results at the next sales meeting. So we turned the presentation into a report on advertising results, introduced by a "quiz." Underneath each salesperson's chair was the quiz, "How Smart Are You About Your Customers?" Attendees completed it privately, then the results of the image study were shown. Each salesperson checked off the responses, comparing their perceptions to the reported attitudes of customers. As expected, the salespeople — as confident and successful as they always are — underrated the company's reputation against the competition, not realizing how strong the brand name was with customers.

REACHING FINANCIAL PEOPLE WITH YOUR MESSAGE

Today's chief financial officer (CFO) wants to know about everything — especially why you're spending all those dollars on advertising. And it's to your advantage if the CFO and the financial department understand the contribution advertising makes to the sale of the company's products.

Financial people respect success in the marketplace. Top management at successful marketing companies have clearly communicated down through the ranks the belief that advertising is their most cost-efficient means for building the business.

Corporations like Procter & Gamble, Philip Morris, and Nestle have succeeded by using advertising to launch new brands, maintain market share against competitive attack, and enter new markets. Today's P&G president has urged brand managers to spend more on advertising to build the brand and less on promotion.

It may be that some advertising managers find it difficult to have a meeting with the CFO. Robert F. Lauterborn urges you to reconsider that position:

"It's a mistake for marketing communications people to think of financial managers as adversaries. Invited into the process, they can become the best allies we have. The key is to get the financial manager thinking about advertising as an investment, rather than as a cost. Then the conversation turns to how do you measure return on investment, and he or she can be surprisingly creative in developing such measures. I believe the only way we as a profession will ever achieve credibility at the senior management level comparable to 'hard science' functions like manufacturing or engineering is when we and the financial people work together on this issue and present a united front." [13]

One CFO for European operations of a large multinational corporation conducts a seminar annually for his people to learn more about advertising. The result is that managers see financial people as internal consultants who understand the business, not as "bean counters."

There are benefits if members of the financial community outside the company understand the value of your advertising. Bankers feel more favorable and confident when giving the company a loan or commercial credit. Wall Street advisors see your company and its products as more desirable by consumers and, therefore, worth further investment. Security analysts pick up your advertising messages as they compile their research reports on companies or industries. In a positive sense, every product ad (if executed well) is a corporate advertisement.

There is another important audience you need to talk to or help others explain advertising to in their presentations.

GETTING THE TRADE EXCITED ABOUT YOUR ADVERTISING

This is any channel of distribution between you and the consumer, for example, manufacturers' representatives, brokers, wholesalers, distributors, or retailers. Unless you have a breakthrough new product or technology, are going to spend a fortune on the campaign, or are going to put Michael Jordan into their stores in person, this audience may give you a big yawn. Here are some alternative ways to build interest and excitement in your advertising.

- Set up a panel of retail chain buyers who meet several times a year to talk about advertising and promotion. One agency that did this found that many of their ideas were used. It was also an excellent opportunity to hear what the trade has to say and to provide sneak previews of upcoming advertising.
- Build an in-store "infomercial" around the TV commercials so consumers learn about product features and how to use the product.
- Hold "extravaganza" sales meetings to announce a new ad campaign. Ford, Dr Pepper, and others do it with their dealers and bottlers. It works because it is 90% show business — entertaining and memorable, as opposed to the boring, routine sales meetings the trade always attends.
- Tie incentive/involvement events to the launch of new advertising. This encourages the trade to participate, and rewards

those who do. Make sure to select something of significant value to encourage participation.

- Hold media seminars for the trade. To help soft drink bottlers understand the value of advertising, how to use it effectively, and how to deal with local agencies, PepsiCo conducted regular media seminars for its bottlers. These were informative, highly interactive seminars that changed the way bottlers handled advertising to support the national brand.

Any good advertising, sales promotion, or public relations agency can give you more ideas. But keep in mind that the trade has been disappointed so many times by national advertisers' promises of promotional support that it may take a really innovative idea or medium or unusually heavy spending to get their attention.

Finally, while advertising in business and trade publications may seem effective, conduct a reality test of your own. How new or rapidly changing is the industry or its technology? (Are there really hard news and must-read topics for those in the industry?) Some publications have outlived their vitality and usefulness. (There used to be a saying, "You can't kill a bad trade magazine.")

How do these media compare with alternatives to persuade the trade? If you want to reach buyers in food stores, can you do better than *Progressive Grocer* magazine? If you are marketing electronic components to commercial aircraft manufacturers and the defense industry, can you find better than *Aviation Week*? Or *Engineering News-Record* for the construction business? Sometimes you can learn the difference yourself by thumbing through these publications, talking to your agency media director, and asking your own sales and marketing people.

TALKING TO EMPLOYEES

Your most importance audience could be employees. They are the front line, the people customers see or talk to. Their enthusiasm or lack of it can build or break a company over the long haul. Someone once said, "Every employee is a salesperson." That's very true.

They think they know and understand advertising. "Yes, it's about jingles," or "Yes, it's keeping your name in front of the public." But most do not understand the value or the benefit of advertising. It is not because the company failed to communicate its new ad campaign. The reason could be any of the following:

- They don't know why it is important to their jobs to have this information;
- Nobody has explained how advertising works to change people's attitudes in the context of the company's or brand's new campaign;
- They are judging the advertising not as the target group, but as themselves;

- Nobody asked them questions, for their opinion, or settled misunderstandings; all the internal communication was one-way.

If employees believe in your advertising, there is a multiplier effect, even with a small number of employees. Word-of-mouth recommendation is the most effective medium of communication in many product categories.

Take the time to kick off your program internally. It's very important to show new ads and campaigns *before* the advertising appears in the press or on the air. It may seem too basic a rule, but some companies do not do this. Imagine a salesperson, customer service representative, or plant manager seeing a new TV spot or campaign for the first time without knowing why it is running. It pays to avoid this because your people will get angry at not being told in advance, and their negative comments destroy the benefits your advertising is trying to communicate. How much better to have them know, understand, and then say, "Yes, it really does that...," supporting and reinforcing the advertising. Or translating the message into their own words and feelings.

Even if you use a standardized or canned presentation to employees, allow some time for feedback to be sure employees understand the campaign and to elicit support. This can be done in a question-answer exchange at a meeting. Without the playback in their own words, you will never know if there is true understanding or support.

Employees may be an important secondary target for your advertising. Metropolitan Life Insurance Company, for example, aims its advertising at adult male heads of households. But the company also wants its thousands of agents to be persuaded and involved. When these agents buy into a campaign, they become motivated to do a better job selling — and serving — customers.

The U.S. Postal Service advertising sells you stamps, but it also wants its one-half-million employees to feel proud giving you good service every day. Copies of videotapes, media flow charts, and suggested scripts are sent to postmasters in the branches to encourage them to talk about the new USPS advertising campaign to their people; copies are also distributed to district offices, so everyone can connect to the new selling idea.

Copies of the famous "We try harder" Avis ads were inserted into employees' paycheck envelopes to show that higher standards were expected. Clerks wore buttons with the slogan, encouraging a dialog with customers who walked in to reserve cars. One ad in the series even showed a mistake that had been made. The last line of copy said, "They will probably never run this ad." Think of the effect this had on Avis employees!

The merchandising or re-use of advertising offers many opportunities to exploit the value of advertising to the "inner market," or those inside the company. Reprints of ads as mailing pieces, brochures, framed ads on walls of factories and lobbies, slide presentations as part of new-employee orientation meetings, previews of new campaigns explained by managers, articles in company newsletters and house organs/magazines, and many other forms of internal communication reinforce the value of advertising to employees.

The result is better informed employees, people who appreciate learning more about their products and take pride in working for their companies.

If you are giving a presentation to employees, consider what they know about advertising (very little) and what they think they know (everything). One approach to such a presentation is shown in Exhibit 8.2.

A LOOK AT SOME OF THE PROBLEMS

While total advertising volume remains large and we are learning more about how to develop effective advertising campaigns, several problems and trends have contributed to the advertising manager's need to question existing plans and raise new questions.

Changing market dynamics need monitoring because they may negatively impact your goals. Increased competition, new segmentation of markets, private-label acceptance by consumers (especially during recessions), and other factors are today's work environment.

Competitive product and marketing strategy changes can decrease the impact of advertising, especially if a product no longer measures up to the competition. General Motors set up Saturn as a different kind of enterprise. Today this low-priced car outperforms Lexus and Mercedes-Benz in customer satisfaction. Not having high-perceived quality advantages may eventually cause a brand to lose, no matter how good the advertising. One observer predicts:

"Businesses that have high and improving customer perceived relative quality can gain on average up to a half percentage point of market share each year while holding other variables constant."[14]

These companies have the momentum to win, advertising or no advertising. It is the advertising manager's job to decode what these "winner" competitors are doing, to diagnose their weaknesses, define their strengths, and recommend changes in advertising and marketing strategies.

Communications barriers to reaching the consumer. Increased noise and clutter in traditional media decrease the chances that your selling message will be seen or heard. Changing attitudes and a decline in credibility of advertising claims and sponsors also affect the perceived value of advertising.

Decrease in the power of advertising to persuade viewers and readers during the past twenty years. "We have been collecting data for two decades that suggest that new product and new service awareness and penetration — both in large part the result of advertising — are increasingly difficult to achieve. Therefore, performance per dollar is slipping."

EXHIBIT 8.2 SAMPLE PRESENTATION TO EXPLAIN ADVERTISING
TO EMPLOYEES

WHAT ADVERTISING DOES FOR OUR COMPANY

What can advertising do for a brand? for a business? for the economy? What are the effects of the advertising in communicating messages to people? One place to start is with the names of products or brands you know.

For a brand like Nike, Coca-Cola, or Xerox, advertising attracts new customers or persuades existing customers to keep buying and using the product. Successful brands like these make sure the ads evoke a favorable attitude or feeling toward the brand. The ads link the brand to the consumer.

Advertising is the engine of branding, of building brand loyalty. It adds value to the brand, creates differences in the consumer's mind. Added value is the single most important function that advertising performs, like continually putting capital investment into an existing brand.

How do ads work? If you examine a good ad, it usually focuses on one important attribute, benefit, or satisfaction that the brand offers. Ads help people consider information before they purchase and use the product like a computer, life insurance, or a video camera. Or for a familiar brand, it may just remind people to try it or use it again.

From hundreds of case histories, test markets, experiments, books, and articles, we know that advertising works. It can help achieve a brand's or company's objectives. Of course success also requires a good product, a creative selling idea, and adequate opportunities for people to see and hear this message in the media. We know that advertising can launch a new brand, expand the market for existing products, or penetrate markets to increase share. It can inform, change attitudes or opinions, predispose people to choose, identify themselves so they can be sold, tempt them to try, keep them satisfied, and more.

We know that great advertising is often remembered years after it stops.

For some of the nonbelievers, the conclusive proof of its value is a real-life demonstration or a personal experience. Work in a retail store the day after a sale ad appears in the newspaper and see the people coming through the doors looking for the advertised products. Seeing is believing.

From a marketing standpoint, advertising does many things for any business.

- It can maintain markets by encouraging customer loyalty to your brand; it can revitalize markets by giving them new reasons to buy.

- It can create new markets. Dannon Yogurt stressed that yogurt is good for consumers at a time when they were getting interested in natural foods.

- It can expand volume, like getting kids to brush their teeth every day; gain or broaden distribution by getting people to go into stores asking for the brand advertised.

- Advertising can respond to competitive threats and make it more costly for competitors to win new customers. Hertz retaliated against the original Avis ("We're No.2, so we try harder") campaign and eventually blunted this successful campaign.

- It enhances the reputation and image of the company. DuPont, GE, IBM, and other companies have used advertising to win friends and customers and enhance their corporate images.

- It shapes people's perceptions about a brand, offers the opportunity of consideration at the time of brand choice, and thereby leads to increase of market share.

- Advertising can reduce unit cost of a product by lowering the selling cost. And increase profits.

- Properly communicated, it can motivate salespeople, the trade, and employees.

- In the broadest sense, advertising benefits the national economy. As more products are advertised, the category grows. Industry grows. The economy grows. As more new products are developed, they compete because brands need to be announced and advertised to enter a market. This inevitably brings better products and lower prices. The cost of selling for consumer or industrial goods would be higher without advertising. It's plain, old-fashioned economics.

How about the general public? While there are some complaints about advertising, it does enrich people's lives, gives them more choices, and widens their experiences. Even among those people who deny that advertising has any influence on them, we find that they own name brands that are heavily advertised. (Just open their medicine cabinets in their bathrooms, or check out the brands of household products they have in their kitchens!)

Fragmentation of media means declining media ratings and changing cost efficiencies. How do you follow target audiences as they migrate from network to cable viewing? How can you cover focused targets as new media emerge and the Internet web sites blossom? Consolidations, acquisitions and mergers with their selling packages may not be more effective in media buys. Convergence, directly competitive companies working in alliances, a trend of the 1990s, is good for the media companies (sharing risks and resources), but may mean more forced choices for the advertiser.

Decline of advertising agencies. Agencies were once dominant in the thinking and planning of brands, acting more as a partner to top client management. Some experts claim the agency's role as a custodian of the brand has diminished, with clients expecting only ads and media placement. (This is partly true, but agencies are striving for more strategic partnerships today.)

It is all changing, but it is manageable.

EXCELLENT OPPORTUNITIES AWAIT YOU

The advertising manager is the gateway to new ideas, helping management, and building brands. Here are just a few more suggestions that may help along the way:

Keep learning. Advertising is not changing as fast as the Internet, but there will be at least two or three new books, theories, models, and seminars you ought to explore each year, in addition to keeping up with news and articles to sharpen your expertise.

Widen your network. Include media research people, sales reps, people who work in distribution, professors of marketing, and others.

Join a good industry organization in which you can learn from others. The Association of National Advertisers is one possibility; it conducts excellent seminars, at least one of which ought to be included on your calendar each year.

Study failures as well as successes. Hardly anyone does, but you can learn much from others' mistakes.

If you have time, teach. Teaching forces you to the outer limits of any specialty, to stay ahead of the students, to search for what is new and important.

Read. At the end of this chapter are references and suggestions for further reading. Every two years you owe it to yourself to read, skim, or spot-read a new advertising textbook. Professor-writers are usually ahead of practitioners. This is an inexpensive way to catch up in your field.

REFERENCES

1. Sandra Moriarity and Tom Duncan. *How to Create and Deliver Winning Advertising Presentations* (Lincolnwood, IL: NTC Business Books, 1991).

2. Magid Abraham and Leonard Lodish. *Advertising Works, A Study of Advertising Effectiveness and the Resulting Strategic and Tactical Implications* (New York: Information Resources Inc., 1990).

3. Bradley T. Gale. *How Advertising Affects Profitability and Growth for Consumer Businesses* in: *The Value Side of Productivity* (New York: American Association of Advertising Agencies, The Strategic Planning Institute, 1990).

4. Naras V. Eechambadi. "Does advertising work?" *McKinsey Quarterly* 3 (1994).

5. Interview with Ghafoor Rawtaer, managing director of Borneo Motors, Singapore, August 1995.

6. Interview with Paul Walker, Asia/Pacific marketing director at Andersen Consulting, Singapore, August 1995.

7. Interview with Laura McCorvie, partner with CSC Weston Group, Wilton, CT, August 1995.

8. "Themes like old times," *New York Magazine* (January 30, 1989).

9. Interview with Paul Best, creative consultant, August 1995.

10. Don E. Schultz, Dennis Martin, and William P. Brown. *Strategic Advertising Campaigns* (Lincolnwood, IL: NTC Business Books, 1995).

11. William F. Foley. "The medium is the salesman," *Advertising Age* (June 9, 1980).

12. Interview with David Mattingly, Mattingly and Partners, Australia, August 1995.

13. Interview with Robert F. Lauterborn, James L. Knight professor of advertising, School of Journalism and Mass Communication, University of North Carolina, November 1995.

14. Interview with Joel Rosenfeld, managing director and chief executive officer of The Strategic Planning Institute, Cambridge, MA, January 1996.

SUGGESTIONS FOR FURTHER READING

Aaker, David A. *Building Strong Brands* (New York: Simon & Schuster, 1996).

American Association of Advertising Agencies. *It Works! How Investment Spending in Advertising Pays Off.* Report by Value of Advertising Committee, New York, 1991.

Hiam, Alexander. *The Vest-Pocket CEO* (Englewood Cliffs, NJ: Prentice Hall, 1990).

Jones, John Philip. *Does It Pay to Advertise?* (Lexington, MA: Lexington Books, 1989).

Jones, John Philip. *When Ads Work* (New York: Lexington Books, 1995).

Kim, Peter. "Does Advertising Work: A Review of the Evidence." *Journal of Consumer Marketing* (Fall 1992).

Kotler, Philip, and Gary Armstrong. *Principles of Marketing* 7th ed. (Englewood Cliffs, NJ: Prentice Hall, 1996).

Lele, Milind M. *Creating Strategic Leverage* (New York: John Wiley, 1992).

Norins, Hanley. *The Young & Rubicam Traveling Creative Workshop* (Englewood Cliffs: Prentice Hall, 1990).

Ogilvy, David. *Confessions of an Advertising Man* (New York: Athenaeum, 1988).

Ogilvy, David. *Ogilvy on Advertising* (New York: Random House, 1985).

Ries, Al, and Jack Trout. *The 22 Immutable Laws of Marketing* (New York: HarperBusiness, 1994).

Salz, Nancy L. *How to Get the Best Advertising from Your Agency* 3rd ed. (Burr Ridge, IL: Irwin, 1994).

Schultz, Don E.; Stanley I. Tannenbaum; and Robert F. Lauterborn. *Integrated Marketing Communications* (Lincolnwood, IL: NTC Business Books, 1995).

Schwartz, Peter. *The Art of the Long View* (New York: Doubleday, 1991).

Stobart, Paul, ed. *Brand Power* (New York: New York University Press, 1994).

Surmanek, Jim. *Media Planning* (Lincolnwood, IL: NTC Business Books, 1995).

Wells, William; John Burnett; and Sandra Moriarity. *Advertising Principles and Practice* (Englewood Cliffs, NJ: Prentice Hall, 1995).

Bill Foley is president of his own consulting firm, William F. Foley & Associates, in Pelham, NY, where his clients include Dentsu, Young & Rubicam, BBDO Worldwide, BDDP, Publi-Graphics, and McCann-Erickson Worldwide.

He has worked in advertising for more than thirty years. After earning an M.B.A. from the University of Chicago's Graduate School of Business, he was national retail advertising supervisor for Montgomery Ward. In sequence, he became a copywriter for Needham, Harper & Steers; account supervisor for Frank C. Nahser, Inc.; research director for Marsteller Advertising; and head of training worldwide for Young & Rubicam Advertising. In addition, Foley has taught marketing and advertising courses at Chicago City Junior College, Manhattan College, and New York University, and has published extensively.

CHAPTER 9

MANAGING CREATIVE RESOURCES

If you think back on everything you've seen so far in this book, you might logically ask, "How can I get it all done?"

The answer is much the same for any supervisor or manager: by planning and by managing all the resources you need to get the job done; your own staff of people, outside suppliers and freelancers, and your advertising agency.

Times are changing. Corporations are flattening departments and downsizing. Agency-client relationships allegedly are deteriorating. How do you manage people in today's climate? How do you hire a freelancer? How does a company go about selecting an advertising agency? What do some of the best practitioners of advertising advise?

Mary Koelle, Xerox manager of marketing for office document products, gives this advice to a new ad manager, "First, you have to recognize and believe in the power of integrated marketing communications. Secondly, because organizations are downsizing, you need to get the most from your agency relationship. Establish a true partnership relationship so that the line between client and agency is almost transparent. Next, get your people to interpret your goals as positive for them, as well; 'What can it do for me?'"[1]

Koelle's philosophy takes a big-picture approach to her business and integrated marketing communications. She wisely intends to lean on what can be her most important outside resource, the ad agency, and will communicate with her people so they understand her vision and goals.

According to Bob Lundin, president of Jones-Lundin Associates, advertising management consultants, the problem of managing internal and external resources is the same: failure to give clear guidelines of expectations and a shared vision.[2] This is true for an advertising manager's own staff or the advertising agency. There must be job descriptions with specific role functions; responsibilities must be clear, or conflicts will arise. Once goals are set, they should be declared, shared, completely understood and committed to.

STARTING WITH YOUR PEOPLE

If you are the new head of this department, to manage your people, your most important resource, you'll need to learn who the people are. Listening and asking questions, getting briefed by each of them is a good first step. You should be committed to them and believe in their competency, and you'll want to form a relationship of mutual respect and sharing your values and goals. They must believe that you care about them.

Is the person just right? If not, can that person change to adapt to your plans for the department? Can you set performance goals for and with him or her with a time deadline like three or six months for review of achievement of these objectives? If not, then perhaps it is in both your interests to transfer or let this person find a job in another company.

Remember that you were given this job because of your management expertise; while you should not play the part of "great dictator," you are expected to be the leader and coach. You will want to set clear expectations early, defining roles and responsibilities. Tell them where theirs begin, end, and how you fit in. You may want to be candid about your style if you are a hands-on manager, so there are no surprises or shocks as you begin working together. Above all, be fair, consistent, and accessible.

While participative managing is preferred, situations will arise when pressure to deliver, must-do, or "slam-dunking" is called for. There is nothing wrong in such a case to announce, "We won't do it this way any more. We are changing the way we do this...." Nevertheless, you must present the dictum in such a way that your staff understands the rationale regardless of whether or not they agree with it.

Managing advertising or marketing communications is probably no different from managing other departments. One weakness of managers and supervisors in any business is delegating. In the creative arena, it may be especially difficult for the manager to encourage and nurture his or her staff members to take the initiative and assume responsibility.

Robert Weinstein, vice president of external relations at Metropolitan Life Insurance Company, said, "My managing style is delegating. Having the right people, setting the general direction, and then letting them go. I've always believed in delegating, and it produces results."[3]

An advertising agency is somewhat like your department in that many of its people must supervise a number of projects at one time and overcome problems and crises that happen.

One of the most creative, and also best organized agencies, is Leo Burnett Worldwide. William T. Lynch, Burnett president and CEO, suggested, "The free flow of creative solutions is essential. Leaders must shepherd this process along, stretching their people's minds while providing focus. A leader must translate smart thinking into knowledge and use this knowledge to provide the vision to help the team stay one step ahead of the business, building opportunities and competition.... Encourage and promote the most talented people who also favor 'being a leader' over 'acting like a boss.'"[4]

Hidden in what Lynch says is the important concept of teamwork. As the boss, if you can get your people to believe in the success of their teamwork and train them in the behaviors that help people perform on their teams, you will achieve your goals and they will enjoy their work.

Making Your Goals Drive Your Actions

One manager says he keeps his five goals in his top drawer to look at every day. A common trait of successful executives and strong leaders is a defined sense of purpose. They are single-minded. The trendy word today is *focus*. You know where you are going.

Stephen Covey, authority on leadership, divides people into "proactive" and "reactive" types. The proactive ones work on things they can do something about. Reactive people concentrate on things like problems, weaknesses of others, and end up using a lot of negative energy.[5] You can guess which type of leader has more influence on his or her people and delivers results.

In summary, the art of leading others begins with you—who you are, what you want to do, and how well you communicate with other people.

Making Decisions About People

What kinds of people do you need? With so many tasks, plans, promotions, and deadlines, you need competent project managers more than anything else. How do you hire them? There are hundreds of these around, but too many tend to be functionally narrow, not the generalists your department needs. It is easy to find someone who knows video production. It is more difficult to find someone who has these skills and understands print production. Some managers say that it is probably better to have people who can work across disciplines, including advertising, direct marketing, and sales promotion. How do you find them?

The flow of incoming resumes and curriculum vitae is one source, but it may not reveal the candidates you want to hire. With the cutbacks in agencies and companies, you can find the talents and skills you are looking for. But you'll need an updated job description before you run those classified ads or talk to a head hunter.

A general rule for interviewing is to study the applicant's resume very closely and ask a few leading questions, probing him or her to tell you about an important project or projects he managed. Be careful not to reveal the competencies you are looking for. Why? Because people will tell you what they think you want to hear. You want to discover inside the story being told how competent someone is in managing many projects at one time, keeping within budgets, getting good work from suppliers, etc.

"Can-do" statements, promises, and generalities are only guesswork. You must play detective, asking open-ended questions and listening within the interviewee's stories for signs of success and ability to do the tasks you want done. Proof or evidence of jobs done from the interviewee's stories may be more predictive of future performance than the cleverly written entries on the resume or CV.

Hoping to get the decision by reference checks with ex-employers is usually not helpful today. Why? Supervisors and managers try to be nice in job reference checks and sometimes fear legal problems from admitting to problems or deficiencies in a former employee's performance.

A list of competencies can become criteria for a job description or an outline for you to use in a job interview. If you don't have a human resources expert to help you determine these, you'll need to do some research inside the organization. Interview someone who was highly successful at the job. It will be easy to make a list of the day-to-day tasks, but be sure to probe for the job or professional skills a more-than-adequate performer must have to do this work well. Observe by spot-visits to someone doing the job; look at the daily or weekly "to-do" list. Ask which are the difficult tasks. You will begin to get insights and make a final listing of core competencies, as well as attitudes, traits, and personal characteristics, all of which now become your expectations for job performance.

Now you are ready to begin talking to someone because you know exactly what you want in the person who will do a great job for you. And this person will know your standards and the performance he or she will be measured on.

You may wish to use a temporary employment agency that can provide creative or other advertising personnel. Get to know them. Ask your peers in other companies which ones have proved to be the best. You then have a short list to use when the next job opening comes up.

Should you hire trainees? Yes and No. On the Yes side, it is generally a good policy to have "new blood," younger people who are learning (and someone training them) and who have growth potential. On the No side, if your department is too small or highly specialized, orienting and working with trainees could dissipate energies. The pay-off may not be there for you and it is unfair to the trainees. Some companies hire trainees and then leave them to fend for themselves, which can backfire on a company's reputation in the marketplace.

Hire straight out of school? You would probably prefer not being the first full-time business experience in this graduate's life. You are looking for some maturity and judgment.

Have we skipped any people you should be managing inside your company? Yes. What about managing your boss? He or she is a resource you can and should use. Learn the art of delegating some tasks upward or seeing how a thing to be done can be done better at a higher level. Or at least gain valuable, needed inputs from the boss. Doing this might change the whole task, or end the meeting with the boss taking it on as his own responsibility.

One president who seemed to act in an autocratic way warned his managers, "You have to learn how and when to use me as a resource." The subtext, or what he was actually saying, was: "I am not going to change my managing style to fit you, but do not be so afraid of me that you make a fatal business mistake by not asking for my opinion."

Some questions and criteria may help in these "boss" situations:

- Is it a crisis situation when the boss can quickly make important decisions?
- Will it be more efficient or deliver better results if the boss does it?
- Does the boss have free time and we are very busy?
- Can one of us team up and do it with the boss, perhaps using this as a developmental or learning experience?
- Are you overloaded with nobody else to whom you can delegate?
- Is this a poorly defined task without an objective or mission?

Managing your boss is an art to be mastered. Delegating upward needs to be done with tact and finesse. No boss will admit to looking forward to being given a task from his subordinate.

Managing your peers may seem like an oxymoron, like managing your boss. But if you don't do it, they'll do it to you. Every product or brand manager eventually has to learn it. The nature of the job is responsibility without the authority.

Your mastery of teamwork is important to your success with your peers and a skill that marks you as a real manager. Some learn it on the job or from a good coach; some get formal training in workshops and seminars. You might learn it from a book, but doing it is far more important than reading about it.

A seminar in team building will help you understand how effective a team can be. Find out what you need to improve your leadership of small groups. There are courses and workshops in interpersonal skills, like listening to others, motivating and influencing others, presenting your ideas, running meetings, coaching, being a champion of change, and building relationships. Where are you strong and where are you weak?

Let's consider some practical suggestions of how to deal with peers.

On some occasions you can enlist their support or advocacy, ask for direct help, partially delegate, borrow resources, or become a member of their task forces. Why do it? Productivity is the biggest argument, getting more done in less time. Or teamwork that accomplishes the work and builds a spirit of networking across the organization. Even in a highly structured corporation, if open lines of communication are understood, new ideas can fly directly from a peer in one division to a peer in another division without the laborious ascent up the hierarchy which is the old way of working.

Guidelines are simple: Does management understand the benefits? Will peers work with ideas based on merit, not on whose turf it is?

Is the corporate culture one that respects ideas and encourages initiative, not just being politically correct?

While corporations and their CEOs expect new ideas to stay alive and grow, marketing departments have been criticized for generating few new ideas, not taking the lead in proposing new directions to their managements. A study by the Strategic Directions Group explains this behavior partially with psychographic segments of the marketing people.[6]

Which type of marketer are you?

- *Sophisticate.* Focus on niche, not mass, markets. Open to innovation, looking for change. I keep up with new developments, read, learn. Send my managers to seminars, training. We rely on external, not just internal, data. Believe in research we bought. Want more insight into customers.

- *Direct Answer.* A marketing niche is a two-dimensional view (key characteristics, not a sophisticated profile). Marketing consultants tell us what we already know. Market research is either not believable or not actionable. Attending seminars is not an important priority.

- *Mass Marketer.* Targeting niches is not central to our marketing strategy. Decisions should be based on "solid research data." Because I am computer-literate, I can use sophisticated information technology.

- *Constrained.* We don't have time to do research (or we wait until the last minute to get it). Like to do more research, but budget prevents it. Anyway, internal and secondary research can give us the answers we need. Pointing out new directions to management is not our job.

- *Networker.* We encourage relationships, working with consultants because they can help us solve problems. We are willing to propose new directions to management, so we are open to new ideas, systems, techniques. Therefore, we are committed to sending managers to training and seminars as much as we can and attending them ourselves.

THE ORGANIZATION OF TODAY AND TOMORROW

Yesterday's advertising department in a large corporation might have had a staff of dozens of people. Today's downsizing and re-engineering have changed the landscape. As every department in a corporation meets new standards of cost reduction and productivity, the advertising department must not only reduce headcount, but also change its process of working. Thus, we hear comments like these:

"We are doing more outsourcing, having 'contracts,' not full-timers, whom we can let go any time when business is down. Each regular employee's benefits cost us almost 40% of that salary."

"I am a single contributor. No secretary, no direct reports, just voice mail. Because I still manage all the marketing but with no administration now, I get a lot more done and I can even work from my 'virtual office' at home."

"One of the hardest things is facing 'deadwood' in your department, especially someone with tenure. It is very difficult to get rid of them or gain their confidence."

"Politically, getting rid of bodies is important right now...."

"Every year that the corporation is not making its target profit we are asked to cut back and this drops to the bottom line. The easiest thing to do is to eliminate one or more staff positions."

The lean organization of today still requires completion of projects on time and on budget. It is much easier to buy creative expertise freelance when you need it than get approval for a budget of full-time staff. More on this later.

You can catch glimpses of the department organization of tomorrow by looking at what is happening in some companies today. A senior manager at Verifone is one of a new breed of nomadic executives called the virtual worker. His meeting places are where he can plug into the company's computer network. Home is where the data port is.[7] A marketing communications manager in a large services company holds on-line meetings with his staff who are in several cities via computer. A New York ad agency creative team cranks out "99-cent" promo ad for a fast food company in just thirty minutes. By fax, the client takes the typeset ad to the local newspaper in Omaha and it runs the next day. In the Online Ad Agency (yes, that's their name), workers in different cities rarely see each other. They communicate via e-mail with one another and with clients.

When asked if his agency represents the future structure of an advertising agency, Jay Chiat of Chiat/Day answered, "I would hope that we're good enough to be the present. The future is bullshit. Eighty percent of what everyone is talking about never happens.... But there are two things that are important ... an intellectual architecture and a team architecture. The intellectual architecture means focusing on doing great work instead of focusing on agency politics. The team architecture means setting up an organization that helps people produce that great work in teams."[8]

How Feedback Helps You to Encourage Creative Ideas

Whether your organization is traditional, transitional (going through downsizing or significant change), or the new virtual organization, your flexibility and openness as a manager will help you adapt to the future. The question is: How open are you?

One way to succeed with your department is to get feedback. Stay confident, but keep assessing the working environment for possible dysfunction. What can go wrong? Many things.

Here is a confidential internal memo from one department where the boss obviously doesn't listen:

One problem is that our people are afraid to make mistakes. The most common operating mode is to anticipate exactly what one's boss wants to see and to deliver it, many times without understanding what that person is thinking. Superficial impressions of what a superior is looking for become rules of the road. The result is that people do not take chances or understand what the real issues and opportunities are so they can come up with innovative solutions. People avoid risk, and big ideas do not happen here. It is a factory-like system in which safety is the rule of the day.

This example is a bureaucracy, not a department with a creative climate or managers who set high standards and are open to fresh ideas.

The "climate" of a department or organization depends on the leader. If you discover what your people need to know, encourage them to share information, encourage even opposite points of view because you are always looking for new ideas, bring your key people into your decision-making, and you are predictable in the sense that they always know what is happening, your organization should run smoothly. As a check on yourself, ask every day what news there is that should be reported to your people and what new assignments lie ahead.

A WORD ON FREELANCERS AND CONSULTANTS

Why is it difficult to find advice on how to hire freelancers? The woods are full of them, but there isn't much written. Experience tells you that film and TV production companies live in a complete world of freelancing, talented people. They have their own informal rules for managing.

Most advertising agencies hire and use freelancers at some time during the year for creative work. How they choose these people varies. Some use databases. More often, it is a "proximity rule" (what you did last time or whom they can remember). Talent sometimes gets chosen based on friendships, networking, or who is currently in vogue because of unusual work or awards or visibility in the media. You hope your system is more rational.

Common sense suggests starting a simple system or planning now before the crisis when you need a freelancer. Start a "best freelancers" file. Under headings (copywriters, designers, photographers, etc.), begin a ranking of the best talents in your market. Candidates for your first list of names can be gotten from company records, headhunters, your ad agency, competitors, local ad club, Yellow Pages, and other sources. Start a screening and evaluation process of having breakfast once a week with one freelancer to get to know each one, then rank this person in your file. Within six months you will have the best freelancers identified for future use.

If you were to consult Paul Best, a European creative consultant, he would say: "If you are going to hire or choose a freelancer, I would do it on three possible criteria: I know him/her/them. I've worked with them. Or secondly, they are stars ... perhaps they can work the miracle. Thirdly, I am told they are pros and I can afford them." [9]

Best might also advise you to consider, apart from personal chemistry and money, how to fit the freelancer into the whole operation of getting advertising running. This connects with the nature of the job. Do you need just copy and layout or more than that, like a relationship? Do you need to get involved in continuous ad making, evaluating, and planning or not?

When should you hire a freelancer? You may have a small, quick creative task that needs doing. You may be frustrated that several attempts by an agency or a sales promotion firm have not yielded the results you want. You want a fresh point of view. Or you may be happy with your agency, but want to experiment with a part of your advertising that might uncover one breakthrough idea to build that segment of your business. In any of these cases, freelancers might provide the help you need.

CONGRATULATIONS: YOU ARE A ONE-PERSON LEARNING ORGANIZATION

Your management expects you to know everything—marketing, strategic thinking and positioning, media strategy/implementation and the new media, integrated marketing communications, promotional marketing, and the technology and cost efficiencies of broadcast and print production. How can you be this renaissance man or woman?

If you are new, you can plead ignorance: "Teach me." Or, "Please tell me everything you know about this business, starting with...."

One way to know is to have experts on staff. Another is to take full advantage of the experts at your agency. And, of course, you should always continue to educate yourself in the business of advertising.

You might consider hiring consultants. They ride the economic waves of change, technology, and other people's problems. They are worth meeting and knowing.

There are people you will meet, for example, media planners, marketing research suppliers, publishers of business magazines, editors, distributors, food brokers or wholesalers, and others, whose opinion you can consult to solve problems. How do you find them?

Your network of business acquaintances and associates can include experts of all kinds. Ask your advertising peers whom they use. Some of them are in your own company. Some are outsiders trying to do business with your company. Your conversations will uncover pockets of expertise you can list as future resources. Some may be sitting next to you at an ANA (Association of National Advertisers, Inc.) seminar. Some you will meet socially. Again, building a resource file is one of the secrets to keeping up with your field.

If you identify yourself as an information-seeker, people will begin using you as a resource.

As long as you are in a learning mode, increase your exposure to books and publications. Add a new publication each year, removing a weak one. Even if only one article of what you scan in a weekly trade magazine is new and worth remembering, that's worth your 20 minutes a week. Don't let them stack up, because old news is useless. One way to discipline yourself is to find 15 minutes the first day important magazines arrive. Tear out all the articles you know you must read and put them in your briefcase; throw the magazines away because you've already decided what you want.

When was the last time you took a course in advertising or marketing? Crack an advertising or marketing communications textbook every two years; scan it for the chapter that has a new theory, interesting case history, or something that changes what you learned before. Professors are most often ahead of the practitioners (and neither really listens to the other for some strange reason). Ground-breaking books or major theories emerge only every two or three years. Visit a good book store and see what's really new in the marketing and advertising sections. Get yourself on the mailing list of universities and organizations that give seminars and workshops. Try to put money in your budget each year to attend these.

SELECTING, MOTIVATING, AND WORKING WITH YOUR AD AGENCY

The first question to address is: Should you use an advertising agency? (Even if you have one, it is good to ask yourself and then see the real value of having one.) It is certainly not essential for every company to have an agency.

Looking at your department, what are its tasks? Generally, there are four main task areas: administration, budgeting, planning, and coordination of programs (like creative, media, research, production, and promotion).

To get the job done, what choices are there? Do it yourself (in-house), hire specialized services, or hire a full-service agency?

Some advertisers prefer the do-it-yourself or in-house agency, giving you complete control. Some retail, pharmaceutical, real estate, apparel, industrial, high-tech and other types of companies do it. Some companies say the disadvantages and risks (less experience, less objectivity, less flexibility) outweigh the advantages (cost savings, more control, increased coordination). But approximately 1,000 companies have their own "house" agencies and a total of 4,000 place their advertising directly with the media. (See "The Red Book," or Standard Directory of Advertising Agencies, under "house agencies" for a listing and partial description of these.)

Common sense tells you there are several natural conditions favoring a house agency decision:

- If your company is new and start-up activities call for new, fast decisions by a small number of insiders;
- Budget is small, product is too technical or specialized, number of assignments is great (ads to be done, amount of sales promotion or merchandising projects), or other special circumstances argue for inside staff versus outside agency;
- Key tasks of creative and media placement can be easily handled by outside services and freelancers, eliminating need for ad agency;
- Management is emphasizing cost reductions and savings in media commissions and agency fees;
- Professional experience of advertising manager and staff suggests competencies inside the company are equal to more than those of outside agency.

A typical organization of a large in-house agency is shown in Exhibit 9.1. Most are smaller house agencies with fewer than 10 people, but include most of these functions.

EXHIBIT 9.1 ORGANIZATION OF AN IN-HOUSE AD AGENCY

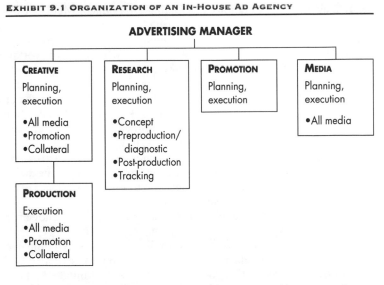

Source: ANA report, *Advertising Services*.[10] Reproduced with permission of the Association of National Advertisers, Inc. © 1991. All rights reserved.

Buying a la carte has increased. Witness the success of creative boutiques, media buying services, strategic marketing consultants, co-op advertising agencies, and more. Sometimes these will compete with the ad agency on specific tasks. Sometimes an ad manager will coordinate the specialized services almost like a full-service agency. Or one specialist supplier will take on a task that the agency of record is unable to perform.

The greatest change or trend in the recent past has been in agency compensation. No longer tied to the 15-percent commission system, many agencies have reduced commissions, charged fees, worked on an incentive basis to be paid based on performance, and have "unbundled" their services. Today, agencies will offer services alone or in combinations at negotiated fees. This, together with the rise of media-buying services, computerized or desktop publishing, and mergers among advertising agencies, has challenged the thinking of advertisers about the traditional agency-client relationship.

Should you be doing your own media buying? Some say it may be worth the $2\frac{1}{2}$ to 5 percent you will pay in commissions or fees because you could save up to half on your media rates.

Donna Kirchman, group media director and senior partner at the Tatham EURO RSCG advertising agency in Chicago, comments: "Doing your own buying to save on buying fees or commissions can be very costly unless you have a great deal of experience. You need a good understanding of the fair market value of the media to be a successful negotiator. If you have an agency it is advisable to take advantage of their buying operations negotiating experience. Media buying services also have extensive negotiating skills and are a valuable resource to advertisers who may not employ a full service agency. If you go the media buying service route, know who you are working with. Ask lots of questions like how they are being compensated and if they provide 'full disclosure.' (This means sharing all the information on the invoice, allowing you, the advertiser, to see exactly what you are paying for, not just bottom line or the package price.) Ask about accountability: Will the schedules be guaranteed? Check references. Have a few companies bid for your business. Keep the number down to two or three of the most reputable companies or you will experience information overload. The more information you have, the better equipped you will be in making the decision to hire an outside party to do your buying or to do it yourself."[11]

So how do you decide which is better—full-service agency or in-house agency?

It's not easy, but it's worth it, according to the many companies who choose the in-house agency route to go. Some have switched back and forth over the years. One in-house agency was eliminated when a new parent company executive, looking for improvement in the brand's national and trade advertising, hired an outside ad agency. After several years, the company went back to an in-house agency setup, claiming a cost advantage.

You will get totally different opinions, depending on whom you ask. The president of a midwest advertising agency: "Some companies have moved in-house and then discovered they need a full-service agency. Companies have become lean. They've learned it is hard to do everything in-house. Not enough talented people. The best people want to work at the agencies. Also, it is impossible for an in-house agency to have total objectivity with its ideas and its management."

"The biggest difficulty for us," reports one in-house ad manager, "is to maintain the respect of our management, to prove we are as good as an outside agency."

The executive vice president of an apparel manufacturer: "The least complex jobs are the national and trade advertising. The agency we had could get immersed in a new product every 90 days or respond to fire-engine calls from us every time. As business gets more volatile, there will be more house agencies like ours."

According to a senior media executive serving both clients and agencies: "Saving money by going in-house is an old idea when it was good to beat the 15-percent commission system, only economy and moving fast were the rule. Today, media are a commodity and you can get good buys with an agency or do it a la carte at reasonable cost. Also, global marketers need the muscle of a worldwide agency crossing boundaries and fitting into different cultures. That's why I would say the trend is not to in-house agencies."

Regardless of whether you have an outside or in-house advertising agency, you will want to explore two important topics now: how to work with your ad agency and how to select a new agency.

Your advertising agency is, or should be, your key resource for objectivity and creativity. Use it thoughtfully and well.

How to Work with Your Ad Agency

It's a combination of being a good manager (because you are in charge), understanding the strengths and weaknesses of the agency (because nobody's perfect), defining your respective roles and your expectations (because you set the standards), and motivating them to work as a team with you and your people.

Your job, when working with an agency, is very important. In your first one or two meetings, you may want to consider these suggestions. (If you want more, read Nancy L. Salz's book.[12])

First impressions establish who you are. What you say may become gospel inside the agency, so you will want to listen first to understand who they are as people and as an organization. How much they know about your business. What their contributions have been to the success of your brand(s), an indication of their possible value to you.

They want to be partners with you, not a vendor (a dirty word among agencies), so establishing mutual trust becomes your goal (and theirs).

Is there a signed contract that defines the relationship? (It is surprising that there are still some agency-client relationships that are based on only a handshake.) Nine out of ten advertisers have a formal, written contract.

Let them understand your high standards and expectations. What are your values and preferred style of working? What are theirs? Do you and the agency agree on procedures and work guidelines?

Has the agency given you a thorough orientation or "How We Work" presentation (maybe even one-half day)? This covers all the nuts and bolts like their forms and procedures, normal work schedules and time required to complete tasks and assignments, how you prefer to work or see a new campaign, who pays for specific services like ad testing or news releases, access to their resources, etc.

A private one-on-one meeting with your account executive is essential. Get to know him or her. State your intention to make this a successful relationship and look for a personal, not just professional, commitment from your AE. Rest your case only when you feel it in your bones or see it in his or her eyes. This is a "personal contract" between the two of you that will work to both your advantages later on when a problem or crisis happens. This is an early statement of trust.

Be analytical. Considering the agency as your resource, what are its strengths and weaknesses? What is its expertise when compared with other agencies? What is the philosophy of advertising (and not just, "We believe in creativity")? How does your management regard the agency, and is there a regular procedure for agency performance evaluation, or is it just a subjective thing?

Help the agency understand your business. While you (or someone else) hired this agency partly because he or she knows your business, there is never 100% knowledge. A wise managing director in Australia confessed once that it took him five years to learn the film business when he worked on Kodak.

If this is a new agency, be sure it debriefs the previous agency, getting the historical reel, masters of commercials and your original artwork; all the other materials. Oversee visiting the factory, traveling in the field with salespeople, doing store checks, and digging into your business.

Give them clear direction based on your marketing plan. It is worth the time to have your marketing manager(s) also brief them so they get his or her interpretation.

Brief them thoroughly, being open with your information. Trust them; tell them everything they need to know. (More on how to brief for a new campaign or task later.)

Motivate them to high performance. How important is the agency to you in your own plans to be a success in your company? Is there any incentive (giving the agency more assignments in the future or helping them win awards)? Can you express your confidence in their talents and achievements? Are you sure that the agency makes a satisfactory profit on your account? Do you encourage them when they do good work?

If problems occur later, be fair. Human error calls for forgiveness, but not repeatedly. Be objective and guard your emotions in a conflict situation; ask yourself what the facts are. Get a senior person from the agency to help analyze the situation with you and arbitrate, if necessary. Remember, too, that this may be an opportunity to learn from a mistake or problem.

Always be accessible, but don't interfere. You may think you have an open-door policy, but does your secretary screen your calls and make it difficult for people to get to you? Have you ever tried calling yourself to see what it is like to be on the receiving end of voice mail? Do you have half of the meetings at the agency's offices? Does your account executive have your home or cell telephone number for emergencies? Do you control your anxiety and not ask ahead of time to see the new advertising? Or are you the kind of person who wants to be in brainstorming meetings at the agency?

Keep looking for new ways to improve your relationship. Manuals, books, articles, and speeches by industry experts will refresh your thinking and actions.

These are links in a chain; break one of them and the quality of the agency's work falls apart.

Some Tips on How to Brief Your Agency

Giving good instructions to anyone or briefing an ad agency demands careful thinking, being comprehensive in scope, and simplifying the communication. Why are so many briefings of agencies inadequately done? Advertising managers made one or more of these mistakes:

- Not understanding management's goals, the company's mission, or the brand's positioning and current problems or opportunities;
- Not connecting with your boss on major agency assignments, with the chance that you may be overruled when the agency delivers on the assignment;
- Rushing into the briefing meeting with incomplete information, resulting in poor direction to the agency; not being prepared to give the agency what they need to do their best work for you;
- Not being open-minded, not asking for new thinking and ideas, but asking the agency to do what you have already decided is the ad or solution;

- Saying you want fresh thinking, but then biasing the agency by letting them know your preference for a style or approach to advertising;
- Wanting to play it safe and not taking any risks, resulting in the agency's limiting its people's creative freedom and resulting in ordinary, not great, advertising.

Long-timers in the agency business say they can remember only three or four good briefs in their entire careers.

Your job is to define the task and goals, giving information that they need. The agency's job is to return with their thinking (strategy) for your approval, then return a second time with their creative recommendations. If you're in doubt, don't hesitate asking the agency to tell you what they expect in an ideal brief. Few clients ask and it shows you care, and you are certain to learn something about briefing and about your agency in the process.

Now for some practical tips:

1. *Time will vary.* Someone has said that anyone should be able to give a good brief in four minutes by simplifying everything. An average brief on an advertising assignment could run between one and two hours. One of the best briefs this author has experienced took one entire day and was quite thorough and inspiring.

2. *Be comprehensive.* Your agency needs to know the facts about the market, product, pricing, competition, distribution, packaging, advertising and promotion, obstacles and problems, and what has worked and failed to work in persuading the consumer.

3. *Be clear, simplifying and setting the stage for ideas.* Prepare for your meeting so you understand what they need to know about the product and its place in the market. Describe it in simple words, as well as competitive performance (objective evaluation) and customer satisfaction (subjective evaluation). Describe the market in words, graphs, and charts, giving numbers in your handouts. Tell them your pricing strategy with examples of your brand versus competitors'. Paint a picture of distribution so they see where your brand is, its strengths and weaknesses, what kinds of dynamics and promotion or advertising that influence its sales.

4. *Share your marketing plan.* Give them a copy. Summarize concisely what your long-term and short-term marketing objectives are (in share, volume, or other specific goals to be met). Profit and return-on-investment goals are OK for your business plan, but market or consumer behavior changes contribute more toward strong strategies you want the agency to develop for you. Explain your marketing strategies and whether or not these are fixed or open to possible changes if

suggested by the agency. Included here might be: positioning, brand equity and portfolio policies, selling strategies with key distributors and retailers, new product plans, marketing research studies of the consumer, timetable and budget.

5. *Make it exciting.* Bring samples of the products, preferably for them to try or for you to demonstrate. Include salespeople's call reports, and evidence or research of consumer preference. Take them through the factory or into the field so they can smell, taste, feel, touch the product and meet those who handle, service, sell it.

6. *Define the problem, but don't write the strategy.* Your job is to give direction. What is the task? What are the facts? What is the real problem? The agency may redefine the problem after conducting their own situation analysis and show you a new advertising strategy, since you are hiring them to do the thinking and creating.

7. *Define your expectations.* Do you just want a new campaign or do you want breakthrough advertising? Fuji told its agency in Thailand that it wanted to overtake Kodak's dominant market share within five years, expected unusually good advertising, and would aggressively outspend Kodak to do it. How much risk will you tolerate? How much freedom does the agency have?

8. *Make it a dialogue.* Expect lots of questions. Push to make sure they got the main points in your brief. The most important ones are your marketing objective, positioning of your brand, where is the advantage or leverage with the consumer today and do you and the agency agree on what you will be seeing at the next meeting, that is, what is their task?

Are Advertisers Getting What They Want from Their Agencies?

According to a survey of 390 marketers,[13] some clients want a broader range of services from agencies, but others complain that they would not turn to ad agencies for help with their three most pressing problems: assessing potential markets, developing new product concepts, or a crisis in branding. (See Exhibit 9.2.)

As ad agencies have expanded their services, they are aware that this is an opportunity to deliver marketing counsel, direct marketing, sales promotion, and other services. There is obviously a communications or perception gap: Marketers see agencies in their traditional function as admakers only, and a source of help in brand equity management or launching a trade promotion.

What is the secret of a good relationship? At the core of the client-agency relationship is how honest and open the communication is on two levels. First, between you and the account executive. Are

EXHIBIT 9.2 PERCENT OF MARKETING EXECUTIVES SAYING THEY WOULD TURN TO AN AD AGENCY FOR THESE TASKS

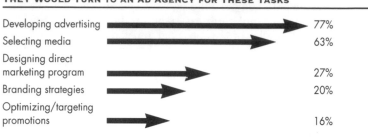

Developing advertising	77%
Selecting media	63%
Designing direct marketing program	27%
Branding strategies	20%
Optimizing/targeting promotions	16%

Source: Strategic Directions Group, Inc., Minneapolis, MN.

EXHIBIT 9.3 RANGE OF CLIENT-AGENCY RELATIONSHIPS

Client is master.	Client is buyer.	Client is employer.	Client is partner.	Client is new or naive.
Agency is slave.	Agency is vendor.	Agency is employee.	Agency is partner.	Agency is boss.
(1)	(2)	(3)	(4)	(5)

mutual roles defined and expectations understood? Secondly, does someone in your company (president, marketing director, or managing director) meet at least once a year with the agency CEO? This is a system of checks and balances that assures a good working relationship and fair settling of problems, if any occur that cannot be worked out at your level.

What is the attitude or mind-set of the client toward the agency? From some agencies' point of view, these relationships might fall on a spectrum something like that shown in Exhibit 9.3.

This is an oversimplified illustration to try to identify distinctions and differences. What happens if the client plays the master? In many cases, only subservient agencies — not the best ones — are willing to work within this attitude. Many clients and some consultants use the word "vendor," putting the agency on the same level as anyone selling anything, rather than treating the agency as a partner.

Many agencies see themselves as equals to their clients and talk about "partnership." But while the intention of equality is a good one, it is an empty promise and most clients say they actually resent it, according to one consultant.

"Partnership is not only a fiction, but an unctuous way of stating a vague promise to the client in agency-ese," cautions consultant Bob Lundin. "The client is the employer, and in the relationship the employee is as valuable to this relationship or the team as the employer. Not superior versus subordinate, but team players with the client in control." [14]

Lundin's formula for all relationships, as well as client-agency, is summed up this way:

$$S = \frac{P}{E}$$

where:
S is satisfaction
P is performance
E is expectations.

When performance meets expectations, one is satisfied. The hitch is that in too many cases there is no clear statement of expectations and true listening by both parties. (Listening is, after a simple statement, feedback, and then verification that what the listener got matches the message the speaker sent.)

One consultant claims that agencies do not listen very well; he says clients usually have a better perception of what is going on in the relationship.

How Well Do You Think Agencies and Clients Understand Each Other?

Compare mutual perceptions of client and agency in this study: [15]

Advertiser: "They have an inbred arrogance. They rely on past creative techniques. And there's been an astounding lack of involvement at the [agency] executive vice president level and higher."

Agency: "At the moment we have a very strong relationship. On our part of the account, at the executive vice president and senior vice president level, we've got a very solid relationship."

In the same study, clients saw the agencies as mainly interested in making ads, not solving problems and developing strategies. The agencies' perceptions were completely different from the clients:

Advertiser: "We expect our agencies to be partners — strategic thinkers who assess problems and recommend solutions — and to be focused on our business rather than just advertising."

Agency: "In general they are interested more in the product we produce ... and less interested in our strategic contributions."

According to the 1993 Salz Survey of Advertiser-Agency Relations:

"The top 100 advertising agencies report that they are able to do their best work for only 59 percent of their major clients. That means only about one out of two advertisers is getting the best advertising for the money.... However, these same advertisers predict that, if they got their agencies' best advertising all the time they would see a 24 percent increase in sales and a 23 percent increase in profits."[16]

It is probably true that the advertiser-agency relationship is a lot like a marriage: You have to work at it to make it a success.

How Do You Know If the Agency Is Doing a Good Job?

The answer is honest feedback on a continuous basis, the good, the bad, and the just average work that is done by the agency. If it is an open and honest relationship, roles and expectations have been defined. And at any given time, the agency knows where it stands.

Do you give positive strokes when the agency does good work? One agency account director confessed to not having received one thank-you or word of praise after four years of good results working on a difficult client's brands.

It isn't easy to assess performance of an agency because there are so many recommendations, decisions, events, transactions, and sometimes no clear, defined results. There is an obvious need for measurement of some kind. On a formal basis, some large companies have an established method of reviewing performance periodically or once a year. For example, some advertiser presidents meet with their agency presidents and privately review this. There is even a manual on it.

The worst situation is no system. Then, when problems occur, a crisis erupts and quick decisions are based on emotions, not reason.

How do you handle problems? There are ways to handle mistakes, differences of opinion, personality conflicts, poor creativity, and lack of initiative. But before the problem reaches the crisis point, your management needs to be advised. And you will want to decide if the relationship is worth saving. The obvious options are asking for new procedures, new people on your account, putting the agency on probation with one last chance to improve, or a performance evaluation with specific recommendations for improvement.

A serious problem was solved by one advertiser who hired a consultant who helped the agency and client work better together. KPMG Peat Marwick national marketing director Mark Linder explains: "I once did a study of clients who changed agencies and what happened to their market shares. Their business usually suffered. Most often, it's not that there's a better agency; rather, there is a better way to manage the relationship."[17]

At the core of such a case is getting each side to share common goals, and sometimes this is best done by an experienced consultant or third party.

Consultant William Weilbacher has learned that there are many potential problems.[18] The four common causes of friction between advertisers and agencies are:

1. Agency cannot grasp strategic essentials of client's business. Weilbacher claims that this is the most important cause of advertiser discontent and can usually be fixed by putting different people on the account.
2. Client is dissatisfied with the creative work.
3. Agency top management is indifferent.
4. Compensation.

HOW TO SELECT A NEW AGENCY

The decision to fire your advertising agency or put your account in review is possibly a wrong decision. Why? For several reasons:

It takes time. As one source warns, "Are you ready for at least three months of agony?"[19] It takes that long on average to search, screen, and hire a new agency. Expect enormous amounts of dead time—yours, your management's. Expect confusion, misunderstandings, calls from competing agencies, reporters looking for a story, headhunters trying to get information, and a fearful attitude of people at your existing agency. The time to change agencies will always be longer than you think.

It costs money. What is your time worth? The time of your boss? Your president's? Multiply these numbers by dozens (maybe hundreds) of hours. What about the opportunity cost; that is, the lost time managing and building your business by these executives, now working in the selection process and indoctrination of the new agency?

It disrupts business. The selection and changeover will interfere with your work and the entire marketing process. It may take the newly hired agency from six months to two years to learn your business, no matter what they promised in the new business pitch.

In some cases, the new agency is just as bad as the previous one.

Still, there are many situations when changing agencies makes sense. Companies with many agencies are consolidating so they deal with one or two agencies; and advertisers gain increased leverage and buying power with the media. Flawed strategies or lackluster creative ideas may have contributed to decreased market share. Loss of key people on the advertiser's account at the agency is a common source of irritation. Conflicts. And other reasons.

Is agency selection a self-perpetuating problem? Yes, suggests a leading consultant for advertisers: "Their [advertisers'] problem seems like a candy store out there, choosing among hundreds of agencies who could serve them. And this is perpetuated by some consultants who want to send questionnaires to forty-five agencies. And this is then carried further by the advertising trade press who pounce on the gossip and treat it as news. There is nothing like a hot agency to make headlines. The wise consultant can come up with a short list of agencies; most of the material is in published sources."

There are books, articles, booklets, seminars, rainmakers, gurus, and lots of advice on how to select an advertising agency.

Eight Steps to Selecting an Advertising Agency

Over the past ten years there have been more than 100 articles and speeches on how to find the right advertising agency. Today, it has become a complicated, time-consuming job for any organization. Weilbacher simplifies this complex task:[20]

1. Make a list of criteria that the agency must meet.
2. Screen all agencies that must meet these criteria. You do not need a questionnaire sent to potential agency candidates.
3. Identify a long list of agencies that meet your criteria, maybe eight or ten.
4. Ask these agencies to present their credentials. Specify that you wish to see the people who will work on your account. Evaluate the agencies on your criteria and the "chemistry" between them and you.
5. Choose a short list of three or four agencies based on their credentials presentations.
6. Give them a specific assignment relating to an existing problem you have. Your goal is to see their strategy, not necessarily the creative executions. You want to see how they think and work. Any freelancer can do a TV spot or print ad.
7. Listen to and evaluate their final presentations, again, using your criteria.
8. Choose the agency.

Some More on Choosing and Starting with a New Agency

Reading and seeing several new business pitches by ad agencies can be an educational, but mind-numbing, experience for an advertiser. All the agencies tend to look and sound the same. They are hard to differentiate. If they have presented creative ideas, you are probably looking at a massive creative effort (including ideas from freelancers you will never meet) based on little or no knowledge of your business. Your brain is swayed by emotion, personal relationships between them and your boss, and whatever your fatigued memory can retain. It's not easy to make an objective, wise choice.

Some advertisers, moving away from traditional presentations, have tried new approaches. A Hong Kong advertiser arranged a work session with its short-listed agencies. Developing the creative strategy together, the client learned exactly how the agency worked and also found itself compatible with the personalities and values of the agency team it then selected.

IBM had each of the competing agencies make their presentations informally across a dinner table, allowing for some of the same insights.

After the search is over, the honeymoon begins. At the high moment of the startup of this new relationship, it is important to go for closure and wrap up the details. For example, you will want a written contract and agreement on compensation, items discussed and resolved during your initial meetings. Make sure your company's attorneys and financial people are involved in the final agreements. Understand the agency's cost and profit structures that are part of the compensation agreement, down to the small items you or they will pay for. Someone said, "It's the little things that can break a marriage."

Remember that the relationship should be a win/win for both sides. If the agency isn't making money on your account, the work done for you will suffer and you will be unhappy.

As one former agency executive confessed, "I've known agency-client relationships that begin on excellent terms and high hopes, and then have gone bad slowly because of misunderstandings about money."

And remember what was discussed earlier about defining roles and expectations.

A few advertisers have "gone public" with their credos or philosophies about their agencies so it is clear to everyone inside the company and at their agencies as to what they believe in. Colgate-Palmolive has "partnership reviews" with its advertising agencies once a year to determine if agency and client are working together satisfactorily and to improve the quality of the creative product. They follow CEO Reuben Mark's guidelines that are on the desk of every product manager worldwide:

Colgate-Palmolive Guidelines for Advertising Agency[21]
1. Be the best client they [the agency] have.
2. We must really care.
3. True partnership and mutual trust.
4. Ask for excellence.
5. Clear, honest direction.
6. Look for the big idea.
7. Streamline approval procedure.
8. Personal involvement of top management of client/agency.
9. Ensure agency profitability.
10. Be human.

According to Tim Pollak, vice chairman of Young & Rubicam Inc., Colgate-Palmolive's agency of record, it works.

Managing your people and other resources can be a very satisfying job, both in results that you see and the relationships you build.

NOTES

There are more than 60 advertising trade and professional organizations for people like yourself. Here are some you might look into
either for information or possible membership:

Advertising Research Foundation
(212) 751-5656
641 Lexington Avenue
New York, NY 10022

American Advertising Federation
(202) 898-0089
1101 Vermont Avenue, NW
Washington, DC 20005

American Marketing Association
(312) 648-0536
250 S. Wacker Drive
Chicago, IL 60606

Association of National Advertisers, Inc.
(212) 697-5950
144 E. 44th Street
New York, NY 10010

Business Marketing Association
(800) 664-4BMA
150 N. Wacker Drive
Chicago, IL 60606

Direct Marketing Association
(212) 768-7277
1120 Avenue of the Americas
New York, NY 10036

International Advertising Association
(212) 557-1133
521 Fifth Avenue
New York, NY 10022

International Exhibitors Association
(703) 941-3725
5501 Backlick Road
Springfield, VA 22151

Magazine Publishers of America
(212) 872-3700
919 Third Avenue
New York, NY 10022

National Association of Broadcasters
(202) 429-5300
1771 N Street, NW
Washington, DC 20036

National Cable Television Association
(202) 775-3550
1724 Massachusetts Avenue, NW
Washington, DC 20036

Newspaper Association of America
(703) 648-1000
11600 Sunrise Valley Road
Reston, VA 22091

Outdoor Advertising Association
(212) 688-3667
12 East 49th Street
New York, NY 10017

Point of Purchase Institute
(201) 894-8899
66 North Brunt Street
Englewood, NJ 07631

Promotion Marketing Association
(212) 420-1100
257 Park Avenue
New York, NY 10010

Public Relations Society of America
(212) 460-1400
33 Irving Place
New York, NY 10003

Radio Advertising Bureau
(212) 254-4800
304 Park Avenue South
New York, NY 10010

Television Bureau of Advertising
(212) 486-1111
850 Third Avenue
New York, NY 10022

Yellow Pages Publishers Association
(810) 244-6200
820 Kiets Boulevard
Troy, Michigan 48084

REFERENCES

1. Mary L. Koelle, marketing manager of office document products, Xerox Inc., Rochester, interview by author, November 21, 1995.

2. Bob Lundin, president of Jones-Lundin Associates, Chicago, interview by author, September 5, 1995.

3. Robert Weinstein, vice president, external relations, Metropolitan Life Insurance Company, New York, interview by author, August 21, 1995.

4. "What Makes a Smart Leader?", *Chicago Magazine*, Graduate School of Business, University of Chicago, (Summer 1994): 19.

5. Stephen R. Covey, *The 7 Habits of Highly Effective People* (New York: Simon & Schuster, 1990), 66.

6. "Marketers as change agents, a report on the second survey of marketing executives," Strategic Directions Group, Inc., Minneapolis, 1996, and Carol M. Morgan, president Strategic Directions Group, interview by author, February 28, 1996.

7. "Virtual Worker: Anyplace I hang my modem is home," *Business Week*, (Oct. 17, 1994): 96.

8. Jay Chiat, Interview, *Wired Magazine* (July 1994): 84.

9. Paul Best, creative consultant, London, interview by author, August 17, 1995.

10. *Advertising Services: Full Service Agency, a la Carte, or In-House?* (New York: Association of National Advertisers, Inc., 1991). Reproduced with permission of the Association of National Advertisers, Inc. © 1991. All rights reserved.

11. Donna Kirchman, senior partner and group media director, Tatham EURO RSCG, Chicago, interview by author, February 15, 1996.

12. Nancy L. Salz, *How to Get the Best Advertising from Your Agency* (Burr Ridge, IL: Irwin, 1994).

13. "Make yourself useful," *Adweek* (October 23, 1995): 26. Report of National Survey of 390 U.S. marketing executives by Strategic Directions Group, Inc., Minneapolis, MN.

14. Bob Lundin, interview by author, op. cit.

15. "Perception and Reality in Agency-Client Relationships: How Senior Agency and Client Advertising Executives View the Crucial Aspects of Their Relationship" (New York: Association of National Advertisers, Inc., 1993). Reproduced with permission of the Association of National Advertisers, Inc. © 1993. All rights reserved.

16. Nancy L. Salz, *How to Get the Best Advertising from Your Agency* (Burr Ridge, IL: Irwin, 1994), 177.

17. Mark Linder, "Unhappy Couple Finds Road to Conciliation," *Adweek* (May 15, 1995).

18. William M. Weilbacher, "Advertising Agency Reviews," *The Advertiser Magazine*, Association of National Advertisers, Inc. (Spring 1995): 40. Reproduced with permission of the Association of National Advertisers, Inc. © 1995. All rights reserved.

19. Allan Gardner, *A Client's Guide to Conducting an Agency Search* (New York: American Association of Advertising Agencies, 1994).

20. William M. Weilbacher, "Advertising Agency Reviews," *The Advertiser Magazine*, Association of National Advertisers, Inc., Spring 1995. Reproduced with permission of the Association of National Advertisers, Inc. © 1995. All rights reserved.

21. Tim Pollak, interview with author, Feb. 24, 1996.

SUGGESTIONS FOR FURTHER READING

Weilbacher, W.M. *Managing Agency Relations: Maximizing the Effectiveness* (New York: Association of National Advertisers, Inc., 1991).

Weilbacher, W.M. *1995 Trends in Agency Compensation* (New York: Association of National Advertisers, Inc., 1996).

Zeltner, H. *Maximizing Your Media Dollars: ANA's Guide to Media Planning and Buying* (New York: Association of National Advertisers, Inc., 1996).

Laura Schoen is president of PResence/EURO RSCG, managing all domestic and international business. PResence is a division of EURO RSCG, the seventh largest advertising and public relations company in the world.

Schoen joined the EURO RSCG group in 1991 after eight years at Burson-Marsteller, where she served as senior vice president and director of the firm's international division in New York. In this capacity, she was responsible for international business development as well as managing accounts.

At PResence/EURO RSCG, Schoen is responsible for the creation and development of its health care division. She develops marketing and communications strategies for non-U.S. companies entering the American market as well as U.S. companies expanding overseas. Recently Schoen completed positioning studies for Sodexho and Sofamor, two leading European companies entering the American market. The list of U.S.-based companies that Schoen is currently counseling includes Bausch & Lomb, Pfizer, and Wyeth-Ayerst.

Schoen has developed more than 50 international programs for a variety of leading multinational companies, including the creation and adaptation of public relations and advertising campaigns worldwide.

Schoen holds a master's degree in international relations from the University of Pennsylvania. She earned a B.A. in journalism.

Chapter 10

INTERNATIONAL AUDIT

The Formula to Building Global Communications Strategies That Succeed in Local Markets

The dynamics of the international marketplace have changed dramatically over the past 20 years. Until the 1970s, the international business environment was dominated by a limited number of nations that promoted products designed and manufactured for their home markets. These products were exported without taking into consideration the needs of local markets. The made-abroad label increased the appeal of products and services. Companies publicized their foreign origins, trusting that that alone would allow imported products (even obsolete ones) to sell at premium prices.

Today's global marketers have to operate in a completely changed environment:

- Global competition has forced companies to develop new price strategies which include manufacturing in the most cost-effective locations, very often outside a multinational's home country.
- Mergers and acquisitions have resulted in an internationalized corporate entity with multiple headquarters and multinational cadre of executives.
- Consumers/clients are better educated and organized in the United States and overseas and are more demanding about the products they buy.
- Due to increased competition, economies of scale and growing deregulation of imports, most companies live or die by their international marketing strategies.

These developments have challenged international companies to find ways to address their customers' global and local needs in order to succeed.

Manufacturers have learned how to customize products to different markets. It is time for public relations and advertising professionals to try to systematize their work and gain a new understanding of the environment in which they will be operating.

Adapting to the Demands of an International Marketplace

Experts in the art of communications describe communications as a complex process relying heavily on a common language and system of symbols. To communicate the value of a product or service, we search for the right words and symbols that will create value in the minds of the ultimate user or buyer.

To find the message that will persuade consumers is tough enough in one market. Multiply that by the number of countries that you are trying to reach, and you quickly understand that a multimarket advertising or public relations campaign cannot achieve its goals without a process that will help to determine the cultural and marketing context in which you will be operating.

For those who work in the communications industry, there are ways to ensure that the campaigns you develop, like the products you represent, address local as well as global needs. You can take additional steps to ensure the international viability of the recommendations that you are making to your clients. One of those steps is the international audit.

THE PURPOSE OF AN INTERNATIONAL AUDIT

An international marketing/communications audit provides information for the development of a unified strategy that works locally as well as globally. Audits are essential tools for savvy marketers of products or services, from industrial manufacturing to advertising. They act as benchmarks of what your company is doing and can do in marketing communications.

The purpose of an international audit is to create general understanding on a country-by-country basis of local markets' trends. In advertising as well as public relations, the initial market audit will allow you to set goals and strategies. One of the most common reasons why international campaigns fail is because they lack a clear goal. Ensure that there is a consensus within your company or client regarding the audit's purpose and objectives.

In the absence of a specific mission, communications professionals tend to play it safe and try to be all things to all people. The analogy to that would be trying to be the quarterback, in American football, without having a set play. It would be the fastest game you have ever played.

Since international audits help to identify local characteristics that influence the acceptance and efficacy of marketing and corporate strategies, an audit also serves as a company's local image barometer, identifying issues which can affect a company's success in specific countries.

An audit allows you, from the start, to demonstrate that your company can operate in a seamless way, taking off the blinders and looking at business from an international as well as national perspective.

An additional benefit of an audit is that it builds team spirit and shared values among all people involved in the process. It is a democratic way to ensure that all voices are heard and that people share ownership of the activities developed as a result of the audit.

Audits are effective ways to develop campaigns with messages and goals that can be used consistently from one country to the next. The valuable information which was compiled through a marketing communications audit will later be incorporated into the campaign and will provide basic guidelines that will be used to analyze local markets' needs.

DEVELOPING CRITERIA FOR AN AUDIT

We have discussed the purpose of an audit and the role it can play in helping to develop a successful strategy which will be the basis of a program that works across borders.

The next question to ask is, "What criteria do we use to evaluate the need for an audit prior to creating an international campaign?" In order to answer this question, we need to review the objectives of the program or campaign that we are about to develop.

Although the main reason for conducting an audit is to ultimately build familiarity and recognition within local markets, you have to make a judgment as to the practical value of the audit in each specific situation.

Exhibit 10.1 shows a checklist that can help you decide if the audit is worthwhile. If you find that your program does not meet a reasonable number of these criteria, it might be smart to reconsider an international strategy. The campaign you plan to develop might not require a multimarket coordinated approach.

PLANNING THE AUDIT

After having carefully considered the costs and benefits of an audit and reaching the decision to go ahead, you need to realize the importance of the project that you are about to undertake: The audit will become a benchmark of what your company or client is doing in the marketing communications area.

Like a marketing survey, you should start by putting in writing the goals, objectives, and process. Work with your clients or associates to create consensus for what the audit will accomplish.

Measurement tools that will help to define what constitutes success have to be defined and agreed upon before you start the process. In general, a successful global or regional strategy requires more than knowledge of a certain area. For example, knowing a great deal about cars helps, but does not necessarily prepare you to launch a car in Japan. The combination of industry expertise and "international smarts" is what it takes to be successful worldwide.

This requirement is even more important when you deal with intangible ideas and concepts, as most communications professionals do. Before making a recommendation, marketing communications pros need to acquire a solid grasp of the situation in the markets, or countries, which they hope to impact through their work.

EXHIBIT 10.1 WHEN AN INTERNATIONAL AUDIT IS NECESSARY

International or multimarket product launch	X
Campaign involving sensitive issues	X
Campaign using a celebrity or theme internationally	X
Campaign to create global awareness for issues	X
Program to establish global partnerships	X
Program to promote a single message worldwide	X
Campaign to encourage cross-fertilization among your company's subsidiaries	X
Multimarket crisis management	X
New logo or corporate identity development	X
International events marketing	X
Global public affairs issues	X
Building an international marketing support group	X
Managing a company's global image	X

Selling the Idea of an Audit

Do not underestimate the amount of reluctance that needs to be overcome in convincing people to spend time and money on a survey.

In selling the idea of an audit, you need to list all the possible advantages that will result from the survey, including:

1. Your company can position itself as a sophisticated player in international markets by doing its homework prior to implementing activities abroad.

2. Today's media explosion has forced adoption of consistent patterns around the world.

3. Good ideas are scarce. Through an audit you can identify successful ideas that work across borders.

4. There are increasing similarities among consumers worldwide which justify the development of a global message, but excessive use of common icons can lead to oversimplification and stereotypes. The audit will become your marker.

5. Successes demonstrate that brand harmonization works. Multinational brands such as Coca-Cola, Levis, IBM, and Tylenol are clear examples of it.

6. Personally, an international audit can be a very effective platform to gain some visibility within the organization. It can be leveraged internally and externally, to gain visibility within your organization and in your industry.

7. In companies which do not have a great deal of information

about overseas markets, adopting an audit to survey relevant markets adds depth and credibility to your organization's efforts.

8. The audit creates a knowledge base regarding the availability and quality of your local resources, including their budgets and existing tools such as video, newsletters, cadre of available consultants, and marketing data.

9. An audit provides assurances that, in the intangible world of marketing communications, the ideas included in a campaign did not come out of thin air. It can help you convince skeptical decision makers that the ideas are worth developing.

If none of the above works, try common sense. For example, a survey can help avoid disasters. A brilliant campaign consisting of a series of 30-second spots for TV might never be used because none of your affiliates have the budget for a television campaign. You should have used radio!

Although the idea of an audit is logical to you, in today's business world, we have become so results-oriented that people are afraid to make any investments. Remind the decision-makers that if they are about to invest a significant amount of money in the development of a multi-market program, it would be wise to make sure that the program will be on target, and in the process, get the buy-in of your local subsidiaries as well.

International communications audits also include inventories of the subsidiaries' activities in the communications area. This provides a database of information both for the external agency and for the client's headquarters. Very often, you will find out that companies really do not know much about what happens outside the home office on a market-by-market basis.

If none of these arguments work, propose to survey a few senior managers on their knowledge of the operations in other markets. Very often you will find that they really don't know as much as they think about what happens on a market-by-market basis.

Finally, do not forget that you need to be sure of something to be able to convince others. Think about the pros and cons of undertaking a multi-market audit and the fee to conduct such an audit. Be certain that this is a battle worth fighting before you actually start.

Choosing the Medium for the Audit

Ideally, it is best to survey all markets personally. However in the lean 1990s, the days of globe-trotting are all but over. Very few companies have budgets that allow their executives to go around the world gathering information to develop a global strategy. Today's austerity programs make the international audit an even more important tool. The information obtained through them will become the blueprint that will be used to build programs/campaigns.

If you are one of few who can actually afford to survey all markets in person, feel free to do so. Nothing is more effective than one-on-one communications. Keep in mind that the process of auditing your affiliates around the world is also an opportunity to build relationships and establish your role in supporting their efforts from the company's headquarters or home office.

Before you plan your trip, make sure to contact your peers and sell them on the purpose of your visit and how it will benefit them in the end. Make them feel like an integral part of the process. You will become the conduit that will ensure their voices are heard and their opinions are taken into consideration.

Develop the audit questionnaire and mail it to the people who you will be meeting with in advance to give them time to prepare for your visit. Make sure to follow up with preliminary findings and let them know when they can expect your final report. It is very frustrating to spend hours briefing someone and then never hear from them again. It is also counterproductive to let people wait for months for your final report. Build expectation, by providing them with preliminary data which will whet their appetite for the final product. When you actually produce the final product, whether it is a campaign or just a report, share the credit with all the people who gave you input.

If you cannot afford to visit each market yourself, consider conducting your audit via phone, fax, mail, or a combination of these techniques. First call all your markets and introduce yourself and the idea of the audit. Follow up with the written questionnaire.

Although it can be more cost-effective to send the audit by mail, think about the message it sends. International mail is not reliable in every single market and does not reflect a sense of urgency. It is unlikely that your international markets will respond to you immediately, nor should you pressure them for immediate responses. That is a sure way of souring the relationship. By faxing the audit, you convey a sense of importance. Always give your correspondents in other markets a deadline.

Getting answers back is also tricky. A letter from the president, introducing you and the objectives of the audit can help. A lot of "shmoozing" on your initial introduction on the phone is valuable. On the other hand, the basic principle that rules every human interaction is still valid here: People will be more motivated to do something if they feel they have something to gain from the process. Make sure you build an incentive mechanism into your audit, such as clear name recognition for all respondents. A chance to come to headquarters to present the results is another strong motivator.

Be prepared to do a lot of follow-up before you get the answers you need. The right people to answer the audit are executives with high-level responsibilities in the local market. They are not there just waiting for your audit. On the other hand, be careful not to choose somebody too senior. That person might be out-of-touch with the day-to-day ins and outs of the business.

Setting the Audit Budget

There is no doubt that when your product is advertising or public relations, you have to be prepared to face additional difficulties selling an audit. When Microsoft is asked to develop a new software for MCI, no one assumes that Microsoft will pay for all development costs. Unfortunately, in our field a lot of our best thinking is done on specs. Often development costs are absorbed by the agency, and many agencies are reluctant to make such big investments on a multinational basis.

Ideally your client will underwrite the cost of the audit. In either case, you should develop a very complete budget estimate, including all the details involved in creating and implementing an audit, before you start the audit. Do not forget to include a generous allocation for telephone and fax charges as well as plenty of time to gather results and organize them in a meaningful way.

If your budget is tight, you may have to establish a good selection criterion instead of surveying every market. If you are working in 10 markets, selecting the ones that will be audited might not be a problem, but for companies that have marketing operations around the world—like Coca-Cola or IBM—a survey can become an expensive project. In this situation, you might be forced to recommend a more limited audit to make the project viable.

There are different ways to establish selection criteria. They include listing countries that are representative of a particular region, culture, or language, and by the size of the market. Again, for budgetary reasons, you might choose to survey your top five markets only. The assumption is that if your campaign does not work there, it will not matter if it has worked elsewhere.

On the other hand, you might decide to take just the opposite approach: Survey markets that are weak in order to develop tools that can boost their sales.

There are no right or wrong ways to do it. You and your clients should agree on a set of criteria that works for you.

Taking the time to complete an international audit is a guaranteed way to develop better communications and support systems that will help you and your firm approach global marketing and get measurable results.

THE AUDIT

Sample questionnaires for extensive and abbreviated audits are shown in Exhibits 10.2, 10.3, and 10.4. Keep in mind that you will have to develop the right questionnaire for your needs. Although each situation is unique, the examples will provide a strong framework from which to start developing your own audit.

EXHIBIT 10.2 INTERNATIONAL AUDIT — SAMPLE 1

To prepare for the international launch of (product name), we are seeking information on the following subject areas. We hope to receive some of these items from you, and others from the international affiliates. Once we have determined the items to request from the affiliates, we will craft an appropriately worded questionnaire.

MARKET ANALYSIS

In Each of the Markets

Current market size and competitors' market share.

Forecasted market size and targeted market share in five years.

Key competitors in that market and their perceived strategies.

The Category

How many potential users of this type of product are there? (Number of people and percentage of population.)

Demographic data on potential users (gender, age group, etc.).

How is category of product perceived culturally (1) by the general public, and (2) by the media?

How is product used and by whom? (Alternative usage and product alternatives.)

The relative importance of family versus other influencers.

Educational/social issues that may affect product acceptance.

Organizations, associations, and interest groups that may or may not support the product.

MARKETING STRATEGY

In Each of the Markets

Short- and long-range marketing objectives.

Short- and long-range marketing strategies.

PRODUCT

Product's competitive advantage over its competitors in the market; its positioning statement.

Current perception of product, if any; reaction to information already published or other information available to the professional or general public.

Schedules of upcoming publications or any other promotional materials, presentations, and other potential milestones.

PROMOTION

Media — Print, Radio, and TV

Demographics of audience.

Pricing.

Suggest media plan for launch and post-launch.

Budget allocations for previous product launches.

Specifications regarding advertising and public relations materials such as formats, moral or religious standards, deadlines, etc.

Regulatory Limitations

Competitive intelligence systems that may be in place, for example, media monitoring, field force reporting, etc.

Target audiences.

PR/advertising staffing and local agencies.

Professional relations and detailing activities.

Consumer-directed activities.

PRICE STRATEGIES

Regulatory or market limitations on pricing.

Anticipated price-point and rationale (e.g., competitively priced to secure acceptance, etc.).

DISTRIBUTION

Primary paths of distribution.

Key players who will be involved in this area.

CORPORATE

In Each of the Markets

Perception of company manufacturing and marketing this type of product — positive and negative aspects.

Recent corporate advertising or PR activities.

Recent media coverage on company.

Can you share any recent corporate advertising or PR activities?

Please summarize recent local media coverage about the company.

(Continued on next page)

MARKET ANALYSIS

What is the current category market size and competitors' market share in your country?

Forecast market size and targeted market share one year after product introduction

a) 5% _____

b) other _____

Name your key competitors and rate them on a scale of 1 to 4, 4 being the most important.

1. _____

2. _____

3. _____

Others _____

What are the competitors' perceived strategies?

What are your short- and long-range marketing objectives in your country?

Can your briefly describe your short- and long-range marketing strategies?

PROFILE OF RETAILERS/WHOLESALERS

Who are the primary purchase influencers and what is their relative importance?

Important _____

Relatively Important _____

Relatively Unimportant _____

Unimportant _____

COALITION BUILDING

Name top professional organizations or associations and interest groups who are allies or foes of this type of product or industry.

PROFILE OF USER

Describe the demographic and psychographic profile of the future user of (product name).

PRODUCT-RELATED INFORMATION

Please describe (product name) competitive advantage over its products in the market.

Do you foresee price being a major issue in your market? Why?

Regulatory or market limitations on pricing.

Anticipated price-point and rationale (e.g., competitively priced to secure acceptance by certain buying organizations).

How do you plan to distribute (product name) in your market?

Can you identify key players other than above mentioned ones?

PROMOTIONAL ENVIRONMENT

Provide a description of the media environment and available, opportunities to promote this product based on your previous experiences.

Are you concerned with any regulatory limitations on promotion? Please describe your main concerns.

What resources do you currently have in place to monitor the competition? Examples: media monitoring, field force reporting, etc.

Are you working with any agencies/consultants to launch (product name) in your market? Please identify agency, contact person, and briefly list areas of responsibility.

- PR
- Advertising
- Professional relations and detailing activities

STAFF

Please identify how many professional staff members you have working with you to launch (product name). Include those in all areas of public relations, marketing, or advertising.

Please provide names and brief relevant biographical details.

RESOURCES

How could you benefit more from the assistance and resources available through headquarter's marketing and communications team? Please provide examples of assistance in the area of marketing/communications that you would find helpful in supporting your efforts to launch (product name).

EXHIBIT 10.3 ABBREVIATED INTERNATIONAL AUDIT — SAMPLE 2

1 — STAFF

How many professional staff members do you currently have working with you? This should include, but not be limited to, personnel in charge of merchandising, advertising, public relations, special promotions, and media relations. Please provide names of professionals only, with brief biographical information and proficiency in English and other languages, if applicable.

2 — ONGOING ACTIVITIES

What is your subsidiary doing to promote sales in your market? This includes advertising, public relations, promotions, merchandising, sponsorships, and other marketing tools.

After listing each activity, please describe your efforts (theme, media reach, messages, slogans, nature, and frequency of each activity). If possible please send us copies of your program and samples of your activities such as ads.

3 — MARKETING NICHE

What is your company's position in your market? If you do not have an image yet, please describe desired positioning.

4 — COMPETITION

Who are your key competitors in your market? Please describe image of each key competitor and provide rating. If possible include key competitors' advantages and disadvantages compared to your company.

5 — COMPETITION'S IMAGE

Provide a description of your key competitors' marketing promotion efforts, including advertising, public relations, promotion, sponsorships, merchandising, and other marketing tools that they are currently using. If possible, please send samples of their activities such as ads.

6 — CONSUMERS'/CUSTOMERS' PROFILE

Provide a description, including demographic and psychographic information, of current customers in your market. If you are interested in reaching other types of consumers, please describe desired target.

7 — KNOWLEDGE OF EXISTING RESOURCES

How much do you know about what your company's current marketing/promotion activities are in other markets, including the United States?

Are you aware of your company's image and positioning in other markets?

Do you currently receive any support in the areas of marketing, advertising, and/or promotion from corporate headquarters?

8 — HEADQUARTERS CONTACT PERSON

Whom do you call when in need of assistance in marketing, promotion, and communications at headquarters?

How frequent is your contact: daily, weekly, monthly?

9 — SUGGESTIONS

Can you benefit more from the resources and experience available at your company headquarters? How? Please provide examples of assistance in the areas of marketing/communications that you would find helpful in supporting your work in your market.

10 — CONTACT PERSON IN YOUR ORGANIZATION

Who is the contact person at your subsidiary in the area of marketing communications? Who acts as liaison with headquarters?

Who should receive copies of any correspondence between headquarters and your organization? We do not want to leave any key players outside the loop.

11 — TRAINING

Would you send a representative to headquarters to participate in professional meetings and seminars regarding marketing communications?

EXHIBIT 10.4 ABBREVIATED CORPORATE ORGANIZATION AUDIT — SAMPLE 3

This type of audit can be done before the development of the full-scale audit. It can be useful as a tool to sell the complete audit and to demonstrate the need for an international audit within an organization that needs to communicate in different markets around the world.

1. What is the structural framework of the company or department?

2. Who makes decisions regarding marketing communications campaigns?

3. How many people or departments are involved in the decision-making process?

4. Which structure best describes your company or department in relation to the marketing communications/promotion area?
   a) Central Strategy/Central Execution
   b) Central Strategy/Local Execution
   c) Decentralized/No Company Employee Is Based in the Local Market

5. Is your brand image the most important company asset?

6. Are decisions made at the local level?

7. Is the company philosophy that greater flexibility allows better market acceptance?

8. Do you believe your company's international affiliates lack an overview of what the company is as a whole?

9. Do you believe that your company's affiliates subscribe to the "not invented here" mentality?

10. Does your company coordinate with your overseas representatives to develop an international campaign or strategy?

And when you're done, remember to send a note to everyone who responds.

Example 1: Thank you for spending time in filling out this questionnaire. If any aspect of the survey is unclear or you have further questions, please do contact (name of company or contact) in the U.S. They have multilingual professionals on staff, fluent in (list languages).

Your responses are important in enabling us to better coordinate our worldwide communications and marketing activities. With this information we will be able to better tailor existing events and resources to your needs, and provide greater assistance where you need it. Please keep in mind that without your assistance we cannot have the tools to develop a successful core program to launch (product name) worldwide.

Example 2: Thank you for your time. If you have any questions please do not hesitate to call us at (telephone number). We have bilingual professionals on staff, fluent in Spanish, French, Italian, and Japanese. [If applicable include:] We can also make arrangements to have a translators available if required.

We appreciate your taking the time to help us develop better communications tools and support to assist our partners around the world. We will forward a copy of the findings of this survey reflective of yours and other markets' input from around the world.

HOW DIFFERENT ORGANIZATIONS BENEFIT FROM AUDITS

Below are some case histories in which multinational audits proved useful for determining the marketing objectives for corporate communications campaigns. The cases cover a diverse set of organizations facing different types of situations.

Finally, don't forget to send a note thanking people for their time and consideration.

Case History 1: International Nonprofit Organization

Problem: Large, nongovernment organization (NGO) faced image problems, which included negative media coverage, budget cuts, and overall lack of credibility. It decided to launch a major effort to create awareness among key audiences around the world about the role it played regarding many major worldwide issues. The strategic platform of its image-building program required the identification of issues that carry universal importance.

Solution: Before developing the program, a multicultural, multilingual department surveyed the NGO's representatives in all major offices around the world. It sought to identify issues that had local repercussion and ways in which the organization could improve its image by publicizing its local and global role in dealing with these issues.

An audit identified the need to create a local advertising and media relations campaign. The program included print, radio and TV productions, as well as special projects, documentaries, and public information campaigns implemented on a global level. All key ideas and campaign strategies originated with the audit.

The NGO's campaign resulted in a broader understanding of its function and contribution and in improvement in its image worldwide.

Case History 2: Worldwide Advertising Agency Responds to Demands of Clients' Globalization

Problem: The demands of economic globalization increased need for advertising services in new geographic markets. The agency's best opportunity to grow was by delivering global services. To gain credibility among clients and prospects, the agency needed to create synergies among existing international and domestic offices, developing programs and systems to provide multinational client services.

Solution: The agency developed an international audit to gauge multinational perceptions of agency's competitors as well as new trends in local markets.

Based on survey results, the agency created a new division with responsibilities for management of worldwide accounts, international training programs, and international personnel issues. Audit results also indicated the need to incorporate new technologies to develop new system and communications tools that would accommodate international clients' demands. The agency established international access to electronic mail and an accounting department able to consolidate charges incurred in different countries into one single invoice in clients' preferred currency. In two years, the agency became the recognized industry leader and the preferred choice of global accounts.

Case History 3: International Liquor Company Makes an Inventory of Vulnerabilities Within Governments

Problem: Around the world, government agencies have implemented programs discouraging excessive alcohol consumption. Programs to discourage drinking and driving, underage drinking, and other alcohol misuse are just a few examples of initiatives now under way in many countries.

A major liquor manufacturer found its potential growth was being fueled by global opportunity. The manufacturer was concerned with monitoring activities and issues related to drinking in its major markets. It also had to coordinate the company's response to these initiatives. For example, its subsidiaries in France refused to recognize the need to address public concerns regarding alcohol abuse. As a result, it had recently received very negative media coverage. The company's headquarters feared the impact that negative media coverage could have in obtaining government permits.

The company decided to undertake an audit to identify key issues which can affect their business. Secondarily, the audit would survey subsidiaries' perceptions and responses.

Solution: The survey identified key issues and local market responses to public and government pressures. Based on the results of the survey, headquarters developed a core campaign to encourage responsible drinking. The fundamental goal of the campaign was to establish a way for the company to demonstrate its commitment to curbing alcohol abuse. Local markets were responsible for tailoring local activities to respond to market-specific issues, such as anti-liquor attitudes and religious issues.

The company received praise from government officials involved in alcohol misuse programs. Several of these officials spoke very positively of the company's role in educating the public. The program generated worldwide media coverage.

MERCHANDISING RESULTS:
GETTING THE CREDIT FOR A JOB WELL DONE

But, the job is not over when the audit is complete. Many executives forget to merchandise the results of their labor. You and your client will have gained insights into how the company operates in many markets, and its strengths and weaknesses. Make sure to translate all the knowledge you have acquired into action. Here are a few suggestions for using the audit results to promote yourself within your organization:

1. Develop and deliver a presentation based on audit results/findings.
2. Write an article in the company's/client's newsletter summarizing the results.
3. Develop a speech based on your experience conducting the multinational audit to present at industry meetings.
4. Prepare and distribute a press release based on your findings.
5. Arrange to be quoted by journalists who write on issues related to the audit.
6. Incorporate information disclosed in the audit to the company training program to encourage global thinking among company employees.
7. Incorporate quotes from the audit into the company's annual report.
8. Leverage audit results to make your superiors look smart.

Dealing with the Politics

Finally, a word of caution: multinational audits can become a multilateral political game in an organization. It's a jungle out there! To implement an audit successfully, you have to be skillful at playing the corporate game.

Be prepared to deal with the general manager of country x, who thinks the audit is just a conspiracy to get him fired.

Be calm when arguing with the big egos who truly believe they have the monopoly on all worthwhile ideas.

Be reasonable when you start hearing complaints regarding marketing and communications campaigns developed at company headquarters. They have a point! A lot of what comes out of headquarters is not appropriate.

Be aware of the chronic "not invented here" disease carriers who basically consider all core international concepts irrelevant to local markets.

Remember, that in part, these complaints are motivated by corporate politics and power struggles inside organizations. Everyone wants to have creative control over the marketing communications tools that are going to be used in their market. Many times, however, subsidiaries have a point when they complain that the global strategies they get are not tailored to their needs.

Keep in mind that one of the reasons why international market surveys play a pivotal role in the successful development of any international advertising or public relations strategies is because the results can lead to rational decisions based on data, not on gut feelings or power games.

Ron Solberg is president of EasyCom, Inc., a Chicago-based management consulting/education firm specializing in counseling communicators on using technology and the Internet. In 1984, he created the first computer-linked network for professional communicators on CompuServe. Called the Public Relations and Marketing Forum, the network has more than 40,000 members worldwide. Ron's Internet address is 76703.575@compuserve.com.

CHAPTER 11

ADVERTISING AND THE INTERNET

The Internet, especially the World Wide Web, has literally exploded onto the scene, providing organizations with multiple ways of advertising and promoting products and services in new and different ways. Advertising and promotion as we've understood it may be impacted as well. A good Internet ad delivers the message, inspires action, generates a response, and measures and reports activity and public opinion. Every "bit" of it is offered up through the same medium with the entire transaction occurring, perhaps, in a matter of minutes. Furthermore, the audiences come to the advertiser. Like that mythic ball field in Iowa, you build it right and they will come. In the end the most important impact on our business may be the effect all of this is having on blurring classic distinctions between advertising, public relations, and marketing. Our idea of what comprises a good communications program may never be the same.

THE STRINGS OF THE "NET"

Established in the late 1960s by the U.S. Department of Defense, the Internet was a series of interconnecting data and telephone lines and systems linking universities doing government research. Essentially free of government regulation, the Internet today has attracted an increasing number of businesses and consumers worldwide who use the lines to transfer electronic mail and other more graphic material between two or more locations. Rather than a place, it is an electronic pipeline for exchanging data.

The Internet is not formally regulated or organized. It's much like the state of America's highways prior to the creation of the interstate highway system. Some of the best directories or indexes for the Internet are on the Internet itself. For example, Yahoo and Lycos are a couple of the most popular web sites that help Internet users search for other sites of interest.

The Net's Web

The most advanced address or connection to the Internet is a page on the World Wide Web (WWW) — an interface, permitting the transmission of text, pictures, graphics, video, and sound through "hyperlinks." The "page" may be set up through one of more than several hundred Internet Service Providers (ISPs), who will, of course, charge you for the page storage, connection, and address.

The WWW was created in 1991–1992 by physicists in Switzerland to automate research footnotes and citations. As a communication medium peculiar to the Internet, the web offers five very important features:

1. It's potentially multimedia. You can post text, pictures, graphics, animation and video, and sound on one page.
2. A page is immediately accessible to a global audience of more than 40 million Internet users.
3. It offers "hyperlinks." (This is the automated footnote feature.) Keywords or graphics on the individual pages marked or highlighted by a mouse will move you to another page at some other part of the Internet within seconds.
4. Pages are interactive. Those who access them can issue commands to individualize responses.
5. The site enlists "pull marketing" techniques to attract an audience. People seek out an attractive site to get what they need.

Elements of the Web

WWW "locations" are generally referred to in one of three different ways — the web page, the web site, and the home page.

The web page is an individual element on which one or more computer screens of material appear.

The web site is the sum total of web pages for the place or location. All of them are usually tied to a specific Internet address. A site may be a few pages or many. The number of web pages may change as the site is modified from one time to another.

The home page is generally the first page you see when accessing a specific web site.

Getting Around

To connect to the Internet and the WWW, you must have a computer, modem, telephone line, and an Internet service through which you can contact the Internet. All of the major commercial on-line services, such as America Online, CompuServe, and Prodigy, provide Internet access.

In addition to the hardware, you need software that allows you to "browse" sites and pages. Using "browser" software such as the popular shareware packages Mosaic or NetScape, you can navigate through the Internet to find what you are looking for on the WWW. However, because there is no single organization operating Internet, searching the system for relevant information may be time-consuming and frustrating for the novice or sometime user.

More than 25,000 businesses (as of late fall 1995) of every size have web pages on the net. They are using the pages to sell products and services, dialogue with their prospects and customers, communicate with the media, generate on-line relationships with other organizations, promote an image, and measure public attitude and interest.

STEADY AS SHE GOES WHEN SETTING UP A WEB PAGE

We're witnessing a real feeding frenzy at the cyberspace trough as growing numbers of individuals and organizations race to get online. The web page, in particular, has generated the most interest because it can offer appealing multimedia effects while easily linking to other remote locations in the Internet. A web page is a communications tool that extends reach and is not limited by time or location. But be warned: although the promises are considerable, so are the perils. WWW is as much an abbreviation for "Wild, Wild West" as it is for "World Wide Web." The Internet is new territory. It's hard to navigate and difficult to measure results. Service may be slow and inconsistent.

As you consider whether or not your organization should set up its own web page, we suggest several steps that will make the resulting product effective and worth the effort. A checklist is included in Exhibit 11.1.

Getting Started

Start by creating an interdepartmental team to study the need for the page and, if appropriate, to put it up on the web. Such a team should include people from marketing, advertising, marketing communications, public relations, MIS, and the graphic arts.

Next, consider your purpose for publishing a page. We suggest six possible reasons:

1. **Enhance your corporate image.** Though the number of web sites is growing at a phenomenal rate, there is still a certain amount of prestige in setting up an attractive and well-designed site. It may communicate to your audience or public that you are progressive and on the leading edge in using communications technologies.

2. **Address target market interests.** More than 40 million people are currently on the Internet. Many of these users are young males. A growing number are seniors with time on their hands and some disposable income. The academic community is well represented, as are any number of other groups. Just as with other forms of electronic communication, a WWW page is readily available 24 hours a day to those who need information, seek advice, or wish to communicate with you.

3. **Build relationships.** This may be one of the most interesting and exciting opportunities. Because web pages can be easily tied through menus and "hyperlinks" to other pages anywhere on the Internet, organizations can create informal or formal connections that were not previously possible.

4. **Create business opportunities.** A variety of businesses are identifying prospects from those who stop by their pages, "raise their electronic hands," and leave e-mail or other kinds

EXHIBIT 11.1 SETTING UP A WEB SITE—A CHECKLIST FOR MANAGERS

Consider the following points if you're preparing a web site on the Internet for your organization.

1. Set up an interdepartmental team to oversee the creation and maintenance of the site.

2. Research the Internet to determine what your industry and competition are doing on the World Wide Web. Note applications that are and are not working. You also want to see if your organization is already represented in one way or another on the net.

3. Identify the needs that a web site would best meet for your organization.
   * Enhancing your company's image;
   * Selling products and services;
   * Communicating with the target audience;
   * Prospecting for new customers;
   * Building on-line business and professional relationships;
   * Measuring interest and response.

4. Organize the web page elements.
   * Apply for a URL (web site address).
   * Establish a theme and business identity.
   * Create a menu of interrelated pages.
   * Identify hyperlinks to other sites.
   * Provide for feedback, measurement, and order mechanisms.
   * Consider "hooks" that will keep people coming back to your site for more.
   * Consider other site features, for example, a searchable database.

5. Collaborate with a web page artist to provide a suitable overall design.

6. Work with a web page programmer, using hypertext markup language (HTML) to prepare your design and content for placement on the Internet.

7. Create webmaster role and establish graphic and editorial policies for maintenance of the site.

8. Provide technical maintenance and storage of the site on a server.

9. Promote the site with news releases, on-line registries, links, off-line references, tie-ins, and advertising and editorial opportunities.

10. Monitor ongoing site activity.

of messages indicating interest. Some businesses are even cutting back on more traditional prospecting initiatives as their web pages attract growing numbers of potential customers. Others who have published web pages were not prepared for the deluge of responses they received.

5. **Sell product.** Businesses are using web pages to promote services, sell products, and accept orders. Although the Internet systems are not yet in place to make the posting of credit card numbers truly secure on-line, these systems will be in place in the very near future as encryption procedures are perfected.

6. **Measure response and public opinion.** A very good reason to set up a web site is to find out what people think about various issues, products, and services. You can ask visitors directly through an electronic questionnaire, which is then automatically recorded and tabulated as responses are completed. You can also use other more subtle systems to discover reactions, such as counting the number of visitors who select one hyperlinked option over another. Because the site is available 24 hours a day, every day of the week, measurement and feedback are continuous.

As your team establishes the purpose for your web page, investigate what is already on the Internet. Is it clear that your customers are now using the Internet? What are your competitors doing? And to what effect? What seems to work? What doesn't? You may wish to contract with one of the Internet clipping services to gauge on-line activity in your industry.

AN ATTRACTIVE WEB PAGE TAKES SMART AND CREATIVE DESIGN

Like a good piece of art, a WWW home page should be as interesting and attractive to the casual first-time visitor as it is to someone who is returning to the location for the umpteenth time. And like a good piece of art, preparation of the page requires a knowledge of tools of the craft combined with creative skills.

Though setting up a page may be similar to designing an effective advertisement, newsletter, or magazine, a web page is a relatively new medium with its own unique characteristics.

The design elements of an effective page include:

Uniform Research Locator (URL). The URL is the name people type in to find you. This is also called your address. Register an address that no one else is using. Include, if possible, your organizational identity into the address. Furthermore, the shorter the better. Longer addresses are difficult to remember and tedious to keystroke.

Theme and organizational identification. You don't want to hit your visitor over the head with what or who you are. But, do make it clear from the outset where the cybernaut has landed. Make sure your corporate logo or organizational name is clearly presented. A solid and creative graphics theme will help tie together your family of web pages more efficiently and add some eye appeal.

Text and graphics. The home page is the "cover" to your web pages. It introduces visitors and users to what follows. Some text, presented with bullets, is helpful. While other linked pages may be predominantly text, keep in mind that some variation in layout and presentation keeps the reader interested. Too much, however, will make it difficult for the viewer to understand what it is you're communicating. Large graphic elements such as pictures can be informative and interesting. But, the more complex and colorful the graphics, the more time it will take for your users to pull down your page into their computers. What might seem to be "wonderful" art on a printed page may be agony to download to a computer with a moderate-speed modem. Temper good graphic and sound elements with ease of access.

Hot buttons and links. Most pages should have hyperlinks, indicated by boldfaced and underlined type or by icons. A web page is a multidimensional medium that allows quick and easy access to other pages — in your home-page system or to other relevant locations throughout the Internet. And the hyperlinks make it so. Use them. Also, make it easy for users to move back to your home page from the other web pages by including a home-page hyperlink at the bottom of the other pages.

The hook. How do you get people to your page? The "honey for the bees" includes novelty, special information, interesting graphics, contests and promotions, and interactive activity, to name a few. Discover these techniques and test out their effectiveness first-hand. Surf some web sites. See what it is that attracts you to a page and what would bring you back for more.

Screens. A page may appear as one or many screens on the computer monitor. That is, each time a person has to physically scroll down to see another portion of the page to fill the viewing area on the monitor, he or she is viewing another "screen." Each screen that you see should be a design whole — both horizontally and vertically. So, a good screen won't be wider or deeper than the natural viewing area of the monitor.

Feedback mechanism. Any good marketer will see the web page as a real opportunity to collect responses from visitors. On-line surveys, questionnaires, and an e-mail address will make your page an interactive mechanism that turns visitors into dialoguing users. Not only will you want to use information from the surveys to build a database about your prospects, clients, and customers, but you'll find that responses will help you address needs and interests in your pages — pages that should be ever-changing to maintain interest among returning users.

YOUR PAGE IS ONLY HALF-BAKED WITHOUT PROPER MAINTENANCE AND PROMOTION

Building in response opportunities is only the first step in a continuing commitment to attract visitors and to keep those who have already discovered your place coming back for more.

Refresh the content of the page, at least monthly. Tell people when you last revised the page. Highlight important areas, especially those that have been changed from last month. Make it easy for visitors to quickly access these areas through the use of hyperlinks. If you don't know what's important to visitors, ask them. You may discover that they find a feature of particular value, while you had dismissed it or considered it parochial. For example, it may be the search function you've built into your page that's particularly appealing. Whatever it is, tout your page's attraction early.

When you put an e-mail response mechanism in your page, be certain to read and respond to e-mail queries regularly. Daily is best. Those who use e-mail know that an electronic message that is left unread and unanswered for more than 48 hours will likely be followed by a second message asking about the status of the first. E-mail messages that aren't responded to promptly will eventually generate more work and bad Internet relations.

Once you have your page up on the net, you'll need to institute some publicity to let people know that it's there. A press release announcing the page is a good idea. Though, the fact that you have put up a home site is probably no longer a story since more than 20,000 pages are already up on WWW. An interesting or unusual application or service offered by the page, on the other hand, may be a story angle. See what others are doing on the Web—especially the competition—so that you know what "unusual" or "interesting" might be.

All of your future press releases should carry a reference to your page and URL (Internet address) in the heading. This is especially important if you plan on posting company or organizational information on your site. Reporters may use the page as a resource.

Be sure to get your page listed on the various Internet directories, the very best guides to what's what on the Internet. The major directories include Alta Vista, Yahoo, Lycos, Webcrawler, EINet Galaxy, and The Whole Earth Catalog. Each directory accepts submissions, will place your page under the proper subject category, and will provide a hyperlink to your site from the directory—at no charge.

You'll probably discover other Internet directories and indexes that specialize in subject areas related to your industry or field. Do some on-line searches to flush them out. Numerous printed (yes, on paper) directories are also published regularly. Contribute your page address and description to the publishers for listing in their next editions.

One of the most important promotional opportunities you have is the mention of your presence on other Internet pages from which your site can be hyperlinked. You'll want to look for such opportunities among related and noncompeting groups and organizations that gain something for their users by listing your site on their page. A little reciprocity may be in order as you do the same for them by posting a hyperlink to their sites on your page.

It's a new era for advertising, public relations, and marketing professionals. Although we may have the traditional communications skills well in hand, the Internet has introduced a venue that offers different tools and new, creative approaches.

How Much Will This Cost?

There is no simple answer to the question. There is no simple answer to "How much will it cost me to run my [traditional] advertising campaign?" There are so many variables, it is impossible to give specifics.

We can give you some 1996 ballpark costs for the various steps that you will be going through to produce the site. The computer work involved in creating and storing your web page will be the least expensive part of the process. The creative time and talent to design the page along with promotion and maintenance, on the other hand, could total more than 75 percent of the bill. Those publishing pages frequently underestimate the program's total price tag, tending to overlook indirect expenses. Although you may be able to handle some of the tasks yourself, you will probably go elsewhere for much of the work, unless you're a real Internet "jack-of-all-trades."

The first step, research, helps you determine what your industry, competition, customer, and prospect presence is on the Internet. Research may even uncover sites put up by enterprising employees or members that unofficially represent your company or organization. Research will cost you $75–$100 per hour.

When you know what others are doing, you are in a position to begin thinking through what you can and should do on your site. With your research in hand, it is a good time to bring in an Internet consultant to discuss content and design. Figure on $125–$175 per hour for this advice.

Simultaneously to planning the content, you should register a URL or name for the site. Plan on spending $75–$150 for a name search and registration, when done on your behalf. The official registration fee is another $100 plus an annual charge of $50 to maintain it. You can register a name before a site is actually up and running.

When you have a content concept, you will be calling in a web-site designer, at $125–$150 per hour. The more elaborate your site (for example, audio, video, feedback mechanisms, site visit measurement tools, etc.), the more design time required. If you need some special copywriting assistance to make your on-line text read well, add fees of $100–$125 per hour for the copy preparation.

With a design and copy that satisfy you, contract with a computer programmer to interpret your material into the web language, HTML (hypertext markup language). Charges for HTML work are running $75–$100 per hour.

You're ready to store your page on a computer with a live link to the Internet. Storage rates are running at about $1 a kilobyte of storage space per month. Assume a minimum charge of $50 per month for a single page. Multiple-page sites with a lot of graphics will hike the tab.

It's important to figure in maintenance expenses. Many of these could be indirect costs. You may require an in-house full- or part-time webmaster to oversee the site activity. If you don't have someone in mind to handle the webmaster work, you may have to go to a search firm to find the right person. Since you'll be revising your web page regularly, set aside some monies for additional HTML support. Also, don't forget promotional activities that would include listing your URL on the major indexing and search sites such Yahoo and Lycos. You will also want to remain on the lookout for other appropriate web-site links both to and from your site.

Then there are training and education. You want to help people with whom you're doing business learn how to use this new medium. That could include fellow employees, customers, members, and suppliers. Customized full-day workshops on using WWW and the Internet cost $1,200–$1,500.

Where do you go for any or all of these above services? Some web-site contractors offer all of these services under one roof. You may wish to serve as your own contractor and arrange with individual providers to handle the various tasks. In either case, don't expect to find a listing of these skills in your local yellow pages. It's too new.

Back to our original question. "How much does it cost to set up a web site?" I can't possibly give you a specific figure. Only ranges. Be warned, however, that the real cost of a good web site is not in its creation. It's in its maintenance — keeping it up-to-date and viable for its users.

INTERNET JUDGES CITE HOME PAGE "NETCELLENCE"

Self-styled judges of web page quality have set up their own Internet sites. Some tell us what's most popular. Others tell us they may not know art, but they know what's "cool." Some establish complicated point systems in different categories letting us know what's best. Some look only at design. Still others have decided they know "bad" better than they know "best" by giving us the "worst" of the web. Some are undecided about the whole thing and let us vote for the best and "zap" the worst. Taken collectively, however, they are helping us develop a critical and "cool" eye about excellence in a medium that's literally exploded into our senses within just months. Yes, even in the undisciplined "wild, Wild West" of the Internet there are certain standards.

Among the most prominent of the virtual critics of "netcellence" are the Internet search engines like Yahoo. It's natural that an index and search help should do so since it knows which subject categories and sites are visited most frequently based on the hyperlinked menu items selected by the users. Yahoo lets you select those sites that are "cool" and those that are "most popular."

It shouldn't be too surprising, by the way, that "Entertainment" is the most popular category, followed by "Computers," "Society & Culture," "Art," and then "Business." Among the "coolest" business sites, says Yahoo, is the friendly and helpful Mama's Cucina by Ragu (Exhibit 11.2). Alamo Rent-A-Car offers up an equally "cool" site (and name) with a fine respite for the traveler.

A host of other sites also keep surfers up on what's hot and what's not, using their own criteria. Some have even created logos that winning sites can post on their pages. The people from Point Communications Corporation in Brookline, Massachusetts, have probably gone the farthest to define overall excellence with numbered ratings using three criteria — Content ("Just how broad, deep, and amazingly thorough is the information?"), Presentation ("Is the page beautiful, colorful, easy to use, etc.?") and Experience ("Is it fun, worth the time, and does it deliver the goods?"). A page that rates a 40 to 49 in any category is "The singing of angels." One that rates 0 to 9, on the other hand, is "The singing of Marcel Marceau."

David Siegel with his "High Five," takes a somewhat different approach to good sites. Always the artist, Siegel says, "I'm not in the cool site business. I'm looking for well-designed sites, sites that are visually sophisticated and refined.... We encourage designers to sweat the details and banish the garbage." His criteria — degree of difficulty, execution, and aesthetics — are ranked using ratings 1 to 5.

Lightning Ridge Ranch offers up its "Golden N Awards," promoting the use of Netscape 1.1N and the HTML 3.0 enhancements, to personal home pages, information pages, entertainment pages, and fun pages — but not commercial pages ("which have more hardware/software resources"). Although no specific criteria are mentioned, Lonnie and K.C. Odom say that "being able to read a page is probably the biggest factor of all." Obviously, the emphasis is on design technique and craft.

Exhibits 11.3 and 11.4 show two examples of the creative use of a web page to reach consumers.

ELECTRONIC MALLS MATCH CONSUMERS WITH PRODUCTS IN VIRTUAL MARKET

Can you really sell product on the Internet? Questions about who is on the Internet and about the safety and security of on-line money transactions have muddied the cyberwaves. Because the Internet is as yet uncontrolled and growing at a phenomenal rate, good and valid

EXHIBIT 11.2 MAMA'S CUCINA WEB PAGE

This web site, sponsored by Ragu, features a warm, welcoming "mother" who invites you into her kitchen. In addition to providing help in cooking delectable meals, the site features a "hook" to get people to come back again and again. The ever-present "mama" encourages all good "sons" and "daughters" to write to her. The site has a catchy, easy-to-remember URL — http://www.eat.com.

EXHIBIT 11.3 SECURITY FIRST NETWORK BANK WEB SITE (APRIL 1996)

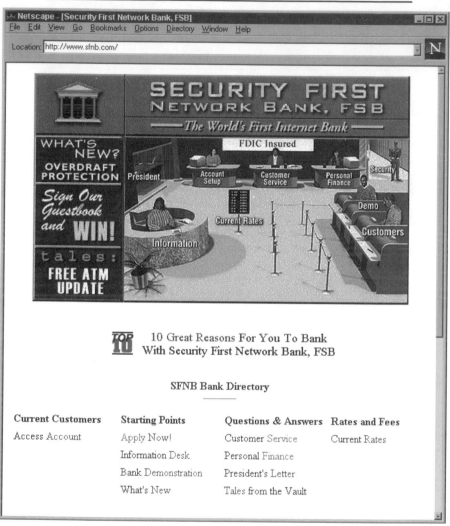

This re-creation of the Security First Network Bank lobby is a good exam-ple of how organizations are making web sites friendly and welcoming to visitors. Real employees are ready to respond to queries with a simple click on the respective hyperlinked icon. Notice that the unseen bank president is in the background, supporting the work of the employees who meet the pub-lic face-to-face. Security First has been so successful with this Internet banking system that it is selling the on-line technology to other banks. The URL is http://www.sfnb.com.

EXHIBIT 11.4 AMP WEB SITE

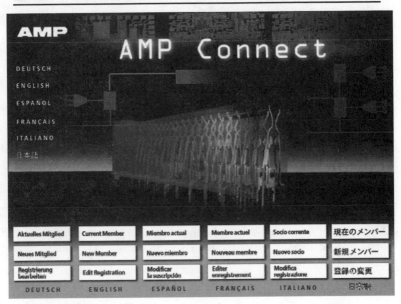

AMP Incorporated, an international firm that specializes in the manufacture of electrical-connection components, put their 30,000-part catalog online. The catalog is accessible in six different languages, including Mandarin Chinese. You can search by part — picture, number, or name — and you can refine your search by submitting specifications. Once the right parts are identified, orders are placed and received. The entire transaction takes place on-line. The company reports that the site is receiving tens of thousands of "hits" every month. The URL is http://connect.amp.com/. Reprinted with permission of AMP.

data are hard to come by. Frankly, much of the information is anecdotal. We just don't know how good the Internet is as a medium for the exchange of products and services.

For nearly twenty years, however, one or another form of the electronic mall has successfully brought product to market. The major on-line services discovered some years ago that people would actually connect via modem and computer to order products and services. The Internet's electronic malls are different, however. They offer everything from automobiles, boats, and tee shirts to advertising specialties, CDs, and graphic services. And, because web pages can easily show off products through pictures, graphics, text and, yes, even sound, consumers can make on-line decisions based on what they see and hear.

Internet's electronic malls are different in a couple of other important ways. On the one hand, the malls are being created out of cyberair by entrepreneurial types who are pulling together diverse (or industry-specific) businesses. On the other hand, cities, chambers of commerce, tourism bureaus, conference centers, and associations are assembling businesses under their URLs (addresses). Of course, you pay for virtual presence on the Internet just as you would for a location in a strip mall in a local community.

There's yet another wrinkle to the virtual mall. If you can assemble the commercial businesses together to attract an audience, why isn't the reverse also possible? We are, in fact, seeing home pages that bring together an audience to attract business. Cyberdevelopments are emerging where users with common interests are encouraged to construct their own personal web pages without charge. Advertisers, catering to these interests, are in turn invited to sponsor pages promoting their products and services. Everyone is happy. The individual has an on-line presence, without charge. The business buys access to its very select market. The mall sponsor makes money.

Internet can't yet guarantee the safe and secure transfer of monies. But it's coming. There is no Internet authority to guarantee satisfaction. That isn't coming. On the Internet, just as on the street, the buyer must beware.

A GOOD SITE MEASURES ACTIVITY
AND ENCOURAGES RESPONSE

With the growing interest in using web sites for advertising and commercial purposes, you should know how to measure on-line activity. If you are using a site to take orders for a product or service, the measure is clear. It's all bottom line. How many orders did you receive, and for how much? In addition to the sale, though, there are other measurement or response systems you can and should use to quantify activity.

At a minimum, you can track "visits" or "accesses"—the number of people who have stopped by to see your site. The same software will tell you the number of visitors as well as when they stopped by, and, on occasion, the locale and system they were coming from or through to get to your site. This is information that most web site developers will provide as part of a basic site maintenance package.

Those selling space on their sites should know how many visits the site and its respective pages receive during an average week. "NandOnet," an electronic newspaper published in Raleigh, North Carolina, recently reported that its web site had more than six-and-one-half million accesses during a single week in early 1996. Individual pages on the site, of course, will receive proportionately fewer accesses. You will pay advertising rates, according to the access or visit activity on the respective page or site. The "visitor" measure, however, cannot tell you who stopped by the site, how long they stayed, or if they are repeat visitors.

A second, more sophisticated level of measurement, is the "hit." This reports how many times visitors have clicked on specific hyperlinking icons or words. This is valuable information for those who want to know what visitors are interested in viewing on their sites. It's a subtle way of soliciting opinions about various products and services.

A major airline, for example, offers a listing of its various airplane types and amenities. When you click on the specific type, you bring up an attractive photo of that airplane along with specifications. By getting a regular reading on these hits, the airline knows that some airplanes are more popular with the public than others. A site becomes a kind of cyber focus-group by providing "hit" levels on product descriptions. Because you know that each site visitor will likely generate multiple hits, you may need to factor in a visit/hit ratio that provides an estimate of how many different individuals have actually activated separate links.

The "hits" are important for those who advertise on WWW. Sites that sell adlinks (display ads that are hyperlinked to other sites and pages) should be able to tell the advertiser how many times visitors clicked on their adlinks. If you can't get that information, you may want to choose other sites for your adlinks.

Sites have begun using e-mail links to attract visitors to their pages. I received an "anonymous" electronic valentine from the State of Virginia to promote the theme "Virginia is for lovers." I received the valentine greeting in my electronic mailbox, inviting me to pick up my "personalized valentine" by visiting the state's site. I was given a specific URL (address) that, when used with my web browser, launched me to "virtual Virginia." When I arrived, I picked up my card. I was also encouraged to send a valentine greeting to another, bringing yet other cyber visitors to Virginia. This chain-valentine provides Virginia with visitors, hits, names, and e-mail addresses. A sweet promotion.

An electronic survey may also provide important feedback. Specific questions are answered. Opinions are given. Though the survey requires more care and support, it's one of the best ways to monitor public response on a variety of subjects. The best sites use the survey to get opinions on the site itself. Miller Genuine Draft's "Taproom," for example, uses suggestions and recommendations from surveys to help build new and interesting site features for the following months. Though you don't necessarily get names and addresses from the surveys, the opinions constantly contributed are a good and continuing measure of public sentiment.

A web site responsive to visitor opinions and suggestions will undoubtedly generate more hits. Columbia University's Healthwise program encourages contributions through its interactive question and answer service, "Go Ask Alice." Visitors may ask health-related questions anonymously. Answers to the questions are posted in a public area. Months-worth of answers are stored for reading by future visitors to the site. In addition to giving the site personality, the "Go Ask Alice" program lets users dictate the topics of discussion.

Personal ongoing electronic dialogue with individuals who have left names and e-mail addresses provide yet another form of measurement for a good web site. Visitors are not inclined to leave their names and addresses unless the site gives them good reason to do so. Oklahoma State University does so by encouraging youthful "student prospect" visitors to talk to the university about building their own home pages. The right medium for the right message.

I'm particularly high on the OSU site. Its creators have obviously given some considerable thought to the audience. It features a "Who Am I?" line under a small headshot on the home page. "Who Am I?" turns out to be a faculty member whom you can learn about when you click on the picture. I discovered the picture and faculty member change every time I logged on to the site. What a wonderful way to recognize a very important audience — and attract them to the site as well!

YOU MAY BE ON THE NET, AND YOU DON'T KNOW IT

Some organizations have decided to stay off the Internet. It's a new medium, and, frankly, they don't want to be pushed into any early decisions about putting up a web site or participating in newsgroups. Sad to say, it's probably not their decision to make. Those organizations holding out are very likely already on the Internet and they don't even know it.

Recently, I was speaking to a high-tech firm that had decided to hold the line on putting up a web site. Unfortunately, they were also holding the line on knowing much about the Internet. I did a little research on the side to see, in fact, what their industry presence was on the net. I wasn't surprised by the high level of industry activity. I was surprised, however, by something else. Through one of the search and directory sites, I found the company and a several-paragraph-long description on a site maintained by one of their suppliers. The description was outdated. Furthermore, the listing suggested a special relationship between supplier and company that was inaccurate.

Companies and organizations should know how they are currently portrayed on the net, especially if portrayals are inaccurate or negative. These may come from employees representing their personal sites as official company pages; students using their own web pages to speak out on behalf of their college or university; dissident members spreading rumors and untruths on newsgroups and listservs about their organizations; divisions and subsidiaries espousing practices that run counter to corporate policy; chapters and affiliates taking responsibilities that aren't theirs to assume; or other groups using trademarked names of corporate products or services.

You can obtain a quick snapshot of your Internet presence with an electronic search using one or more of the search and directory sites—Yahoo, Lycos, Webcrawler, Alta Vista, etc. This will provide you with today's picture only. Because things change very quickly on the Internet, you'll need to do this research regularly for accurate information.

Needing to stay current is especially important when monitoring material that appears in the discussion areas of the net—the newsgroups and listservs. A general search using the search and directory sites would not pick-up the transitory exchanges occurring daily. However, you can "clip" the newsgroups using one or another of the Internet monitoring services. For a relatively modest charge, the service will provide an organization with a monthly report on cyberspace discussions of interest. You may even download newsgroup-monitoring software off the net if you have the time and interest to do the research work yourself.

If you discover that your organization is on the Internet and that it is being portrayed inaccurately or unfairly, there are several things you should do. Ask the webmaster of the site to remove or update the information. Then, return to the site to make certain that changes or deletions have been made. If the webmaster or site has no official relationship with your organization, you won't be able to enforce your request—unless it's an issue of trademark or copyright.

On the other hand, webmasters and sites with special relationships with the organization—employees, students, members, divisions, departments, chapters, affiliates—create special challenges, especially if they already have a page on the web. It may not be "politic" to demand changes. One corporation I know has created a "mega" home page, bringing into the fold the subsidiaries and divisions that had already created sites. It has begun enforcing Internet standards through example and by establishing a WWW interdivisional marketing team to oversee cyber activity.

That an enterprising department or division has created a web site may just prove to be an opportunity. With just a few modest changes, the site may very well serve as an important component for the organization's new official site.

Rumors or bad information appearing in electronic exchanges should be tracked down and corrected in the discussion group where they appear. If they persist and are serious, you may have to speak to the newsgroup's sysop (or moderator) about correcting the "slander" and dealing with the offender. You may be able to identify the person leaving the offensive messages and threaten legal action if the material is patently untrue, malicious, or libelous. If the offending messages are receiving wide attention and given some credibility, press alerts and advisories to relevant reporters are appropriate.

There is another option, especially if the offending messages left on the newsgroups or listservs are solicitous. A "Blacklist of Internet Advertisers" site has been established to keep those at bay who would advertise or solicit in the discussion groups. The "Blacklist" uses publicity and other informal (but effective) measures to enforce the "nonsolicitation" rules of the Internet. Working with sysops of the respective groups, you should report offenders to "Blacklist."

In the end, we really shouldn't expect that we can or should control all Internet activity on our organization's behalf. We do need to be continuously aware, however, of how we are being represented there, creating change when necessary and possible.

THOSE WHO WISH TO PROMOTE
ON THE INTERNET MAY BE "TOOL-LESS"

Possibly the most frequently asked questions by professional communicators about the Internet are about advertising, promoting, and publicizing on the superhighway. "Can I do it?" "How do I do it?"

There is a long informal Internet tradition of no advertising on the Internet. That tradition is still generally accepted in all areas of the net, except for the WWW. Although some try to advertise on the Internet, others who are using the Internet for discussions and e-mail exchange will have none of it. Most consider it bad "netiquette" for someone to post one or more solicitations or promotions in a civil discussion. Those leaving multiple solicitations to a particular newsgroup are accused of a "spam." Others who post the same message to many different newsgroups or boards are accused of a "velveeta." Both types of violators are swiftly "flamed" or criticized by others who don't wish to be bothered by on-line advertising.

Repeated offenders of the nonsolicitation rule are in for even more serious consequences. The home page, the "Blacklist of Internet Advertisers," publicizes a list of the worst violators of the nonsolicitation rule. "It is intended to curb inappropriate advertising on usenet newsgroups and via junk e-mail. It works by describing offenders and their offensive behavior, expecting that people who read it will punish the offenders in one way or another."

And how are the offenders punished? The "Blacklist" suggests: "Boycott the advertising business.... Send them or their system administrators a message informing them that you disapprove of their behavior.... If a phone number is given, you might want to try to call them collect. 1-800 numbers are also always warmly welcomed... Put them in your kill file.... Filter them out of your mailbox.... Use proc-mail and an AI engine like emacs doctor to engage them in a fake mail dialog." The "Blacklist" goes on to list other more serious "punish-ments," as well, to match the severity of the offense.

There are newsgroups, however, for selling and advertising on the Internet. The biz.* and *.marketplace groups have been established specifically for such activity. Check them out, however, before you post your solicitation. Some were created to accommodate users who want to sell personal items. Others are for commercial products and services.

The nonsolicitation rule is generally enforced on non-Internet bulletin boards and forums, as well. Increasing numbers of users who are new to on-line communications see these electronic collectives as wonderful places to publicize their respective services. However, it is very bad manners and a serious intrusion on professional exchanges.

And what are the consequences for those who continue to leave their solicitations even after being warned not to do so? After the third such violation, the offender is barred from further access to the forum.

Because the use of e-mail to solicit business is generally frowned upon, journalists may feel your e-mail news release is unacceptable. We suggest that media relations people send out initial queries to jour-nalists on-line, asking their permission to send out future material via e-mail. Some reporters will welcome the e-mail news releases, since they should be able to more easily review, use, save, or discard the material electronically. Others who think of e-mail as a medium for personal business communications only might consider it an invasion of privacy.

Generally speaking, the on-line services have addressed on-line solicitations by setting aside areas like electronic malls for the promo-tion of products and services. The Internet has no such formal organi-zation or structure, however, for the separation of advertising and promotion from editorial matter. Informally, home pages have become accepted places to promote and solicit business.

Some pages are noncommercial sites created by individuals or organizations to inform, while others are commercial operations creat-ed to sell a service or product. Still other pages are commercial ven-tures by independent entrepreneurs who are selling space on their pages. Yet other pages, just like commercial publications, are a mixture of advertising and editorial material. The webmasters welcome both kinds of contributions.

Is there a directory of Internet addresses and locations of acceptable promotion opportunities? Not yet; the Internet is too new, too ever-changing. Ultimately, your individual research and investigation is required to discover how and where you can best advertise, publicize, and promote on the Internet.

Some web pages that may be helpful include Spam's Own Page, Netiquette for Usenet Site Administrators, How to Advertise on the Net, and Information on Advertising newsgroups.

GO SURF WHERE THE MEDIA ARE

There are multiple ways of communicating with the media on-line. Although e-mail will continue to be an important communications link with selected reporters, editors, and freelancers, consider the opportunities afforded by the media presence on the World Wide Web.

More than 150 newspapers worldwide have their own web pages. A surprisingly large proportion of the newspapers — 70 — are posted from Europe, according to Media-Link, itself a web page published in Amsterdam. Although newspapers dominate the media types with their own pages, television and radio stations, magazines, wire and press services, and film companies are also well-represented. Many student-operated publications from colleges and high schools also have their own pages.

These web pages are not simply experiments in one-way communications. More often than not the media-operated pages encourage site visitors to dialogue with them via a posted e-mail address.

Although pages are frequently organized around the traditional sections — general news, sports, financial reports, entertainment, and lifestyle, many are testing new options and alternatives offered by the Internet. For example, *The San Francisco Examiner* reports on special topics through a kind of "advertorial" section. A recent topic was "Care Givers," adults who are providing living support to elderly or infirm parents, other relatives, or friends. In addition to articles, the section includes hyperlink pointers for home pages of groups and organizations who offer one or another kind of help for care givers. Newspapers, like the *Examiner*, will typically reference related Internet services and product home site hyperlinks in the section. As an aside, the *Examiner*'s selection of "Care Givers" as a focus is interesting and suggests that the Internet audience may be fast becoming more diverse.

Once the plans for the special electronic supplements have been determined, you can suggest links with your business and product interests. This works best if the links are hyperlinks to your client's or company's own home pages.

The appearance of the electronic publications and their special features requires that advertising and media relations people maintain a new category of editorial calendar. In "olden times," one could have subscribed to a media service for a listing of editorial calendars. Today, it requires some heavy, and creative, individual surfing research.

Because media presence on the net is growing so quickly, there simply is no one single source for these electronic supplements. But there is more. Internet is spawning a whole new category of nonmedia media. Commercial (and noncommercial) enterprises are introducing web pages that are evolving into "electronic publications." For example, the Miller Genuine Draft folks started by creating a congenial place for their target market — young males — to gather. The MGD "Taproom" has become something more; it publishes monthly lifestyle features of interest to its audience. As any good publication, it has become a very quotable news source for other media. Any good editorial calendar should include the Taproom plans.

All of this is a way of saying that good and effective advertising and marketing on the Internet requires considerable personal ingenuity. Sure, there will continue to be sources of good information. But, more and more of those sources will be identified through personal discovery — and surfing.

INTERNET ADLINKS MAY BE THE SIGN OF ADVERTISING'S FUTURE

The Internet is like one gigantic virtual laboratory where communicators are testing, experimenting, developing, and introducing new advertising, public relations, marketing, and promotional techniques and devices. One such device that is receiving a lot of attention is the "adlink."

Popping up on web sites all over the Internet, the adlink is a small display advertisement that promotes another site or page. The adlink may be less than an inch square or it may stretch across the screen in a rectangular-shaped block. Usually, the adlink promotes another site with a tantalizing line of copy and a bit of art. In addition, the adlink will automatically hyperlink you to the site referenced if you click on it with your mouse.

This very popular form of advertising and promotion on the net also provides some measurement possibilities. Frequently, the site that hosts the adlink will give the advertiser a daily and weekly figure, reporting the hits (the number of times people have clicked on the ad) generated by the adlink. An adlink "hit" report can quickly tell you how effective a particular ad and its placement has been, giving you a cost per hit.

Just as in any advertisement, a good adlink must be matched with an appropriate placement. And there are opportunities galore for effective placement on the Internet. One of the most promising is that offered up by the search sites like Lycos and Yahoo. Many people start out their trips on the Internet's web by first accessing one or another of the search sites. The search sites give advertisers the opportunities to list their adlinks on specific pages relevant to user interest. So, for example, if you're advertising a real estate web site, you can have your adlink appear at the top of the page that appears when someone has keyed in "real estate" as his or her search term. The more terms you wish to key on your adlink, the more you pay the site sponsor for your placement. Electronic newspapers, like NandOnet (News & Observer), offer a similar site service, though not necessarily linked to searches. Just as in their real paper versions, you can request to have your adlink appear on a page related to your interest — sports, news, finance, etc.

The adlink is an important way for site sponsors to generate income since most are not collecting subscription fees to access them. Other intriguing wrinkles to the adlink phenomena are appearing. MapQuest offers pages of maps and itinerary help for travelers. MapQuest sells adlink sponsorships, as well. When someone makes an inquiry on types of businesses or services available in one or another part of the country (or world), the sponsors' listings will appear on the map, along with the URL (address) and link to their site, if they have one. In addition, sponsors can make provision to link their site to that map page (or pages), showing business locations.

The costs for placing an adlink range anywhere from something less than a hundred dollars to many thousands per month. It all depends on the numbers — the volume of visits and hits generated by the site. It's been my experience that the adlink rates on many sites are underpriced — due, probably, to the inexperience of the site operators and sponsors. Other site rates are extravagant when you consider that we still have much to learn about the effectiveness of the Internet as a medium for the sale of products and services. Ad set-up charges for an adlink may be less, too, since there aren't the color separation and multicolor printing fees one has to normally figure into print publication.

There is one downside to all of this. Because the Internet is an unsupervised medium, there are no rules governing the indiscriminate mixing of advertising and sponsorships with editorial matter. Even newspaper-sponsored sites don't always effectively separate one from the other. Unless Internet users are given clear clues as to what is a promotion and what isn't, adlink effectiveness could be limited over the long haul.

How Like an Elephant Is the Internet

One realizes just how like a shadow this thing we call the Internet really is when we review a year's worth of related reports and studies. Like the proverbial elephant "seen" and described by the blind men, it's not always clear if Internet researchers are describing the same thing. Yet, if we are to make commercial sense of this new medium to judge its marketing value, we are forced to pay some attention to what research is telling us.

One of the more interesting and "comprehensive" reports was that completed by Nielsen Media Research and reported in late October 1995. It said that "some 24 million people in the United States and Canada alone are already on the Internet—fully 11 percent of the North American population over age 16." In addition, it said that 17.6 million people use the World Wide Web. Nielsen went on to report that about one-third of all Internet users are women and that Internet users spend an average of five hours on-line each week. Users tend to be upscale, educated professionals with a household income of more than $80,000.

Shortly thereafter, Vanderbilt University business professor Donna Hoffman contended that the Nielsen study "is skewed toward people more likely to be on the Internet." It makes inflated estimates, particularly in respect to household income and education level, she said, in a piece reported in *The New York Times*. It turns out that Ms. Hoffman also serves as a key adviser to Nielsen Media Research, a unit of Dun & Bradstreet Corporation. One wonders when and how she was advising Nielsen. And if they were listening.

An October 10 to November 10, 1995, study by the University of Michigan Business School indicated that 79 percent say the top reason for using the web is for fun. Only 11 percent listed shopping as a primary reason for using the web. Sixty percent of the respondents cited security as a primary reason for not shopping on-line.

This survey suggests that the growing numbers of users are more diverse and less computer-sophisticated than those responding to an earlier survey by the University of Michigan. The implication is that this newer user will be more impatient with the speed and complexities of the Internet. The average income of users surveyed was $63,000 or 21 percent less than the Nielsen survey figure.

Demographer John Quarterman, in a December 18, 1995, Associated Press report, said there were 16 million people on the Internet at the start of 1995. The projected estimate for January 1996 was 32 million.

The three major on-line services, America Online, CompuServe, and Prodigy, began offering full access to the Internet last spring, which has undoubtedly helped to escalate Internet user activity. And, in fact, one has probably affected the other. Growth of subscribers to the on-line services, such as CompuServe and America Online, was even more impressive, according to Information and Interactive Service Report, growing from 4.6 million at the beginning of the year to 11.3 million by the end of November. In late December, CompuServe reported that its worldwide membership had surpassed 4 million people and that it would reach 5 million in the spring.

There have been reports, as well, as to the amount of business that actually has been transacted on the Internet. A study by Input, a California-based information services research firm, estimated that $20 million in business was done on-line in 1994, $40 million in 1995 — and $260 million estimated in 1996. The Nielson survey, mentioned earlier, reported that "roughly 2.5 million Internet users" have purchased products or services over the web.

Globally, according to SIMBA Information, Inc., a Wilton, Connecticut, information services company, North America accounts for 72 percent of web accesses; Europe, 23 percent; Australia, 4 percent; with the remaining 1 percent scattered among other countries. SIMBA also predicts that "personal access to the web is expected to grow to 7 million by the year 2000." This is somewhat different from the 17.6 million people that Nielsen says are currently using the web.

More than 20 Internet reports sponsored by different organizations were published in the last half of 1995. The sheer volume suggests intense interest in this medium. The diversity of the results and projections, however, tells us that Internet research is still very immature. Because the Internet is growing and mutating so rapidly, we simply don't have adequate benchmarks to judge change. Furthermore, this "elephant" is not necessarily the sum of its parts. Research still tends to lump all of the elements of the Internet and electronic communications together as one medium. In fact, they represent different and diverse media, including the web, newsgroups, FTP sites, Gopher sites, bulletin boards, commercial on-line services, and e-mail.

The bottom line is that the research measures and numbers vary, depending on the criteria and terminology used, the questions asked, the audience surveyed, and the representations offered up by the sponsor of the study. Advertising managers need to be both vigilant and discerning when using current research to make Internet marketing decisions. And, perhaps we should be demanding more and better figures from those putting the touch on the real pachyderm.

NOTES

Advertising and the Internet was taken from a three-part series in Ragan's Interactive Public Relations (June 15, 1995, July 1, 1995, and July 15, 1995). For subscription information, please contact: Lawrence Ragan Communications, 212 W. Superior Street, Chicago, IL 60610.

USEFUL ADDRESSES

The following services are mentioned in this article.

Service/Site	On-line Address
For Internet Directories	
Alta Vista	http://altavista.digital.com
Yahoo	http://www.yahoo.com
Lycos	http://www.lycos.com
Webcrawler	http://www.webcrawler.com/
EINet Galaxy	http://www.einet.net/
The Whole Earth Catalog	http://www.gnn.com/gnn/wic/ newrescat.toc/html
For "Cool" Business Sites Identified by Yahoo	
Mama's Cucina	http://www.eat.com/
Alamo Rent-A-Car	http://www.freeways.com/
For Information on Advertising on the Net	
Spam's Own Page	http://spl.berkeley.edu/ findthespam.html
Netiquette for Usenet Site Administrators	http://ancho.ucs.indiana.edu/ FAQ/USAGN/
How to Advertise on the Net	Gopher://gopher.internet.com: 2200/00/News/cmd-ibiz
Advertising Newsgroups	http://www.phoenix.net/ ~lildan/FAQ
For Web Site Ratings	
Point Communications Corp.	http://www.pointcom.com
David Siegel	http://www.best.com/~dsiegel/ high/five/high_five.html

For Media Information

Media-Link	http://www.dds.nl/~kidon/media.html
The San Francisco Examiner	http://www.sfgate.com/examiner/index.html
NandOnet (News & Observer)	http://www.nando.net

For General Interest

AMP Inc.	http://connect.amp.com
"Blacklist of Internet Advertisers"	http://www.cco.caltech.edu/~cbrown/BL/
Columbia University's Healthwise	http://www.columbia.edu/cu/healthwise/
MapQuest	http://www.geosys.com
Miller Genuine Draft	http://www.mgdtaproom.com.
Oklahoma State University	http://pio.okstate.edu/
Security First Bank Network	http://www.sfbn.com
State of Virginia	http://www2.virginia.org

Andre de Zanger is the founder and director of the Creativity Institute, in New York City, which is dedicated to stimulating and actualizing creativity. Andre is an international consultant, author, entrepreneur, and seminar leader. He has facilitated creative-innovation projects at AT&T, Bell Labs, Ogilvy & Mather, United Technologies: Otis Elevator and Carrier Air Conditioning, Airco, and the Federal Reserve Bank of NY. He has developed and leads Creative Selling seminars and has worked with advertising firms, conducting Creativity On Demand seminars. Andre has taught at numerous universities, colleges, and centers around the country and abroad. He is a faculty member of the Creative Problem-Solving Institute (CPSI), Buffalo State University. Andre is the author of a number of books on creativity and is the inventor of the FLASHER, an anti-theft auto device.

Judith Morgan is co-founder and co-director of The Creativity Institute. She works with both individuals and organizations and is an international consultant in the field of creativity. She is a specialist in the psychology of creativity, combining her background as a sculptor and psychotherapist. She brings practical skills and unique information to her work in creativity. She has written for many professional journals and has authored a number of books on creativity. She teaches at a variety of universities and organizations. Judith is a faculty member of the Creative Problem-Solving Institute (CPSI), Buffalo State University.

Andre de Zanger and Judith Morgan are available for speaking engagements and workshops, and can be reached at the Creativity Institute, 1664 Third Ave., N.Y.C., 10128, (212) 289-8856 or e-mail (creativityinstitute@juno.com). Other books on creativity as well as a computer program (The Creativity Machine) designed to stimulate creativity are also available.

CHAPTER 12

CREATIVE SOLUTIONS

In today's world there is tremendous pressure for "Creativity on Demand." The tools and techniques that are presented here will help you use your creativity to come up with new ideas ("on demand"), and to see things from a new perspective.

The myth that only a select few are born creative is not true. Our natural creativity is often educated out of us by the time we reach college. What happens to our creativity may be similar to what occurs to the little girl in the following story:

> Once there was a very little girl who started to go to a very large school. She was excited to go to school because she loved to learn and express herself. She was curious and loved to try new things. One day, her teacher said, "Okay class, today we are going to learn to draw." The little girl was very pleased because she loved to draw. She quickly got out her crayons and paper and began to draw very beautiful green flowers with purple and blue stems. Suddenly, her teacher said, "Stop, wait, I will show you how to draw a flower the correct way." She drew a red flower with a green stem and then told the class to copy it. The little girl thought her picture was much prettier but she didn't say anything and quietly drew a red flower with a green stem. The teacher was very pleased.
>
> Several weeks later, the teacher said, "Today we'll use clay and learn how to make a bowl." Again, the little girl was very excited because she loved to make things with clay and already knew how to make all kinds of shapes and animals. She started right away. Again, the teacher said, "Stop, wait, I will first show you how to make a bowl the right way." The little girl liked her bowl better but followed the teacher's instructions and made one that looked exactly like hers. The teacher was pleased.
>
> Gradually, the little girl learned to always wait to hear how to do something before she started. She squelched her natural enthusiasm (from the Greek word, "en-theos," meaning the "god within") and learned to keep quiet. The little girl became so good at following instructions, that she soon forgot that she already knew how to create.

Instead of finding the "right" way or "following directions," the model of creativity presented in this chapter will help you find "your" way. The tools and techniques are aimed at helping you discover that the answers are within.

> "A man should learn to detect and watch that gleam of light which flashes across his mind from within, more than the lustre of the bards and sages. Yet he dismisses without notice his thought, because it is his."
> — Ralph Emerson

GAINING NEW PERSPECTIVES

Can you read the word above and see the something in the nothingness? The white spaces are the letters (Success). Creativity can be defined as the ability to create "something" out of "nothing" and to see things in new ways.

Yield to Nothingness
From nothingness,
All things are created,
Arising from not being,
Being is born.
Once born,
All things open to life,
All life, Yields to nothingness.
> — The Tao of Creativity[1]

> "Every creative act involves...a new innocence of perception, liberated from the cataract of accepted belief."
> — A. Koestler

We all have a dominant way of seeing things that sometimes gets in our way of "seeing" a solution. Practice changing your perspective on the figures below.

Man on a horse   Duck and rabbit   Plane coming and going

Flexibility or the ability to change your perspective is one of the characteristics of successful people.

THE PYRAMID OF SUCCESS

What are the characteristics of successful people? Research was conducted on more than 1,000 successful people in business. It was found that they all had three characteristics in common. They all knew their *purpose*, and had a high degree of *awareness* and *behavioral flexibility* (with creativity being the highest degree of flexibility).

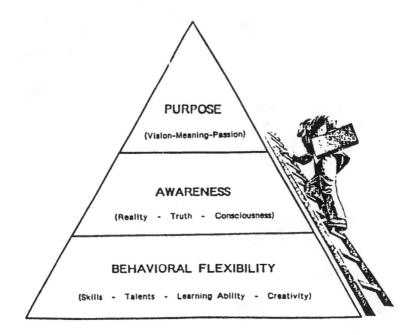

PURPOSE

(Vision-Meaning-Passion)

AWARENESS

(Reality - Truth - Consciousness)

BEHAVIORAL FLEXIBILITY

(Skills - Talents - Learning Ability - Creativity)

These characteristics can be practiced and are the ones that are used in creativity. All of the tools and techniques in this chapter will help you increase your awareness and flexibility. Purpose is our natural enthusiasm, curiosity and desire to create. It, too, can be practiced.

WHAT IS CREATIVITY?

Is it...   *Or, is it...*

Art.. Science
Vision Seeking..................................... Problem Solving
Exploring... Data Collecting
Play.. Work
Possible... Practical
Intuitive... Analytical
Spirit.. Mind
Right Brain .... Left Brain
Yin.. Yang
Spontaneous .... Procedural
Mystery.. Material
Beauty.. Functional
Joy .... Satisfaction
Revelation.. Resolution

Or is it both?

Perhaps creativity is a dialectic paradox. It contains opposing forces, the dialectic, and brings them together into a resolution, the paradox. The opposing forces—the analytical and intuitive, art and science, play and work—are brought together into the wholeness of creativity. The Dialectic Model of Creativity includes both sides of creativity. One part of the model explores the Visionary Focused (intuitive) aspects of creativity, while the other looks at the Problem Focused methods.

Einstein started with a question, "How does the universe work?" (Visionary Focus)

Edison asked, "Is it practical? Can it be produced? Is it marketable?" (Problem Focus)

Aristotle felt we all have a need for "emotional expression" and a "formative impulse." (Visionary Focus)

Socrates asked, "What do you mean?" (Problem Focus)

Michelangelo said, "The form is already there and will be revealed." (Visionary Focus)

Plato thought there were "ideal forms." (Visionary Focus)

Spinoza taught balance. (Both)

THE DIALECTIC MODEL OF CREATIVITY

Some of us are triggered into creativity by a *need*—a problem or situation that needs resolving (the bottom or *Problem Focused* side of the model). Others are spurred on by a *wish*, a desire for new ideas or creative stimulation (the top or *Visionary Focused* side of the model.

All of us tackle problems in different ways. Some of us move toward a *work* mode of problem solving. We go *searching* (gathering data, using logical analysis), *doing* research, synthesizing information, etc. Others move into *play* (*exploring*, experiencing, entering into a *being*, rather than a doing, state).

Still others move back and forth between the two modes. The problem-solving side of us wants a *resolution*, while the visionary side moves toward a *revelation*. This may vary according to what kind of situation you are facing. It's important to follow your way.

THE DIALECTIC MODEL OF CREATIVITY

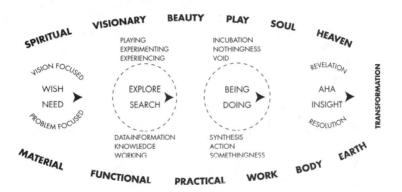

Source: Judith Morgan and Andre de Zanger, *Creativity on Demand* (New York: The Creativity Institute, 1995).

It is important to go with your style of creativity. You may prefer a more linear sequence or a more intuitive exploration. All models of creativity seem to suggest that the creative process has phases.

CREATIVITY AS A PROCESS

1. **Motivation.** The process starts with either a problem or vision/wish.
2. **Saturation.** This step involves both gathering and absorbing information as well as experimenting, exploring, and playing with the problem. Doing several of the exercises in this chapter around one problem would be a form of saturation.
3. **Incubation.** Often this takes place outside our awareness when we have let go of the problem consciously.

4. Illumination. The "Aha!" phase, the moment of insight.
5. Actualization. Bringing the idea into form, into a product, into new behaviors, etc.
6. Verification. The validation process, getting positive and negative feedback.

Sometimes we go back and forth between phases or repeat them totally.

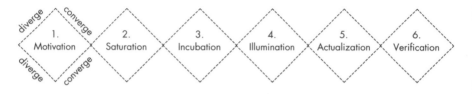

The creative process includes both divergent and convergent thinking. In divergent thinking, we are asked to suspend judgment and to come up with as many ideas as possible. We are encouraged to be wild and imaginative, to combine and build on thoughts or ideas. In convergent thinking, we need to make judgments and decisions in order to give our process a focus and direction. Often our creativity is blocked because we use convergent thinking (judgments, evaluations) when we are in the divergent phase. The tools and techniques that we will be presenting in this chapter will help you stay in the divergent phase to broaden creative output and expand options.

QIM

The Tools and Techniques presented here can be applied to problems in the form of QIM (Question, Input, Meaning). First there is a Quest or Question that needs an answer (one's motivation). Then a tool or technique can be used as an Input or Stimulus (related or random) to activate your creativity. The "stimulus-response" reaction of the Input generates the energy, joy, and excitement of creativity. Finally, we make Meaning or Connections and apply it back to the problem as a solution.

THE CREATIVE STATE OF CONSCIOUSNESS

How can we "create on demand"? It may be a process of combining QIM with entering into a creative state of consciousness. Research has shown that creativity is related to "Alpha and Theta" states of consciousness. Our alert waking state is "Beta," in which our brain waves are oscillating at 14–28 cycles per second. "Alpha" is a slower, more relaxed, intuitive state of consciousness at 7–14 cycles per second. "Theta" (3.5–7 cycles) is sleeplike, meditative, and creative. "Delta" (0.5–3.5 cycles) is that of deep sleep.

BETA 14–28 cycles per second (can go higher under certain circumstances)	**Conscious Mind** Input from 5 normal senses: Sight (about 80%)　　Touch Hearing　　　　　　Smell Taste **Level of** Daily coping with world Stress, anxiety, apprehension, tension, competition **Left side of brain** logical, reasoning, verbal	Simplified idea of way print-out might look

——— Input from ——— 　——— 5 imaginative senses ———

COMMUNICATION **ALPHA** 7–14 cycles per second	**Subconscious Mind** Input from 5 paranormal　Level of: senses: Sight—clairvoyance　　　Absence of stress 　　　　　　　　　　　　Concentration Hearing—clairaudience　Relaxation 　　　　　　　　　　　　Creativity Taste, Touch, Smell　　　Awareness 　　　　　　　　　　　　Meditation Clairsentience—　　　　Healing psychic knowing **Right side of brain** intuitive, feeling, nonverbal	
THETA 3.5–7 cycles per second	May be sorting–classifying level Creativity Relaxation Reduced awareness except for people experienced in meditative techniques (yoga, Zen masters, etc.)	
DELTA 0.5–3.5 cycles per second	**Level of** Deep sleep May be state of sleep-walking, sleep-talking May be state of astral projection	 Deep trance

Source: Graph of Beta-Alpha-Theta-Delta courtesy of Anne Durrum Robinson.

Application

There are many ways of entering the "Alpha" state of consciousness, and, in fact, we do it on a regular basis — when driving, watching TV, etc. However, to create on demand, it is important to learn to do it at will. Practice some of the methods listed below until you find one that suits your style.

Movement: Gently move your head from side to side while repeating a two-syllable word (Sufi). Slowly move your head back and forth (Dovening). Defocus the eyes while walking (Zen). Slow dancing, running, exercising, or any rhythmic movement can induce "Alpha."

Smell: Some of us become relaxed and slow down while "smelling the roses." Or you can be smelling apples, mint leaves, etc.

Breathing: Focus on your breathing; begin to breath slowly and deeply.

Color: Different colors tend to relax us — see or visualize one.

Visualizing: Imagine yourself in a place which is pleasant and calm.

Being Present: Focus on the moment, your environment, bodily sensations, colors, sounds, smells, textures.

Music: Different beats and tones can trigger an "Alpha" state.

Thoughts: Positive, optimistic thoughts, or laughter. Positive thoughts release healthy neuropeptides, chemicals which are produced in the brain and help us enter into a relaxed state.

ZINGERS: CREATIVE WARM-UPS

Zingers are creativity word games. Think of them as a Creativity-Gym for the mind. They can help warm up your creativity by having you practice Flexibility, Reverse Thinking, and Playfulness. Try your hand at some of the Zingers[3] on the following pages.

1. Legal Separation 2. Splitting Hairs 3. Setback 4. Tongue in Cheek
5. A Hole in One 6. Out of the Ordinary 7. Balancing Act 8. Drinks All
Around 9. André 10. A Lucky Dog 11. A Countdown 12. Undercover
Agent 13. Eternal Triangle 14. Pennsylvania 15. Peter out 16. The Last
Roundup 17. Bottom Line 18. Slim

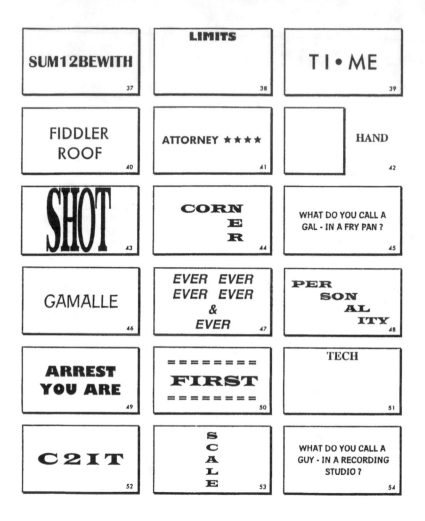

37. *Someone to Be with* 38. *Upper Limits* 39. *Point in Time* 40. *Fiddler on the Roof* 41. *Attorney General* 42. *Handout* 43. *Big Shot* 44. *Turn the Corner* 45. *Pam* 46. *All in the Game* 47. *Forever and Ever* 48. *Split Personality* 49. *You Are Under Arrest* 50. *First Among Equals* 51. *High Tech* 52. *See to it* 53. *Upscale* 54. *Mike*

217. *Bend over Backwards* 218. *Square Deal* 219. *Generation Gap*
220. *Little by Little* 221. *Sleeping at the Wheel* 222. *Work out*
223. *Go for It* 224. *Upset over You* 225. *Candy* 226. *In Hot Water*
227. *Hand-Me-Downs* 228. *Bee Line* 229. *Push Comes to Shove*
230. *Sign of the Times* 231. *Quarterback* 232. *Overcoming All Odds*
233. *Black Eye* 234. *Jim or Mat*

PARADIGM SHIFTS

A paradigm is defined as "the dominant or habitual way of seeing or thinking." We can severely limit our creativity and effectiveness if we see and think about things in only one way. We all tend to have dominant paradigms and think that the way we see things is the "right" way.[4] However, the same phenomenon can have two equally valid interpretations. To increase your flexibility, practice "shifting" the form below. The form has a dominant way of being seen, yet it can be seen in an entirely new way.

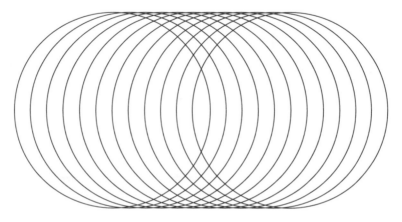

Application

Practice shifting your problem by asking new questions, such as: Don't ask what you can do to solve the problem, but what can it do for you?

PARADIGM SHIFT 1

Here's another opportunity to practice seeing things in new ways.

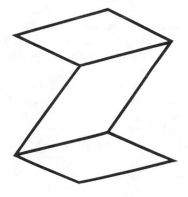

Application

Shift perspective on your problem. What would happen if you minimized it? if you maximized it? or reversed it?

PARADIGM SHIFT 2

Here's another opportunity to practice seeing things in new ways.

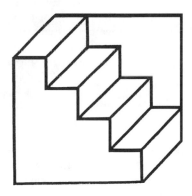

Application

Look at your problem in a new way. Break it down into its separate components. Now try rearranging them or combining them in different ways. Substitute a component with something else.

EMPATHIC METAPHOR

Metaphors are often used in creativity to stimulate our imaginations, suggest new perspectives, and help solve problems. We use metaphors all the time in our language: "Time is money"; "Business is war"; and "A relationship is an investment." Using them consciously can offer a new perspective on situations. This exercise combines the use of Metaphors with Empathy — the ability to become "one with."

Application 1

1. Sit back, relax, and think about your problem situation.
2. Choose an object at random from around the room or from the objects on the next page.
3. Become that object (Empathic) and write from its perspective. Start with "I am ..." and just keep writing for a few minutes.
4. Read what you have written and see what it tells you. Look for words or themes that have power or energy for you. They often reveal something about the problem situation or even yourself.
5. Force-fit these ideas back into your problem.

Example 1: Situation = Finding my Purpose/Object = Window

Free-Associate: "I am ... a window, letting in light while keeping out wind and rain. I protect, yet allow people to look out and feel good. Light is important for mental health, especially in winter. I serve many useful purposes. I am something and nothing. I am strong yet fragile."

Force-Fit: I notice the opposites, "something and nothing" and "strong yet fragile." I wonder if looking at opposites might be the answer. Am I looking only one way? I notice the emphasis on serving, being functional, and having a purpose. Maybe I just need to be myself, have fun, and do things that move my spirit?

Application 2

In business, becoming your customer, your product, or your problem, can give you greater insights and understanding of the real issues.

Example 2: Situation = Customer service/ Object = Customer

Free-Associate: "I am ... a customer. No one is thinking about my needs. Salespeople only think about closing the sale. Will they take care of me if I have problems? Am I getting a good deal and the best product? Do I have all the facts? Is the company really reliable? Can I talk to someone who has bought from them? What is going to happen in the long run? Are there guarantees?"

Force-Fit: Am I thinking about my customers enough? What are their needs and how can I really serve them? Spend quality time with them, building a lasting and trusting relationship.

Random Objects

TRIANGULATION

Triangulation is a way of gaining new insights into problems by breaking down the elements surrounding a situation and recombining them into new associations, analogies, and symbols. It is the process of "differentiation" and "integration" that nature uses in creating new life forms.

Methodology

1. State the issue you are working on in *one* word and place it in the center of the circle.
2. Brainstorm 12 words that describe the situation (characteristics, traits, or associations) and place them around the circle (from 1 to 12).
   Example: How to stay energized? Word = **ENERGY**

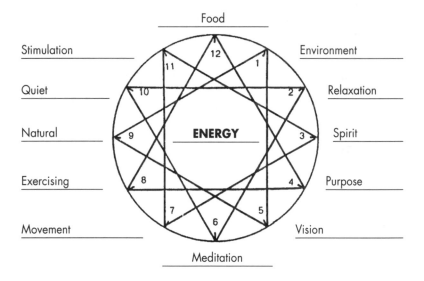

3. Triangulation — Connect the numbers and rearrange the words in any order that makes sense (change any word ending in -*ing*, -*ly*, -*ment*, etc.).

Purpose – Food – Exercising

Vision – Natural – Environment

Stimulation – Relaxation – Meditation

Exercising – Quiet – Spirit

4. Analogy — What would be an *example* of each triangulation in nature or the world?

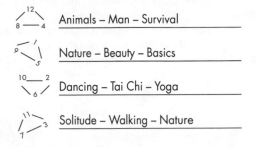

Animals – Man – Survival _____

Nature – Beauty – Basics _____

Dancing – Tai Chi – Yoga _____

Solitude – Walking – Nature _____

Triangulation

In the boxes below, draw a symbol to represent each of your analogies. Look for a common theme, and explore how it might help you to resolve your issue.

"The soul never thinks without a picture."

—Aristotle

Analogy: Animals – Man – Survival

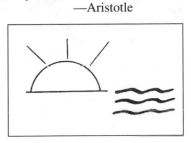

Analogy: Nature – Beauty – Basics

Analogy: Dancing – Tai Chi – Yoga

Analogy: Solitude – Walking – Nature

Common Theme: Being in Nature, The Opposites of Action and Nonaction, Health

Connection to problem: Be active and then rest well/Be in nature/Go for walks – Park/ Dance/Run/Eat right/ Rest/Relax/Naps/Write/Get Right Stimulation/Fresh Air/Sunlight/ Less Alcohol/Less Red Meat/Meditate/Focus on Purpose/Spirit

SCAMMPERR

Alex Osborn, a leader in the field of creative problem solving, developed ways of shifting a problem or its components to come up with new ideas. These nine ways of shifting perspectives were later put into the mnemonic, scammperr, by B. Eberle. Michael Michalko developed the Thinkpak, a series of cards around each of the processes to trigger new ideas.[5] Scammperr can be useful individually, in groups, and especially in meetings.

S = Substitute
C = Combine
A = Adapt
M = Magnify
M = Modify
P = Put to another use
E = Eliminate
R = Rearrange
R = Reverse

Substitute: What other person/place/part/time/dimension/direction/process/emotions/benefit/pain/consequence/reward/goal/strategy/procedure/theme/package/message/environment could be substituted?

Combine: What could be combined? How could you combine new ideas/emotions/people/science-art/function-beauty/body-spirit/intuition-logic/play-work/heaven-earth/procedure-spontaneity/data-mystery?

Adapt: How can you adapt something from nature/politics/science/art/finance/philosophy/sex/religion/circus/sports/psychology/medicine/comics/history/television/nutrition to your situation?

Magnify: What would happen if you exaggerated/enlarged/overstated/dramatized/added more value/made worse/higher/longer/safer/stronger/thicker/global/extended/optimized your issue?

Modify: What can be modified or altered? Its size/shape/use/meaning/purpose/process/character/color/sound/smell/functions/name/rules/package/components/benefits/appearance/destiny?

Put to another use: Can you find other uses/meanings/context/function/purpose/relationship/location/colors/forms/processes?

Eliminate: What can you delete/minimize/simplify/streamline/condense/compact/understate/separate/cut back/subtract/omit?

Rearrange: In what ways might you change the order/interchange components/change the sequence/timing/energy/rewards/transpose?

Reverse: What are the opposites? End first/envision results/negatives into positives/positives into negatives/worst result?

THE TAO OF CREATIVITY

The poems in *The Tao of Creativity*[1] can give new insights into your problems. They are a way of practicing using your intuition and discovering answers within. These poems have survived 2,500 years because they contain wisdom that is universal and ageless. They were originally written by Lao Tzu, who lived in China around 600 B.C. This version of the Tao focuses on the Creative Spirit. The poems emphasize Being in the Moment, Effortless Actions, Enjoying the Journey, and the Importance of Nothingness in order to allow the Somethingness to Emerge. These qualities speak directly to the creative process. They, therefore, can be used as triggers for stimulating creativity or for gaining new insights into problems.

Application
1. Think of a problem or situation that you are facing.
2. Choose a poem at random; reflect on its meaning.
3. Write down any associations or insights.
4. Force-fit these ideas back into your problem.

Example: Situation = New Packaging / Poem = Thirty Spokes

Free-Associate: Thirty Spokes = Round/Wheel/Thirty/Empty/Hole/Different Materials/Stone/Hard/Wood/Grains/Clay/Mold/Depth/Void/Space/Nothingness/Somethingness/Form/Cozy/Play/Comfortable.

Force-Fit: Bubble Air-Nothingness/Different Materials and Textures/Round-Angular/Soft-Hard/Serious-Playful/Sturdy-Flexible/Empty-Full/Allow Inside to Create the Outside/Shape and Function are One.

11. THIRTY SPOKES
Thirty spokes has a wheel,
But it's the hole,
The emptiness,
That makes it real.
A bowl is made from clay,
But it's the center, the depth,
That gives it play.
Wood and stone shape a house,
Yet it is the spaces,
The emptiness,
That form a home.
Just as nothing and something,
Combine to become more,
We are helped by the void,
To create the form.

26. GRAVITY AT THE CENTER
Gravity is at the center,
Of all things,
Speed, time and light all obey,
It conserves and maintains,
Yet stillness is at its core.
A creative man centers himself,
Staying in balance,
No matter how fast the day.
There is a call for action,
Opportunity awaits,
Yet the master within,
Keeps a calm head,
Sets a pace rooted in gravity,
In stillness,
Transforming the chaos into grace.

6. THE MORE IT IS USED
Intuition is like a timeless valley:
It lies deep,
Is sometimes dimly seen,
Yet is always present
Giving birth to the planted seed.
Because it lies so low
It cannot fall,
And to it all things flow.
Draw from it all you wish,
The more it is used,
The deeper it grows.

45. SUSPEND JUDGMENT
Great perfection,
Is always incomplete.
Great fullness,
Often appears empty.
The straightest of lines,
Seems curved.
The wisest of men,
Often act like children.
Since the truth,
Often appears opposite,
Suspend judgment,
Step out of the way,
Keep to what is,
And you will find your way.

39. STONE GROWING

Those who are in harmony with life,
Experience the strength of wholeness.
The heavens appear clear,
The earth is firm,
Minds are free,
And everything flourishes.
When the wholeness of life
Is forgotten,
The heavens appear cloudy,
The earth infirm,
Minds are enslaved,
And everything decays.
Would you rather hear
The tinkle of jade pendants,
Or listen to stone growing
In a cliff.

64. SEEDS GROWING TALL

Pay attention to what is,
In order to prevent what is not.
A cut needs cleaning,
A hurt needs caring,
A relationship needs tending.
Pay attention to what is,
In order to grow what is not.
A joy needs sharing,
An idea needs nurturing,
Creativity needs expressing.
The greatest of pine trees,
Is deeply rooted,
Yet easily grows,
From the tiniest of seeds.

2. VARYING TONES MAKE MUSIC

People finding one thing beautiful,
Think another unbeautiful,
Finding one creation sound,
They judge another unsound.
Yet, creation and destruction,
Difficult and easy, long and short,
High and low, all arise from each other.
Since something and nothing
Give birth to one another,
And varying tones make music,
Offer texture to a life,
And nourish imagination,
A creative man accepts no rules,
And believes in no set laws.
He accepts everything as it is,
Lets it come and go,
As something to participate in,
Yet not to dominate,
To nourish, yet not to possess.
In union with what is,
He gives birth freely,
Without claiming authority,
For creativity is all around,
And within us all.

16. RETURN TO THE STILLNESS

Quiet your mind of thoughts,
So your heart shall be at peace.
Being at peace,
Your imagination may more easily arise.
Creativity, like all healthy vegetation,
Arises, flourishes,
And then returns
To the root, to the stillness,
From whence it came.
Through returning to the stillness,
Each living thing,
Fulfills its own destiny.
Awareness of this cycle,
Is to face life with open eyes.
With open eyes,
You will see,
That stillness is both the source,
And the destiny of all creativity,
Of all living things.
And, by entering, into the stillness
With an open heart,
You become one with all of life.

OBJECT METAPHOR

"Creativity is finding unexpected likenesses."

—Michael Ray

Object Metaphor:

How is a _____ like _____?

(object)   (the problem)

Innovations are frequently discovered by people who are able to bring new perspectives to the problem. This is often done by consciously exploring areas that are unrelated to the situation. Working with random objects and their characteristics can help to bring fresh insights to a problem.

Example

Problem Statement: How can we sell a new candy bar?
Random Object: Combination lock.

Curved Steel Bar:
It won't throw you a curve
Round but strong
Soft yet hard

Steel:
Make a shiny silver wrapper
It will make you as strong as steel
We need iron in our diet
Bite the bullet packaging

Round Edges:
Won't hurt you
Soft but strong
Easy to hold
Soothes the sharp edges

Combination:
Combine it with romance
Combine it with sports
Combine with other foods
    to unlock secret formula
Secret combination

Dial:
Turn on
Around you go
Circle it
Choose the right one
Move through the steps
Clicks open

Numbers:
Sequence of events
It has the right number
    of calories
It's got your number

Lock and Unlock:
Lock in flavor, unlock energy
Unlock potential
Unlock flavor

Hard:
It won't crumble in your pocket
Show someone eating it while
    arm wrestling
Package in nut and bolt form
Combine with nuts and hard candies

Application
1. Describe your problem in one sentence. What is its essence?
2. Choose one of the objects below.
3. List all of its characteristics.
4. Free-associate and Force-fit these attributes to your problem. "In what ways can characteristics be applied to your situation?"

*Free-Associate:*_____

_____

Force-Fit:
In what ways can _____ be applied to _____?
In what ways can _____ be applied to _____?
In what ways can _____ be applied to _____?
In what ways can _____ be applied to _____?

HEROES

How would your favorite Hero solve a problem? Use this idea generator to gain new insights about your problem situation. Ask "How would (your favorite Hero) deal with (this problem situation)?"

Application

1. Reduce your problem situation into one or two words.
2. Think of a number from 1 to 15 at random or choose one of the Heroes from the list below (add your Heroes in spaces 16–20).
3. Apply your random number or choice and make a sentence [Ex. 5 — Thomas Edison, Situation = Dynamic Presentation]. "How would (Thomas Edison) handle a (Dynamic Presentation)?"
4. Free-Associate and Force-Fit any ideas back to your original problem situation.

HEROES

1. Superman	16._____
2. Gandhi	17._____
3. Christ	18._____
4. General Patton	19._____
5. Thomas Edison	20._____
6. Batman	
7. Socrates	
8. Tarzan	
9. Martin Luther King	
10. Alexander the Great	
11. Mother Theresa	
12. Captain Kirk	
13. Buddha	
14. James Bond	
15. Moses	

How would _____ deal with _____?
        (Hero)   (Situation)

Free-Associate:_____

_____

Force-Fit:_____

_____

Example: "How would (Thomas Edison) handle a (Dynamic Presentation)?"

Free-Associate: Invent/Light Bulb/Generator/Phonograph/R&D/ Tried Over 1,000 Times/White Hair/Entrepreneur/Financial Backing/ Functional

Force-Fit: Electrify/Use Energy-Lights-Sounds/Older Person Presents/Tried and True via R&D/Experimental/R&D Best Presentation Methods/Invent New Ways/Be an Entrepreneur/Functional and Practical Ideas.

WORST IDEA

Sometimes our ability to discover new ideas is limited by our desire to be good and come up with the best answer. A way to bypass this restriction is to brainstorm ideas on the worst resolution.[6]

Application

1. Reduce your problem to one sentence.
2. Choose one word from the list below that suggests the worst possible scenario or choose one at random.
3. Brainstorm associations to this word and Force-Fit any ideas back into your problem.

Example: Problem = Developing a new soup. Worst Word = Vomit

Free-Associate: Predigested/Smelly/Acidic/Small Chunks/ Green-Yellow-Orange/Bathroom/Relief/Bad Taste/Contractions/ Force/Fluid

Force-Fit: Strong taste and smell/Predigested for babies or elderly/Bright colors/Small chunks/Medicinal soup/Less acid/Soothing soup/Chicken-Penicillin soup/Strong yet healing soup.

Worst Words

Bad, Evil, Illness, Vomit, Corrupt, Inferior, Hostile, Earthquake, Fracture, Break, Crash, Cancer, AIDS, Death, Paralysis, Decay, Diarrhea, Diabolical, Satanic, Black Magic, Voodoo, Enemy, Rape, Frightening, Defeat, Frustrate, Impotence, Burglary, Theft, Murder, Fired, Divorce, Drowned, Overwhelmed, Stress, Heart Attack, Ulcers, Panic, Terrorists, Trauma, Amputation, Incapacitated, Feeble, Plague, Bomb, Assassination, Plane Crash, Deception, Lying, Cheat, Embezzlement, Fraud, Violence, Depression, Default, Bankruptcy, Helpless, Incontinent, Alcoholism, Addiction, Compulsion, Failure, Sabotage, Criticism, Abuse, Delinquency, Loser, Deterioration, War, Imprisonment, Threat, Menace, Intimidation, Blackmail, Sinister, Impoverished, Hopeless, Mean, Malicious, Starvation,

Electrocution, Suffocate, Choke, Strangle, Berserk, Coma, Insane.

DIALECTIC-PARADOX
(THE RESOLUTION OF OPPOSITES)

Dialectic: To better understand a problem, the Dialectic can be used to probe a situation for what it *is* and what it is *not* and in doing so uncover more of its essence. [Definition: the investigation of truth by logical argumentation; opposite in direction.] Examples: (Using opposites, synonyms and antonyms can open up new dimensions of a problem that might not be obvious.) If we are *pushing* what would happen if we *pulled*? If we are *maximizing* what would be the effect of *minimizing*? As *above* so as *below*, *rich* to *poor*, *more* to *less*, *male* to *female*, *somethingness* to *nothingness*, etc.

Paradox: A Paradox is the resolution of opposing forces and a possible solution to problems. [Definition: a statement or proposition seemingly self-contradictory or absurd, yet expressing a truth.] Resolving the Dialectic paradoxically could generate creative solutions to the opposing forces within a problem (usually expressed as the "Present-State" and the "Desired-State," where one is *now* and where one would like to *be*). Examples: A resolution of the Dialectic — *Healthy-Disease* could be a *Vaccine*, A *Peaceful-War* = a *Truce*, *Quiet-Loudness* = a *Dirty Look*, *Weak-Strength* = *Homeopathy*, etc.

Application

1. Write down your problem/situation in *one* sentence.
2. Identify the key concept in *one* word.
3. What is *it*? (Synonyms) What is it *not*? (Antonyms)
4. Force-Fit the Synonym-Antonym to create an = Paradox.
5. Apply the Paradox/Resolution to the original problem.

Example:

1. How to stay motivated
2. "Motivation"
3.

Synonyms	Antonyms	Force-Fit	4.= Paradox/ Resolution
move	stable	stable-movement	= Exercise/Yoga/ Tai-Chi
induce	allow	allow-inducement	= Seduction/Sex
provoke	rest	provocative-rest	= Meditation
catalyst	lazy	lazy-catalyst	= Time-Release Vitamin

incite	sleep	sleep-excitement	= Dreams
stimulate	relax	relaxed-stimulant	= Reading
push	pull	push-pull	= Dialogue
propel	repel	propel-repel	= Climbing
prompt	ignore	ignore-prompt	= _____
incentive	retard	_____	= _____
influence	_____	_____	= _____
inspire	_____	_____	= _____
elate	_____	_____	= _____

5. (Apply to problem)

Dialectic Paradox

Synonyms	Antonyms	Force-Fit	= Paradox/Resolution
disease	health	healthy-disease	= Vaccine
provoke	rest	provocative-rest	= Meditation
catalyst	lazy	lazy-catalyst	= Time-Release Vitamin
war	peace	peaceful-war	= A Truce
quiet	loud	quiet-loudness	= Dirty-Look
strength	weak	weak-strength	= Homeopathic Medicine
move	stable	stable-movement moving-stability	= Yoga/Tai-Chi/Tree
stagnant	growth	stagnant-growth growing-stagnation	= Hibernation/Meditation
conflict	harmony	conflictual-harmony harmonious-conflicts	= Orchestra/Negotiation

autonomy	tampering	autonomous-tampering tampering-autonomy	= Supreme Court
serene	anxiety	serene-anxiety	= Entrepreneur
		anxious-serenity	= Actor
compulsive	procrastination	procrastinating-compulsiveness	= Incubation
secure	freedom	secure-freedom	= Marriage
push	pull	push-pull	= Dialogue
stimulate	relax	relaxed-stimulation	= Reading
propel	repel	propel-repel	= Mountain Climbing
bright	dark	bright-darkness dark-brightness	= Black Hole

RANDOM WORDS

When you need a fresh approach to a situation try *Random Words*. Pick a word at random. Free-Associate to it and then Force-Fit the associations to your problem situation.

Application

1. Reduce your problem situation to one or two words.
2. Choose a Word at Random from the list beginning on the next page. Pick one as far from your problem situation as possible.
3. Free-Associate to both your problem situation and the random word and then Force-Fit any ideas back to the problem.

Example: Situation = Sell Fertilizer to Farmers/ Word = Blue

Free-Associate: Fertilizer = Nitrates/Beans/Fix/Molecules/Components/Natural/Manure/Solids/Liquids/Amount/Timing/Monitor Blue = Blue Sky/Blue Heaven/Feeling Blue/Sing the "Blues"/Blue Bird of Happiness/Blue Horizon/"Blue Beard" the Pirate

Force-Fit: Don't feel blue with poor growth/Look to a bright horizon/Right amount and right timing/Nature's components/Fixed molecules /There are Pirates out there/Not a "pie in the sky"/Grow a hill of beans/You'll be in "Blue Heaven"/Blue Ribbon.

Random Words

Acropolis, Green, Picture, Sky, Thunderstorm, Teacher, Red, Pill, Afghanistan, Apple Orchard, Leader, Lightning, Student, Feelings, Brainstorming, Effectiveness, Purpose, Paint, Pure, Flying, Spaceship, Clock, Salesperson, Complaint, Issue, Wisdom, People, Pretend, Acting, Improvisation, Gossip, Competition, Awareness, Busy, Discovery, Invention, Order, Nothing, Win, Groups, Light, Blind, Instant, Trust, Silence, Growing, Emerging, Storm, Rage, Calm, Resolution, Transformation, Africa, Complex, Ability, Theory, Balance, Trouble, Akido, Martial Arts, Generals, Battle, Enemies, Errors, Administrators, Production, Manufacture, Good, Motivation, Alaska, Obligations, Opportunities, Practical, Careers, Artist, Counseling, Algeria, Ship, Ocean, Potential, Alps, Work, Satisfying, Desire, Action, Steps, Cement, Mood, Shoe, Perfume, Bubble, Doughnut, Ghost, Queen, Jester, Gambler, Athletic, Artist Studio, Interpret, Indian, Smoke, Dinner, Date, Harmony, Rapport, Initiate, Conclusion, Archeological Site, Objective, Results, Love, Empathy, Ideas, Island, Asia, Butterfly, Cat, Clay, Purple, Daisy, Atlantis, Garden, Misery, Hermit, Spider, Cobweb, Harbor, Winds, Bali, Bank, Baseball Field, Broken, Bone, Teeth, Key, Auditorium, Pencil, Ink, Sand, Water, Catalog, Brochure, Chapter, Fear, Symbol, Earrings, Wedding Ring, Ceremony, Traditions, Australia, Bakery, Pizza, Cookies, Jam, Poetry, Bahamas, Ice Cream, Chocolate, Jazz, Museum, Dough, Tough, Ballroom, Reward, Enlightenment, Match, Leaf, Dew, Ruler, Grass, Content, Noble, Lethargic, Bathtub, Bubble Bath, Trap, Game, Beach, Botanical Garden, Laughter, Mask, Honor, Behind, Jeans, Advertisement, Library, Mark Twain, Heart, Learning, Chew, Coupon, Success, Toothpaste, Rotten, Feast, Battleship, Sources, Volunteer, Directory, Phone Book, Control, Manipulation, Throwing, Scissors, Cleaning, Repairing, Bee Hive, Camera, Television, Operation, Harvest, Bordello, Analyzing, Reporter, Gathering, Pet, Snake, Dirt, Test, Boxing Match, Campground, Buddhist Monastery, Coral Reef, Brazil, Sponge, Budget, Figure, Model, Fashion, Octopus, Snail, Squirrel, Oak Tree, Cherry Orchard, Florist, Postman, Card, Letter, Trick, Index, Jar, Gum, Foundation, Buenos Aires...

NATURISTICS

Nature has been creating and experimenting for over 4 billion years. To solve your problem, use Nature as a model: "How would nature solve it?" Choose a random element of nature, list its characteristics and those of your Problem/Quest, recombine them, and gain new perspectives and possible answers.

> *Example:* Problem = "How can I motivate myself?"
> Problem in one word = "Motivation."
> Nature element = "Seed."

Elements of Seed	Components of Motivation
1. Water	1. Energy
2. Soil	2. Desire, Passion
3. Right Temperature	3. Colleagues, Support
4. Weeding	4. Purpose
5. Time	5. Survival
6. Cycles of blooming and rest	6. Caring
7. Sun	7. Knowledge

Three ways of using these elements to gain new perspectives are through (A) *Intrigue*, (B) *Connectedness*, and (C) *Randomness*.

A. Intrigue: Choose those elements that intrigue you or have some meaning for you and try force-fitting them back into your problem. Example: "Cycle of blooming and rest" suggests that my motivation has cycles and perhaps I need to look at my expectations of "always being motivated" versus needing time to "rest." Maybe my "rest" times are part of "being motivated."

B. Connectedness: Look for connections between the two lists. Example: "Soil" and "Temperature" seem connected to the idea of "Colleagues, Support." The common or connecting element is environment. Just like seeds need to be nurtured by soil and temperature, my motivation may need more nurturing through a support system.

C. Randomness: Connect the two lists randomly (close your eyes and think of two numbers) and try for a force-fit. Example: I'll choose #4 (Weeding) under seeds and #7 (Knowledge) under motivation. Perhaps I need to weed out my knowledge and get to essentials = choose priorities? Extraneous knowledge is choking my motivation? Too much knowledge has me confused and I'm not taking action? I think I need more knowledge when maybe I just need to clarify what I do know?

NATURISTICS

1. Armadillo	29. Quartz	57. Barracuda
2. Cactus	30. Venus Flytrap	58. Beehive
3. Bird's Nest	31. Canyon	59. Cave
4. Cobweb	32. Desert	60. Forest
5. Garden	33. Jungle	61. Iceberg
6. Marsh	34. Meadow	62. Mesa
7. Mountain	35. Ocean	63. Pond
8. Prairie	36. Puddle	64. Rain Forest
9. River	37. Swamp	65. Tundra
10. Volcano	38. Earthquake	66. Bat
11. Cat	39. Cheetah	67. Chicken
12. Clams	40. Cow	68. Dog
13. Dolphin	41. Dove	69. Dragonfly
14. Duck	42. Eagle	70. Eel
15. Goose	43. Gorilla	71. Hamster
16. Hawk	44. Horse	72. Goat
17. Falcon	45. Fox	73. Leopard
18. Lion	46. Lizard	74. Monkey
19. Mouse	47. Octopus	75. Owl
20. Pig	48. Platypus	76. Rabbit
21. Rat	49. Shark	77. Shrimp
22. Snake	50. Tiger	78. Turkey
23. Turtle	51. Whale	79. Wolf
24. Ant	52. Bee	80. Beetle
25. Butterfly	53. Caterpillar	81. Cockroach
26. Firefly	54. Fly	82. Grasshopper
27. Mosquito	55. Moth	83. Praying Mantis
28. Scorpion	56. Spider	84. Termite

ZEN-HAIKU

A Haiku is a form of Japanese poetry that puts words together in a unique, nonlogical order. It is a method of using the Zen way of focusing on the essence or "heart of the matter." This can be a useful tool in creative problem solving as it helps us to shift our perspectives, to think in a nonanalytical way and to obtain intuitive insights.

Innovations, discoveries, and solutions often occur when you allow your mind to leap forward into the future, to the Ideal Resolution. We can get stuck in a problem by referencing the past and struggling with it in the present. (Someone once said that the difference between a neurosis and wisdom is that, in wisdom, we know when to let go of the struggle.)

Application

1. Think of your problem as well as its Ideal Resolution. If your problem was already solved, what would it look like, feel like?
2. Free-Associate words that come to mind while you are thinking of the Ideal Resolution.
3. Underline five to ten words that have energy or importance.
4. Count their syllables and place that number next to them, for example, beautiful (3), motivated (4), vision (2), good (1), and so on.
5. Put them into Haiku form:
   The first sentence has five syllables.
   The second has seven syllables.
   And the third has five syllables.
6. Place in unique, nonlogical order, no sentences. Play with it.

Example: Situation = Selling / Ideal Resolution = Have Fun. Being of real service, feeling connected and satisfied.

Free-Associate: comfortable/easy/balanced/service/music/dance /excited/empathic/motivated/fun/joyous/repeat/grounded/good /relationships/alignment/abundant/committed/worthy/purpose /grow/improvement/satisfied/mission/spiritual/contribution.

HAIKU: mission (2), worthy (2), purpose (2), spiritual (4), contribution (4), service (2), empathic (3), grow (1), balanced (2), motivated (4), fun (1)

Purpose Empathic
Grow Mission Service Worthy
Motivated Fun

METAPHORICAL MATRIX

The Metaphorical Matrix is a random idea generator. It is a way of stimulating one's creativity by asking how a particular person would handle your situation in a specific environment.

Application

1. Reduce your problem situation into one word.
2. Think of a number from 1 to 10 at random. Do this two times, for example, 1 and 7.

3. Apply these numbers to the lists below and formulate a sentence, for example: 1-Psychologist, 7-Wild West: "How would a Psychologist deal with (your situation) in the Wild West?"
4. Free-Associate and Force-Fit any ideas back to your original problem.

Metaphorical Matrix

Person	*(Your Situation)*	Environment
1. Psychologist	"	1. Theater
2. Shaman	"	2. Monastery
3. Biologist	"	3. Prison
4. Gypsy	"	4. Caribbean
5. Poet	"	5. Gallery
6. Minister	"	6. Museum
7. Lawyer	"	7. Wild West
8. Entrepreneur	"	8. Church
9. Akido Master	"	9. Acropolis
10. Cowboy	"	10. Ghetto

"How would a _____ deal with _____ in _____?"
      (Person)   (Situation)   (Environment)

*Free-Associate:*_____

_____

*Force-Fit:*_____

_____

Example: "How would a Psychologist deal with (selling a new candy) in the Wild West?"

Free-Associate: Psychologist = Perceptions/Measurement/Motivation/Persona/Authority/Psycho-Priest/Analyzes-Cures Emotional Problems/West = "Strong and Silent" Type/Hard Life/New Frontier/ Work Hard/Make It on Your Own/Be Independent/Be a Good Neighbor/Gunslingers — Life Is Short/Simple Life/Simple Values

Force-Fit: Candy Will Taste or Make You Strong/Sell as Western Candy (Marlboro Man) Persona/Simple Taste with Good Value/ Independent, Real People Like It/Cures Low Energy/It's a Hard World, You Deserve a Luxury, Sweeten It Up/ Life Is Short, Enjoy Now.

REFERENCES

1. Judith Morgan and Andre de Zanger, *The Tao of Creativity* (New York: The Creativity Institute, 1992, 212-289-8856).

2. Judith Morgan and Andre de Zanger, *The Idea Generator* (New York: The Creativity Institute, 1994).

3. Andre de Zanger, *Zingers* (New York: The Creativity Institute, 1994).

4. Andre de Zanger, *Paradigm Shift* (New York: The Creativity Institute, 1994).

5. Michael Michalko, *Thinkertoys* and *Thinkpak* (Ten Speed Press, 1991).

6. Bryan Mattimore, *99% Inspiration* (American Management Association, 1994).

INDEX

Page numbers in italics refer to exhibits.

A

B

C

D

F

G

H

I

M

N

O

P

Q

R

S

W

Y

Z